ALEISTER CROWLEY
in India

"Relying to a large degree on unpublished documents, Churton's narrative account demonstrates the extent of Crowley's engagement with both the theoretical *and* practical dimensions of Hindu and Buddhist teachings and their enduring influence on his magical philosophy. Crowley's efforts in conjoining the spiritual systems of the East and West have important implications for the study of comparative esotericism, and Churton deserves praise for his eloquent treatment of this fascinating subject."

GORDAN DJURDJEVIC, PH.D., AUTHOR OF *INDIA AND THE OCCULT*

"The devil is in the details when it comes to the study of Aleister Crowley, and in this groundbreaking book Tobias Churton offers a compelling look at this all-too-overlooked period of Crowley's sojourns in South Asia. Much praise and credit is due to Churton for revealing the many strands of Crowley's life and relationships during this formative period—from his poetry to his mountaineering and from his interest in the yogi Śrī Sabhāpati Svāmī to his humorous and often purposely offensive social commentaries. Scholars of early modern Hinduism, Buddhism, and Western esotericism as well as general Crowley aficionados will all find much of interest here, especially given the wealth of historical context that Churton provides for the colonial-era history of India, for early Theosophy, and of course for Crowley right in the thick of it all with his mystical and magical aspirations."

KEITH CANTÚ, PH.D. CANDIDATE IN RELIGIOUS STUDIES
AT THE UNIVERSITY OF CALIFORNIA, SANTA BARBARA

"In this excellent book, Tobias Churton examines Crowley's critically productive time as a student of yoga and Buddhism under his brilliant mentor Allan Bennett and sheds light on the wider context of the cultural push to bring Eastern mysticism to the West, a movement that has shaped both modern spirituality and world history itself."

JASON LOUV, AUTHOR OF *JOHN DEE AND THE EMPIRE OF ANGELS*
AND TEACHER OF MAGICK AND MEDITATION AT MAGICK.ME

"Tobias Churton has once again uncovered—and more importantly, interpreted—some critical aspects of Aleister Crowley's life and legacy. As with *Aleister Crowley in America,* he has leveraged his unprecedented access to long-hidden archival material by and about the Great Beast; with these records Churton fills in additional pieces of the grand puzzle that is Crowley, so the reader can see a more complete picture of the experiences that shaped the development and interpretation of his mandate to spread Thelema to the world."

TOBY CHAPPELL, AUTHOR OF *INFERNAL GEOMETRY AND THE LEFT-HAND PATH*

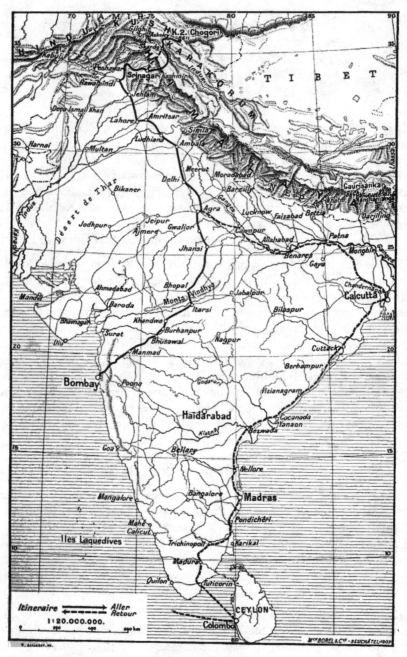

INDIA, as traveled in 1902 by Dr. Jules Jacot-Guillarmod,
member of Aleister Crowley's Kangchenjunga Expedition
(from Guillarmod's Six Mois dans l'Himalaya,
Neuchâtel, Switzerland: Sandoz, 1904).

ALEISTER CROWLEY in India

The Secret Influence of Eastern Mysticism on Magic and the Occult

TOBIAS CHURTON

Inner Traditions
Rochester, Vermont

Inner Traditions
One Park Street
Rochester, Vermont 05767
www.InnerTraditions.com

Text stock is SFI certified

Cataloging-in-Publication Data for this title is available from the Library of Congress

ISBN 978-1-62055-796-9 (print)
ISBN 978-1-62055-797-6 (ebook)

Printed and bound in the United States by Lake Book Manufacturing, Inc. The text stock is SFI certified. The Sustainable Forestry Initiative® program promotes sustainable forest management.

10 9 8 7 6 5 4 3 2 1

Text design and layout by Debbie Glogover
This book was typeset in Garamond Premier Pro with Heirloom Artcraft, Gill Sans MT Pro, and ITC Legacy Sans Std used as display fonts

Because hyperlinks do not always remain viable, we are no longer including URLs in our resources, notes, or bibliographic entries. Instead, we are providing the name of the website where this information may be found.

To send correspondence to the author of this book, mail a first-class letter to the author c/o Inner Traditions • Bear & Company, One Park Street, Rochester, VT 05767, and we will forward the communication, or contact the author directly at **tobiaschurton.com**.

Contents

PART TWO

INDIA IN CROWLEY

Acknowledgments

This project could neither have gotten off the ground nor—to mix metaphors—reached its summit without the kind encouragement of William Breeze, Outer Head of the Ordo Templi Orientis. I thank him deeply for making available not only vital documentation—much of it previously unpublished—but for his advice, patience, good humor, and many tips as to which forgotten cases it might yet prove worthwhile to investigate. I should also like to thank James Wasserman and Stephen King, both shining members of the same order, for their good will and friendliness toward this special book project.

My dear friend in Florida, Renate zum Tobel, has been enormously helpful in making me look deeper into the work of Madame Blavatsky and the Theosophical Society, without whose labors Aleister Crowley would never have followed the path he did across the Indian subcontinent. Renate is herself a responsible member of the T.S. today, and it is thanks to her that I was permitted access to a digitized copy of Col. Henry S. Olcott's personal copy of Sabhapaty Swami's book on Vedantic rāja yoga, which would prove so influential to Crowley's understanding of the potential of jñāna yoga. I am most grateful to Janet Kerschner, who coordinated the digitizing project between the Henry S. Olcott Memorial Library and the Archives Department of the Theosophical Society in America, and the Adyar Library and Research Centre of the Theosophical Society, Adyar, India, for permitting the publisher to draw on her and her colleagues' important work.

Persons who find the figure of Alpinist, keen photographer, doctor, and natural scientist Jules Jacot-Guillarmod an impressive and inspiring one will share my appreciation for the work of the Fondation de l'Hôtel de Commune de Lignières, Switzerland, for providing biographical information about Crowley's mountaineering colleague on the K2 and Kangchenjunga expeditions, along with extracts from Guillarmod's climbing journal on the foundation's website. Dr. Guillarmod lived in Lignières, serving the sick there between 1904 and 1905, and again from 1906 to 1910.

Other helpful sources of ideas and information include LAShTAL, the remarkable website of the Aleister Crowley Society, run so ably by Paul Feazey, and the cyber-archive project devoted to Crowley's works that is the 100th Monkey Press who continue to augment their useful database, including an archive of Crowley's many appearances in world newspapers and magazines, from the 1890s to this day.

I should like to thank Dr. Philip Young, Assistant Librarian at the Warburg Institute, for his kind assistance in making me so welcome to study the Yorke Collection of Crowleyana, a most vital resource for serious Crowley studies.

Not far from the Warburg Institute stands the wonderful Atlantis Bookshop on Museum Street. Thanks are due to Geraldine and Bali Beskin, who daily open its doors to the seekers and *curiosi* of our times, for their long and caring encouragement of my work, which would never have begun, had my mother not pushed me through the Atlantis's doors back in the summer of 1979.

Finally, I must express my indebtedness to the inspired, tireless work of Inner Traditions International: to Jon Graham and Ehud Sperling for commissioning the book, to my superb editor, Mindy Branstetter, to Jeanie Levitan for love and discipline, to Ashley Kolesnik for publicity, and to Kelly Bowen, and all the marvelous staff at Rochester, Vermont's, hive of determined, practical idealism.

To everyone I have mentioned by name and all who care about its subject, I dedicate this book, that we may all look higher than mountains, to that "One Star in Sight."

TOBIAS CHURTON,
ENGLAND, 2019

INTRODUCTION

❖

Tipping Point for India: Catalyst for Crowley

From Ind—shall her summons awaken?
Her voices are those of the dead!
By famine and cholera shaken,
By taxes and usury bled,
In the hour of her torture forsaken,
Stones given for bread!

FROM *CARMEN SAECULARE*,
ALEISTER CROWLEY, 1900

In 1897, while the British Empire celebrated Queen Victoria's Diamond Jubilee, western India was wracked by famine. Exacerbated by bubonic plague and other killer diseases, Plague Commissioner Walter C. Rand employed brutal methods to prevent infection spreading. Oblivious to custom, troops destroyed private property considered contaminated. Amid reports of rapes, with males and females segregated into plague camps, over-vigorous searches damaged religious shrines. On June 22, Indian revolutionaries, the Chapekar brothers, assassinated Rand and army lieutenant Charles Egerton Ayerst at Rand's base at Poona.

British power in India had reached both summit and tipping point. An empire born from competition first with the Portuguese, then the Dutch, later with the French, Britain's East India Company eventually triumphed over competitors for influence over a decaying, corrupt, and

1

periodically anarchic late Mughal Empire. Mughal conquest of India having begun in 1526, India was already a conquered country. East India Company commander Robert Clive's 1751 to 1757 campaigns to keep the French from ejecting the British from Madras and Bengal left much of eastern India under British control. In September 1803, war with remaining independent Marathas in the west climaxed in the capture of Delhi and of Mughal emperor Shah Alam. As Michael Edwardes expressed the British achievement: "In less than eighty years, a company of merchants from a small country thousands of miles away had managed to gain control of a vast Empire."[1] Most of India was now under dual government: Crown and Company. Complete control would take some decades yet, with costly wars fought in Sindh, the Punjab, Burma, and elsewhere.

Aleister Crowley's account in chapter 34 of his *Confessions* concerning the psychology of effective British rule reveals—sometimes, note, with irony and full tongue in cheek—what *he* believed it took to govern India and, especially ironically, what it would take for the British to maintain dominance:

> England conquered India by understanding the minds of the inhabitants, by establishing her own standards of conduct as arbitrary, and contemptuously permitting the native to retain his own wherever they did not conflict with the service of the conqueror. England is losing India by consenting to admit the existence of the conquered races; by consenting to argue; by trying to find a value for incommensurables. Indian civilization is far superior to our own and to enter into open competition is to invoke defeat. We won India by matching our irrational, bigoted, brutal manhood against their etiolated culture.
>
> We cannot even plead that we have lacked a prophet. The genius of Rudyard Kipling, however aesthetically abominable, has divined the secrets of destiny with cloudless clarity. His stories and his sermons are equally informed by the brainless yet unanswerable argument based on intuitive cognition of the critical facts. India can be governed, as history proves, by any alien autocracy with sufficient moral courage to dismiss Hindu subtlety as barbaric and go its own way regardless of reason. But India has always conquered its invaders by initiating them. No sooner does the sahib suspect that he is not Almighty God than the attributes of Jehovah cease to arm him with

unreasonable omnipotence. Our rule in India has perished because we have allowed ourselves to consider the question of divine right. The proverb says that the gods themselves cannot contend with stupidity, and the stupidity of the sahib in the days of Nicholson* reduced India to impotence. But we allowed the intellectual Bengali to invade England and caress our housemaids in the precincts of the Earl's Court exhibition. He returned to Calcutta, an outcast indeed from his own social system, but yet a conqueror of English fashions and femininity. We admitted his claim to compete with us, and our prestige perished exactly as did that of the Church when Luther asserted the right of private judgment.

We conquered the peninsula by sheer moral superiority. Our unity, our self-respect, our courage, honesty, and sense of justice awakened the wonder, commanded the admiration, and enforced the obedience of those who either lacked those qualities altogether, possessed some of them and felt the lack of the others, or had, actually or traditionally, sufficient of them to make them the criteria of right and ability to govern. As elsewhere observed, our modern acquiescence in the rationally irrefutable argument that the color of a man's skin does not prevent him from being competent in any given respect, has knocked the foundations from underneath the structure of our authority. . . .

India could be kept in order, even now, to its own salvation and our great credit and profit, if we would eliminate the European women and tradesmen, the competition wallah, and the haw-haw officer, and entrust the government of the country to a body of sworn "samurai" vowed like the Jesuits to chastity and obedience, together with either poverty or a type of splendour in which there should be no element of personal pride or indulgence, but only prestige. Like the Jesuits, too, these men should be sworn never to return to Europe as long as they lived. The capacity of such men to govern would be guaranteed by the fact of their having volunteered to accept such conditions. They would enjoy universal respect and absolute trust. They would require no army to enforce their authority. All the best elements of India would spontaneously

---

*John Nicholson (1821–1857); East India Company soldier and hero of the Siege of Delhi in the 1857 Indian Mutiny against British rule.

unite to support it. One further condition. They would have to be guaranteed against the interference of any ignorant and indifferent House of Commons. The stupid callousness of the India Office is as much to be dreaded as the silly sentimentalism of sympathizers with "national aspirations," "the brotherhood of man," and all such bunkum.[2]

Crowley's reflections not only reveal much about his personal philosophy, but, interestingly, also intuit British rule in India as being practically finished; he interpreted the signs.

The point of view of administrators on the ground is well expressed by historian of British India, Michael Edwardes: "Anglo-Indian administrators determined on successful, peaceful and prosperous rule. They performed miracles of construction that laid the foundations of modern India . . . but as they did so they created for themselves an enclosed world consciously designed to separate the rulers and ruled."[3] Even after 1858, when East India Company functions passed to the Crown, Indians were barred from upper levels of administration, regardless of Queen Victoria's post-Mutiny proclamation that all her subjects be "impartially admitted to Office in Our Service."

Access to governance dominated the Indian National Congress's founding in 1885 (under Theosophist inspiration; see page 20), while lack of progress in this regard fueled frustration, with reformers' attitudes diverging ever more widely. While middle-class Congress leader Gopal Krishna Gokhale favored gradual progress in partnership with "the genius of the British people,"[4] religious nationalists inspired in Bengal by civil servant (until 1891) Bankim Chandra Chatterji—who identified love of country with love of God—saw the Raj as prelude to a Hindu India revived. Bal Gangadhar Tilak (1856–1920), founder of the Indian Independence Movement, also opposed Gokhale. Imprisoned for sedition in 1897 (suspected of using the Bhagavad Gita to incite the Chapekar brothers into assassinating Rand), Tilak looked provocatively to former Maratha independence as an ideal. Radically inspired young men gathered in secret societies, waiting for an opportunity to launch revolution. In 1905 opportunity came when Bengal was divided to assist a Muslim majority in the east. Crowley witnessed the tension during his third Indian sojourn.

In 1899, thirty-nine-year-old George Nathaniel Curzon (1st Marquis Curzon of Kedleston) became viceroy of India. He would be viceroy throughout Crowley's presence in India. Bringing brilliance, dynamism, and originality to the task—as well as specialist knowledge of a perceived Russian threat from Afghanistan's northern border—Curzon was creative, sensitive, flexible, and highly industrious. In 1902, around the time Curzon called for Oscar Eckenstein's detention from the Eckenstein-Crowley K2 expedition, Curzon confessed to his private secretary "that under the intense pressure of business he sometimes felt as if he were going mad."[5] When Crowley arrived at Colombo to study rāja yoga with friend Allan Bennett in August 1901, Curzon was presiding over a conference on education at Simla, personally drafting 150 resolutions. Predictably, Curzon endured disappointment with lack of initiative at the top of India's incorruptible Civil Service, and the sense that his reforming interests were neither shared by India's ruling Council nor by London. Time would prove Curzon India's last great viceroy.

Crowley gazed beyond Curzon's practical concerns. Convinced the world had entered a new era of liberty and insight, Crowley believed the spiritual keys to that future required recovering the workable essence of past knowledge, and reintegrating it with science. Madame Blavatsky and the Theosophical Society had, he believed, already laid first ground for reconstruction. Founded in the year of Crowley's birth—1875—the Society moved from New York to Bombay in 1879, engaging directly with Indian religion. The Theosophical Society advanced a new consciousness of parity between Hinduism, Buddhism, and Christianity subversive of British assumptions of dominance (as well as of Hindu and Buddhist particularity).

Crowley, meanwhile, grew to manhood amid strictures of an upper-middle-class, exclusive and fundamentalist Plymouth Brethren household, against which he began rebelling, aged eleven, when his wealthy father—gentleman-preacher Edward Crowley (1830–1887)—succumbed to cancer.

Raised in Leamington, Warwickshire, and Redhill, Surrey, Crowley attended a string of private schools, with tutors providing his largely classical and scientific education. Bullying led him to embrace mountaineering for strength, and by the time he entered Cambridge in 1896—nominated by Prime Minister Lord Salisbury with a diplomatic career expected—he was fit, handsome, highly intelligent, profoundly romantic, artistic, and bisexual.* At Cambridge, Crowley's mind underwent a major turnabout. In 1897, awareness of life's sorrowful, fatal nature—and worldly ambition's ultimate futility—overwhelmed him. Attracted to a philosophy of spiritual causes, he sought the attention of beings he believed held the levers of human destiny in their power; *them* he chose to serve, an ambition that led him into the Hermetic Order of the Golden Dawn, specializing in Western, neo-Rosicrucian magic, founded in the wake of scandal that beset the Theosophical Society in 1888, leading many members to demit from its pro-Hindu-Buddhist agenda. The Golden Dawn itself split in spring 1900, and a disappointed Crowley began traveling around the world as an adept on a quest. The world, he believed, was on the cusp of spiritual revolution, and the adept was dimly aware he had come to India to learn how to play his part in it.

---

*For knowledge of Crowley's background and upbringing, my *Aleister Crowley: The Biography* (Watkins, 2012) may be consulted.

PART ONE

CROWLEY IN INDIA

ONE

⬡

Go East,
Young Man!

Sail due west from Great Britain and you hit the coast of North America; continue westward and you'll reach the Pacific on the west coast; keep heading west, and you'll find yourself in the Far East. The world is a circle, and we find ourselves at the beginning.

Self-exiled from his British homeland for nearly a year, twenty-five-year-old Aleister Crowley boarded steamship *Nippon Maru*, bound westward for Honolulu at San Francisco on May 3, 1901. Reading matter included *The Astral Plane, Its Scenery, Inhabitants and Phenomena*, published in 1894 by C. W. Leadbeater when secretary of London's lodge of the Theosophical Society.

Theosophy was in the air. *Theosophy* means thinking about spiritual things. Its aim: a system accommodating science while embodying spiritual knowledge, or wisdom about God.

Docking at Honolulu six days later, Crowley noted a local paper's announcement of a "White Lotus Day" at a local Theosophical lodge to commemorate Helena Petrovna Blavatsky's death, which had occurred a decade before, on May 8, 1891. Crowley planned to visit the lodge during his month in Hawaii, before venturing on to Japan, China, and India. Without Theosophy, Crowley's first journey to India in 1901 to 1902 would never have happened. Understanding why this is so entails understanding Crowley's early relations with Theosophy, whose organization, more than any other, revolutionized Western perceptions of Indian religion.

Crowley confessed two main motives for quitting the Americas for the East. First was a quest for further mountaineering achievements with friend Oscar Eckenstein. Having scaled Mexico's peaks in early 1901, the pioneers anticipated hurling themselves against the mighty Himalayas in 1902. Second, Crowley wished to interview Allan Bennett, his admired friend and fellow member of the Hermetic Order of the Golden Dawn. Bennett had been studying rāja yoga and Buddhism in Ceylon (today's Sri Lanka) since early 1900. Crowley sought to resolve a dilemma, involving Bennett, derived from the tangled story of the Golden Dawn and the Theosophical Society, a story that explains Crowley's interest in both Bennett and India.

The Hermetic Order of the Golden Dawn in part represented a reaction to the Theosophical Society's preoccupation with Indian religion. Conversely, Bennett's quitting London for Ceylon represented his own reaction to the Golden Dawn magic he'd mastered, discarding it for an Indian spiritual idealism fostered by the Theosophical Society. Since Bennett had been Crowley's guide in magic, Crowley needed to know whether Bennett's departure from former mentor and Golden Dawn founder Samuel "Macgregor" Mathers was philosophically motivated, or whether it was rooted in doubts over Mathers's integrity, for which wavering reed Crowley himself had expended considerable time, energy, reputation, and money in 1900.

Shortly before Crowley's arrival in Ceylon in August 1901, Bennett gave his first address on the subject of Buddhism's Four Noble Truths. Significantly, it was delivered to the Theosophical Society's Hope Lodge, in Colombo.

MADAME BLAVATSKY AND INDIA

If we credit her accounts, the woman born Helena Petrovna von Hahn—the woman Crowley came to regard as his spiritual predecessor—entered India in 1852 in search of an alternative spiritual system to that of the Russian Orthodox Christianity in which she'd been raised. Blavatsky explained to friend Countess Constance Wachtmeister how her first Indian adventure was rooted in childhood, when she'd experienced the astral form of a being close to her. Like a guardian angel, he was particularly close in times of danger.¹ During a visit to London in 1851, this being appeared as a living person on her twentieth birthday.* That person gave his name as "Morya," a Rajput by birth, participating in a political delegation to Britain's capital. Blavatsky subsequently claimed Morya explained how a new society to reform spiritual knowledge could be formed, a task requiring three years' training in Tibet.†

Having toured the Americas, Blavatsky claimed she arrived in Bombay in late 1852, but failed to enter Tibet via Nepal. Welcoming a few merchants, Tibet restricted entry to foreigners at its remote borders. Sylvia Cranston's biography of Blavatsky offers evidence to support elements of Helena's story. In 1893, Theosophical Society co-founder Col. Olcott met Major General C. Murray, Seventieth Bengal Infantry (rtd.), chairman of the Monghyr Municipality, by chance on a train. According to Olcott's account—signed as true by Murray in Olcott's diary—Murray was captain of the Sebundy Sappers and Miners when he met Blavatsky in 1854 or 1855, 19 miles south of Darjeeling at Punkabaree (Pankhabari), due south of Mount Kangchenjunga, and some 81 miles south of the Tibetan border. Hearing about a European lady abroad, Murray instructed a subordinate to fetch her. Murray recalled the woman telling him she wanted to go to Tibet "to write a book." Staying with the Murrays for about a month, she finally realized it was impossible. Murray heard of her again at Dinajpore (Dinajpur)

---

*A variant account emerges in contemporary notes made in Blavatsky's own hand, with a drawing of boats in a harbor, indicating that on her twentieth birthday she was at Ramsgate in East Kent, encountering her "Master" there (Cranston and Williams, 46).

†Skepticism over the name "Morya"—whom Blavatsky often referred to simply as "M"—persists, since it appears to have no etymological basis as an Indian name; this is not strictly the case. Chandragupta Maurya founded India's greatest empire before the Mughals (circa 322 BCE–84 BCE). Buddhist sources, compiled centuries later, claim both Chandragupta and grandson Ashoka—a great patron of Buddhism—were of noble lineage. Not surprisingly, some Buddhist texts link Chandragupta to the Ksatriya warrior caste, as well as to the Sakya clan from which the Buddha came, further suggesting his epithet "Moriya" (Sanskrit: *mayūra*) derived from the Pāli *mora*: a peacock. Buddhist texts also refer to a legendary city, "Moriya-nagara" built of bricks colored like a peacock's neck. In India and Persia, the peacock can symbolize royalty, enthronement, spirituality, vision, the creative deity, awakening, guidance, protection, watchfulness, and the night sky.

in faraway West Bengal.[2] Murray thought her about thirty years of age. Age and dates differ with Blavatsky's account, as her account has her returning to England via Java in 1853.

Blavatsky insisted she again attempted to enter Tibet via Kashmir and Ladakh, arriving in India via Japan in late 1855. Biographer Cranston sees no reason to doubt the idea that Blavatsky's Indian tour and alleged Tibetan sojourn of 1856, helped by her "Mongolian" appearance, provided material for articles on the caves and jungles of Hindustan, published under the name "Radda Bai" in the *Moscow Chronicle* after the Theosophical Society was founded.

Blavatsky claimed instruction under a Siberian shaman in Tibet who wanted help with Russian authorities to return to his homeland: a curious detail. Murray's account to Olcott indicated Murray himself once met a Hindu gentleman in Bareilly (about 124 miles east of Delhi) who recalled a European lady who tried to enter Tibet via Kashmir, and identified her with the Blavatsky who came to India on T.S. business in 1879.

Ladakh, meaning "the land of high passes," in Jammu and Kashmir, known collectively as Baltistan, is also known—when we include the Karakoram mountains—as "Little Tibet." People of Tibetan origin dwell in Ladakh, and Little Tibet may be deemed better than no Tibet at all, though Blavatsky never claimed to have achieved her objective of visiting Lhasa, the Dalai Lama's home in southeastern Tibet. She did, however, claim to have studied Mahāyāna Buddhism in Tibet.

The term *Mahāyāna* possibly originates in the word *mahājnāna*, that is, "a great knowing," consisting of how an individual may achieve spiritual liberation in this life if sorrow and the temptation to bad practices and tendencies can be overcome. Good practices advocated in the tradition include ascetic self-denial, and, in the *Lokakṣema sūtra* corpus, retirement into forests for meditative concentration to the stage of *samādhi*. Such conditions were held to expand spiritual consciousness and stimulate fresh revelation.*

The detail about the Siberian shaman, whom Blavatsky says could

---

*It is significant to note not only that Crowley followed this path, but that his two great mountaineering expeditions, of 1902 (K2) and 1905 (Kangchenjunga), both occurred in those two parts of India and Nepal's borders with Tibet allegedly explored by Blavatsky half a century earlier.

transfer thoughts and images to far distant persons by mind power, is interesting, especially his desire to return to the Russian Empire. Contacts between the Russian court and Tibetan medicine do in fact date to the 1850s, when Buddhist Buryat lama Sultim Badma (died 1873) arrived in St. Petersburg in 1857. Appointed to the Nikolayevsky military hospital, he was authorized to practice the three-humor-based herbal medicine that southern Siberian Buryat doctors shared with Tibet, establishing a Tibetan pharmacy—the first in Europe—on Suvorovsky Street in St. Petersburg, inviting younger brother Zhamsaran to join him.

Rechristened Pyotr Aleksandrovich Badmayev, Zhamsaran became Tibetan medicine's leading advocate in Russia, with a clinic on the Poklonnaya Hill just outside of St. Petersburg. Count Sergei Witte (1849–1915), minister of finance from 1892 and later prime minister, became one of his patients. The count was Blavatsky's cousin.

Closely related to important figures in nineteenth-century Russian military and diplomatic history, we may wonder what British military intelligence officers might have made of such a well-connected woman exploring hidden passes that led out of Tibet (as she claimed to have traveled) and back into India—the kind of thing the British mounted expeditions to determine in the "Great Game," as British India's diplomatic and not very diplomatic engagement with Russia was known.

Helena's relatives gave her more than access to corridors of power. Blavatsky's mother Elena's maternal grandfather, Prince Pavel Dolgorukov (died 1838), possessed hundreds of books and manuscripts on alchemy, magic, Freemasonry, and Rosicrucianism. After Elena von Hahn's death in 1842, Helena Petrovna joined her grandmother's household, gaining unrestricted access to the late prince's library. According to K. Paul Johnson, absorption in the library brought Helena to the idea of "Unknown Superiors" familiar to "Strict Observance" Templarist and neo-Rosicrucian Freemasonry,[3] an experience that probably shaped her perception of "the Masters"—and Crowley's too, in due course.

In 1847, aged sixteen, Helena Petrovna had moved with her family to Tiflis on the appointment of grandfather and diplomat Andrey Mikhailovich Fedeev (or Fadeyev) to the Council of Secret Governance for the Transcaucasia region. Tiflis resident Prince Aleksandr Golitsyn, Freemason, magician, and seer, paid a call on Helena's grandparents, greatly impressing young Helena. According to the memoirs of the wife of Tiflis's governor, Madame Ermolov, Helena and Aleksandr's long conversations kindled such passion that the couple ran away, an adventure that encouraged Helena's family to condone her hasty marriage on June 7, 1849, to the older Nikifor Vladimirovich Blavatsky, vice-governor of Erevan, Armenia. Ermolov suggested it was Prince Golitsyn who gave Helena contact details for Coptic magician Paolos Metamon, considered Blavatsky's first "master" in occultism.[4]

Escaping marriage, Helena went first to relatives in Tiflis, then to Odessa where she took English sailboat *Commodore* to Kerch before moving on to Constantinople, where she met Russian countess Kiseleva with whom she traveled to Egypt, Greece, and central Europe. In Cairo in 1851, Blavatsky met American writer, artist, Freemason, and archaeologist Albert Rawson (born 1828). Fascinated by ancient and esoteric religion, Rawson enthusiastically joined American fringe Masonic orders. In later life he recalled of their encounters—he and Blavatsky were together in Paris and the States in the early 1850s—how she claimed her destiny was to liberate the human mind, a work not "hers" but of "Him who sent me," a phrase from Saint John's Gospel used by Jesus.

Madame Blavatsky claimed that having left "Tibet" at the end of 1856, her occult guardian insisted she leave India, shortly before the Indian Mutiny (a near-catastrophic revolt of Indian troops against British rule) and before completing the three years in Tibet expected of her by Master Morya. It seems unwise to discount other, possibly covert, objectives in Blavatsky's attempts to investigate the Himalayan borders with India.

While Russians intrigued with Afghanistan's emir throughout the 1870s, Blavatsky went to the United States. Investigating "spiritist" phenomena, she met Colonel Henry Steel Olcott, together forming the "Theosophical Society" in New York to investigate spiritual powers that might force science to abandon materialism. News of the Society reached Ceylon, whence came enquiries that encouraged Olcott and Blavatsky to reestablish the Society among sympathizers in India.

Reports of Blavatsky and Olcott leaving New York for India, via England, appeared in New York on December 10, 1878. Having secured

American citizenship to obtain an American passport to protect, if necessary, a Russian woman from British Government restraint, Blavatsky informed a *Daily Graphic* journalist: "I am going to Liverpool and London, where we have branch Theosophical Societies: Then I shall go to Bombay. Oh! How glad I shall be to see my dear Indian home again!"[5]

Arriving in Bombay harbor on February 16, 1879, Blavatsky and Olcott were taken to a small house in Girgaum Back Road, in Bombay's native Hindu quarter. There they established headquarters. Hindu and Parsee gentlemen called on them. Olcott would soon be giving lectures telling Zoroastrians how they should commit more deeply to their traditions, as against modernist or European learning.*

It was not long before Blavatsky attracted fame for feats such as producing at will new designs on embroidered handkerchiefs, letters falling from the ceiling, sounds, manifestations of the "Masters," and apparently miraculous transplacing of lost or familiar objects. Such feats would certainly be a problem for science. It appeared Blavatsky could out-do a guru with all the *siddhis,* and, it should be noted, in India, as in medieval Europe, miracles were signs of holiness.

Alfred Percy Sinnett, editor of popular daily paper the *Pioneer,* founded in Allahabad, joined the Bombay Theosophists, whereupon the triumvirate embarked on a tour of northwest India: an interesting time, one might think, to be promoting indigenous religions (excepting Christianity) through the gauze of miraculous (unless you knew the secret "science") "spiritualism."

While violent conflict flared up with Afghanistan, the Russian Blavatsky and American Col. Olcott returned to Bombay in October 1879 to publish the *Theosophist:* "A Monthly Journal devoted to Oriental Philosophy, Art, Literature, and Occultism, embracing Mesmerism, Spiritualism, and other Secret Sciences. Conducted by H. P. Blavatsky." The Theosophical Society grew rapidly. Young native men with mystical visions of beings from spiritual worlds could feel elevated in a "universal brotherhood" dedicated to "spiritual science." Many Europeans also were looking for something to bolster religious faith and to under-

---

*See Col. H. S. Olcott, "The Spirit of Zoroastrianism," Adyar Pamphlets, No. 23, "A Lecture delivered at the Town Hall, Bombay, on 14th February, 1882" (Adyar, Madras, India: Theosophical Publishing House, 1913).

mine what they perceived as gross materialism in mercantile and scientific progress. India, it transpired, had hidden knowledge, secret glories, revelatory truth: all to be brought into a transcendentalist phase of transnational universalism or spiritual messianism. It was as if Blavatsky projected a suppressed Western spirituality onto the British "possession" that was India, rendering it new and strange, pregnant with "Aryan" mystique. It came as a novel surprise to Indians, many of whom considered Theosophy's message foreign and strange, albeit interesting and politically helpful.

It is evident from reports and letters that abounded in this period concerning Blavatsky that what drew most interest was not her Society's idea of a future marriage of religion and science, or the search for "truth," or even a "secret doctrine," be it Gnostic, Vedantist, or Buddhist, or all of them in an esoteric mélange, but rather the instantaneous duplication of documents and articles of clothing, the making of inscriptions in golden letters in oriental texts, mysterious musical sounds, "raps" with no source, tables held to the ground by unseen force, the production of paintings and writings on paper by placing her palm on blank sheets, and other curiosities: a lost piece of crockery appearing with no rational explanation buried outside in the grounds of a house, trinkets appearing as by magic in a person's pocket—all done in plain view, with the Madame herself visible and benign. And, most influential of all, the mode of communication between the Mahatmas and their star pupil, and her followers: letters sent without benefit of the (very efficient) Indian postal service, messages that fell from thin air, their contents exhibiting knowledge of recent discussion or future requirements—all working overtime in a rush to convince the most skeptical skeptic or to bathe in hope the supine believer.

As A. P. Sinnett wrote: "The raps gave me a complete assurance that she was in possession of some faculties of an abnormal character."[6]

Quite.

While little Edward Alexander Crowley celebrated his fourth birthday at 30 Clarendon Square, Leamington Spa, Warwickshire (on October 12, 1879), Emir Yakub's brother Ayub Khan seized power in Kandahar, Afghanistan, initiating the Second Anglo-Afghan War. While Ayub secured his position, intriguing against the British,

Col. Olcott and Madame Blavatsky decided to go stirring things up in Ceylon, or, as Theosophists see the period May–July 1880: "Col. Olcott laid the foundations for his later work to stimulate the revival of Buddhism. They [he and Blavatsky] both took Pansil,* that is, Pancha Sila, a formal recitation of five precepts renouncing harmfulness, stealing, sexual immorality, lying, and alcohol, preceded by taking refuge in the Buddha, the Dharma, and the Sangha. The public ceremony of repeating these vows after a leader of the Buddhist community is the official profession of Buddhism."[7]

THEOSOPHY IN CEYLON

When Crowley's friend Allan Bennett delivered his maiden speech at Colombo's Theosophical Lodge in July 1901, it was thanks to Blavatsky and Olcott's visit. As Olcott put it: "Early in May 1880, I took passage from Bombay for Colombo in Ceylon on one of the comfortable little coasting steamships of the British Navigation Co. A visit to Ceylon, long urgently requested by the leading priests and laity of the Buddhist community, had been determined upon, and the preparations occupied us."[8] What—or who—had made the priests and "laity" to urge such a thing?

On May 16, the Theosophists' arrival was heralded by a large boat. Aboard it stood voluble Buddhist orator-priest Migettuwatte (or Mohottiwatte) Gunananda Thera (1823–1890), John Robert de Silva, later celebrated Sri Lankan playwright and satirist (1857–1922), and some junior priests. De Silva had become a "Fellow" of the T.S. when it was based in New York. Olcott described Gunananda as "a middle-aged, shaven monk, of full medium stature, with a very intellectual head, a bright eye, very large mouth, and an air of perfect self-confidence and alertness, the most brilliant polemic orator of the terror of the [Christian] Missionaries. HPB had sent Migettuwatte from New York a presentation copy of *Isis Unveiled*, and he had translated portions where she described some of the phenomena she had personally witnessed in the course of her travels.† He requested us to proceed with the steamer to Galle."

---

*See Crowley on "Pansil" on page 253.
†Migettuwatte Gunananda had distinguished himself in written debate with Wesleyan missionaries at Baddagame, Ceylon, in 1865 and across the island in subsequent years.

Influential Buddhist revivalist and anti-colonialist Anagarika Dharmapala ("Defender of the Dharma"; 1864–1933) was sixteen when he first saw Olcott and Blavatsky "regally entertained" in Ceylon. Anagarika would work with Olcott and got to know Blavatsky quite well. She advised him to learn Pāli and serve humanity. Anagarika described attending a Migettuwatte Gunananda debate in about 1874. His account helps us understand one factor in what stimulated the Blavatsky-Olcott Ceylon mission:

> When I [Anagarika] was ten years old, I attended a great debate in a temple pavilion sixteen miles from Colombo, Ceylon, where the Christians on one side and Mohottiwatte Gunananda on the other argued out the truths of their respective religions. Thousands came from the most distant parts of the island to hear the famous debate. Mohottiwatte Gunananda supplied the oratory; and the Venerable Sumangala furnished him with the scholarly material and references. The debate lasted three days.
>
> Dr. J. M. Peebles, an American Spiritualist, who was visiting Colombo at the time, obtained an English report of the controversy, between the Buddhists and Christians. And upon his return to the United States, showed it to Col. Henry S. Olcott and Madame HPB. . . . Deeply impressed, they wrote to Gunananda and Sumangala that, in the interests of universal brotherhood, they had just founded a society inspired by oriental philosophies and that they would come to Ceylon to help the Buddhists. The letters from Col. Olcott and Madame Blavatsky were translated into Sinhalese and widely distributed.[9]

Ground prepared, and following Migettuwatte Gunananda's direction, the Theosophist party approached Galle before dawn on the seventeenth, as the monsoon burst. According to Olcott, "Monks who had read Migettuwatte's translations pressed her to exhibit her powers."[10] Even the Buddhists wanted a bit of magic, it seems, or was it proof of her blessedness they sought? Madame satisfied curiosity with two of her handkerchief demonstrations. She then made "fairy bells ring out sharp in the air near the ceiling and on the verandah. I had to satisfy the crowd with two impromptu addresses during the day."[11] Yes, old

Olcott's addresses might have been of some interest, but it was wonder woman people came for, and the frisson of challenging the missionaries with things *they* couldn't do.

While Ayub gathered his deadly forces in Afghanistan, closely observed by Russia, metaphysical discussions took place in Ceylon with high priest Bulatgama Sumanatissa, a "persistent disputant," as Olcott describes him. Psychic powers were displayed again: ringing bells in the air, a booming explosion, "spirit raps" that caused a dining table to tremble, then move. The audience was amazed. Not surprisingly, "the people could not do enough for us; we were the first white champions of their religion, speaking of its excellence and its blessed comfort from the platform, in the face of the missionaries, its enemies and slanderers."[12]

May 25 was the date chosen for the bombshell. HPB and Olcott took Pansil from the Venerable Bulatgama at a temple of the Ramanya Nikaya "and were formally acknowledged as Buddhists." Olcott added: "We had previously declared ourselves Buddhists long before, in America, both privately and publicly—so this was but a 'formal confirmation' of our previous professions. HPB knelt before the huge statue of the Buddha, and I kept her company. We had a good deal of trouble in catching the Pāli words that we were to repeat after the old monk."[13]

Olcott and Blavatsky left Panadura, just south of Colombo, by train for Kandy on June 9, and after an hour and a half's journey through what Olcott found to be one of the most picturesque tracts of country in the world, arrived at about 7:00 p.m., received at the station by a deputation of Kandyan chiefs. They were then led in great procession, with torches, tom-toms, and "ear-splitting trumpets," to an address given by a committee of chiefs and a Buddhist society linked to the Temple of the Sacred Tooth of Buddha, the Dalada Maligawa. Seeing the somewhat incongruous tooth, Blavatsky slyly declared: "Of course, it is his tooth: one he had when he was born as a tiger!"[14]

While Blavatsky and Olcott toured villages and initiated people into a new Ceylonese Theosophical Society until late at night, Ayub, ruler of Afghanistan descended upon a British and Indian brigade, 2,500 strong, at Maiwand, leaving one-third wiped out, then advanced on Kandahar's British garrison. On August 27, five days before General Roberts famously relieved Kandahar by defeating Ayub's numerically superior force, Blavatsky and servant Babula left Bombay to see A. P. Sinnett at Simla, where Viceroy Lord Lytton—when not anxiously dealing with news from Lord Roberts and myriad other responsibilities—was completing his viceregal plans for fully Anglicizing the government's summer mountain-station location. Sinnett was soon guided by correspondence apparently received from Blavatsky's Masters, Morya and Koot Hoomi. That correspondence formed the substance of Sinnett's books *The Occult World* (1881) and *Esoteric Buddhism* (1883), books familiar to Crowley that generated enormous public interest in Theosophy. Crowley particularly disliked *Esoteric Buddhism,* realizing there was no such animal, nor the persistent (as he saw it) romanticizing of Buddhism's austere creed by equating the "bliss" of nirvana with Christian ideas of heaven.

Sinnett asked for the impossible: that the Masters manifest a copy of the London *Times* in India on its day of issue! The Masters declined the test, but Blavatsky's propensity for wonders would soon overtake her.

HOW INDIANS BECAME ARYANS

It is interesting to observe that in India, people felt drawn to Theosophy not so much as a restatement of familiar religion, but as an exotic and troubling novelty from America. In his book *From Hinduism to Hinduism* (Calcutta: W. Newman Co., 1896), Parbati Churn Roy, B.A., F.T.S., familiar with T. H. Huxley, Herbert Spencer, and Tyndall's Western scientific and skeptical philosophy, devoted three chapters to his personal relations during the early 1880s with Blavatsky, Olcott, the Mahatmas, and the Theosophical Society.

> What I would not accept as true from Hindus, whom I looked upon as too credulous and superstitious, I was prepared to accept as such when it came from Europeans. . . .
>
> During his short stay at Dacca, Colonel Olcott delivered a lecture, one evening, in the Town Hall, in which he praised the Aryan Rishis of old, and advocated the more general study of Sanskrit. But the same spirit of hostility towards the Rishis and their teachings which had induced me to deliver, at Darjeeling, in 1881, a counter-lecture in answer to Babu Protap Chunder Mozoomdar, roused me up again, and at the conclusion of Colonel Olcott's address I said all

manner of things against the ancient Hindus. I attributed our present degraded condition to the too great importance they attached
to the spiritual side at the expense of the material. The study of
the Sanskrit language and literature, which had such charms for
Sir William Jones, T. Colebrooke, Max Müller, and others, meant
to me a mere waste of time. Sanskrit, I argued, was a dead language,
and contained none of the sciences and arts which had contributed
to the greatness of the Europeans, and so it deserved no revival. My
remarks wounded the feelings of the audience, who were mostly
Hindus, and must have also wounded those of Colonel Olcott,
though he was far too good to betray any sign of being hurt. He
was too noble to take offence at my rudeness and want of patriotic
feelings.[15]

She [Blavatsky] was at first suspected by the Government to be
a Russian spy, but, far from being a spy, she was an admirer of the
British Rule. In her opinion it was the best Government that India
could have in her present condition.[16]

Churn Roy's note about Blavatsky's apparently positive view of
British rule in current circumstances may not be quite the benign
observation it first appears. On August 21, 1881, demoted civil servant
(retired) and leading ornithologist of India, Allan Octavian Hume
(1829–1912), and his wife, Mary, formally joined the Theosophical
Society, having met Blavatsky and Olcott with Sinnett at Allahabad in
1879 and in Simla in 1880. Interestingly, Hume's only daughter, Maria
Jane Burnley ("Minnie"; 1854–1927) would join the Hermetic Order of
the Golden Dawn after moving to England.

As a leading Theosophist, Hume strongly supported Calcutta
undergraduates who backed the founding of an Indian National
Congress, which occurred as Blavatsky left India in 1885. Initially at
least, the Congress demonstrated belief in British institutions, liberal
democracy and British law and justice, the greatest desire being for
active participation in government. The Congress's moderate position
of 1885 was clearly that which Blavatsky suggested to Roy, though the
Congress may be seen as first step to an independent India, a perception
doubtless apparent to Blavatsky.

In September–October 1882, shortly after Roy's objection to honoring the "Aryan Rishis of old," since Blavatsky disdained residence with a European or in a European hotel, she abided awhile at Roy's cottage, Willow Dale, in Darjeeling, where they discussed contrasting philosophies.

I also had no sympathy for the exclusiveness of the Tibetans, who would not let any foreigners into their country, and so I wished that the English might go and conquer them and throw their country open to us. She [Blavatsky] felt greatly pained at my then attitude of mind and said that I was an unworthy descendant of the great Aryans.[17]

Readers will note the stress on an alleged superiority of an ancient "Aryan" race. It is important to understand how the word *Aryan* explains the importance attached by sympathetic Westerners—especially Theosophists—to Indian religions. Indeed, if it had not been maintained that India represented survival of an "Aryan race" whose genius had spread westwards, neither Blavatsky's, Allan Bennett's, nor Aleister Crowley's particular respect for the Vedantist philosophies of Hinduism, or of the system of Buddha, may be properly accounted for. Furthermore, since the use of the term *Aryan* has had such catastrophic effects on world history, having been used by extreme German nationalists to distinguish themselves from an allegedly "Semitic" race (Jews in particular), it is essential we understand how the error and pseudo-science of an "Aryan race" came about. The term's significance among those desiring to transplant Indian ideas in Western minds is plain in Allan Bennett's own work, *The Wisdom of the Aryas* (1909), at page 11, written under Bennett's Buddhist name, "Ānanda M[aitrēya]":

Be that as it may, the fact is obvious enough, and of all the various great root-races that have successfully appeared on earth there can be no doubt as to the intellectual and moral supremacy of the Aryan Race. Cradled somewhere in Central Asia, it developed bud after bud like some great zoophyte, each branching bud, as it reached its adolescence, destined to break off from the parent body and wander forth to occupy new lands. Earliest of all came that branch which emigrated through the Himalayan passes into India; and, in the forcing-house provided for it by that tropical climate, and the easy conditions of life in the fertile valleys of the great Indian rivers, it burgeoned into maturity of growth almost before the later buds from the same parent stem had individualized, and, breaking away, had emigrated westward into Europe. Thus it followed that, at a time when the Greeks and Latins were developing the first rudiments of their civilizations; when, in their harsher northern climes the Celtic and Teutonic and Slavonic Aryans remained yet plunged in the semi-savagery of racial childhood, India became the earliest home and centre of Aryan civilization known to our histories.*

The myth of an "Aryan race" began on February 2, 1786, when Bengal's High Court judge Sir William Jones (1746–1794) addressed the "Asiatick Society of Bengal" in Calcutta with a demonstration that Sanskrit bore similarities to Greek and Latin, something explicable, he believed, only by direct biological link, since language was understood as fount of a race's soul.† Apart from his own linguistic mastery, Jones leaned on the work of Jacob Bryant (1715–1804) whose *A New System; or, Analysis of Ancient Mythology* (1774) gave us the names "Shemitic," "Hamitic," and "Japhetic" for race-families believed extended from three sons of Noah. The word *Aryan* had appeared—probably for the first time in Europe—in 1771, in the course of translating a text from Avestan into French where French pioneer orientalist Abraham-Hyacinthe Anquetil-Duperron (1731–1806) linked the name given to the Medes in Herodotus and Diodorus (the Greek *aroi*), the country "Iran," and a Persian self-designation in Avestan (*airyanamvaejah*).

---

*From lectures delivered in the studio of Clifford Bax, 1917–18. Crowley absorbed Bennett's enthusiasm. Fellow Golden Dawn member, poet W. B. Yeats, would publish an edited version of the Upanishads, or commentaries on the Vedas, whose philosophy is called "Vedanta" (or "late Vedic"), which philosophy Crowley would both occasionally challenge, or be captivated by.

†See Prof. Stefan Arvidsson's crucial study *Aryan Idols: Indo-European Mythology as Ideology and Science* (2006), which I reviewed for *Nova Religio, the Journal of Alternative and Emergent Religions* 14, no. 1 (August 2010): 129. Arvidsson's is an original, insightful, convincing analysis of the development of Aryan and "Indo-Aryan" mythology, science, and pseudo-science.

In French, the word was *aryens,* in German, *arier.* Then in 1794, William Jones in Bengal, while translating Indian legal text *Mānava Dharmaśāstra,* the "Laws of Manu," found the Sanskrit *arya,* roughly translated as "noble" and referring to a higher caste. Scholars' alacrity to seize upon the word *Aryan* (in English) may suggest the very high price eventually to be paid for snobbery; the word *Aryan* seemed to have particular appeal to German academics.

Popularity for calling Indo-European languages "Aryan" accrued quickly after 1819 when Karl Wilhelm Friedrich Schlegel saw a connection between the word and the German for "honor": *Ehre.* This sealed a link between a (theoretical) race and deeds of chivalry. Norwegian-German Indologist Christian Lassen lent his weight to Schlegel's idea, and with that, *Arier* and *arische* entered German scholarly discourse. Widely regarded as a word that had sprung directly from an "Aryan" people, it entered all major European languages. As Arvidsson expresses it, there was "no more fatal use of language than the one that separated 'Aryans' from the descendants of Shem."[18] Through Germany it entered the mind of influential Oxford-based orientalist, Friedrich Max Müller (1823–1900), whom Crowley repeatedly referred to as his authority and justification on matters regarding the importance of Indian philosophies.

Arvidsson makes an important point: "As far as Indo-European scholarship was concerned, the fascination with India and with Sanskrit meant that the image of the ancient Indian became prototypical for the image of Indo-Europeans in general—the ancient Indian became the Indo-European *per se.*"[19] They shared a romantic identity, the one "race" in the past, with the newly vivified European now in a position to rejoin the ancient thread. Romanticism proliferated. Johann Gottfried Herder (1744–1803) wrote of how the Brahmin had educated youth for millennia: an unequivocal service to humanity. Arvidsson draws attention to how "the romantics created an image of ancient India as being lost in contemplation of the spiritual nature of the world, the migration of souls, and the recurring incarnation of the gods."[20]

As we have noted, Crowley was drawn to Müller's flame, and it seems no accident then that much of his occult study, evinced in his unfinished compendium of comparative religion, symbol, language, and parallel magical doctrine, *777,* and in copious diaries written in Sicily 1920–22, concern themselves with elemental properties of words and significant etymologies. In later life, Crowley was seldom without his "Skeat," that is, the *Etymological English Dictionary* (four parts, 1879–1882) by Cambridge lecturer in philology and the English language Walter William Skeat (1835–1912), the principal British philologist able to compete with German university professionals. Rev. Professor Skeat, though a no-nonsense, realistic Englishman (part of his appeal to Crowley) disinclined to jump to linguistic conclusions based on arch theories of "family" and root-elements, still showed his respect for Max Müller and the Sanskrit theory in his *The Place-Names of Hertfordshire* (Hertford, 1904, 7):

> But, as was long ago pointed out by Professor Max Müller, the discovery and study of Sanskrit have entirely changed our point of view. We can now recognize the no longer disputed fact that the various languages or dialects of the Indo-Germanic family stand to each other in a sisterly relation; and, consequently, that Old Celtic and Old English must be placed side by side.

The years 1884 to 1885 saw criticism of the T.S. and doubts over Madame Blavatsky's credibility intensify, culminating in damning revelations of alleged fraud on her part, assisted by the disgruntled Coulombs—Blavatsky's housekeepers at Adya—who, if their testimony to hostile missionaries be accepted at face value (and it need not be), assisted Blavatsky by arranging masks and dressed dummies to appear as Mahatmas, and by arranging trapdoors and other means to assist in "materializing" letters in a boxed shrine, and through temporary gaps in ceilings.

The gathering controversy was coolly assessed shortly before the Coulomb dam broke, in Moncure D. Conway's article "The Theosophists," published in the *Religio-Philosophical Journal* in Chicago, after he visited Adyar in January 1884. He describes "the new cult called Theosophy," whose center is at Adyar, Madras,* "whose believers see in it the fulfillment of past visions and prophecies, while

---

*It is curious that Britain's empire in India began in Madras, and that the arrival of the T.S. there may arguably be taken as symbolic of the start of its decline.

unbelievers find a repetition of the pious frauds which have attended the history of religious enthusiasm in all time."[21] When Moncure asked whether he could send a note to the Mahatmas through the cabinet-shrine, he was quickly informed that a previous letter forbade further correspondence; Moncure wondered if a Theosophist friend in Sydney had forewarned Adyar of his journalistic intentions.

Undoubtedly this American has shown the vast possibilities of a new non-Christian agitation that should strike the Indian heart and imagination. These Hindu scholars have always been aware that they have a great history and religious literature. After all the generations in which missionaries sent here have ignored that literature, despised their philosophy, counted their religion mere idolatry and them as idolaters on their way to hell—there has risen a new race of scholars like Max Müller, who have shown the high value and profound religious idealism of their systems. . . .

I have just met an educated gentleman who has arrived here from the United States—Dr. [Franz] Hartmann.* When I was in Colombo, the Chief Priest of Ceylon told me that he had received from Colonel Olcott a request for "permission" to administer the *pansala* [Pansil] ceremony to Dr. Hartmann, and had granted it. . . .

The scene of two men advanced in years coming from Christendom to take refuge with Buddha is unique even in the anomalous history of religion. It has touched the Hindu imagination and heart. In Ceylon Theosophy has given a distinct check to the missionary successes reported in recent years.[22]

Moncure Daniel Conway's *My Pilgrimage to the Wise Men of the East* further illuminates his visit to the new T.S. headquarters at Adyar, Madras, including a remarkable disclaimer to Conway, uttered in timely fashion by Blavatsky herself.

I [Conway] said, "I wish to find out something about the strange performances attributed to you. I hear of your drawing teapots from under your chair, taking brooches out of flowers, and of other

---

*Later co-founder of the Ordo Templi Orientis.

miracles. If such things really occur I desire to know it, and to give a testimony to my people in London in favour of Theosophy. What does it all mean?"

She said with a serene smile, "I will tell you, because you are a public teacher [here she added some flattery], and you ought to know the truth; it is all glamour—people think they see what they do not see—that is the whole of it."[23]

The significance Conway so adroitly placed on the Theosophy phenomenon was precisely that which Aleister Crowley recognized seventeen years later when correcting English writer G. K. Chesterton's understated jibes at Blavatsky's Theosophy that appeared in a review of Crowley's *Soul of Osiris* (see page 58). For Crowley, it signaled the beginning of a new era, a preparatory stage in the initiation of humankind to a "new Aeon of light, life, and liberty." The seed of the idea came to him through Theosophical channels, but he would see himself and, eventually, his synthesis of "Thelema" as Blavatsky's true successor, establishing a new aeon marked by, among other phenomena, a renaissance of India's authentic will.

By the end of 1884, serious doubts about Blavatsky and her secret Mahatmas induced London's recently founded (1882) Society for Psychical Research to approve Australian Richard Hodgson (1855–1905) conducting an investigation. Hodgson presented his preliminary report at two meetings of the S.P.R. on May 29 and June 26, 1885. While necessary for the S.P.R.'s credibility to treat extraordinary claims with some skepticism, Hodgson may have relied too heavily on Emma and Alexis Coulomb's testimony. The precise provenance of the "Mahatma letters" has never been established satisfactorily to all parties.*

Hodgson had trouble fixing a motive for what he considered fraudulent phenomena, not grasping that among devotees of "spiritualism," strange phenomena were *expected* as "proof" of spiritual activity.

---

*Those wishing to explore the Mahatma letters issue further may consult the following websites: Dr Vernon Harrison's examination in the early 1980s, which can be found on the Theosociety.org website, supports the defense case. Further research may be found on the Prajnaquest.fr website.

Followers were seldom content with Saint Paul's dictum that "spiritual things are spiritually discerned" (I Corinthians 2:14). Blavatsky's letters appearing "out of nowhere" seem almost like an ironic joke on public expectation. Having put aside a political motive, and expressed doubt that Blavatsky was a "spy"—how could Hodgson judge such a thing?—he concluded the following as a supposition of his own:

> But a conversation with Madame Blavatsky, which arose out of her sudden and curious excitement at the news of the recent Russian movement upon the Afghan frontier, compelled me to ask myself seriously whether it was not possible that the task which she had set herself to perform in India was to foster and foment as widely as possible among the natives a disaffection towards British rule.
>
> I cannot profess myself, after my personal experiences of Madame Blavatsky, to feel much doubt that her real object has been the furtherance of Russian interests. But although I have felt bound to refer to my own view on this point, I suggest it here only as a supposition which appears best to cover the known incidents of her career during the past thirteen or fourteen years.[24]

In June 1885, while new British prime minister Lord Salisbury threatened war if Russia would not quit the Zulficar Pass, with its commanding position over the north Afghan plains, Madame Blavatsky prepared to move to Würzburg in Germany, putting her energies into thoughts of a new book, *The Secret Doctrine* (1888), determined perhaps to clarify that the only secrets she was serious about were those that profane or materialist consciousness hid from itself. In late December, following an announcement in March made at Theosophist Allan Octavian Hume's initiative, the Indian National Congress held its first sessions in Bombay.

Blavatsky's work in India was done.

TWO

Fall-Out and Fall-In

Founded by esoteric Freemasons Samuel Liddell Mathers, William Wynn Westcott, and Edward Woodman in 1888 out of the Masonic *Societas Rosicruciana in Anglia* (founded circa 1865), the Order that shaped Crowley's life appeared in the wake of the Coulomb scandal. The Hermetic Order of the Golden Dawn—which attracted former T.S. members—may also have been inspired by the premature loss of mystic Anna Kingsford (1846–1888). Anna had served as president of London's Theosophical Society in 1883 but disagreed with Blavatsky's overwhelming promulgation of Hinduism and Buddhism, at Christianity's expense.

Kingsford's rejection of materialism and fervent interest in gnosis and Graeco-Egyptian Hermetic thought won an admirer in fellow vegetarian and anti-vivisectionist Samuel Mathers, who would make such an impact on Allan Bennett and Aleister Crowley. Before the G∴D∴ was established, Mathers lectured on Kabbalah to London's Theosophists, and attended Anna Kingsford's talks on a universal and spiritually transformative Hermetic gnosis.*

Medical graduate Anna Kingsford and colleague Edward Maitland in London deviated early from the Indian emphasis. If esoteric wisdom of a spiritual nature was to be found among orthodox and heterodox

---

*Doctrines expressed in Kingsford's posthumous book *The Perfect Way, or the Finding of Christ,* edited by Edward Maitland (London: Watkins, 1909), and in *The Mother: The Woman Clothed with the Sun* (1885), which latter work impressed Aleister Crowley in early 1900.

Western mystics, and in the annals of Hermetic magic and Freemasonry, as Helena Blavatsky also believed, need one really look further than Western traditions for the "light that lighteth the world"? Reaction against the T.S. leadership's absorption in Hindu and Buddhist thought-categories, coupled with the Hodgson Report's conclusions, led Samuel (self-named) "Macgregor" Mathers, French Martinist "Papus" (Gérard Encausse), and, in Vienna, Rudolf Steiner (1861–1925), to step outside a strictly Theosophist tide, favoring instead "Western" esoteric, Christian, and classical-pagan spiritual traditions, for not only was Rosicrucianism inherently pietist-Christian (with heterodox elements), but there had long existed a Masonic-Rosicrucian prejudice in Egypt's, not India's, favor.* The Western Hermetic tradition in Masonic Rosicrucianism, including alchemy, astrology, and magic, was Christian-mystical, gnostic, or Neoplatonist-Hermetic in philosophy, and romantic in spirit. The ideal source for an arcane primal "Tradition" of spiritual-cosmic knowledge was thus divided: between Egypt and/or Atlantis (or something earlier), and "Masters" in (or under) the Himalayas: Agarttha, Shambhala, Shangri La.

Nevertheless, while British Theosophists favoring the "Golden Dawn" approach to Western magic, gnosis, and Kabbalah thus were able to avoid overt apostasy to Hinduism or Buddhism, there remained an elephant in the room, formed of awareness that Indian spiritual categories, however poorly understood, impacted strongly on the minds of spiritual seekers as being analogous, fundamental, or even mysteriously primary (*Aryan*) to the historic evolution of "God consciousness."

ALLAN BENNETT

Probably the most striking example of reaction *to* reaction against India appeared in the career of Charles Henry Allan Bennett, despite twenty-one-year-old Bennett's having entered the Golden Dawn in 1894 as, apparently, *adopted son* of Order founder MacGregor Mathers. Bennett's heart belonged elsewhere. It was Allan Bennett who turned Crowley on to yoga, and to Buddhism, and Bennett's path to yoga can be traced directly

---

*Note that according to Crowley's account, his own fundamental spiritual impulse-event of 1904 occurred in Egypt, following invocation of Egyptian gods Thoth and Horus.

through enthusiastic Theosophist circles in Ceylon, mainland India, and in Europe, stimulated by the Buddhism-for-Western-consumption purveyed in Sir Edward Arnold's epic poem *The Light of Asia* (1879) and Dr. Paul Carus's *Gospel of Buddha* (1894). Nevertheless, as Sandra Bell has argued convincingly in her research article "Being Creative with Tradition: Rooting Theravāda Buddhism in England,"[1] it was "not unusual for members of the colonial service in Asia and European travelers to learn about Buddhism from local people, usually monks."

Sri Lankan monk Yatramulle Unnanse, for example, collaborated with Thomas William Rhys Davids (1843–1922), after Rhys Davids had learned Tamil and Sinhala while working at the Colonial Secretary's office in Colombo, teaching the latter Pāli when Rhys Davids was appointed to Galle's police magistrate court (see page 85). Notably critical of Theosophy, Rhys Davids went on to found the Pāli Text Society in 1881 in London, providing a benchmark of "unimpeachable scholarship" (Bell) and long-term institutional support for Buddhism in Britain. Rhys Davids would support Allan Bennett's own pioneering efforts to evangelize an authentic Buddhist message, and he became Britain's leading scholar and translator of Buddhist works, whose translations are still widely consulted.[2] He also expanded Max Müller's conception of the Aryan race, writing papers and giving lectures alleging that the British peoples shared Aryan ethnicity with the Buddha's family and followers in Ceylon, thus suggesting a controversial theory that British people possessed racial affinities to Buddhism itself, and were therefore especially adaptable to India's governance.

Another notable collaborative exercise—this time friendly to Theosophy—came from the work of *Daily Telegraph* editor, Sanskrit scholar, and poet Sir Edward Arnold. His *Light of Asia* received a glowing review in the first issue of Blavatsky and Olcott's the *Theosophist*. Arnold's work directly stimulated Bennett's turning from magic to Buddhism. In 1885 the *Daily Telegraph* published articles by Arnold drawing attention to the dilapidated state of the Buddha Gaya (or Bodh Gaya) temple, where Gautama Buddha had achieved enlightenment. Six years later, Anagarika Dharmapala (whom we encountered welcoming Blavatsky and Olcott in Ceylon) was fired up to restore the site after visiting it with Japanese priest Kozen Gunaratna, resulting, in May 1891, with the founding of the Budh-Gaya Mahabodhi Society. Arnold was a founder member, with Ceylon's high priest H. Sumangala as president, Dharmapala as general secretary, and Col. Olcott as director. Representatives of seven Buddhist countries appeared in the Society's inaugural constitution; the Society continues to this day. As Sandra Bell makes plain, Asian Buddhists were not a passive source plundered by Westerners: "A more accurate picture delineates a quite sophisticated pattern of interaction between intellectual elements of both the European and Asian cultural elites, resulting in Asian Buddhists reexamining their own religious texts in the light of European ideology. The nineteenth century was altogether a period of reformation throughout the Theravāda world."[3]

Knowledge regarding Allan Bennett's early life is scarce. Numerous mini-biographies tell us he was born in London (but where?) on December 8, 1872, that his mother was a Roman Catholic, and that he trained as an electrical engineer, with a serious interest in chemistry. He is supposed to have been schooled at Hollesley College, and at Bath.

Hollesley (Colonial) College at Ipswich in Suffolk provided training for unemployed men intending to emigrate. On one salient matter only do extant accounts of Bennett agree: Bennett was poor. Largely self-educated in science and religious philosophy, both esoteric and exoteric, his path was dogged—as would Crowley's be—by asthma, exacerbated to alarming levels of misery by London's dense, polluted air in that period.

At some point in his youth Bennett had befriended Samuel Liddell Mathers (1854–1918), and after initiation into Mathers's and his Masonic-Rosicrucian colleagues' Hermetic Order of the Golden Dawn in 1894, supported Mathers against detractors in the Order during the 1890s, when several members lost patience with Mathers for being a careless debtor, supporter of immoral doctrines and subversive political Legitimism, and being subject to autocratic, ill-mannered impulses, among other perceived misdemeanors. More detail concerning Mathers's relationship with Bennett occurs in Elizabeth J. Harris's careful biographical treatment, "Ānanda Metteya: The First British Emissary of Buddhism."* Harris cites reminiscences from prominent Sri Lankan

---

*The Wheel 27, nos. 420–22 (1998): 161–222, in Collected Wheel Publications (Kandy, Sri Lanka: Buddhist Publication Society, 2014).

Buddhist Dr. Cassius Pereira (later Ven. Kassapa Thera, author of *The Dhammapada: The Gift of Truth Excels All Other Gifts*) who first heard Bennett in Ceylon in 1901. Following Bennett's development closely, Pereira claimed, importantly, that Bennett had been adopted by a Mr. McGregor and kept McGregor's name until McGregor died (this must be Samuel Liddell "MacGregor" Mathers). In support of this, Bennett's name appears as "A. MacGregor" on his Adeptus Minor Golden Dawn certificate of 1896. Crowley occasionally referred to his friend as Allan MacGregor, which doubtless tickled Jacobite Crowley, aficionado of Scottish rebelliousness.

According to Harris, Bennett was born December 8, 1872, in London, his father a civil and electrical engineer who died when Allan was young. Information about "McGregor" was repeated to Harris by Buddhist scholar and Sri Lankan spiritual leader Ven. Balangoda Ānanda Maitreya Thero (1896–1998). Balangoda entered the Bhikkhu Sangha in 1911 and was one of the few Harris met who remembered the Ānanda Metteyya era.* Harris mentions Crowley's view that Bennett was raised a strict Catholic by his mother, so she was still caring for him, presumably, at some level. He was educated in Bath, afterward trained as an analytical chemist, eventually employed by Dr. Bernard Dyer, public analyst and consulting chemist of repute, based in London as official analyst to the London corn trade. (This latter detail derives from Kenneth Grant's *The Magical Revival* [London: Frederick Muller, 1972], 82n.)

Sensitive and serious, Bennett was alienated from Christianity on account of the suffering he saw about him that seemed to deny a personal God of love. His asthma obstructed regular employment. Pereira thought Bennett's prāṇāyāma exercises may have worsened his asthma.

---

*In Buddhist eschatology, Metteyya (Pāli) or Maitreya (Sanskrit) is a Buddha yet to appear. Bennett sometimes used the Sanskrit *Maitreya* after becoming a bhikkhu in Burma in 1901–02. The Maitri Hall in Sri Lanka, for the international friends of Buddhism, was founded and named by Pereira in the 1920s in honor of Ānanda Maitreya (Bennett). Maitreya or Metteyya is derived from the word *maitrī* (Sanskrit) or *mettā* (Pāli) meaning "loving-kindness," derived from the noun *mitra* (Pāli: *mitta*): "friend." *Metteyya* first appears in the *Cakavatti* (*Sihanāda*) *Sutta* in the *Digha Nikāya* 26 of the Pāli Canon. In the *Amitabha Sūtra* and the *Lotus Sūtra,* Maitreya is described as "Ajita Bodhisattva": a bodhisattva who will attain complete enlightenment at a future time on earth, and deliver the pure dharma.

Bennett's partiality for Mathers was likely based on his relationship with his adopting guardian (if that relationship has basis in fact) but seems, anyway, to have been significantly reinforced by a general lack of respect for the wits of Mathers's opponents, among them Frederick Leigh Gardner (with whom Bennett corresponded on magical matters) and Annie Horniman.*

Crowley entered the hornet's nest of the Golden Dawn in November 1898 with the best intentions, hoping to find himself among the enlightened, on a higher plane to a mediocre world outside the portals of initiation. It would not take very long before *Perdurabo* (his Order name) became aware, by degrees, of Order politics, and it would not take Order members long to realize an unusual bird had flown into their simmering glasshouse, a creature whose projected demeanor seemed a perpetual boast, and whose physical, eccentric, and assumed aristocratic manner came over as both blunt and obscure by turns; Perdurabo was not trusted by all members. In spring 1899, Allan Bennett latched on to him after an Order meeting. Presumably reading something amiss in Crowley's "aura," Bennett accused Crowley of meddling with the "goetia." This was the old term for magic involving evocation of demons, or spiritual entities bound to the material world and its concerns, magic traditionally condemned as abominably black in contrast to "Magia": august, noble pursuit of the hidden principles of all Nature, reliant on the light and will of Almighty God and his angels, progress in which required denuding self of impurity rather than self-aggrandizement—the proverbial wager of the demonic pact. When Crowley protested innocence, Bennett replied: "Then the goetia have been meddling with you." Taken aback by what he took for Frater Iehi Aour's direct perception of his deepest struggles, Crowley was doubtless also struck by Bennett's appearance.

Bennett's 1896 certificate of entry into the Golden Dawn's Inner Order grade of Adeptus Minor ($5° = 6^\square$) has survived.[4] Most of the certificate consists of a composite photo showing a twenty-three-year-old Bennett coming forth from darkness behind an ancient Egyptian pylon emblazoned with hieroglyphics. Illuminated by light before him, the adept wears a full-length Eastern robe, embroidered at the edges

---

*See my *Aleister Crowley: The Biography*.

and wrapped at the front by a bright, broad silken sash, gripping his slim body like a golden amulet. His youthful face looks surprisingly late twentieth-century-hip cool for a man of the mid-1890s. He has a mop of black hair over his ears and a thick black moustache. The "beautiful and divine one" (as the adept is described in a panegyric below the photograph) has large, emotive eyes, a gentle presence, and looks not unlike a young Carlos Santana, a pinup for rock-oriented fans in the 1970s. Crowley, with his eye for decadence, much indulged at the time, was surely attracted to a man a little older than himself who had soft, compelling looks backed by knowledge Crowley did not yet possess, and a clean will backed by an air of quiet authority. Brother "Let there be light" also expressed that kind of inner suffering from spiritual sensitivity that racked Crowley's own poetry with agonies of ecstasy. We can be reasonably sure Crowley found Bennett attractive, but whatever he might have dreamed of doing was strictly off limits. Crowley asserted that, to Bennett, the existence of sex was a blight on life. He related how a youthful Bennett recoiled with shock when introduced to the facts of human reproduction, vowing never to have anything to do with sex whatsoever: lust was the absurd snare that bound the angel to earth. One might just imagine Crowley teasing his new friend on this matter, but one suspects Crowley knew when not to overstep the mark. As far as we can tell, they grew close. According to a manuscript of Crowley's included by Kenneth Grant in his *The Magical Revival* (82):

> We called him [Bennett] the White Knight, from *Alice in the Looking Glass*. So lovable, so harmless, so unpractical! But he was a Knight, too! And White! There never walked a whiter man on earth. He never did walk on earth, either! A genius, a flawless genius. But a most terribly frustrated genius.

Crowley got the noble and gentle Bennett out of his crowded digs (described by Crowley as a "grim tenement") and let him share his London flat at 67 Chancery Lane where Crowley had constructed two simple temples, one for evoking demons to serve the magician, one for invocations of higher spirits. Bennett greatly aided Crowley in understanding this process and other aspects of ceremonial magic, including the assumption of "god-forms," to identify with divine energies, and the correspondences between gods and magical elements (such as plants and precious stones, colors and planets) from different magical, mythical, and religious traditions. This knowledge was integrated with Hebrew Kabbalah (gematria in particular). Bennett had worked on tables of correspondences with Mathers, and Bennett lent Crowley copious notes on the subject, to which Crowley later added his own researches to produce the current text of *777,* intended as research in progress.

Bennett also introduced Crowley to the world of combining stimulants with magic to intensify concentrated effects. Bennett's asthmatic condition had rendered him dependent on medicines to palliate his condition, and once the benefit of stimulants was clear to him, there seemed no reason not to experiment with other, possibly beneficial uses in order to "open the veils beyond the gates of matter," or to expand inner consciousness and imaginative awareness, or to "break the bonds of the body" (anesthesia). Quite legal drugs such as hashish, opium, and ether were easily obtainable through E. P. Whineray's pharmacy in Stafford Street near Piccadilly Circus, London, though Crowley was quite squeamish on scientific and health grounds about going over anything like an absolutely minimal dose. Bennett had other tricks up his sleeve, such as a notorious "blasting rod" of his own invention he apparently preferred to the usual kind of "wand" Golden Dawn members were supposed to construct and imbue with their will. Crowley saw Bennett use his rod on an annoying person, whose arm suffered temporary paralysis. While the implication was that Bennett had charged it with psychic forces, its effectiveness may have derived from knowledge of electrical engineering, and that it was effectively a battery (stored energy) with the means to deliver an electric shock to adversaries. At this time, analogy between magical ("spiritual") phenomena and an invisible world of electricity and electromagnetism was common. No one could deny any more the real, scientifically quantifiable existence of invisible forces, and much was made of this analogy in Theosophical discourse. Effects of electricity were commonly described as "magic," and "vibrations" of sound and thought had long been inherent to magical invocation. Pulse and rhythm had obvious electrical analogies.

However, perhaps due in part to the tiresome Order politics and bickering in the Golden Dawn, and the pull of a profound spiritual idealism, Bennett became disenchanted with manipulating the lower

Fig. 2.1. Boleskine House, Loch Ness, circa 1899.
(from Crowley's "autohagiography," The Spirit of Solitude, 1929;
courtesy Ordo Templi Orientis)

universe and sought a spiritual realm beyond the material altogether: clearer air to be absorbed in. Again, there is an analogy with his increasingly desperate asthmatic condition, for which Crowley hoped to contribute the cure. Fumes from incense of evocation and invocation cannot have helped Bennett, even if the entity evoked might have been supposed possessed of powers beneficial to health, such as demon "Papus" from the *Nuctemeron* of magus Apollonius of Tyana.

Crowley's opportunity to assist Bennett achieve his desire of going out to Ceylon to immerse himself in yoga and Buddhism came in the new year, 1900, a few months after acquiring Boleskine House on Loch Ness in Scotland, where Perdurabo had invited Lilian Horniblow, wife of (then) Lieutenant Frank Horniblow of the Royal Engineers, to stay before Christmas 1899, along with Cambridge graduate and journalist William Evans Humphrys. A magical ceremony "to obsess Frederick Leigh Gardner," who had apparently contacted the police in November, possibly over Crowley's living in Chancery Lane with another man (Bennett?), and allegedly having sexual relations with an unnamed

Cambridge chum, or brother of said chum, led to Humphrys's fearful departure, as well as that of "Laura Grahame" (Mrs. Horniblow's name for assignations), with whom Humphrys appears to have fallen in love.

Crowley had already begun preparations for the perilous requirements of the "Sacred Magic of Abra-Melin the Mage," to acquire the "knowledge and conversation of the Holy Guardian Angel," and expected all kinds of demonic interference to his aims; he was certainly subject to interference, being warned by "Laura," by Humphrys, and by girlfriend Evelyn Hall that he was in trouble with the police. On February 24, 1900, Bennett wrote to him, that the "Angel of the Lord" had appeared with the message that his friend was in deep trouble over a number of issues, some spiritual. Meanwhile, Mathers had overridden the London Inner Order's refusal to permit Crowley to the Adeptus Minor Grade, and brought Crowley into the Inner Order himself in Paris on January 23.

Crowley prayed and submitted himself to the "Providence of God," while Laura, wishing to prolong the affair with Crowley (he had gone cool on it—chastity being a, perhaps convenient, component of Abra-Melin discipline), had asked how she might do *her* bit for the cause of spiritual evolution, a cause that meant so much to the fancied man exposing himself to chastity and enemies visible and invisible. Crowley's story is that he persuaded her to forego some of life's unearned luxuries and achieve spiritual merit by securing the survival of a good man, that is, paying Bennett's fare to India. Laura provided either cash or a ruby ring in lieu, but in March, with the sex turned off, and under pressure from Order members such as Gardner, and possibly Humphrys, "Laura" demanded the gift's return—already spent on Bennett's ticket. Rebellious Inner Order members informed police that Crowley had stolen a large sum of money from a lady. The lady, however, surely desirous of keeping her affairs from public—or her husband's—scrutiny, did not press charges.

For Perdurabo ("I will endure"), caught in the spiritual logic of the Abra-Melin preliminaries, settling with Laura was a snare because, he surmised, powers resisting Abra-Melin success were exploiting the Laura situation to break his will to subdue them. Abra-Melin required Crowley's treating every event as a "dealing of God with his soul." Capitulating to Laura threatened his Adeptus Minor promise to regard suffering as an initiator of the heart.

By the end of March, the London rebels had renounced Mathers as leader and begun investigations into Mathers's allegations that the Order's founding documents were forgeries produced by William Wynn Westcott, which bombshell Mathers interpreted as meaning authority was his, for he was close to the "Secret Chiefs," required authorities for the Order as a spiritual body. Pledging himself to aid Mathers against what he was convinced was a war of spiritual opposition to the Secret Chiefs, Crowley dropped Abra-Melin.*

By the time Crowley left Great Britain for America at the end of June 1900, Bennett was ensconced in Colombo, Ceylon.

BENNETT IN CEYLON 1900–1901

According to Cassius Pereira, Bennett went to Kamburugamuwa in the Matara region, some ninety-three miles south of Kandy on Ceylon's southern coast, to study Pāli for six months under the Ven. Weraganpita Revata, an elderly Sinhalese monk.[5] This study brought him close to the text of the earliest extant copies of the Buddha's teachings; original manuscripts have not survived. Expert in Buddhism's earliest history Richard Gombrich reckons Gautama died in about 410 BCE after forty-five years of preaching, but a period of oral tradition ensued before accounts of his teachings were committed to the Pāli written language (*not* Sanskrit) in the first or second century BCE. Those adhering strongly to the earliest Buddhist traditions are called Theravāda (elder school) Buddhists, dominant in Sri Lanka, a feature of whose teachings is greater emphasis on the psychological state of people (especially monks) advancing views and theories, rather than the content of the views and theories themselves. As Gombrich maintains in his vital study of early Buddhism, the concern of the Buddha was more with *process* than definition.[6] According to Gombrich, "The central teachings of the Buddha came as a response to the central teachings of the old Upaniṣads, notably the Bṛhadāraṇyaka [Upaniṣad]."[7]

---

*For the detailed story of the Golden Dawn rebellion, consult my *Aleister Crowley: The Biography* (2014), Ellic Howe's *Magicians of the Golden Dawn* (1978), and R. A. Gilbert's *Revelations of the Golden Dawn: The Rise and Fall of a Magical Order* (1997).

The first noble truth is the single word *dukkha,* and it is explicated to mean that everything in our experience of life is ultimately unsatisfactory, so that it follows that for true satisfaction we must look outside that experience.[8]

It is worth lingering a while here on doctrine, since it will have major repercussions on assumptions that Crowley, after his sojourns in India, would carry with him for the rest of his life, and helps to explain some of the denials of basic Christian and liberal expectations that made him and his ideas seem threatening and dangerous to some minds. As we shall see when examining Crowley's writings that emanated from his Indian experiences (doubtless discussed with Bennett in detail), he was inclined to be critical, sometimes dismissive, of Vedānta—chiefly the teachings of the Upanishads and their commentaries—and of the Advaita school, which to varying degrees identified fundamental essence (Brahman) with the soul or spirit (*ātman*). In this he was following the logic of Buddha's critical teachings of the Brahmins as preserved by Theravāda Buddhists. Buddha engaged with Brahmin pundits and found them wanting in realism, that is, by asserting claims unsubstantiated by experience. Crowley would come to agree with the general criticism, but years later found the Buddha's teaching wanting also, at least insofar as Gautama's teachings were understood.

The Buddha taught life as experienced bore three features. It is impermanent (*anicca*), unsatisfactory (*dukkha*), and not the "self" (*anatta*). The idea of the "self" here is taken from what Brahmins received from the Upanishads, namely, that ultimate essence is one, in origin (Brahman) and in the soul (ātman), expressed explicitly in the phrase *tat tvam asi* ("Thou art that") in *Chāndogya Upaniṣad* 6, 8, 7 and elsewhere. The Buddha sees this as wrong in the Pāli text, *Alagaddūpama Sutta* (*Majjhima Nikāya* I, 135–36) where the Buddha says people worry unnecessarily about something that neither exists externally, nor internally. According to Gombrich: "The Buddha was attacking Vedānta and in effect denying Descartes: from the fact that there is a process of thinking he would refuse to draw the conclusion that 'I exist.' But remember that for the Buddha existence implies stasis: it is the opposite of becoming."* Life as experienced cannot be of the

---

*Gombrich, *How Buddhism Began,* 40.

self because life changes, and *essence* does not change. What changes is therefore not the self. That life ends in death is clear enough proof of its unsatisfactory nature *and* its lack of essence. So the Buddha, in the first instance, accepts the Upanishad teaching: a dichotomy between the unchanging and the life of continual rebirth, but he then denies the unchanging character of the "self" known in the world. Gombrich notes that while the Upanishads reduce the microcosm and the macrocosm to an equation of 1 = 1, the Buddha denies existence of an essence in either sphere, making a "parallel equation: 0 = 0." We shall see how important a 0 = 0 equation is to Crowley in chapter 11 where he uses it to create an original ontology of his own, in his work *Berashith,* inspired by his time spent with Bennett and his own spiritual and intellectual puzzles. In Gombrich's view, it was not that the Buddha wished to make a doctrine out of a lack of essence in the world, but that he was making fun of the Brahmins from a standpoint of commonsense approach to their own logic. Crowley would do precisely the same thing, and in doing so comes very close to the perception of Buddha's sense of humor so brilliantly highlighted by Gombrich.*

Now, Bennett was certainly not in this position when he became acquainted in Ceylon with the earliest traditions of Buddhism; he was

Fig. 2.2. Allan Bennett in Ceylon (Sri Lanka), 1901. (from The Spirit of Solitude, *1929; courtesy Ordo Templi Orientis)*

---

*See chapter 11, "The Works."

awestruck, highly respectful, not critical, as was Crowley. Buddha's promise of a reality beyond painful phenomena was his deepest hope. Besides, Bennett was soon to be immersed in rāja yoga practices whose underlying philosophy was Advaitist, involving the substitution of false conceptions and experience of "I" with a transcending "I" or Self that obliterated distinctions between "I" and "not I" in a bliss of being itself.

According to Pereira, such was Bennett's brilliance that after six months in Ceylon, he could converse fluently in Pāli—a simpler language than Sanskrit.[9] Pereira recorded how he learned much from Bennett about meditation, thinking it Buddhist in origin, but later realized Bennett had included "mystic Christian, Western 'occult,' and Hindu sources." As to Bennett's knowledge at this point, Pereira concluded it was "vague, wonder seeking, and really only played about the fringe of a truly marvelous avenue for study and practice."[10]

Bennett's health also improved, and he was able to cut down on medicinal support while seeking employment. A job transpired as tutor to a son of Hon. Ponnambalam Ramanathan, Ceylon's distinguished lawyer and politician (1851–1930). Appointed solicitor general in 1892, having been made Companion of the Order of Saint Michael and Saint George in the 1889 royal-birthday honors list, the Shaivite Ramanathan had three sons and three daughters from his first wife, and a daughter, Sivagamisundhari, from his second wife, Australian R. L. Harrison (later known as Lelawathy). His wife wrote the preface to her husband's commentary on Saint John's Gospel that impressed Crowley after it appeared in 1902.

Bennett's employment had the added advantage that the Tamil Hindu solicitor general wrote about religion under his yogic title, Sri Parānanda, and taught Bennett techniques of hatha yoga: prāṇāyāma = breathing control, *asanas* (physical postures), and acquainted the Englishman with knowledge of *jñāna* yoga as a path to the meaning of ascending trances "*dhyāna*" and "samādhi." Crowley noted in his *Confessions* that even these "spiritual joys" would soon be rejected by Bennett as he believed they impeded control of his mind, which he wished to direct to the "ultimate truth" he sought.[11]

While Crowley was intrigued by Ramanathan's use of jñāna (gnostic or spiritual knowledge) yoga to penetrate the mysteries of the Gospel of John in his *Eastern Exposition of the Gospel of Jesus According to*

St. John (London: William Hutchinson, 1902)—where the phrase "I and the Father are one" (John 10:30) is interpreted as a state of samādhi, the highest yogic experience of divine union*—Crowley was dismissive of the author's intellect exhibited in the religious work for which Ramanathan was best known when Bennett arrived in his employ, *The Eastern Exposition of the Gospel of Jesus According to St. Matthew* (1898), where the author accounted for the Hebrew parallelism of Jesus arriving "on an ass, and a colt, the foal of an ass" (a quote from Zechariah 9:9) as suggesting Jesus rode two beasts in the manner of a circus performer! Sometimes comparisons between Jesus and gymnosophist yogis' accomplishments could be taken too far! Crowley thought it his duty to whisk Bennett away from Colombo to Kandy in the island's interior as soon as possible, though he allowed that Shaivite devotee Ramanathan was yet superior to the Vishnaivite devotee on account of what he observed as a healthy pride.

Nevertheless, Bennett was fortunate to meet a senior Sri Lankan politician whose academic background led to a topflight career in law and administrative heights under a benign colonial administration Ramanathan labored to reform, founding the Ceylon National Society in 1880, striving with the imperial government for constitutional improvements and better administration of justice for all in a country where Tamil migrants such as Ramanathan had endured prejudice.

---

*Sri Parānanda's actual text commentary on this theme (pp. 200–201) reads as follows: "The soul after sanctification (v. 36) is perfect (Matt. V.48) or pure, and is in this respect the same in being as God." The solicitor general defines *sanctification* on the following page thus: "Sanctification or saintliness, derived from the Sanskrit *Sánti*, through the Latin *Sancio*, to make holy (Greek *hagios*), means pacification of the soul. The soul that has attained the peace that passeth all thought (Phil. IV.7) is said to be saintly or sanctified; and this Peace (from Sanskrit *paksha*, love, through Latin *pax, pacis*) is Infinite Love; or the Love that has neither length nor breadth, nor height nor depth (Eph. III.18)." Commenting on verse 38 "The Father is in me and I in Him," Ramanathan says: "First know your own Spirit by isolating it from all that is flesh, and then the alone-become Spirit, or Christ, will most assuredly know God. Jesus meant to say that the popular idea of the Jews that God was far away from man, somewhere beyond the region of the clouds, was a great mistake, and that the truth was that God has been connected with the Spirit of every man inseparably from eternity. Only, the worldly man is much too blind to perceive this connection in his own case, whereas to the spiritual man no fact is more patent than that the Father is in him, and he is in the Father." Which is to say: Saint John's Gospel is Advaitist!

In July 1901, shortly before Crowley's arrival in Ceylon, Cassius Pereira witnessed Bennett's maiden address on the subject of Buddhism's "Four Noble Truths" at the Theosophical Society's Hope Lodge, in Colombo. Profoundly moved, Pereira would insist Bennett's address initiated his own renunciation unto Buddhist enlightenment.[12] As Elizabeth Harris observes, it hardly surprises that the call came over so strongly from Bennett to Pereira, as it embodied what was now becoming Bennett's conviction, that he too should renounce all, take up the yellow robe of the bhikkhu, and commit to the core of his study of the Tripitika or "three baskets of the [Buddhist] law." Crowley's arrival in August may then have constituted something of a distraction to Bennett's objectives, but Bennett was nonetheless generous with his time, patience, and knowledge. Crowley appreciated the opportunity to the full, bequeathing us the fullest contemporary account extant of the extraordinary Allan Bennett. Besides, without Crowley's machinations on his behalf, Bennett would never have made it to Ceylon in the first place, to begin a career now finally being recognized as profoundly courageous and pioneering.

THREE

The Beast in Colombo

On August 1, 1901, aboard German steamship *Bayern* in the Andaman Sea, having left Hong Kong via Singapore and Penang, Crowley started the diary he titled "The Writings of Truth."[1] It is headed, in very neat Sanskrit, with the common Buddhist salute to the master: *Namo tassa Bhagavato arahato sammasambuddhasa*—"Glory to the Blessed One, the Perfected One, the Enlightened One," followed by an introduction:

> The Seeker after Wisdom, whose Bliss is non-Existence, the Devotee of the Most Excellent Bhavani, the Wanderer of the Samsara-cakra, the Insect that crawls on Terra, on Seb beneath Nuit, the Purusha beyond Ishwara: He taketh up the Pen of the Ready Writer, to record those Mysterious Happenings which came unto Him in His Search for Himself. And the beginning is of Spells and of Conjurations and of Evocations of the Evil Ones: Things unlawful to write of, dangerous even to think of: wherefore they are not here written. But he beginneth with his Sojourning in the Isle of Lanka [Ceylon]: the time of his dwelling with Maitrananda Swami [Allan Bennett]. Wherefore, O Bhavani, bring Thou all unto Proper End! To Thee be Glory. ॐ [AUM].
>
> I exist not: there is no God: no time: no place: wherefore I exactly particularise and specify these things. August 1, 1901 A.D.[2]

Crowley was continuing with arduous concentration exercises recommended by Oscar Eckenstein in Mexico, but was now applying them

44

experimentally on other people, attempting to make them aware of what he was focusing on. He chose some interesting targets:

> I succeeded in causing a Chinaman of high rank to believe that there was an insect on his left cheek. Instant success.
> I succeeded in causing Prince Chun himself to look round upon me!

The Chinaman of high rank would have been either Yin Chang (China's new ambassador to Berlin) or Chang Yi, Reader of the Grand Chancellery, who accompanied eighteen-year-old Manchu prince Zaifeng, Prince Chun of the Qing Dynasty, on an "expiatory mission" insisted upon by the eight foreign powers that subdued China in 1901, after one En Hai murdered German ambassador Baron Clemens von Ketteler in Peking (now Beijing) during the Boxer Rebellion on June 20, 1900, shortly before Crowley sailed to America.

In July 1901, Prince Chun left China for Germany by sea on the SS *Bayern* captained by German Captain Bleeker; China had upset the Germans. Prince Chun would meet Kaiser Wilhelm II in Berlin in September.* Judging from the lightness of the diary entry, Crowley

Fig. 3.1. Prince Chun (1883–1951).

*Prince Chun—father of China's last emperor, Puyi—served as prince regent from 1908–11 during his son's brief reign (dramatized in Bernardo Bertolucci's movie, *The Last Emperor,* 1988). The Xinhai Revolution overthrew the Qing Dynasty in 1911.

appeared indifferent to having touched a figure from history by power of mind! It was, however, typical for Crowley to make no reference to the Chinese mission's contemporary importance. He took the world and its powers for granted; to him, their relevance was purely temporal, the stuff of ordinary men's minds.

On August 6, Crowley disembarked at Colombo. Over twenty years later he declared both love and loathing for it, dismissing its climate as chronic, its architecture an "unhappy accident," its natives nasty:

> The men with long hair cooped up by a comb, smelling of fish, the women with waists bulging black between coat and skirt, greasy with coconut oil, and both chewing betel and spitting it out till their teeth ooze with red and the streets look like shambles; its English are exhausted and enervated. The Eurasians are anaemic abortions; the burghers—Dutch half-casts—stolid square-heads; the Portuguese piebalds sly sneaks, vicious, venal, vermiform villains. The Tamils

Fig. 3.2. Swimmers in Colombo Port, 1902.
(*From* Six Mois dans l'Himalaya (1904) by Dr. Jules Jacot-Guillarmod)

are black but not comely. The riff-raff of rascality endemic in all ports is here exceptionally repulsive. The high-water mark of social tone, moral elevation, manners and refinement is attained by the Japanese ladies of pleasure.

In the matter of religion, the Hindus are (as everywhere else) servile, shallow, cowardly and hypocritical; though being mostly Shaivites, adoring frankly the power of Procreation and Destruction, they are less loathsome than Vishnaivites, who cringe before a fetish who promises them Preservation and (as Krishna) claims to be the Original of which Christ is a copy.[3]

Crowley was even more abrasive about Christians in Colombo, sparing not his rod from generalizations about the average Ceylonese Buddhist that would have shocked old Blavatsky and Col. Olcott, who greeted everything they saw in Ceylon with the wonder of a small child let out of school into the park on a sunny afternoon. Crowley pulled no punches:

The Christians are, of course, obscene outcasts from even the traditional tolerance of their clan; they have accepted Jesus with the promise of a job, and gag conscience with assurance of atonement, or chloroform superstitious terrors by ruminating on redemption. The Buddhists are sodden with their surfeit of indigestible philosophy and feebly flaunt a fluttering formula of which the meaning is forgotten; the debauchery of devil dances, the pointless profession of Pansil (the five precepts of the Buddha), the ceremonial coddling of shrines as old maids coddle cats, voluble veneration and rigmarole religion: such is the threadbare tinsel which they throw over the nakedness of their idleness, immorality and imbecility.[4]

Having echoed an Indian jibe that some god had packed all the worst devils into Ceylon before cutting it off by the straits, Crowley then eulogized Colombo on account of its richness, softness, and peace. Feeling an invitation to dream "deliciously of deciduous joys" he would write how he felt as if there was no longer need to do anything more. He paints a picture of palm and flower, the "swooning song of the surf" over a delicate atmosphere "heavy with sensuous scents" while one enjoys the "idle irresponsible people, purring with placid pleasure" like an orchestra performing a nocturne by some oriental Chopin, quite removed from disquieting realities. So it was not *all* bad, but it was his style to make a judgment in one quarter balanced by another. Crowley then waxed prophetic:

> But more, Colombo is the "place where four winds meet," the crossroads of the civilized world. Westward lies Europe, the energetic stripling, who thought to bear the world on his shoulders, but could not co-ordinate his own muscles. Northward lies India, like a woman weary of bearing, a widow holding to her ancient habits without hope. Southward, Australia, topsy-turvy as our childhood's wisdom warned us, sprawls its awkward adolescence and embarrasses its elders by its unconscious absurdity. Lastly, look eastward! There lies China; there is the only civilization that has looked time in the face without a blush; an atheism with good manners. There broods the old wise man, he who has conquered life without the aid of death, who may survive these strenuous youths and even the worn barren widow mumbling meaningless memories in her toothless mouth.
>
> In Colombo this world problem solves itself; for the Indian toils, without ambition or object, from sheer habit; the European bosses things, with self-importance and bravado; the Australian lumbers in and out, loutishly, hoping not to be seen; and China, silent and absent, conveys majestically patriarchal reproof by simply ignoring the impertinence. Slightly as I had brushed against the yellow silken robes of China in the press of jostling cultures, its virtue had so entered into me that the positive and aggressive aspects of Colombo, tumultuously troubling though they were, failed to command my full attention. As you vainly ply an opium smoker who craves his pipe with wine, with woman and with song, so the insolent insistence of the actualities of Colombo merely annoyed me; I was intensely aware of one thing only, the absence of the colossal calm and common sense of China.[5]

Crowley says he greeted Bennett with "sang froid," with no sense of shame or guilt. His skirting the mainland of China had, he maintained, rid him of the folly of the European's perpetual anxiety about conduct.

He found in the Far East that sex was merely an appetite, to be sated as any other appetite: an attitude fitting to Crowley's taste and habits. He would later learn how to harness even raw appetite to a higher cause, and to cease—as he castigated himself for, at the time—"confusing the planes." He would learn to hold the planes of the physical, the moral (human judgment and custom), and the spiritual world distinct. If Allan frowned on pleasure, that was his right. They were two men who shared a common quest; it was right they conversed.

Crowley tells of a Bennett who at about eighteen had, by accident, stumbled into the trance "Shivadasharna," in which the universe, perceived as single phenomenon, independent of space and time, was annihilated. The experience had changed Bennett's life, and he desired one thing: to return to that state. Solicitor General Ramanathan, as Sri Parānanda, undertook to illuminate a practical path back to that trance, but Bennett had found himself not entirely in tune with his employer/teacher's recourse to traditional dogma, and was critical of variance between his master's practice and his principles. Crowley found Ramanathan, yogi of the Shaivite sect and Tamil of high caste, a gentleman of "charming personality, wide culture and profound religious knowledge,"[6] but he was not necessarily the right teacher for the

Fig. 3.3. Sir Ponnambalam Ramanathan (1851–1930).

would-be Buddhist bhikkhu.* Crowley found Bennett "almost puritanically strict." Offered a job managing a coconut plantation, he had rejected it on learning vermin would have to be destroyed, failing, in Crowley's view, to see that all kinds of life involve acquiescence in some kind of murder; to eat rice makes one an accomplice in the destruction vital to agriculture. As I have been wont to say: "Nature eats herself for breakfast." There is no escape from the facts of life.

It was time to put the question to Bennett that had been nagging him. Mathers had told Crowley of a curious disagreement that had escalated between himself and Bennett. According to Mathers, he and Bennett "had disagreed upon an obscure point in theology, thereby formulating the accursed Dyad, thereby enabling the Abra-Melin demons to assume material form: one in his own shape, another in that of I.A.[†] Now, the demon that looked like I.A. had a revolver, and threatened to shoot him (D.D.C.F.),[‡] while the demon that resembled himself was equally anxious to shoot I.A. Fortunately, before the demons could fire, V.N.R. (Mrs. Mathers) came into the room, thus formulating the symbol of the Blessed Trinity."[7]

Interesting, but what had *really* happened?

Bennett's account was that he and Mathers were arguing about the god Shiva, the Destroyer, whom I.A. worshipped because, as Crowley put it, "if one repeated his name often enough, Shiva would one day open his eye and destroy the universe, and whom D.D.C.F. feared and hated because He would one day open His eye and destroy D.D.C.F. I.A. closed the argument by assuming the position Padmasana and repeating the Mantra: 'Shiva, Shiva, Shiva, Shiva, Shiva, Shiva.' D.D.C.F., angrier than ever, sought the sideboard, but soon returned, only to find Frater I.A. still muttering: 'Shiva, Shiva,

---

*Serving the British administration in Ceylon, Ramanathan was much concerned with improving conditions for fellow Tamils brought over to work tea plantations. The East India Company took over the island's commerce from the Dutch, while government fell to a governor responsible both to Company and British Government. Lord North's son Frederick became first governor when Ceylon was named a Crown Colony in 1802 after Holland officially ceded the island to Great Britain at the Peace of Amiens.

†Bennett's Golden Dawn Hebrew motto *Iehi Aour* = "let there be light."

‡Mathers's Golden Dawn motto *Deo Duce Comite Ferro* = "God my Guide, my Companion a Sword."

Shiva, Shiva, Shiva.' 'Will you stop blaspheming?' cried D.D.C.F.; but the holy man only said: 'Shiva, Shiva, Shiva, Shiva, Shiva, Shiva, Shiva, Shiva, Shiva.' 'If you don't stop I will shoot you!' said D.D.C.F., drawing a revolver from his pocket and leveling it at I.A.'s head; but I.A., being concentrated, took no notice and continued to mutter: 'Shiva, Shiva, Shiva, Shiva, Shiva, Shiva, Shiva.' Whether overawed by the majesty of the saint or interrupted by the entry of a third person, I.A. no longer remembered, but D.D.C.F. never pulled the trigger."

According to Crowley, "Frater I.A.'s account was less of a strain upon P[erdurabo].'s faculties of belief." Crowley regarded this peculiar event as having a bearing on whether Mathers was properly fitted for authority in the Order. Crowley had already forfeited much in terms of personal security by supporting Mathers in his conflict with anti-Mathers rebels in the Golden Dawn's Inner Order in London. The story as Mathers had told it in Paris a year earlier left a nagging doubt in Crowley's mind over Mathers's fitness to advance the work of the Order's supposed "Secret Chiefs." Bennett's response added weight to Crowley's misgivings, and the question then naturally arose as to whether Mathers's Golden Dawn was the vehicle whereby the Secret Chiefs of planetary destiny would inspire spiritual revolution. On that question, Bennett had already decided for himself: the future lay with Buddhism, pure and simple, and Crowley opened his mind to Bennett's scheme.

FOUR

✦

To Kandy

Crowley perceived Colombo was sapping Allan's strength, despite his friend's asthma having vanished on entering the Red Sea, freeing him to cast aside his panoply of drugs. Crowley insisted Colombo's enervating climate be exchanged forthwith for the less damp Kandy, and single-minded devotion to Master Patañjali's āsana, pratyāhāra, prāṇāyāma, dhāraṇā, dhyāna, and samādhi! Bennett accordingly exchanged one aspect of the dream or illusion of life for another and begged permission to quit the solicitor general's presence "whose arrogance and mean-ness," Crowley commented, Bennett naively equated with scholarship and sanctity. Crowley, as ever, saw the other side of the guru's eyes.

In fact, Crowley had bagged his own guru: Allan, whom Crowley soon introduced to his interior world of ongoing concentration exercises. What Eckenstein had goaded Crowley into—focusing on a single idea, sound, or image without breaks—was now joined to the meditative practice dhāraṇā, whose meaning may be summed up in words attributed to Jesus: "if therefore thine eye be single, thy whole body is full of light," (Matthew 6:22) on the polyvalent assumption that "the lamp of the body is the eye." The utterance has obvious yogic analogies in concentrated mindfulness and spiritual enlightenment, involving denial of distraction, where myriad distractions inhibit progress in meditation, or indeed any concentrated exercise requiring one-pointedness, such as magic, bricklaying, or exam review. The modern world is a Babel of distractions, and therefore a setting for thoughtlessness and intemperate reaction.

Crowley's "Writings of Truth" diary shows that the day after arriving in Colombo (August 7, 1901), he and Allan were already testing the effect of speech as a "disturbing factor in dharana." Crowley concentrated on a white *tau* symbol for five minutes. Allan spoke six times. The first time caused a "bad break." The second caused two bad breaks, but Crowley maintained concentration from the third to the sixth time Bennett spoke. Despite the concentration, Crowley could repeat what Bennett had said to him, bar a final remark.

Crowley experimented with prāṇāyāma, or breathing techniques, the next day. He muttered to himself in his mind "Namo Sivaya Namaha Aum." *Oṁ namaḥ śivāya* is a mantra important to Shaivism (devotion to Shiva), and so very likely came from Allan's training with Sri Parānanda. It means: "salutations to Shiva," with "Om" (or "Aum") as a devotional syllable—"ya" at the end of *śiva* means an offering, so the mantra may be translated as "I offer Shiva his name's respectful invocation." The mantra may be sung as prayer or repeated in meditation. Its deeper explication involves calling on the "destroyer" aspect of Shiva to subdue ego and promote rebirth into the higher self, which "higher self" is identified with Shiva.

Crowley noted that with "recakam"—slow expiration through the nose—the "Voice" sounded "as if from the confines of the Universe," while with "pourakam" (*sic: puraka* = slow inspiration through the nose), it sounded "as if from the third eye" (the "single eye" that perceives true light). Crowley added: "The eyes are drawn up to behold the third eye without conscious volition of the yogin." The third eye has become the "single eye."*

On August 10, Crowley heard the sound "as of a broken bell" in his head while practicing prāṇāyāma, while the next day, while slowly breathing out, found the "Voice of the Mantra" was "terrible and tremendous," while slowly breathing in through the nose, the Voice was "still and small."

He wrote to Gerald Kelly, safely ensconced in Camberwell Rectory with his parents in London, signing the letter off:

P.S. I have chucked all nonsense, except a faint lingering illusion that anything exists. This (with my breathing practice) should go soon.[1]

---

*Compare the Masonic maxim: "At the center of the circle, the Master Mason cannot err."

A week later, a steam engine carried Crowley and Bennett to Kandy.* There they rented a furnished bungalow called "Marlborough." Crowley gave Gerald Kelly the address as 34 Victoria Drive—now Sangaraja Mawatha—which skirts the edge of Kandy Lake close to what was once the Victoria Esplanade in the town. This, 34 Victoria Drive, may have been the postbox address, for in his *Confessions* Crowley describes Marlborough as being on the hill by a stream, with a waterfall overlooking the lake, Kandy's temple of the Buddha's tooth, and "an amateur attempt at a hotel,"[2] that is clearly higher in elevation to the drive clinging to the lake below. More details of the site emerge from Crowley's account of some of his and Allan's mild adventures on the hillside.

Near my bungalow at Kandy was a waterfall with a pool. Allan Bennett used to feed the leeches every morning. At any moment he could stop the leech, though already fastened to his wrist, by this breathing trick.† We would put our hands together into the water; his would come out free, mine with a dozen leeches on it. At such moments I would bitterly remark that a coyote will not eat a dead Mexican; but it failed to annoy him.

On the shores of the lake stands a charmingly situated hotel. We used occasionally to go down there for a meal. It is some distance by road, so I used to take the short cut through the jungle. One day I had run down the hill at the top of my speed in my mountain boots, followed by a breathless servant. He arrived at the hotel ten minutes later with a dead cobra, four feet eight inches in length. I had come down with my heel right on his neck and never noticed it![3]

Kandy Lake, known also as Kiri Muhada or the Sea of Milk, is shaped like an alligator's head with long, wobbly jaws, the work of King Sri Wickrama Rajasinghe, completed in 1807, though reduced in size since, and the old Victoria Esplanade was at the top of the alligator's

---

*The British administration had constructed a rail link between Colombo and Kandy, completed in 1863.

†The breathing trick is explained earlier in the *Confessions*: "Again, you can prevent things from biting you by certain breathing exercises. Hold the breath in such a way that the body becomes spasmodically rigid, and insects cannot pierce the skin."

head, so to speak. The lake is still an image of calm, fitting for the aim of a stilled mind.

> We hired a hopeless headman, who sub-hired sleepy and sinister servants and dismissed all these damnable details from our minds, devoting ourselves with diabolical determination and saintly simplicity to the search for a spiritual solution to the material muddle. Our sojourn, short as it was by worldly reckoning, proved to be pregnant with events of internal import. The tyrant time took his first wound in Kandy.[4]

Crowley and Bennett got seriously down to work. Searching for "a spiritual solution to the material muddle," they experimented with yoga, laudanum, cocaine, and hashish, and soon lost sense of fixed time. At one point, Crowley found Bennett's body in the difficult padmāsana (lotus position) familiar from images of the Buddha. Allan was so adept he impressed Crowley by swinging his lower body with only his hands on the floor. On this occasion, however, Allan was in the position as normal, but slightly tipped sideways as if his body had either risen like a leaf and come down uncentered, or else had somehow jumped whole to another position perfectly intact like a "Jack" unsprung. Crowley

Fig. 4.1. Victoria Drive, Kandy, in the days of the Raj.

presumed something resembling the idea of levitation had occurred to Allan's physical vehicle in the course of trance, which, by the way, remained unbroken by the movement; Allan's mind was levitated already.

> When I looked into his room I found him, not seated on his meditation mat, which was in the centre of the room at the end farthest from the window, but in a distant corner ten or twelve feet off, still in his knotted position, resting on his head and right shoulder, exactly like an image overturned. I set him right way up and he came out of this trance. He was quite unconscious that anything unusual had happened. But he had evidently been thrown there by the mysterious forces generated by Prāṇāyāma.
>
> There is no doubt whatever about this phenomenon; it is quite common. But the yogis claim that the lateral motion is due to lack of balance and that if one were in perfect equilibrium one would rise directly in the air. I have never seen any case of levitation and hesitate to say that it has happened to me, though I have actually been seen by others on several occasions apparently poised in the air. For the first three phenomena I have found no difficulty in devising quite simple physiological explanations. But I can form no theory as to how the practice could counteract the force of gravitation, and I am unregenerate enough to allow this to make me sceptical about the occurrence of levitation. Yet, after all, the stars are suspended in space. There is no a priori reason why the forces which prevent them rushing together should not come into operation in respect of the earth and the body.[5]

Crowley's first experiences with a suitable āsana were excruciatingly painful. For a long time he went through five minutes agony just straightening out at the end of a practice. At last he achieved success, losing body consciousness quite suddenly, after which what had been the most painful part of the practice became the sole position ensuring freedom from discomfort. Writing the bulk of the *Confessions* in 1922, Crowley remarked that though shamefully out of practice, he could still obtain the benefits of a long rest by just a few minutes in the position—which position specifically he does not mention, but his trials suggest it was a basic padmāsana posture.

Body consciousness was a big issue. On August 18, Crowley observed that if he concentrated his mind on any point of the body, a throbbing became evident at that part. Apart from meditative exercises, however, his mind hovered wryly between two worlds. He had discovered that even a little time spent on his manuscript for *Tannhäuser* seriously affected concentration when meditating, and thus grasped how the many rules enforced upon the bhikkhu, many of which might seem absurd, had been arranged to deal with any number of distractions that might bring an illusory world to a point of disturbing the aim of meditation, annihilation of self, that is: perfect detachment. To build up steam for the next intense period of concentration, Crowley apparently took some nine days off spiritual disciplines, devoting time to poetry: *Orpheus* and *Tannhaüser,* and his play *The Argonauts,** while—judging from a reference in the *Confessions* to sampling Kandy's delights "unsuspected by Mary Elizabeth"—local courtesans also received attention.

Showing *Tannhaüser* (begun in Mexico) to Allan brought disappointment. Allan didn't think it hit the mark. Crowley shared his sorrow with Kelly in a letter:

> O Gerald of all the Festuses! [Gerald Festus Kelly] I am the most miserable of mankind. Allan McG[regor]. doesn't like *Tannhaüser* says it isn't as good as *the Soul of Osiris*—says it's obscure in the beginning, too long and lacks a motive. What in h-[el]l does he mean by motive? He explains it as "the literary transmigration of a moral." This means "As a moral is to a fable, so is a motive to a work of this sort" I answer It is the history of a soul therefore my soul therefore every soul therefore no soul. He answers "Rats."
>
> . . . Address is A.C. 34 Victoria Drive Kandy Ceylon. What a fool I was not to come home instead of this maniac jaunt. "Excuse me, sir, I think I'm going mad." You shall have more Argo[nauts] and Orph[eus] &c. soon. Write and tell me exactly what you think of all you have got, and do it for all what you did for poor T[annhaüser]. Does my work *advance*? Do be good and tell me all about it. Bye-Bye. Ever A.C.[6]

---

*See chapter 11, page 211.

Perhaps Bennett appreciated poem no. 24 in *The Soul of Osiris,*
dedicated "To Allan Bennett MacGregor":

> O MAN of Sorrows: brother unto Grief!
> O pale with suffering, and dumb hours of pain!
> O worn with Thought! thy purpose springs again
> The Soul of Resurrection: thou art chief
> And lord of all thy mind: O patient thief
> Of God's own fire! What mysteries find fane
> In the white shrine of thy white spirit's reign,
> Thou man of Sorrows: O, beyond belief!
>
> Let perfect Peace be with thee: let thy days
> Prosper in spite of thine unselfish soul;
> And as thou lovest, so let Love increase
> Upon thee and about thee: till thy ways
> Gleam with the splendour of that secret goal
> Whose long war grows the great abiding peace.

The Soul of Osiris (1901) had reached famous English critic and
writer G. K. Chesterton earlier in the year. Chesterton responded to
it on June 18, in the *Daily News,* a copy of which reached Crowley in
Kandy, inspiring him to write to Kelly of his excitement. He was "on
ten pinnacles of fame all at once," he wrote, delighted at being noticed
at last! But as for "fame," well, this might have been as famous—as
opposed to infamous—as he would ever be in his long and infinitely
difficult career. Chesterton was hardly an instant fan of Crowley's work:

To the side of a mind concerned with idle merriment there is certainly something a little funny in Mr Crowley's passionate devotion
to deities who bear such names as Mout and Nuit, and Ra and Shu,
and Hormakhou. They do not seem to the English mind to lend
themselves to pious exhilaration. Mr Crowley says in the same poem:

> The burden is too hard to bear,
> I took too adamant a cross;
> This sackcloth rends my soul to wear,

> My self-denial is as dross.
> O, Shu, that holdest up the sky,
> Hold up thy servant, lest he die!

We have all possible respect for Mr Crowley's religious symbols, and we do not object to his calling upon Shu at any hour of the night. Only it would be unreasonable of him to complain if his religious exercises were generally mistaken for an effort to drive away cats.

Moreover, the poets of Mr Crowley's school have, among all their merits, some genuine intellectual dangers from this tendency to import religions, this free trade in gods. That all creeds are significant and all gods divine we willingly agree. But this is rather a reason for being content with our own than for attempting to steal other people's. The affectation in many modern mystics of adopting an Oriental civilisation and mode of thought must cause much harmless merriment among the actual Orientals. The notion that a turban and a few vows will make an Englishman a Hindu is quite on a par with the idea that a black hat and an Oxford degree will make a Hindu an Englishman. We wonder whether our Buddhistic philosophers have ever read a florid letter in Baboo English. We suspect that the said type of document is in reality exceedingly like the philosophic essays written by Englishmen about the splendours of Eastern thought. Sometimes European mystics deserve something worse than mere laughter at the hands of Orientals. If ever was one person whom honest Hindus would have been justified in tearing to pieces it was Madame Blavatsky.

That our world-worn men of art should believe for a moment that moral salvation is possible and supremely important is an unmixed benefit. But to believe for a moment that it is to be found by going to particular places or reading particular books or joining particular societies is to make for the thousandth time the mistake that is at once materialism and superstition. If Mr Crowley and the new mystics think for one moment that an Egyptian desert is more mystic than an English meadow, that a palm tree is more poetic than a Sussex beech, that a broken temple of Osiris is more supernatural than a Baptist chapel in Brixton, then they are sectarians, and only sectarians of no more value to humanity than those who

think that the English soil is the only soil worth defending, and the
Baptist chapel the only chapel worthy of worship. But Mr Crowley
is a strong and genuine poet, and we have little doubt that he will
work up from his appreciation of the Temple of Osiris to that loftier
and wider work of the human imagination, the appreciation of the
Brixton chapel.[7]

Crowley should have recognized with due humility the clear note of
promise attaching to his name at the end of the article. Unfortunately,
he determined, as the folly and pride of youth would have it, to
show the world that he was as smart or smarter than the respected
G. K. Chesterton and not one to be trifled with. He responded to
Chesterton in writing and then, in his collection of arguments with
the Buddha written mainly while in Ceylon and mainland India, *The
Sword of Song (called by Christians the Book of the Beast)*, (1904), he
confided to immortal print his clever, but vain riposte:

I must take this opportunity to protest against the charge brought
by Mr Chesterton against the Englishmen "who write philosophical
essays on the splendour of Eastern thought."
    If he confines his strictures to the translators of that well-known
Eastern work the "Old Testament" I am with him; any modern
Biblical critic will tell him what I mean. It took a long time, too, for
the missionaries (and Tommy Atkins) to discover that "Budd" was
not a "great Gawd." But then they did not want to, and in any case
intelligence and sympathy are not precisely the most salient qualities
in either soldiers or missionaries. But nothing is more absurd than
to compare men like Sir W. Jones, Sir R. Burton, Von Hammer-
Purgstall, Sir E. Arnold, Prof. Max Müller, Me, Prof. Rhys Davids,
Lane, and the rest of our illustrious Orientalists to the poor and
ignorant Hindus whose letters occasionally delight the readers of the
Sporting Times, such letters being usually written by public scribes
for a few pice in the native bazaar. As to "Babus" (Babu, I may mention, is the equivalent of our "Mister," and not the name of a savage tribe), Mr Chesterton, from his Brixton Brahmaloka, may look
forth and see that the "Babu" cannot understand Western ideas; but
a distinguished civil servant in the Madras Presidency, second wran-

gler in a very good year, assured me that he had met a native whose mathematical knowledge was superior to that of the average senior wrangler, and that he had met several others who approached that standard. His specific attack on Madame Blavatsky is equally unjust, as many natives, not theosophists, have spoke to me of her in the highest terms. "Honest Hindus" cannot be expected to think as Mr Chesterton deems likely, as he is unfortunately himself a Western, and in the same quagmire of misapprehension as Prof. Max Müller and the rest. Madame Blavatsky's work was to remind the Hindus of the excellence of their own shastras [sacred books], to show that some Westerns held identical ideas, and thus to countermine the dishonest representations of the missionaries. I am sufficiently well known as a bitter opponent of "Theosophy" to risk nothing in making these remarks.

I trust that the sense of public duty which inspires these strictures will not be taken as incompatible with the gratitude I owe to him for his exceedingly sympathetic and dispassionate review of my "Soul of Osiris."

I would counsel him, however, to leave alone the Brixton Chapel, and to "work up from his appreciation of the 'Soul of Osiris' to that loftier and wider work of the human imagination, the appreciation of the *Sporting Times*!"

Mr Chesterton thinks it funny that I should call upon "Shu." Has he forgotten that the Christian God may be most suitably invoked by the name "Yah"? I should be sorry if God were to mistake his religious enthusiasms for the derisive ribaldry of the London "gamin." Similar remarks apply to "El" and other Hebrai-Christian deities.[8]

While considering Crowley a genuine poet, a gifted poet, Chesterton clearly wondered whether this poet might yet be unrelated to the real world. Like so many things that can be said of Crowley, this latter judgment contains a half-truth; Crowley's intention had been to penetrate the real world to the physical and spiritual causes that he believed underpinned it. Chesterton, for one, was apparently unmoved by the results of that attempt. Crowley's verses were frequently too sensual and too ribald for respectable English taste, and Crowley knew it, though he considered himself to be on what we now call the "cutting edge" of his era, a pioneer. I should say that the essential problem with the bulk of Crowley's ever ambitious poetry in his early period is that it lacks *music,* being meter-, rhyme-, and grammar-bound. Had the modern musical existed at this period, Crowley would have made an excellent lyricist, with just that level of vulgarity the modern audience craves to anchor them in familiar waters when greeting the unfamiliar.

After a nine-day respite, Crowley and Bennett undertook a three-day meditation program under condition of a vow of silence, and reduced food.

> Aug 27, 28, 29. Under following condition: Vow of silence: reduced food: constant muttering of "Pranava Mani Padme Homm" [mantra] with meditation on Buddha and anahata. I lost consciousness when meditating Buddha: Voice of Nadi* became "Aum" alone, sounding like far-off solemn song. Chequers and colours appear-tatwic.† Meditation [on] Buddha—a great luminous gold Buddha appears. Will and Control become weakened after some 24–48 hours of constant yoga.

A common mantra, which Crowley himself recommended with an authentic tune in his *Magick in Theory and Practice,*[9] was "Om Mani Padmē Hum [or Hom]"‡ and it is therefore not surprising that in the mantra repeated by Crowley in Kandy that the word *praṇava* occupies that of *Om* or *Aum,* for "praṇava" refers to cosmic sound-energy, the energy of the sacred syllable, or first sound from which the universe appeared: *Aum* or *Om.* The Sanskrit *praṇava* means the controller or giver of prāṇa, and this life-force enters the cosmos with the first cosmic sound—*Aum*—that embodies Brahman. Praṇava yoga, accord-

---

*Crowley refers to a background "hum" in meditation; "nadi" comes from a Sanskrit root *nad,* meaning channel, stream, or flow. The "flow" refers to the flow of prāṇa—energy or life-force—in the hemispheres of the brain.

†That is, like the "tatwas" or simple shape-images used in the Golden Dawn for astral concentration exercises: gateways for consciousness projection.

‡In Buddhism the reference "manipadme" is to the bodhisattva of compassion, and means "jewel-lotus" and may be a name invoked for that enlightened being, rather than the usual translation of "jewel in the lotus." *Mani* means jewel, or bead, and *padme,* the lotus flower. "Hum" is associated with the spirit of enlightenment.

ing to sūtras attributed to Patañjali, following the Bhagavad Gita and the Upanishads, involves meditating, or holding the mind, upon the sound *Aum*. The sound is, as it were, Brahman (absolute reality) made audible (the "word made flesh," if you like), and the merit of the meditation is expressed in *Prashna Upanishad* (Praśnopaniṣad) 5:1, 5.7 thus:

> What world does he who meditates on Aum until the end of his life, win by That? If he meditates on the Supreme Being with the syllable Aum, he becomes one with the Light, he is led to the world of Brahman who is higher than the highest life. That which is tranquil, does not age, is immortal, fearless, and supreme.

The sound may be traced as a thread (one may imagine beads) to its source, intended to take the meditator to ever-subtler aspects of being. A mantra is *ideally* intended to carry one across this world to what Jesus perhaps suggested by "the kingdom of heaven," the atmosphere that is divine, potentially "within us," above the world of sorrow and transience. Correctly uttered, a mantra should stimulate transformation in the yogi. The devil, one presumes, is in the detail.

Crowley says he combined the mantra with meditation upon the Buddha, which gave him a vision of the Buddha, accompanied by the sound of the "Nadi," and meditation on the "anahata," that is, the fourth primary chakra: the heart chakra. As adjective, *anāhata* refers to something unhurt, or unstruck, or unbeaten, and therefore *anāhata nād* means an unstruck sound (or "hum"), the sound of a celestial or heavenly realm. It is thus clear why Crowley was convinced by his practice in India that one of the components of the (to him) composite figure of the gospel "Jesus" was that of the yogi, a figure with whom he could identify from personal experience. The name of the heart chakra also carries the connotation of cleanliness, purity: something pristine and unbound. Therefore the heart chakra is associated with openness, freshness of vision, and discovery through loosening the bonds of selfishness and attachment, becoming detached, and therefore experiencing spiritual freedom, clarity of thought. Thus, the chakra may play its part in reconciliation of opposing forces, seen from a higher level, and therefore peace. The chakra may be imagined as a lotus unfolding its twelve petals in the spine's central channel, close to the heart, and meditation upon it is said to bring many benefits to the yogi.

On August 30, Crowley again heard the voice of the nāda, described in the diary as "Sweet as a singing rain of silver dew"—Shelley's musical line from *Prometheus Unbound*. "Cleaning" of the nadis is recommended as a preliminary to successful prāṇāyāma, and that seems to have been integral to Crowley's *haṭha* (willful, forceful, or physical) yoga practice.

In his *Confessions,* Crowley states that he purified the nadi while at Kandy, with the result that his complexion became strangely clear, while his voice lost the harsh timbre natural to it. His appearance became calm, his eyes unusually bright, and he was constantly conscious of the nada, whose sound varies considerably, but in his case it most frequently resembled the twittering of nightingales.

Crowley then records "Got into sukshma-kumbhakam. Rigidity." As hatha yoga regards breath as manifest *prāṇa,* then control of breath is believed to control subtle prāṇa within. The word *kumbhakam* refers to the pause between inhalation and exhalation, so when prolonged, means holding one's breath. "Sūkshma" is subtle breath, the vital force of prāṇa, which Crowley was attempting to control. As yogic theory holds that mind requires prāṇa to operate, control of prāṇa controls states of mind. All latent forces, such as heat and light are regarded as prāṇa in its different manifestations, but *sūkshma prāṇa* is applied particularly to the prāṇa of the mind. Naturally, the seat of prāṇa is the heart. As prāṇa is power behind all things, the yogin that controls all aspects of prāṇa is capable of controlling the universe, in theory. One can then see its immediate applicability to the requirements of the magician's will.

Crowley then notes "Dharana on ajna prevents sleep: ditto on anahata causes it." The *ājñā* is the sixth primary chakra and is associated with the third eye, sometimes identified with, or located at, the pineal gland. He notes this phenomenon as a "practical" point, of use when wanting to sleep, or not, and not "when doing it for Yoga purposes." He then adds a pencil note that "Dharana on ajna often causes sleep when trying Yoga."

On September 2, he noted the "Voice of nada" was as a "Far siren or rubbed glass."* It is perhaps a pity that Crowley was not encouraged to

---

*The same sound was registered in the diary for September 30: "The 'rubbed glass' again. I do not here record *repeated* phenomena. I assume like causes like effects."

work more on nāda yoga as it may give reverence for music, or the spirit of music, something Crowley never properly acquired—possibly due to a confessed hearing defect. He fully grasped that music carries spiritual properties that can harmonize inner and outer worlds. Music for him was generally relegated to the role of *accompaniment*. His poetry might have benefited from seeing *sound* behind words as being on occasion more powerful than words themselves. His addiction to alliteration picks up a symptom of musicality within articulate sound, but not its essential cause. His words only flow when he truly lets himself go. I think Crowley's scientific, *objective* attitude may have inhibited this understanding, as well as his aesthetic disinterest in music generally. Music for Crowley had to have a definite rhythm or a strong sensual aspect to appeal to his ear. Spirituality for Crowley was, I think, primarily intellectual, a means of acquiring intelligence. He never tired of reiterating that "yoga means union," a means of joining, but did not value nāda yoga as union through flow of sounds, the "good vibrations" of the universe. We now know that sound alters the movement of the fundamental particles of the universe, and is profoundly related also to light. Music is believed to affect the chakras, and therefore health.

Direct sensory effects of his yogic practice fascinated Crowley. On September 4, he notes looking at a "Siva pentacle"* while "muttering 'Aum Sivayavasi'" and noting that he *believed* (underlined) that its corporeal weight lessened. The mantra "Aum Shiva-ya-Va-shi," if the "va shi" is taken as a pun from the two syllables of the name "Shiva" (itself meaning propitious, auspicious, or destroyer) may represent the universe as a unified course, from zero through the finite, back to zero, on the grounds that *shi* means "rest," and can be interpreted as the absolute or male aspect of the divinity, and *va* is "blowing" or going of air or life energy—arguably the female side manifested—while *ya* here may be Sanskrit for going, proceeding, moving or advancing, or an offering.

He then did "Dharana on tip of nose." He heard an audible voice saying: "And if you're passing, won't you?" noting the effect was not unknown to him "in certain states of mental fatigue." His nose became so sensitive physically that a "fleck of down lighting on it gave him

---

*The pentagram appears in Hinduism as a "star of initiation" and caste mark for priests of Shiva by adding a dot inside the star as a sun symbol.

'jumps.'" He would go back to his nose on September 5, remarking that dhāraṇā on the nose gave a clear *understanding* (underlined) of the unreality of the nose, that is: "its difference from 'Me.'" An hour after the dhāraṇā, lying in bed, he felt hot breath on his arm and asked, "What can this be from?" The normal link between nose and mind had been broken. He noted that with prāṇāyāma, "one may get confused—dizzy—and unable to see clearly e.g.: the second-hand of the watch." He also noted that he "definitively" heard the "Astral Bell," not his, but "M's"—Metteya's (Allan's). The "astral bell" was a phenomenon most famously associated with Madame Blavatsky, about whom colleagues sometimes heard its sweet sound, associated with spiritual presence, an echo from a place independent of this world.

Another curious phenomenon Crowley adumbrated when reflecting on the Kandy experience over two decades later, in his *Confessions,* recalling how prāṇāyāma produced, firstly, a peculiar kind of perspiration; secondly, an automatic rigidity of the muscles; and thirdly, the phenomenon of causing the body, while still absolutely rigid, to take little hops in various directions, as if he'd been somehow raised, possibly an inch from the ground, and deposited very gently a short distance away.

More work on his nose on September 7, produced an even more baffling phenomenon:

> Lost my nose: could not think *what* I wanted to find and then (when I remembered) where to look for it! (This approaches "neighbourhood concentration.") As before, but muttering "Namo Sivaya" &c. I was (a) conscious of physical background seen after nose had vanished (b) conscious that I was *not* conscious of these things. These (a) and (b) were simultaneous. This seems absurd: is inexplicable: is noted in Buddhist Psychology: yet I know it.

Crowley was seriously worried by this phenomenon and considered curtailing all yoga for his own good. Allan told him, however, that "neighborhood concentration," as he called it, was at this point a sign of progress.

On September 8, Crowley concentrated consciousness on the "Ajna Cakkra" (*sic*) describing it as having the "misty blue-grey texture of fine hair. Flame-cone in shape. At intervals it opens out like a flower." Then he heard his own astral bell. This is not unusual for those whose meditation requires utter silence; a ringing begins like a little Tibetan bell whose reverberation does not cease: the "sound of silence." Practicing dhāraṇā again Crowley experienced an effect similar to that of September 4, but this time with the added "feeling of intense pleasure."

On September 9 he went to sleep in dhārāṇā and woke up on his left side. Thinking this unusual he:

> supposed the open door to middle hall to be the outer door and deduced burglars. Writing above note, saw door at foot of bed and mistook that too. P.S. Writing is firm and clear; I was not dozing. Also time is given exact 1:23 A.M. Mind blank: I did not know I had been asleep: the time surprised me. The one dominant thought was "That's it!" i.e. dhyana. [note in pencil by A.C.: This is A. Crowley, whose "sense of direction" is so wonderful. With an ordinary man this would not be an especially remarkable phenomenon.]
>
> Prāṇāyāma culminated in a wet dream.
>
> N.B. Sept. 8. The perspiration of khumbakam has the smell and taste of Semen—much intensified.

Perhaps the latter experience alerted him back to his unsubtle bodily existence, for in mid-September Crowley's restlessness with asceticism led him to the fleshpots of Colombo for some "R & R." One experience with a prostitute seems to have inspired an acid poem (see chapter 11, page 209).

Getting back into his stride gently, he spent an hour in āsana on September 21, before concentrating on the ājñā chakra the next day. He heard the "bell" repeatedly above his head slightly left of the median line (bisecting the body vertically through the navel). It would appear he was aware of some kind of spiritual or subtle light emanating from the chakra at the center of his forehead: "Dharana on ajna-effect of Light gradually glimmering forth and becoming v[ery]. Bright." He added a pencil note that the "Bell" was "conceivably physical," derived, he speculated, from "gradually relaxing strain on eye muscles."

On September 23 he made a guiding note for himself that when engaging with prāṇāyāma it was helpful to "be fresh, cool, not excited, not sleepy, not full of food, not ready to urinate or defaecate, nor anywhere near that." He did dhāraṇā on his tongue-tip and felt a burning sensation: "Every separate tooth can be felt, as if each had an ego, almost."

Next day he attended to "sūkshma kumbhakam," the subtle prāṇa associated with suspension of breath. He "certainly got" it but felt it was not yet under control of will, it being stigmatized by "rigidity and loss of vision." He noted an occasion when loss of vision occurred when breath suspension was impossible as he was reciting his mantra audibly. The next day during prāṇāyāma he forgot what he was doing and breathed out gently after ten seconds of "khumbakam" on the seventh cycle—the cycles being repeated sequences of breathing in, holding, and breathing out again. He now found he was losing consciousness or concentration with repetition of the mantra. "At one particular rate the 3rd eye throbs violently in time with mantra ([the mantras being:] Aum Sivayavashi; also Aum Tat Sat Aum)."

On September 26, he exceeded the time set for khumbakam and forgot himself. He also observed that he was now frequently sleeping on his left side, "contrary to a habit of many years."

Experimentation into the mind took another direction altogether from September 28 to 29 when he and Allan took the opiate laudanum.

The following entry is not part of "The Writings of Truth," but was a stray entry written in the 1901 Mexico diary notebook. Perhaps Crowley did not want it to break the progressive yoga record.

Experiment of taking laudanum.

Having got myself into a poetical frame of mind after a fairly active day (2 hours work, photographing, etc., I took doses of laudanum as follows: 10 drops in water at 5:52, 6:12, 6:29, 6:45, 7:02, 7:17, 7:32. 70 drops in all. Writing poetry: no appreciable physiological result.

7:46. 15 drops.

8:05. 20 drops. This last dose made me rather sick and dizzy. I lay down and soon recovered and went on writing. No contraction of pupils very slight change of pulse. Allan thinks my eyes were dilated forcibly with cocaine from the day before when I had bust up a tooth. My eyes were somewhat aching with the glare of lamps.

8:18. 20 more drops. Talked lay in bed and wrote a little more—very fast.

8:50. 25 drops.

9:46. 30 drops. Took some tea which made me better able to write.

10:20. 30 drops more.

Discussing with Allan why result so small. Wrote a bit more of poem. Feeling unwell from the quantity of water inside me—the vehicle of the Laudanum!

About 11:30 went to bed. Occasional slight dizziness. Very sensitive to sound and "nervous." But latter normal to me at this time from practicing concentration. Wrote 4 sonnets in French (in bed). Went to sleep; this was light refreshing and several times gently disturbed; I had some dreams not remarkable in any way.

[on facing page of notebook:] I got some imaginative effects of a slightly grotesque kind; and after magnificent visions of Himalayas best mountain scenery I ever had and later Japanese-Albrecht Dürer-esque village-river scenes. But these latter shifty and unreal though exceedingly quaint and lovely.

Sept. 29.

Woke about 5:45 for a minute or two.

Woke at 7:45 and got up for breakfast.

Slept 8:30–10:00.

Strong pipe made me feel dizzy again. So lay down and wrote this account (10:40). Nothing to call a "headache"; dullness as if from waking too early or rather weariness and the sleep-toxin feeling the drinking of so unusual a quantity of water gave me fairly full bladder on waking—to my horror I found the urethral muscles partially paralyzed. I could only micturate in short jerks. Quantity of urine certainly not increased considering my drink (1 pint tea and about 1¼ pint water).

The total dose was thus 210 drops.

Pupils much contracted.

Sleeping uneasily off and on all day.

9 P.M. 29th. Pupils pretty normal.

Took Strychnia Iron Hypophosp. AS$_2$O$_3$ this afternoon,* had a good dinner and feel all right.

Yoga impossible after taking laudanum.†

Following this two-day interlude, a significant breakthrough occurred to Crowley on October 1, concerning which date he added a pencil note to the diary: "This Oct. 1 is the 2nd or 3rd jhana of Buddhist phraseology—samādhi of Hindu ditto." This note warrants explication.

In Theravāda Buddhism, the term *jhāna* is close to the Buddhist (not Hindu) interpretation of the word *samādhi*,‡ akin to the word *samatha*, which means "serenity." Buddhist samādhi is concentration, unalloyed one-pointedness. The jhānas apply to the two phases of Buddhist meditation, the first, serenity, the second, insight. The jhānas apply most to the first stage of mind preparation and denote states where the mind is unified with the object of concentration. The early Buddhist suttas (scripture concerning the Buddha) refer to four jhānas. The Buddha referred to them as his "heavenly dwelling," to which he would resort. Progress in his search for enlightenment in adulthood began when the Buddha remembered the first jhāna, experienced as a boy during a plowing festival. When the Buddha passes away, it is in the fourth jhāna. To attain the jhānas, followers need to be rid of five hindrances: sensual desire, ill will, sloth, restlessness, worry, and doubt (this might explain Crowley's preparatory trip to Colombo: to "get it out of his system" perhaps).

The equivalent Sanskrit word to the Pāli word *jhāna* is *dhyāna*.

---

*A footnote to William Breeze's unpublished edited diaries: "Strychnia, with brucia, is an alkaloid in Nux vomica. Like Arsenic Trioxide (AS$_2$O$_3$) or Fowler's solution (1%), it is a poison, but was then part of the Materia Medica; both were prescribed, with iron, for anaemia. What about hypophosphorous? No medical use."

†This last statement is from "The Writings of Truth" for September 29, 1901.

‡*Samādhi* derives from the prefixed verbal root *sam-a-dha*, meaning "to collect" or "to bring together." Concentration or unification of the mind is suggested. In Vedantic rāja yoga, however, *samādhi* means "consciousness of union with God," Brahman: the absolute aim of rāja yoga, though any samādhi attained may vary in quality and sublimity, depending on the individual. Crowley would eventually equate Vedantic samādhi with "the Knowledge and Conversation of the Holy Guardian Angel," or goal of the "Sacred Magic of Abra-Melin the Mage," begun by Crowley 1899–1900, but interrupted by the Golden Dawn imbroglio.

And we are about to witness Crowley's first dhyāna, a major experience for him.

Fifth-century CE Buddhist commentator Buddhagosa playfully traces one derivation of these words from the verb *jhapeti:* to burn up. Jhāna, is, he says in his work, *Path of Purification,* the burning up of opposing states; what we in the West would call the subject and the object, the poles of rational discourse. For the Buddhist, what is burnt up is that which opposes serenity and insight, namely, we might say, "the world," and its suffering, the which is absence of nibbana. In order to move forward to supramundane states, the defilements that inhibit concentration need to be progressively burned up. Eventually this goes for the four primary jhānas also, after which the follower enters transmundane jhāna categories beyond space and time's limitations. Anyone with a good knowledge of Western gnosis will see how very close these ideations of the spiritually possible are in essence.

For Buddhists, samādhi is undistracted one-pointedness,* with of course no reference to Brahman, or "union with God," but Crowley's note shows his concern that dhyāna matched the second and third Buddhist jhānas. In other words, he had the attainment of samādhi on his mind. For him then, dhyāna was just a step away from the supreme attainment, for which he was not yet ready, but to have attained in reality the second and third jhānas showed he was headed in the right direction.

So, on October 1, 1901, Aleister Crowley, withdrawing his consciousness from the hills about him and centering it on the "Cakkra Ajna" in the middle of his brain—with *prāṇāyāma* "at intervals"—repeated his mantra *Aum Tat Sat Aum.*†

A Retirement. Mantra "Aum tat sat aum" [Sanskrit]. Cakra ajna.
After some five hours of this discipline arose The Golden Dawn.

---

*Pāli tradition sees samādhi in three levels: *parikammasamādhi,* that is, preliminary concentration resulting from initial focusing of mind on its subject; *upacarasamādhi,* concentration involving the five hindrances's suppression, presence of the jhāna factors, and the appearance of a luminous mental replica of the meditation object—the *patibhaganimitta* or counterpart sign; and *appanasamādhi,* when the mind is completely absorbed in its object. Such concentration is regarded as fruit of the jhāna factors.

†Where *tat* denotes "reality" and *sat,* "being" for hour after hour.

While meditating, suddenly I became conscious of a shoreless space of darkness and a glow of crimson athwart. Deepening and brightening, scarred by dull lines of slate-blue cloud arose the Dawn of Dawns. In splendour not of earth with its mean sun, blood-red, rayless, adamant, it rose, it rose! Carried out of myself, I asked not "Who is the Witness?" absorbed utterly in contemplation of so stupendous and so marvellous a fact. For here was no doubt, no change, no wavering: infinitely more real than aught "physical" is the Golden Dawn of this Internal Sun! But ere the Orb of Glory rose clear of its banks of blackness—alas, my soul! That Light Ineffable was withdrawn beneath the falling veil of darkness, and in purples and greys glorious beyond imagining, sad beyond conceiving faded the superb Herald of the Day—But mine eyes have seen it! And this, then, is Dhyana! With it, yet all but unremarked, came a melody as of the sweet soul'd *viña*.*

> O Dawn of Rose and Gold, thy memory at least
> shall never fade!

Crowley was moved to the poetry of beatitude and invocation, in praise and wonder of the simultaneousness of creation and destruction, of light and darkness, of life and death:

> Blessed be Thou, O Bhavani, O
> Isis my Sister, my Bride, my Mother!
> Blessed be Thou, O Shiva, O Amoun,
> Concealed of the Concealed. By thy most
> Secret and Holy Name of Apophis be
> thou Blessed, Lucifer, Star of the Dawn,
> Satan-Jeheshua [Jesus], Light of the World!
> Blessed be Thou, Buddha, Osiris, by
> Whatever Name I call Thee Thou art nameless
> to Eternity . . .
> Blessed be Thou, O Day, that thou hast
> risen in the Night of Time, First Dawn

---

*A viña is a musical instrument similar to a sitar.

in the Chaos of poor Aleister's poor mind!
Accurséd be Thou, Jehovah, Brahma,
unto the Aeons of Aeons; thou who didst
create darkness and not Light! Mara,
Vile Mash of Matter!
Arise, O Shiva, and destroy! That in
destruction these at last be blest!

Aum Tat Sat Aum [in Sanskrit]

The import of the experience was profound not only to Crowley's spiritual understanding, but to his rationalism. To have effectively absorbed subject and object in one another, to have temporarily annihilated their distinction, and experienced their union, Crowley had, to his way of understanding, transcended the rational dialectic of Western philosophy and science and opened a path to intelligibility beyond the Western god of reason. He had seen the other side of reality, and it shone.

Like a man who has discovered a fortune in an attic, and then, leaving it briefly, doubted if it had ever happened, and went back to touch once more the precious trove and absorb once more its tactile reality, Crowley resumed his posture the very next day.

Oct. 2.
"Ego sed si sileam, teque quaterque felix!" ["But if I am silent, I am three times, four times happy!"] The discipline as before. About 5 P.M. again, by the Grace Ineffable of Bhavani to the meanest of the devotees, arose the Splendour of the Inner Sun. As bidden by my Guru, Isolated the Dawn with Pranara. This, as I foresaw, returned the Dyanic Consciousness. The Disk grew golden: rose clear of all its clouds, flinging great fleecy cumuli of rose and gold, fiery with light into the midmost aether of the subtle space. Hollow it seemed and rayless as the sun in ♐ [Sagittarius] yet incomparably brighter: but rising clear of cloud; It began to revolve, to coruscate, to throw off streamers of jetted fire! This from a hilltop I beheld, dark, as of a dying world. Covered with black decayed wet peaty wood, a few dead pines stood stricken and unutterably alone. But behind the

glory of its coruscations seemed to shape, an idea, less solid than a shadow! An idea of some vast Human-seeming Form!*

Now grew doubt and thought in Aleister's miserable mind and the One Wave grew many waves and all was lost. Alas! alas! for Aleister! And Glory unto Her. She the Twin-Breasted that hath encroached ever the other half of the Destroyer! ॐ [Aum] Namo Bhavaniya ॐ [Aum]

Crowley's latter mantra would soon bear fruit in Madura on the mainland where he would sacrifice a goat to Bhavani in the temple there. As for yoga, after the breakthrough experience on October 1, he would not resume active yoga for nearly two years, the last entry in the "Writings of Truth" (October 3, 1901) referring to his waking in the night repeatedly, saying his mantra.

YOGA—THE ESSENTIALS

Crowley would summarize what Allan—and experience—had taught him of yoga in his *Confessions*. This account stands today as a first-rate introduction to the essence of a subject that for so many has become little more than an exotic twist on conventional exercise. On the other hand, Crowley was one of the very first to demystify the subject

---

*Compare Ezekiel 1:26–28. where Ezekiel sees the "glory of God" in the form of the likeness of a man: "And above the firmament that was over their heads was the likeness of a throne, as the appearance of a sapphire stone: and upon the likeness of the throne was the likeness as the appearance of a man above upon it.

"And I saw as the colour of amber, as the appearance of fire round about within it, from the appearance of his loins even upward, and from the appearance of his loins even downward, I saw as it were the appearance of fire, and it had brightness round about.

"As the appearance of the bow that is in the cloud in the day of rain, so was the appearance of the brightness round about. This was the appearance of the likeness of the glory of the Lord. And when I saw it, I fell upon my face, and I heard a voice of one that spake." This vision, according to scholar of Western Gnosis Gilles Quispel, was the "stock-vision" of Gnosticism, the revelation of the divine Anthrōpos, primal or Heavenly Man, unfallen, the "image of God," or Phōs, that is: "Light," or radiant glory. The one vouchsafed this vision is called "Son of man," a designation that in the first century CE became associated with a messianic figure (namely, the later portions of the Ethiopic Book of Enoch).

completely and make it accessible to Westerners of all walks of life.

He reduced the essential principles of yoga to one: *how to stop thinking.* The theory regards the mind as made for dealing symbolically with impressions, and its nature is to take such symbols for reality. Thus, conscious thought is regarded as false insofar as it inhibits reality perception. Thus, yoga practices are means to slow down and then curtail thought process. Crowley was proud to observe that it was he, and not the yogins themselves, who had realized this, on account of the fact he was not concerned with religious doctrines and ethics he believed had obscured the scientific essence of the practice. In his dealings with Buddhism also, this assumption that moral considerations were inhibiting accretions to a science of mind is frequently asserted.

Crowley claims to have reached the conclusion from observation of comparative religion, so that, for example, when a Catholic repeats "Ave Maria," the rhythm inhibits thinking processes, resulting in an ecstatic vision of Mary. Similar methods may bring visions of Vishnu, or whatever superior being the practitioner desires access to. Crowley observed that the mechanics of what was essentially a physiological phenomenon transcended the language used, whereas repetition over years in religious contexts made the language and sectarian terminology the transcending feature, leading to the erroneous conclusion that the experience "proved" the religious belief system, rather than the method's own virtue.

Through this understanding, Crowley claimed to have been able to streamline initiation considerably by elimination of dogma, and the temptation to lean on dogma. "Virtue is only necessary in so far as it favours success; just as certain diets, neither right nor wrong in themselves, are indicated for the athlete or the diabetic."[10] Not only would Crowley foreshorten the time required for spiritual breakthrough (typified as "the knowledge and conversation of the Holy Guardian Angel"), but he had "saved the successful from the devastating delusion that the intellectual image of their experience is a universal truth." This is an extremely important point for our times, dogged as we are by various "fundamentalist" or reactionary hysterias, for Crowley believed that while the higher trances represented spiritual progress, their communicable *content* was still relative to the limitations of the mind of the being experiencing them. Unenlightened persons formerly were apt to turn their experiences into visions vital for *everybody* in the form in which they occurred to them. All religious tyranny, Crowley wrote, springs from intellectual narrowness. Thus, in Crowley's estimation: "Mohammed's conviction that his visions were of imperative importance to 'salvation' made him a fanatic."[11] The problem, Crowley believed, was that the high trances produce spiritual energies that give the seer formidable force, and "unless he be aware that his interpretation is due only to the exaggeration of his own tendencies of thought, he will seek to impose it on others, and so delude his disciples, pervert their minds and prevent their development."[12]

Crowley believed the best such "victims of vision" (to coin a phrase) could do was to publish the methods by which their illumination came about, which would at least be useful to science. Crowley himself maintains this had been his own practice, and any illuminations received were of relevance to himself, while his methods could well require adaptation in the light of his own idiosyncrasies. This is quite different from the usual seer of visions, unable to separate himself objectively from his experience. Thus in such a one, the visions inevitably come from "God," even when "God" contradicts himself. The contradictions lie in minds only relatively illuminated.

So, for Crowley, yoga stands as a scientific system for reaching a psychological state. Thus *yama* and *niyama*—"control" and "super control" respectively—are simply restraints to prevent disturbance of ideal conditions (as in a laboratory). Passions disturb equilibrium, so things that rouse passion—"sins" such as greed, lust, and the like—should be eliminated from experiments. "Relax" translates as: take up the āsana that (after practice) calms. Prāṇāyāma: control of breath, has a specific aim of mind control. Experience had shown Crowley that these precautions were not exaggerated. The mind in its normal state has simply no idea how much "interference" prevents the calm through which higher influence may be received, that is, the absorption into silence. Conversely, *pratyāhāra,* being introspection, permits the analysis, and awareness of the complexities and wonders of the simplest things or movements, like clicking one's fingers or crossing one's leg. By analysis one sees symptoms that may disturb, and one attains greater control. By-products include seeing thoughts for what they are and gaining an idea of the elements of the universe as a whole.

Having learned to cope with the tendencies of the mind to multiplicity, confusion, and distraction of thoughts, one may cut one's teeth on the objective of simply concentrating on one thought, and staying so concentrated. That is dhāraṇā (in Sanskrit). In Crowley's *Book Four, Part I*, he examined his yoga diaries to give a concise list of the kinds of ideas that invade the yogin in his self-ministrations. These invasive elements he called "breaks."

Breaks are classed as follows:

Firstly, physical sensations. These should have been overcome by Āsana.

Secondly, breaks that seem to be dictated by events immediately preceding the meditation. Their activity becomes tremendous. Only by this practice does one understand how much is really observed by the senses without the mind becoming conscious of it.

Thirdly, there is a class of breaks partaking of the nature of reverie or "daydreams." These are very insidious—one may go on for a long time without realizing that one has wandered at all.

Fourthly, we get a very high class of break, which is a sort of aberration of the control itself. You think, "How well I am doing it!" or perhaps that it would be rather a good idea if you were on a desert island, or if you were in a sound-proof house, or if you were sitting by a waterfall. But these are only trifling variations from the vigilance itself.

A fifth class of breaks seems to have no discoverable source in the mind. Such may even take the form of actual hallucination, usually auditory. Of course, such hallucinations are infrequent and are recognized for what they are; otherwise the student had better see his doctor. The usual kind consists of odd sentences or fragments of sentences, which are heard quite distinctly in a recognizable human voice, not the student's own voice or that of any one he knows. A similar phenomenon is observed by wireless operators, who call such messages "atmospherics."

There is *a further kind of break, which is the desired result itself.*[13]

The idea seems to be that dhāraṇā may, when perfected, segue, without warning, into dhyāna, whose "characteristic is that whereas in normal consciousness two things are always present—the percipient and the perceived—in dhyāna these two have become one. At first this union usually takes place with explosive violence. There are many other characteristics; in particular, time and space are abolished. This, however, occurs with almost equal completeness in certain states of normal abstract thought. The attainment of this trance is likely to upset the whole moral balance of the student.[14]

Crowley is particularly good on this because he has looked so deeply into the question of what makes religious people of a certain kind become "mad" on a diet of religion, whether theirs or someone else's. He notes quite accurately that people's memory of dhyāna will conform to their pet ideas, or delusions, because the experience itself cannot be translated into normal thought, since normal thought has been abolished in the experience. He notes how the subject in such a case will feel his ideas have become armed by supreme spiritual sanction, and may soon become a fanatic or megalomaniac. Crowley sees the cure in analysis of all ideas, combined with rigorous skepticism. How many might have been saved from religion-induced psychosis if Crowley's guidance had been heeded!

Attaining dhyāna washed out Crowley's brain. He felt like he'd expended the stored energies of years; he had nothing left. So he became a tourist, and Allan, now sure he was going for the yellow robe, did his best to join in, accompanying his friend on an exploratory journey about the island: the last time they would be together as free men—depending, of course, on how you understand the word *free*.

FIVE

Big Game, Small Games

Allan's idea of the expedition was a pilgrimage to what remained of Buddhism's sacred cities; he had found devotion even to high trances distractions from the spiritual progress he envisioned, as though, Crowley comments, they were to him but akin to the enticements of physical love that dupe the lover into accepting the evil of existence. Crowley himself felt impatient, ready to refocus solely on light matters, aesthetic, historical, and ethnological, while getting his "kicks" by taking a "demoniac delight" in shocking Allan with scurrilous comments on current events, disturbing Allan the more by occasional bouts of shooting wildlife.

Crowley says in his *Confessions* that when he first embarked for the Far East, he imaginatively enveloped its splendors in the same romantic folly he had heaped upon the Jacobites. But he found he had already now learned to use his eyes, partly attributing the change to observing nasty political realities within the Order of the Golden Dawn. Experience of people's real nature had lessened the power of romance to persuade. He did not, however, react from one extreme to the other, but rather embraced the wisdom of "Blessed are they that expect nothing; for they shall not be disappointed!" He would not, he claimed, judge Buddhism by the behavior of Buddhists, observing that while Ceylon's Buddhism was based on the earliest body of Buddhist scripture (the Pāli Canon), the people's perennial customs had adapted to it similarly to that process by which Europe's old paganism persisted beneath Christianity's "camouflage," until the ass of Priapus became the ass of the Nativity, Jupiter became Jehovah, Isis became Mary, and Osiris's crown became the papal tiara. In Ceylon, the old demonology and fetish and ancestor worship were adapted to Buddhist theories. He noted that religious reformers and philosophers cannot alter people's primitive instincts, their fears and passions. While Allan was shocked by the continuity of the devil dances that so upset Christian missionaries, Crowley found the natives' unhypocritical simplicity and savagery pleasing, despite the superstitious substructure.

Allan and Crowley were permitted to witness the annual inspection of the "Buddha's tooth," preserved in Kandy in seven concentric caskets of precious stones. Crowley got a close look and reckoned that, while he wasn't sure, the holy gnasher looked most like that of a dog or crocodile, and definitely not human: a conclusion Helena Blavatsky came to some twenty years before him. The men also witnessed Kandy's "Perahera" ceremony in the tooth's honor. Crowley enjoyed its excessive, unsedate wildness, the cacophony of drums, elephants, barking horns, bustling of officials, monks, dancers, and general torch-lit pandemonium. Allan was saddened; desiring to raise people to a higher level of existence, he was disillusioned by the gross tendency of the unenlightened to abandonment rather than dignity in detachment.

Crowley, however, felt a forceful compulsion amid a rather sinister, darkened atmosphere about the lake, to do something "demoniac." He felt what he called the voices of "ancestral appetite," a terror in the face of an unknown force that one suspects might be in oneself. Having great trouble holding himself back, he compared the experience to the mythical presence of Pan: the frightful "All," raw nature in essence, overwhelming, subsuming individual consciousness. He also perceived the original magical value of such occasions, which, by repetitions of dance and chant, might have been devised so that the "subconsciousness" could rise through a sympathetic psychological mass medium and "miracles" be accomplished impossible to the sober. Thus he understood the "barbarous words of evocation" of the Gnostics, ancient Egyptians, and invocations in magical languages such as "Enochian": to open the doors of the soul through rents in the body rational.

Crowley writes in *Confessions* of his relations with British officials on the island. He compares them with well-established and well-understood relations between rulers and ruled on the mainland, and found comparison favored the mainland. He reckoned the officials, surrounded by mixed-race Dutch and Portuguese, felt somehow compromised and inhibited, somewhat unconvinced of their authority—unlike the "heaven-born" mainland official—with the result that the Sinhalese government tended to be "snappish."

Crowley would later lament his folly in calling the police when his cashbox was stolen. An "inspector" duly arrived and stole his compass, thinking it a watch. The imposter was caught but released on a technicality. The magistrate's demeanor enlightened Crowley as to a bestial nature secreted in at least one respectable, cultured Englishman. Describing the punishment the culprit had avoided—flogging—the official's apparent shudder could not hide from Crowley a distinct sadistic pleasure in imagining cruelty Crowley himself claims not to have understood. He wondered if there wasn't something in the island's atmosphere that, if one remained too long on the island, "stupefied" the finer parts of man. Crowley found the local tea's flavor somewhat "symbolic" of this! Pleading with a shopkeeper for some Chinese tea, the seller said he could put the Chinese flavor into the tea; Crowley begged he first remove the Ceylon flavor!

Meanwhile, Crowley told Allan he intended to forego the expedition to K2 (28,250 feet) he had discussed with Eckenstein in Mexico, attending instead to "spiritual progress." Allan insisted he change his mind for Eckenstein's sake, so Crowley wired Eckenstein and agreed. As a result, he began to grow a beard, knowing the journey would take him

Fig. 5.1. Crowley in Ceylon, September 1901. (From The Spirit of Solitude, *1929; courtesy Ordo Templi Orientis)*

into areas predominantly Muslim. The Sinhalese, like Europeans later in Rawalpindi, took the bearded sahib for a Boer prisoner!

DAMBULLA, SIGIRAYA, AND ANURĀDHAPURA

As the railway to Anurādhapura was not completed until 1905, Crowley and Bennett had to make the excursion to the buried cities of Ceylon by coach and horses. Crowley was stunned by the callousness with which the horses were treated; not one, he observed, was sound in limb as a result—and this in a country allegedly dedicated to the first precept of Buddha: not to take life!

First stop was Dambulla, some forty-four miles north of Kandy. Dambulla's wondrous cave temples earned Crowley praise for enthusiasm and sublimity of conception. Five caves in the temple complex opened below a vast overhanging rock like a flat, gray pillow. As the temple entrance he visited was so tiny, Crowley was driven to wonder how the dozens of statues of the Buddha, and other figures, such as local kings, could have been assembled. Then it occurred to him that the statues had been cut from the rock of the caves themselves.

Constructed in the second and third centuries BCE, the complex represents the most intact of Sri Lanka's most ancient Buddhist sites. Crowley wondered who the artisans were who built it in ancient times, as he observed nothing like such skills among contemporary Sinhalese, and lamented how the magnificent wall paintings that garnish the experience of the inner temples had been obscured by later generations, while many statues had been smothered in gamboge by the ignorant—gamboge being the saffron to mustard colored pigment of Buddhist monks' robes. Today, the statuary and many of the wall paintings have been carefully restored, revealing episodes in the Buddha's life, and there is far more to see now than when Crowley and Bennett visited in 1901.

Some seven miles northeast of Dambulla lay the ancient buried city of Sigiraya, and the outstanding "Lion Rock," which place somehow inspired Crowley to write his poem *Anima Lunae* (see page 209). Sri Lankan tradition records a wonderful palace having been built upon the rock four and a half centuries before Christ, the entry to which wonder was a vast stone lion, while the walls of the rock were once adorned with fresco after fresco of art, looking down on some of the oldest landscaped gardens in the world. Around the rock was laid out a city on intricate geometrical patterns. After the fortress fell, the site became a Buddhist monastery. The first archaeology on the site had begun within a decade of Crowley and Bennett's arrival, and would subsequently reveal the extent of the original structure, confirming much tradition, when the massive stone lion's paws and part of the body were revealed, though the ancient head of the monumental lion was gone. Exquisite paintings of unique style were also uncovered, and it would take little imagination to conjure in the mind the picture of a great, lost spiritual civilization to rival any in the ancient world.

Crowley recorded in *Confessions* how he and Allan hung about there several days in the hope of finding a way up the vast rock, but such proved impossible on account of thick jungle, and even if the summit had somehow been reached, foliage was so dense Crowley reckoned only a monkey could get a view from it!

Crowley was engaged on a ramble through the forest in the vicinity of the Lion Rock when he approached a clearing with a shallow lake. Before him was the first buffalo he'd seen, a bull with two cows enjoying a drink. As usual, Crowley carried a Mauser .303-inch rifle and got within a hundred yards before the bull grew alarmed.* Crowley raised the rifle and fired. To his horror, nothing happened: a faulty cartridge. Luckily, the bull thundered past. Close to death, he learned a lesson, though not one that would have appealed to Allan. In future, Crowley carried a double-barreled rifle.

A more charming encounter with Ceylon's wildlife—this time with Allan Bennett—while rambling was described by Crowley in an article published by *Vanity Fair* in 1909:

> I ought to have told you when talking of Ceylon, the delightful story of Allan's adventure with a krait [a deadly snake]. Going out for a solitary walk one day with no better weapon than an umbrella,

---

*Crowley most likely obtained a modified, or had himself modified, a Mauser 1895 Model, which normally took a 7 × 57mm cartridge, whereas the British .303 cartridge was 7.7 × 57mm. Boer farmers (at war with Great Britain) could purchase the German rifle for £3 sterling; whether its rebellious connotation explains why Crowley chose a Mauser rather than a British .303 Lee Enfield, we know not.

he met a krait sunning himself in the middle of the road. Most men would have either killed the krait with the umbrella or avoided its dangerous neighbourhood. Allan did neither; he went up to the deadly little reptile and loaded him with reproaches. He showed him how selfish it was to sit in the road where someone might pass, and accidentally tread on him. "For I am sure," said Allan, "that were anyone to interfere with you, your temper is not sufficiently under control to prevent you striking him. Let us see now!" he continued, and deliberately stirred the beast up with his umbrella. The krait raised itself and struck several times viciously, but fortunately at the umbrella only. Wounded to the heart by this display of passion and anger, and with tears running down his cheeks, at least metaphorically speaking, he exhorted the snake to avoid anger as it would the most deadly pestilence, explained the four noble truths, the three characteristics, the five precepts, the ten fetters of the soul; and expatiated on the doctrine of Karma and all the paraphernalia of Buddhism for at least ten minutes by the clock. When he found the snake was sufficiently impressed, he nodded pleasantly and went off with a "Good-day, brother krait!"

Some men would take this anecdote as illustrating fearlessness, but the true spring is to be found in compassion. Allan was perfectly serious when he preached to the snake, though he is possibly a better man of science than a good many of the stuck-up young idiots who nowadays lay claim to the title. I have here distinguished between fearlessness and compassion; but in their highest form, they are surely identical.[1]

Crowley found the thirty-seven-mile journey northwest to Anurādhapura a weary one. While the old coach was an ordeal, the flat tangle of vegetation on all sides evoked a sense of desolation. Around sunset his tired eye was caught by what appeared to be graceful wooded slopes whose enchantment broke the monotony. Next day the men were delighted to find the slopes weren't hills, but stone mounds of ruined dagobas (Tibetan pagodas or Buddhist stupas), long overgrown. Crowley found these "buried" cities mightily impressive, comparing them with Egyptian counterparts, which he nonetheless preferred as he felt greater inner connection with Egypt. But he could not but marvel at the scale of the ancient architects' work, opining: "They thought in acres where others think in square yards."[2] He was particularly impressed by one pagoda whose lowest terrace was about a mile in circumference, around which was a ring of stone elephants almost life-size in scale. "Most of the ornamentation has perished," he observed, "but the loss does not really matter. The point of the place is the prodigious piety which erected these useless enormities merely as memorials to the Master."[3]

Situated in Sri Lanka's north central province, Anurādhapura is one of the world's oldest continuously inhabited cities. For many centuries the center of Theravāda Buddhism, the belief spread thence to mainland India and beyond. Judging from articles about it that would appear in Bennett's periodical *Buddhism,* published in Rangoon in 1903 and 1904, Bennett was deeply moved by this city of Buddhist temples and watering pools so richly endowed by the region's ancient kings.

THOMAS WILLIAM RHYS DAVIDS

One notable contributor to the November 1904 edition of *Buddhism* was Pāli expert Caroline Augusta Foley Rhys Davids, M.A., wife of founder of the Pāli Text Society, Thomas William Rhys Davids (1843–1922), distinguished scholar of Pāli, Sanskrit, and of Buddhism.

In 1871 Rhys Davids had been posted as assistant government agent of Nuwarakalaviya, whose administrative center was Anurādhapura. Rhys Davids participated in digs in the city undertaken by the Archaeological Commission, founded in 1868 by governor Sir Hercules Robinson. The old city had been abandoned following an invasion of 933 CE, leaving inscriptions collected by Rhys Davids, who would later publish articles about them in Max Müller's seminal *Sacred Books of the East* and in the *Journal of the Royal Asiatic Society* with its Calcutta base, which Crowley would shortly visit himself. Rhys Davids's paper on the "Lion Rock" would be published along with two other papers in the 1875 journal.

Here was the kind of man Crowley could admire, for not only did Rhys Davids get to know his subject "on the ground" by learning local languages and taking local people into his confidence, but he also fell foul of jaundiced superiors. Dismissed for minor indiscretions involving money, Rhys Davids did not leave Ceylon without having accomplished pioneering studies of the many early Sinhalese inscriptions he uncovered across the island. As Crowley and Bennett explored the ruins, Rhys Davids lectured as London University's professor of Pāli, writing a notable book on Buddhism, based on the Pāli Canon, for the SPCK, in marked contrast to missionary accounts of the subject. In 1905, Rhys Davids accepted Manchester University's new chair in Comparative Religion: a subject significant to Crowley, many of whose writings relate to this discipline, with whose essence he enjoyed instinctive affinity.

For all his breadth of interest, by the beginning of November 1901, Crowley found himself "fed up with marvels." Habitual restlessness again rose to the fore, and he longed to be off the island. When Allan received news of a teaching post at a girls' school in Rangoon, Crowley knew the time had come to part:

> All subjects bore me alike after a short time; they cease to stimulate. I was thoroughly pleased to find myself at last in India. The psychological change from Ceylon is very sudden, startling and complete. What is there about an island which differentiates it so absolutely from the adjoining mainland? No amount of similarity of race, customs and culture gets rid of insularity. The moment one sets foot in India, one becomes aware of the stability of its civilization.[4]

A guru-in-the-making, Crowley was in his element.

SIX

The Aim Is Being: Calcutta

If thought is life, and the want of thought is death,
Then am I a happy fly, if I live or if I die.

WILLIAM BLAKE

Descartes regarded the phenomenon of thought as proof, even sole proof, of existence; such was the credo of the Western Enlightenment: *I think, therefore, I am*. And Crowley had found that to *stop* thinking was yoga's aim, as a means to higher consciousness. Naturally, this reverse would take some accommodating were it ever to contribute to a fresh approach to the science of mind. Crowley's personal discovery had Blake on its side: a fly does not think, but it exists, and seems content enough not knowing it. In the meantime, Crowley knew another yoga: mountaineering, and the realization of that practice constituted his next marker, if still some distance away. He would make his serpentine way, as fate or will might dictate, to the Karakorams, where Nature's raw, overwhelming majesty would stuff his self-awareness into a cocked hat, and deliver that peace of mind in the face of immensity the world cannot give: how infinitely small is man; what a relief to feel it!

Despite any relief of mind he expected from an expedition to K2 in 1902, Crowley's brain was restless. Leaving Ceylon on Friday, November 15, 1901, he spent several weeks wandering about India's southern provinces. At Tuticorin (now Thoothukudi, Tamil Nadu state) on the southeastern Coromandel coast, some 105 miles across the Gulf of Mannar from Ceylon, Crowley sought intellectual solace in his vellum edition of Robert Browning's poems "Christmas Eve" and "Easter Day" (1850).* Their subject was Christianity, and Crowley, smarting at attitudes of Christian missionaries encountered on the island, didn't think Browning had gone far enough, so, parodying Browning's style and blending it with his own, he conceived of both answer and commentary on Browning to be entitled "Ascension Day" and "Pentecost."†

Judging by the finished poems, his bounteous wit trundled forward as steadily and rhythmically as the welcome train that took him to Madura (now Madurai), a populous city some 75 miles north, inland from Tuticorin. Perhaps it was while waiting upon this train that Crowley experienced what he called a "charming incident":

> At some station or other, I was about to take the train. A white man with a long white beard came down the whole length of the train in the blazing sun to my carriage. He had seen that I was strange to the country and asked if he could be of any service. (Unless one knows the ropes, one has to put up with a lot of petty discomforts.) The man was Colonel Olcott. It was the first act of kindly thoughtfulness that I had ever known a theosophist perform—and the last.[1]

This was the same Col. Olcott who had "taken Pansil" in Ceylon with Madame Blavatsky all those years before, vows whose basis Crowley would soon demolish to his own satisfaction in his treatise "Science and Buddhism," which, like his Browning-inspired poems, would appear in *The Sword of Song* (1904).

On a November Sunday, "Ascension Day" and "Pentecost" were committed to writing outside Crowley's "dak-bangla," that is, traveler's hostel

---

*Crowley also carried vellum-bound editions of what he called "my family, the great men of the past": Chaucer, Shakespeare, the best editions of *Atalanta in Calydon, Poems and Ballads* (First Series), Shelley, Keats, and *The Kabbalah Unveiled*. Crowley's vellum coverings ensured their survival, even when his rucksack was soaked through.

†These works appeared in *The Sword of Song* (1904); my analysis begins on page 250, in chapter 12.

or bungalow, at Madura.* Very witty and sometimes wise, these poems were brief drafts of what would become extended published versions.

MADURA

Situated on the River Vaigai, the predominantly Tamil city of Madura had been a major center since ancient times when in the third century BCE a Greek ambassador traveled there during the Maurya Empire period. Shiva-worshipping, its name may be derived from the word for "sweetness," *madhura,* in reference to the divine nectar sprinkled over the city from Shiva's matted hair. Thinking of Sir Richard Burton's successful pretense in gaining entrance to Mecca, and knowing a white man would probably be denied access to the more interesting *prakarams* (precincts), Crowley went to a nearby village and mimicked a holy man, sitting by the wayside in only a loincloth, with a bowl for offerings. Suspicious villagers observed the stranger from the jungle's edge, but seeing him adept at yoga, approached him and made friends. One of those who addressed him not only spoke good English, but was also a "great authority on yoga," introducing Crowley to the writings on "Vedantic Raj Yoga" by Sabhapaty Swamy (see page 290), which work Crowley found of great practical interest. The same friendly cove further introduced Crowley to the authorities at Madura's great Meenakshi Amman Temple, around which the city is laid out.†

Its precincts are dominated by six massive, stepped towers, carved out of rock like narrow truncated pyramids, or tall but compressed Sumerian ziggurats, dense with elaborately colored and impressively worked carvings of living beings. Numerous smaller towers form striking gateways

---

*Crowley made good use of dak bungalows in India and Burma. Those erected by the government were used as staging posts for the "dak" or imperial mail, put up in basic form every twelve to fifteen miles, offering free accommodation to officials, and extremely cheap accommodation to travelers. As Raj officials carried their own beds, beds were rare. Egg and chicken dishes could be provided by a "khansamah" or attendant. Legal hearings were heard there when district officials visited, and they had been used as refuges by British civilians escaping from the ravages of the Indian Mutiny. Kipling observed that many tragedies and wild events occurred in them, and that they had all the attraction, as buildings, as a pile of hay.

†Crowley's initial village contact could have been male or female; see chapter 22, page 448.

from grandly pillared and adorned corridor to further corridors, with ceilings inlaid with radiant enamel work of turquoise, gold, mauve, and purple. Holy Crowley was proud to relate how he'd been permitted entry to some of the secret shrines, in one of which he sacrificed a goat to mother Bhavani, avatar of goddess Parvati, happy to join in with the life-giving cult (her name means "life-giver"). The only people who accused the devotees of Madura of black magic were the missionaries, for were they not worshippers of idols, sensually sculpted?

Crowley wrote in his *Confessions* how one of south India's great sights was "the great temple of the Shivalingam." Unfortunately, he does not say which temple this was, for there are several Shiva temples that could have fitted the bill, and he must have forgotten its name, for it does not appear in any of his extant diaries. Likely candidates relatively close to Madurai in Tamil Nadu state are the Arulmigu Jambukeswarar Akhilandeswari temple at Tiruchirapalli, and the Brihadisvara Temple, Thanjavur, with its 210-foot tower and interior filled with frescoes. Crowley's chief interest lay not in frescoes or towers, however, but in seeing the "Shivalingam," stone symbol of the deity, and not, as some consider, a "phallic symbol." Crowley took his own view on this matter. While he understood the emphasis on the deity's supreme spiritual creative force over the object apparently chosen as its symbol, he could not help noticing barren women circumnambulating it in hope of fruitfulness. Crowley was at the time prepared to accept what he later saw as sublimation, since he says he had not yet got over the "shame of sex," even as instinct compelled assent to Blake's dictum: "the lust of the goat is the bounty of God." Crowley relates his thoughts to one of many observations on sin and repression.

The result of my training had been to obsess me with the hideously foul idea that inflicts such misery on Western minds and curses life with civil war. Europeans cannot face the facts frankly; they cannot escape from their animal appetite, yet suffer the tortures of fear and shame even while gratifying it. As Freud has now shown, this devastating complex is not merely responsible for most of the social and domestic misery of Europe and America, but exposes the individual to neurosis. It is hardly too much to say that our lives are blasted by conscience. We resort to suppression and the germs created an abscess.[2]

The Shivalingam would come to be a personal symbol, included in what would be his trademark signature. Crowley observed how "the Hindu" was as superstitious about sin as English men and women of his time, but then, Indians were serious about their soul's welfare. He related coming across a tribe who did not take tobacco, but when Crowley suggested the reason might be that it was forbidden by their religion, they answered, no, but since it was not *recommended* by their religion, there was no point doing it. He still considered Hindu attitudes to sin a cut above what he'd known in Europe, where the squeamishness about facts of sexual life led to a panic that the very hint of such facts would lead to a bottomless pit of bestiality, where, Crowley observed, their minds, in fact, wallowed already. We perhaps find it a little hard to grasp these points today, when much of our culture has gone some way toward Crowley's perception of the matter.

Hinduism proved attractive to Crowley, naturally enough, he opined, since what he saw as its fundamentally egocentric consciousness garners sympathy from Westerners. Repelled by Buddhism's anti-action quiescence, and insistence on sorrow as inherent to everything, Crowley found Hinduism's positivity refreshing. While Buddhism suited Allan's temperament, it did not square with Crowley's lust for pleasure in adventure, and sheer enjoyment of the fun and thrill of life, which joys he'd only found after a highly restrictive childhood, and which had come to him as such a cleansing revelation. Happiness might be unstable; it was, but that didn't mean it could not be savored to the full while it lasted. Fortune's wheel goes up and down; the miserable lows were likely preludes to delicious highs. And even base contentment could be enjoyed for its own sake. Fortune promised adventure that is never all ascending; like the mountains, there are variants, crevasses, glaciers, and ups and downs of all kinds.

Nevertheless, his immediate sensitivities to the India he discovered were, as he put it, "a shade disconcerting." He felt keenly the degradation of the woman, once wealthy, who, bent double with a small brush, swept out his dak bungalow: "a grotesque hag at thirty." Once she had worn heavy earrings, for he recalled how he could have put his hand through her lobes, so wide had they been stretched by weight of former wealth.[3] In the dust of the floor as she swept extended two trails, results of her sagging breasts hanging "idly out of her cotton cloth." For

Crowley the vision of this woman was somehow symbolic of the human situation that confronts any visitor to India who scratches beneath the surface just a little.

In late November, Crowley found himself farther up India's east coast, at Madras. Did he visit the Theosophical Society's headquarters at Adyar? If he did, his *Confessions* do not confess, remarking only that Madras— where Britain's Indian empire was born—was "sleepy, sticky, and provincial." He resolved to head some five hundred miles northeast for Calcutta, West Bengal. The cause given was that on one of his steamship journeys (this might have been during his time between Hong Kong, Shanghai, and Colombo, or indeed between Colombo and mainland India), he had met a "delightful" man. From a passing note in a magazine article,[4] we learn that tea-trader Harry Lambe was Anglo-Indian, and that Lambe's kind invitation to stay with him in Calcutta confirmed, for Crowley at least, the Anglo-Indian's reputation for hospitality.*

Research yields that "Mr. H. Lambe" had been engaged before 1905 with Walker Lambe & Co. in London, later representing that company under his own name in Calcutta.† Harry Lambe obviously made a strong impression, for Crowley booked passage to Calcutta on a small

---

*"Anglo-Indian" can mean a person of mixed British and Indian descent, or a British person who had lived long in India, or who was born there. It is unclear which meaning is intended by Crowley here. While the surname is British, Lambe may have had an Indian mother, or grandmother.

†See *All About Tea* by William H. Ukers (2 vols. New York: Tea and Coffee Trade Journal Company, 1935), which features a photograph of Mr. Lambe. The chapter entitled "The Tea Expert Bureau," (124–25) informs us that in 1905, on the initiative of Mr. F. D. Cochius of brokers Dunlop & Kolff, of Batavia, the Tea Expert Bureau was established, first at Bandoeng, then Batavia. It gave planters opportunity to send tea samples for testing, greatly contributing to improving Java tea quality. Testing was formerly done after shipments arrived in London or Amsterdam. The Tea Expert Bureau's tea tester eliminated delay. Mistakes in manufacture could be corrected before the tea was shipped. Thirty-three gardens were represented in the bureau by the end of 1905. Having moved from Calcutta to Batavia as manager of the former Tea Export Corporation, Mr. H. Lambe was the first expert employed, remaining with the organization until 1910. According to vol. 2, (325): "The first collaborative attempt to create new markets for Java tea was the shipment, in 1909, of 2300 chests to Australia, where the consignment was sold by Mr H. Lambe, the tea expert in charge, at public auction and private tender."

French steamer, the *Dupleix,* named after the commander of French forces in India whom Robert Clive defeated nearly a century and a half earlier. According to the *Confessions,* Crowley would have found it more natural to take the train but had decided to put himself deliberately in unpleasant situations, provided they were new.*

Adventure was not long in coming. A storm had beaten the *Dupleix* back down the coast and the vessel approached Madras's harbor several days late. So rough was the sea, however, that Crowley had to venture to the steamer by rowboat, the sole passenger, having dismissed his servant in Madras. At this point, he tells us he felt he had broken with his past, cutting off communications, but his new life was immediately drenched in two days of cyclone, in a ship reeking of engine oil, smelly cooking, and a similarly malodorous crew. The weather abated to some extent on the third day and was calm enough by the time the *Dupleix* reached the mouth of the Hooghly. A thick fog, however, obscured the light-ship, but with effort, a pilot managed to get aboard for guiding the way by the Hooghly's extremely treacherous sandbanks. Since their position changed constantly, a large staff was employed taking depth-soundings and erecting signs to indicate false banks and shallow water. Joining the pilot on the bridge, Crowley found his zigzag course reminiscent of a European figure skater.

> On arriving at the landing stage [at Calcutta] I was, much to my surprise, met by my friend Lambe. I had informed him of my arrival, it is true, but I had not the least idea that he would trouble himself to meet me, much less that he would drive me off to his bungalow and put me up for a month. The Anglo-Indian is indeed hospitable. It must be remembered that our previous acquaintance had only been of some twelve hours' duration.
>
> Of course, Calcutta represents civilization and, consequently, nothing of interest can happen. The time I spent there was filled up with tennis and cricket, billiards and Ping-Pong, while every Saturday we went off to the racing.[5]

---

*It may be of interest to some readers that G. I. Gurdjieff also, in the formative period of his self-mastery, made a point of exposing himself to danger, with an interest in the psychology associated with that condition. See my *Deconstructing Gurdjieff: Biography of a Spiritual Magician.*

Lambe's house was a large building in a compound, that is, gardens surrounded by a wall. Four men lived in the colony, one of them especially appealed to Crowley, who "struck up an intimacy based on implicit sympathy in the matter of philosophical speculation."[6] Crowley's interlocutor was Edward Thornton, and it is reasonable to wonder whether the men may have shared more than philosophy.

Crowley's unpublished diary reveals he was still at Calcutta "with one H. Lambe" on January 1, 1902.[7] An interesting story appears in the *Confessions*, describing Crowley at dinner with Lambe and the other men shortly after his arrival. Crowley recalled how he "awoke" from interior thinking to hear the table talk: conversation about peculiarities of the native mind. Apparently, the compound's servants were very excited to have a man among them who had sacrificed a goat in Madura, and not only that, a magician too! Crowley was astonished. He had told his hosts nothing of his interests in magic and religion, and had ceased communicating with anyone at Madras. "Was it true?" his hosts asked. "Yes, it was." How could the servants have known such things? Conversation turned to the "native telegraph," of how news of an officer's death in a frontier skirmish was often reported in a Bombay bazaar before field telegraph transmitted the news. Crowley's intuition suggested verbal communication did not explain it, on account of distances, and felt something more was involved. He then related a story of how he had once wanted some accurate words for a ritual, and not knowing, communicated by astral traveling with a Brother of the Order some 8,000 miles away, acquiring the words he needed.*

Crowley justified his being in Calcutta on grounds of needing Hindustani and Balti to render him useful as interpreter on the Chogo Ri (K2) expedition. While making desultory progress through a Balti grammar, he easily found a munshi to teach Hindustani, two or three hours a day sufficing for the purpose. Even the munshi knew his

---

*The first rail link between Madras and Calcutta was completed in 1900. It had wooden coaches, with no catering services and the journey took thirty-six grueling hours to cover a thousand miles-plus. If someone had wanted to beat Crowley to Calcutta, and tell stories, they could have taken the train and got there ahead of him. Crowley does not explain *why* he cut communications in Madras, and he doesn't say with whom communications had been established. Was he trying to hide his trip to see Harry Lambe? Why did he say he had broken with his past? The story does not quite satisfy as it stands, I think.

English pupil was a magician. Crowley was adamant he'd done practically no magic since arriving in Ceylon, and anyway, he felt at the time that "Magick" was of no relevance to mountaineering—a viewpoint later regarded by him as flawed, not then understanding the "possibilities of Magick." He had not, he said, "realized that it [Magick] was the practical side of spiritual progress."[8] Finally the munshi gathered courage enough to ask the omnipotent mage if he could work his wonders by killing the munshi's inconvenient aunt. Crowley told him that only reasons incomprehensible to the uninitiated could possibly persuade him to kill strangers. The munshi then asked Crowley to ensure his brother passed his exams by softening the examiners. Crowley refused, whereupon the munshi asked whether his brother would pass. Crowley said that the brother would not—it didn't require magick to see that someone in need of "supernatural" assistance had little chance of passing anyway!

For leisure in Calcutta, Crowley felt it best to follow the line of least resistance and attend the races, something of little interest to him, though, as in Mexico, he did take interest in the psychology of the swindler. A horse had arrived in the city tipped to be a surefire winner. Of course it attracted bets, but lost race after race, until the odds of success duly declined. Crowley calculated that having been pulled by its owners to such a degree, the time had come to bet on it. Needless to say, he won a pocketful of rupees, but obtained no satisfaction. Fathoming the bestial mind of the criminal was no joy and the winnings did not compensate.

> My cynical disgust with the corrupt pettiness of humanity, far from being assuaged by the consciousness of my ability to outmanoeuvre it, saddened me. I loved mankind; I wanted everybody to be an enthusiastic aspirant to the absolute. I expected everybody to be as sensitive about honour as I was myself. My disillusionment drove me more and more to determine that the only thing worth doing was to save humanity from the horror of its own ignorant heartlessness. But I was still innocent to the point of imbecility. I had not analysed human conduct: I did not understand in the least the springs of human action. Its blind bestiality was a puzzle which appalled me, yet I could not even begin to estimate its elements.[9]

His health did not help matters. Down with malaria since leaving Ceylon, ever since New Year he'd suffered from ague, fever, indigestion, and mental depression. He sought comfort in Deussen's account of Vedanta, the flower of Hinduism, the which, while it was certainly a progressive step from what Crowley called the "crude animism" of the Vedas, seemed still to push him back toward Buddhism. His diary reveals the depth of thought pulsing through his questing mind.

Jan. 13
Early morning walk—deep meditation. Developed a sort of inverted Manichaeism. Nature as evil and fatal force developing within itself (unwittingly) a suicidal will called Buddha or Christ.

The entry shows up the apparent paradox, or indeed contradiction, within Darwinian theory when applied to the human mind and experience. If Nature evolves solely through selection of traits necessary for rude survival, and the "mind" is deemed a "part" of Nature, how is it that the human mind can thoroughly entertain the idea that Nature itself is a negative, or evil aspect, which, in Manichaeism, for example, is regarded in its materiality as an evil to be fled from? As for Buddhist doctrine, Nature is regarded, when we perceive it, as the home of sorrow and corruption.

Jan. 15.
It is a fallacy that the Absolute must be All-Good, etc. There is *not* an Intelligence directing law = line of least resistance, Its own selfishness has not even the wit to prevent Buddha arising.

Jan. 16.
We cannot call nature *evil*. "Fatal" is the exact word [certainly in the Buddhist perspective]. Necessity implies stupidity—this the chief attribute of Nature. As to "Supreme Intelligence," consider how many billion years were required to develop even so low a thing as emotion.[10]

This is a typical chip off the block of Crowley's intuitive and analytical genius. Meanwhile, in quest of perfect detachment, Allan had taken his vows as a bhikku, donning the yellow robe at the Lamma Sayadaw "Kyoung" (or monastery) on Burma's west coast, at Akyab (now Sittwe). Crowley thought it a good idea to cross the Bay of Bengal to visit him, and to combine that adventure with a greater one: to cross the Arakan Hills, the barrier between the Irrawaddy valley and the coast. Reputed to be all but impassable, even the north Burmese army, when fighting the British in 1825, were not expected to survive a march through the Arakans to the east. "I have always had this peculiar passion for putting myself in poisonous perils," wrote Crowley of his motive. "Its source is presumably my congenital masochism, and the *Travellers' Tales* of Paley Gardner had determined its form of expression."[11] So Crowley determined to follow the initial route taken by the first British military expeditions to Burma: sail to Rangoon, then follow the Irrawaddy to Thayetmyo, north of Prome. He would then hire a guide and head west across the Arakans to Akyab, where he would surprise his Buddhist friend somewhat in the manner of Stanley and Livingstone.

Edward Thornton elected to join him on the adventure.

EDWARD THORNTON

When Crowley averred to Thornton and himself sharing philosophical interests, he could have been thinking of a visit Crowley made in Calcutta, as Thornton's guest, to the famous Asiatic Society of Bengal, in which Sir William Jones had first drawn attention to Sanskrit's affinities with Greek and Latin, so launching the "Aryan" race fallacy. It was exciting for me to locate the printed "Proceedings" of the Society, which reveal its monthly general meeting was held on Wednesday, January 8, 1902, at 9:00 p.m. Members present were the Honorable Mr. C. W. Bolton, Major W. J. Buchanan, Dr. A. Caddy, Mr. B. Chandhnri, Kumar Satindra Deb Rai Mahasai, Mr. W. K. Dods, Mr. W. A. Lee, Mr. J. Macfarlane, Kumar Ramessur Maliah, Mr. J. D. Nimmo, Mr. F. E. Pargiter, Captain L. Rogers, Mr. M. J. Seth, Mahamahopadhyaya Haraprasad Shastri, Mr. J. Wyness—and Mr. E. Thornton, A.R.I.B.A. Visitors are listed as Mr. A. Crowley, Kumar Kshitindra Deb Rai Mahasai, and Kumar Maumdra Deb Rai Mahasai.

After the minutes were delivered, including proposals for disposing of present premises and acquiring a new site and building, the following papers were read: Rev. T. G. Bailey's account of the secret language of a tribe of hereditary thieves and cattle poisoners in the Punjab; "On Trilokinatha (Shiva) in the Kalpa Valley," by Dutch Sanskritist, Jean Philippe Vogel LL.D.—who worked with the Archaeological Survey of India—concerning different representations and names for the Bodhisattva Avalokiteshvara in the Chandrabhaga Valley, the southern side of the mid-Himalayan Range, and Patan, Nepal; and "On the Organisation of Caste by Ballala Sen," by Mahamahopadhyaya Haraprasad Shastri, M.A. The latter paper drew on newly discovered ancient sources also used for a paper on the existence of ancient Magi in India, delivered at the previous general meeting. Crowley would undoubtedly have found great interest in the latter gentleman's researches, and in the rare, exotic, and scientific character of the other papers.

The acronym following society member Edward Thornton's name tells us he was an Associate of the Royal Institute of British Architects (R.I.B.A.). Born in 1869 and educated at King's College, London, Thornton was proposed to R.I.B.A. by F. T. Baggalay. He emigrated to Calcutta in about 1897,* where he became principal architect for India's most prestigious architectural firm, Martin & Co., founded by the remarkable Sir Thomas Acquin Martin (1850–1906).

An industrial pioneer in India, and agent-general for Afghanistan,† Martin had left Birmingham, England, in 1874 to establish engineering firm Walsh-Lovett's new Calcutta branch. A superb business brain, Martin founded his own firm at Clive Street, Calcutta, which in 1889

---

*Edward Thornton (1868–1916); obituaries in the *Builder* 110 (June 23, 1916): 453; *RIBA Journal* 23:307.

†In 1887 Abdur Rahman Khan, emir of Afghanistan, appointed Martin as agent, resulting in Sir Salter Pyne's being dispatched to Kabul, the first European to live there since the 1879–80 Anglo-Afghan war, excepting a French engineer who resided briefly in the city before disappearing. Pyne secured for Martin construction of the emir's arsenal, a mint, factories, and workshops, introducing modern industries run as state monopolies. The amir's reliance on Martin and his agents for policy questions enabled Martin to offer his own country important political service. Chosen by Abdur Rahman as chief of the staff for second son Prince Nasrullah Khan's mission to England in 1895, Martin received his knighthood in August that year. Despite the emir's lack of success in diplomatic relations with Britain, Martin remained a trusted confidant, along with his younger brother Frank Martin, who succeeded Pyne as engineer-in-chief.[12]

assumed management of the Bengal Iron and Steel Company, inaugurating steel and iron production at Burrakur, in successful competition with imported steel and iron. The firm also pioneered Indian light railways along district lines to feed into main lines. Martin controlled jute mills and collieries in Bengal, as well as the Hooghly Docking & Engineering Company. His Tansa Duct Works provided Bombay with constant water from a lake forty miles away. Allahabad, Benares, Cawnpore, Lucknow, Agra, Srinagar, and Calcutta all benefited from Martin's provision of water supplies. Vital to Martin's success was his partnership with Sir Rajen N. Mookerjee, born in Bhabla village, Barasat, near Calcutta. Fascinated by engineering since he was a child, young Mookerjee had marveled at how the Taj Mahal was constructed. The firm would have been called Martin & Mookerjee but for the Bengali's insistence that a firm with a native name would suffer prejudice: hence "Martin & Co."

Having acquired Edward Thornton's architectural expertise, Martin & Co. erected important public buildings throughout India, including palaces for maharajas, to one of which Crowley would receive a personal invitation in October 1905 (see page 340). Martin & Co. were contractors for Calcutta's magnificent All-India Victoria Memorial Hall, and provided the city with numerous other fine structures.* So, when we take all that into account, we can perhaps gain a richer picture of the kind of society Crowley had entered into in Calcutta, and this perhaps helps us to understand why he was content to attend the Calcutta races and other collective sporting events in what was clearly élite company. Besides, what with malaria and intense musings on Nature's fatality, he doubtless needed light, undemanding relief. Such could not be said of the proposed trip to Burma, which would prove taxing in more ways than one.

---

*The *Statesman* reported King George V and his consort's reception at Prinsep's Ghat, Calcutta, on December 30, 1911, and his departure from the same landmark January 8, 1912. The *pandal* (temporary structure erected to venerate Ganesha during Ganesh Chaturthi, or goddess Durga during Durga Puja) for the pageant on the Maidan between Chowringhee and Jail Road was described as a "handsome structure of Oriental design." Its designer was "Edward Thornton of Martin & Co." contracted by Motilal Radha Kissen, with Stephen Wilkinson as superintending architect.

SEVEN

Burma—by Train, Boat, and Paddle Steamer

Thornton informed Crowley his motives for going were need of sea air, change, and opportunities to sketch. He received all in abundance. After a pleasant crossing of the Bay of Bengal, the Rangoon River seemed wild. Running from the confluence of two rivers by the city of Rangoon (now Rangon) to the Gulf of Martaban, the estuary reminded Crowley of the Neva at St. Petersburg for its "terrifying breadth of torrent," rapid turbulence, and visceral rush. Observing raw Nature led Crowley, typically, to analogies with the universe:

> one gets the idea of sterile, heartless passion in the midst of a wilderness, and somehow or other this seems obscenely unnatural. One instinctively associates vehemence with detailed result; and when one sees such stupendous forces running to waste, one is subconsciously reminded of the essence of human tragedy, the callousness of nature about our craving to reap the reward of our efforts. One has to be a philosopher to endure the consciousness of waste, and something more than a philosopher to admire the spendthrift splendour of the universe.[1]

Crowley and Thornton entered Rangoon on January 24. Visiting the city's imposing Shwe Dagon pagoda the following day, Crowley found it annoying, partly because of its grand gilded scale, partly because he found Burmese architecture a cut below India's in formal

100

magnificence, and partly because the temple was ringed by what he called "commercial piety." Beggars, devotees, diseased and deformed people offered gifts to the monks to acquire "merit," or relief from further incarnations. For Crowley, the practice ill fitted canonical doctrine: there is no deity in Buddhism to placate or persuade by sacrifice. He therefore considered the psychology underlying the "merit" motive a living remnant of primitive fetishism, running on in the people's subconscious, and conscious, along with demonology and much else that Buddhist authority either tolerated, elaborated upon, ameliorated, or as Crowley observed in Rangoon, exploited. Offerings of gold made such temples the attractions they were, not the spiritual quality of the devotees, or indeed, guardians. He was more impressed by the sight of a poor boy aged about fourteen, lying on a litter in the pagoda's shadow, suffering from severe hydrocephaly. The pagoda showed years of great care; the boy exhibited for Crowley the Buddha's insight, that Nature has neither purpose nor pity, and senseless suffering is its modus operandi and is as nothing to it, where there is no "it" to register anyway. All syllogisms of optimism, Crowley considered, were based on suppressing unwanted premises. Then again, generalizations from selected phenomena were also misleading. What was more impressive as symbol: the hydrocephalous boy or the great pagoda? The sight of the boy subjected to "freak of misfortune," and everything else he saw, made Crowley feel despair for the state of humanity, exacerbated perhaps by ongoing malarial fever. But there was a gain: he now felt he had shared the Buddha's essential insight into the nature of the cosmos, as perceived in thought.

Malaria was doubtless another instance of pitiless Nature; Crowley treated it with quinine and iced champagne, while observing malaria's curious effects. He felt terribly tired, too fatigued to lift a cup at times or swallow his breakfast, but conversely, it put him in such a state of mind that he could bear his rucksack and walk in a personal haze of indifference for miles, hardly feeling anything, with no expectations. He felt something of the kind that afflicted many colonials who stayed in like climates too long; they just about kept up appearances, but spirits were broken by perpetual monotony, indifference, solitude, and meaninglessness. He recalled a trip with Allan to visit a forest officer up-country in Ceylon. Having no conversation, the man cranked up his sole relief, an old gramophone. He had lost interest in life, a future, or of returning to England; quite old, he had become part of the jungle, just about clinging to threadbare tassels of civilized formalities, but otherwise, dank and lost amid the rotting undergrowth of the East. Crowley recognized the symptoms in those who entered such a life without sufficient intelligence and energy to extract some sense, meaning, or interest in the surroundings, and so avoid being overcome by that eternal silence that "has neither shape nor soul."

Having left the Shwe Dagon pagoda, Crowley confided to his diary: "Will go and take refuge in the Triratna,"[2] that is Sanskrit for the "three jewels" (Pāli: *Ti-ratana*) or the "Threefold Refuge" of the Buddha, the dharma (teaching), and the sangha (monastic order or Buddhist community). He was traumatized by the sun, and with a temperature of 103 Fahrenheit, called the doctor, who pronounced him well again the next day (January 26, 1902).

Two days later, Crowley and Thornton's *bandobast* (Anglo-Indian for security or travel arrangements) completed, he engaged a Madrassee boy called Peter at 1.8 rupees per day and warm clothes, advancing him 10 rupees and deducting 5 as fines. When Crowley asked Peter his religion, the lad replied he was "a free man, a Roman Catholic." Crowley's comment: "Some people's ideas of freedom are peculiar. Needless to say, he was a scoundrel of the first water."[3] Crowley wouldn't have taken a Christian if there'd been anyone else with English and Hindustani. The boy's pettiness in continual thefts and duplicity astonished his employer, who was unsurprised that the "native Christian" of his day "invariably" called on his deathbed for the minister of his original religion, after a life built shakily on fraudulent piety.

Before leaving what he considered Rangoon's exceeding dullness and intense, dry, sticky heat, he got a letter to the forest commissioner of the district to which he was heading for provision of elephants. Crowley, Thornton, and young Peter took the train north to Prome (now Pyay), arriving on January 29. *Pyay* means "country" and derives from the Sanskrit *srīkṣetra* ("blessed place, country"), once the main city of the Pyu city-states whose ruins lay five miles southeast in Hmawa village. Eschewing more ruins, Crowley's party immediately boarded steam ferry *Amherst*, named after India's governor general, the Lord Amherst, who had secured victory in Britain's first war with Burma three-quarters of a century earlier.*

THE IRRAWADDY FLOTILLA COMPANY

The five-hour journey upstream to Thayetmyo was stimulated by glorious scenery and the geniality of the *Amherst*'s captain. I should imagine churning up the shallow waters of the Irrawaddy in a paddle steamer was an engaging enough novelty by itself.

> By the old Moulmein Pagoda, lookin' lazy at the sea,
> There's a Burma girl a-settin', and I know she thinks
>   o' me;
> For the wind is in the palm-trees, and the temple-bells
>   they say:
> "Come you back, you British soldier; come you back
>   to Mandalay!"
> Come you back to Mandalay,
> Where the old Flotilla lay:
> Can't you 'ear their paddles chunkin' from Rangoon
>   to Mandalay?
> On the road to Mandalay,
> Where the flyin'-fishes play,
> An' the dawn comes up like thunder outer China
>   'crost the Bay!

—as Rudyard Kipling wrote, and Frank Sinatra sang. Kipling's "old Flotilla" was the "greatest river fleet on earth"—the Irrawaddy Flotilla Company—founded in 1865 originally to ferry troops up and down Burma's main artery, managed by Paddy Henderson & Co. of Glasgow.

---

*William Pitt Amherst, 1st Earl Amherst (1773–1857) was governor general for the East India Company from 1823 to 1828 when Britain responded to Burmese attacks on company officials and armed incursions into Bengal. After a short war, the British flag flew above Arakan province on the west coast at April's end, 1825, and in February 1826, the Treaty of Yandabo ended the first of the three Burmese wars that eventually gave Britain complete control of Burma in 1886, sixteen years before Crowley's arrival in Prome.

Fig. 7.1. A paddle steamer of the Irrawaddy Flotilla.

At its peak in the 1920s the I.F.C. employed over 11,000 men, operated over 600 vessels, and carried millions of passengers and millions of tons of cargo annually.*

Doubtless, the captain filled Crowley in on the ship's details, and Crowley would have been delighted to hear of its Scottish connections—most of the I.F.C.'s British staff hailed from Scotland, where of course, Crowley's Boleskine estate was situated.

Built in 1886 at Dumbarton's Leven Yard in Scotland by William Denny & Bros., paddle steamer *Amherst*'s original 96 nominal horse-power engine from Rankin & Blackmore of Greenock had been replaced in 1897 at the flotilla's Dalla dockyard, across the river from Rangoon, with a salvaged engine from *Pulu,* sunk on the Irrawaddy off Shenwaga in collision with PS *Mandalay.†* To save weight against the tough current *Amherst* had a steel box hull (vital for shallow waters) 160.5 feet long, 24 feet wide, with a depth of 7.8 feet. Denny's paddle steamers typically carried crew, clerical staff, and light cargo, with first- and second-class cabins and space provided for Burmese

---

*When the Japanese invaded Burma in 1942, the flotilla's manager, John Morton, ordered the scuttling of the entire fleet to prevent the Japanese having usable transport up the Irrawaddy.

†PS *Amherst* No. 93331 was hulked in 1924 and converted to a station flat at Dedaye.

deck passengers whose colorful liveliness added to the pleasures of Irrawaddy river travel.[4]

I have some idea of those pleasures as I was fortunate enough recently not only to go on a short river "cruise" on a paddle steamer of the imperial era, but even to spend the night on one in a tiny cabin. Paddle steamer *Emmylou* first went into service at the tiny port of Echuca on the Murray River that divides Victoria from New South Wales, Australia, in 1902, and I had Crowley's trip up the Irrawaddy of that year very much in mind as we paddled through remote waters up and down the Murray in a vessel similar to the *Amherst*. As tropical branches waved by, their roots clawing into the swampy river like so many aged hands grappling onto life, the twin paddles stirred up the bright waters while the wood-fired engine grunted and growled, with a pounding rumble like beating sheets on a clothesline, or a muffled drum, as spurts of steam hissed from frantic pistons to blend with the paddles' wet splash, like cymbals keeping rapid time, at a top speed of 7.5 miles per hour—all rather glorious, like a ride on a benign monster, glad of your company as it munched wood, breathed friendly fire, and contentedly puffed black smoke into the clear blue sky. Happy, bygone days . . .

Crowley, Thornton, and Peter arrived in the heat of the day at Thayetmyo (now Thayet), a port on the Irrawaddy's western bank. Annexed by the British with all Pegu in 1852–53, Thayetmyo was administered by a deputy commissioner as part of "Upper Burma." Crowley just missed Major Eden Vansittart's raising at Thayetmyo, later in the year, of the Eighth Ghurka Rifles.[*]

Service at the dak bungalow was, according to Crowley's diary, "bad." Nevertheless, on the morning of January 30, he secured three suspension-free bullock carts from a man called "Kaveem" at 12 rupees per cart, and the party began the cross-country journey west to Mindon at 6:45 a.m. Ten miles of extremely noisome jolting of bullock carts

---

[*]In 1903 the Eighth Ghurka Rifles became the Second Battalion, Tenth Gurkha Rifles, and Seventh Gurkha Rifles in 1907, being one of only two Ghurka regiments out of ten to recruit from communities along the Himalayan foothills east of Nepal's capital, Kathmandu, whence came also the famous Sherpas vital to Himalayan mountaineering expeditions. An authority on the Ghurkas and Nepal, Eden Vansittart (born 1856) wrote *Notes on Nepal* (Calcutta, 1896).

brought them to the Baha dak bungalow at 10:45 where Crowley shot parrot, which he found made poor eating, though some thought it tolerable in a pie. The party lunched at Natha (possibly on unpleasant parrot), before continuing for Kyoukghyi (spelt in Crowley's diary as *Kyonk ghyi*), arriving there at 7:30 p.m. That night, Crowley was troubled by a bad dream, so made a magical invocation of "H.P.K," that is "Hoor Paar Kraat" or Harpocrates, learned in the Golden Dawn as a means of banishing unclean spirits. The "air" somewhat cleared, Crowley then had a second "love dream" involving "one Princess Oviosonoff." Taken in adultery, the husband twice attempted to murder him, the second attempt being successful, but "by will" Crowley survived and the dream went on.[5]

At 7:15 a.m. on the thirty-first, they journeyed three hours to the "Leh-Joung" dak bungalow. They "lunched like Gods" after Crowley shot some pigeons and partridges with his double-barreled .577, then at 12:30 headed on to Yegyanzin. After four hours, they reached their destination, between Ta La Bar and Mindon, some three-quarters of the way between Thayetmyo and Mondon. At Yegyanzin they met district forest commissioner Mr. Garr and assistant, Hopwood. Crowley's luck was poor. A shooting jaunt with Hopwood bagged nothing, while Hopwood's superior regretted no elephants could be spared from essential tasks. Crowley might get some ponies, however, and finding porters would be easy. Despite the setback, a delightful dinner ensued, and Crowley uncharacteristically remarked on how nice Englishmen really are when encountered in out of the way places, before adding caustically (in his *Confessions,* written twenty years later), "Sometimes not even then."*

A 3:30 early start on February 1 brought them to Mindon at 2:30 p.m., but not without a last seven hours of "fearful jolting" on the springless bullock carts, so severe Crowley arranged with Thornton that each would do advance lookout duty for oncoming declivities in the track. Nevertheless, one particular slipup led several feet down into a paddy field and a terrible shock. Exhausted, Crowley bathed at Mindon before interviewing the village headman with orders for men to help

---

*This sardonic aside did not appear in the 1909 *Vanity Fair* article "On a Burmese River," which Crowley appears to have been using for the relevant section of the *Confessions.*

with the cross-country journey to Kyaukpyu. Grudgingly, the headman obeyed, sending Crowley a "shikari"—or hunter—to assist buffalo shooting the next day. Crowley then went off to shoot pigeon and woodpecker.

Rising early, Crowley departed at 6:40 a.m. for the jungle. Soon it was hot, and the heavy .577 began to weigh on him as he covered some fifteen to twenty miles, up and down hills, in eight hours. For all the effort, however, the buffalo proved shy, and the white hunter came back with nothing more than oriole, red-crested woodpecker, and parrot.

Back at the dak bungalow at 2:30, Crowley and Thornton went bathing together at a pool, just under the hill on which the bungalow stood. Crowley took a shotgun with him, hoping to kill a big paddy bird—valuable for its "aigrette" or feathery crest—visible from the bank. His first shot having somehow missed, he passed the gun to a Burmese boy servant and resumed his outdoor bath. Impudently, the bird paid a return visit. Crowley signaled for the gun, donned a ghurka's topi (hat) and, with nothing but a towel round his waist, stalked the bird. Thornton said he'd never laughed so much in years seeing Crowley maneuvering about the ford thus dressed, shotgun in hand. Crowley had the last laugh. Ten minutes of "infinite pains" was all it took to dispatch the paddy bird into memory, and subsequently, literature.

Fatigued, Crowley passed much of the next day (February 3) reading Henrik Ibsen and Walter Pater. Despite the lethargy, he was keen to show Thornton a spectacular view of hillside and river he'd found the previous day, suitable for Thornton's sketchbook.* Setting out for a stroll, Thornton carried his sketchbook and a kukri. Crowley wondered why his friend always armed himself with such a blade. Tired out on the edge of a hill, Crowley pointed to a tiny path down the slope that would lead Thornton to the place. He then waited—and waited. About to get up and go searching, Crowley heard Thornton's porter, then saw Thornton, his kukri splattered with blood. Asking his friend jocularly where he'd fallen and cut himself, Thornton related how he'd disputed with "an animal" over rights to the path, necessitating his hitting it on

---

*For a comparison of what Edward Thornton might have had in mind, see R. Talbot Kelly, *Burma Painted and Described,* Adam & Charles Black, 1905. Kelly's book features a painting of a dak bungalow (70–71), and a description of Thayetmyo (138).

the head. The beast fell down the slope toward the river. Crowley examined the creature's tracks, concluding that Thornton came out of the engagement rather well. The tracks belonged to a full-grown leopard! Crowley didn't ask about the kukri again.

Back at the bungalow, the headman returned to announce he could not supply porters for a journey into the Arakans. Nobody had been there, he said, and it was very dangerous, and everyone who went there died, and more of the same dire stuff made Crowley skeptical of the headman's next suggestion. Porters (known at the time by Crowley as "coolies") were available for the next twenty miles only, but more would be found after that for the crossing. On consideration, Crowley decided returning to the Irrawaddy via the Mindon Chong was preferable,* so he hired a dugout canoe, some thirty-five feet long, with an awning at its center, and started out down the river the next day.

4th. [Feb.]
Started down the Mindon Chong. Shot many birds. Got fever. I think sun 101°–102°. Slept at Sakade. Got sick. Bad insomnia.[6]

Crowley remembered the journey down the stream with affection. Sitting in the stern, taking shots at snipe, heron, and anything else that seemed fair sport, he delighted in the country, with its bamboo-fortified villages and "charming" population. Burmese boy servants loved retrieving game not swiped by kites watching overhead, careless of Crowley's gun. The afternoon was marred slightly from a bout of fever, but in the evening, when the dugout was tied up at Sakade, he found solace under the stars with a gorgeous "Nat" or nature spirit of a teak tree.

The effects of my continued bouts of fever had been to make me spiritually sensitive. The jungle spoke to me of the world which lies behind material manifestation. I perceived directly that every phenomenon, from the ripple of the river to the fragrance of the flowers, is the language by which the subtle souls of nature speak to our senses. That night we were tied up under a teak tree, and as I lay awake with my eyes fixed ecstatically on its grace and vigour, I found

---

*Crowley writes "Chong" phonetically; the Burmese word is *chaung,* that is: "river."

myself in the embraces of the Nat or elemental spirit of the tree. It was a woman vigorous and intense, of passion and purity so marvellous that she abides with me after these many years as few indeed of her human colleagues. I passed a sleepless night in a continuous sublimity of love.[7]*

It was rare of Crowley to refer directly to his affinity to elemental spirits in nature; perhaps he came to take it for granted, or regarded the matter as, generally speaking, personal to himself as a magician; I can understand that from my own experience (see footnote below).

The next morning (February 5) was something of a comedown. It being winter in Burma, the early hours were bitter, and Crowley felt the chilly damp from the thick white mist that covered the river and did not dissipate until well after sunrise. Crowley kept quiet for the day, for while the fever seemed to abate, his digestive system was upset. Perhaps he felt the many jungle fires that punctuated this and the next day mirrored his gastric condition. Feeling better around nightfall, he saw two deer descend to the bank, barely visible amid the foliage. He appears to have had some Burmese men helpers, for he refers to "the men" holding the boat while he took aim—successfully. The deer provided the party with a "first-class dinner."[8] He finally got to sleep at Singoun.

---

*The experience inspired Crowley's poem "Rondel," included in the collection, *Ahab* (1903), begun at Allan Bennett's Buddhist monastery in Akyab (see chapter 12, page 277), shortly after Crowley's Irrawaddy adventure, which includes the lines:

O woman of deep red skin! Carved hair like the teak! O delight
Of my soul in the hollows of earth—how my spirit hath taunted—
Away! I am here, I am laid to the breast of the earth in the dusk of the night,
By palm and pagoda enchaunted.

I can testify to the experience of encountering a feminine nature spirit, and the lasting sense of a bond following a sensual, spiritual experience with such a being (in my own case—using Paracelsus's classification of elemental spirits—an "undine.") The experience occurred in a hidden pool at Fontjoncouse, Aude, France, in July 1987, and was so extraordinary and affecting I put the story into my first novel, *Miraval* (Weidenfeld & Nicolson, 1989), which I owe to her. Aleister Crowley's ability to get in touch with nature spirits was referred to during a forest walk in Germany at the time of the O.T.O. "Weida Conference" in 1925 by an awestruck Eugen Grosche (1890–1964). (See my book *Aleister Crowley: The Beast in Berlin*, pp 70–71.)

Fig. 7.2. Strand Road, Prome, circa 1901.

The party set off next morning at 7:30. Crowley felt more up to the challenge and felt he had to save his reputation by bagging a "Brahman duck," (also known as a Ruddy Sheldrake) some two feet long known with orange-brown body plumage—his having missed one on the first day. After several attempts, including stalking it on land, Crowley finally got it when it flew back toward him, exposing its breast in flight, offering the target he'd lacked earlier. The party spent the night at Toun Myong.

The next day, February 7, went well, with Crowley shooting two Brahman ducks, a big stork, and other fowl. Finally the party rowed into Kama on low hills on the Irrawaddy's western bank, a village of just under 1,800 souls.* At Kama they were able to signal the southbound paddle steamer, which deposited them at Prome, where Crowley paid Peter 15 rupees and they all slept.

The next day was spent at Prome's pagoda, with Thornton making sketches and Crowley writing a "Buddhist poem" and starting the

---

*Kama was the headquarters of the Kama District of Thayetmyo from the Irrawaddy to the Arakan Yoma in the west, covering 575 square miles, with 201 villages and a population of 39,570. With 50 square miles under cultivation, it paid 53,000 rupees in land revenue. Source: *The Imperial Gazetteer of India,* Oxford, 1908.

poem later entitled "Rondel," which alluded to his amorous experience with the Nat of the teak tree. Crowley's diary informs us he also "did some Mitri Bhavana, taking my refuge in the Triratna."[9] The "Maitri Bhavana" is a Buddhist meditation on expanding loving kindness or unlimited friendliness without limits. The Sanskrit *maitri* means "friendliness" or "loving-kindness" and *bhavana* indicates virtue, quality, generosity of spirit. The meditation may begin: "May I be well, may I be happy, may I be free from enmity, may I be free from ill will toward myself," or thoughts of that kind. Penetrated by feelings thus generated, the second stage involves projecting this feeling onto others, visualizing people and extending the feeling in their direction. Compassion even for those one hates is desirable. In a sense, it is a way of getting out of mind-sets we generate as we move from innocence and trust into the hazards of human society, where anger and hatred fester and manifest in so many ways.

At 8:00 p.m., Crowley, Thornton, and Peter took the Rangoon–Prome railway: 163 miles long, it was the first the British built in Burma, opened in May 1877 after three years' construction, chiefly by imported Indian laborers from areas affected by the Bihar famine of 1873–74. By 1902, three railway companies had been amalgamated into the state-owned Burma Railway Company.

Awaking in Rangoon after many strange dreams, Crowley spent the day driving round Rangoon, wondering why he was dreaming of losing teeth. The "Rule of Agra" stated that dreaming of lost teeth meant the death of relatives. Several of Crowley's relatives had died recently, but the dreams of losing teeth were frequent in Ceylon and had started again.

On Monday, February 10, Peter was finally paid off, after a last attempt to swindle his employer by overcharging, claiming to have lost his account of what he'd taken from stores. Crowley wisely kept a second copy and, having made an accurate summary of what was truly coming to Peter, he offered a bottle of champagne and three tins of food as a backsheesh gift for Peter's otherwise decent services—these items Crowley knowing Peter had stolen already! Peter was somewhat taken aback that Crowley had been so closely "on to him," and his threat to complain to whosoever he could think of duly subsided.

On the eleventh, Crowley was down with fever again. Vomiting attacks called for a doctor who recommended "iced simpkin"

(Anglo-Indian champagne) after a dose of sodium bicarbonate as an alkali emetic. At 5:00 p.m., Crowley was fit enough for eggs and toast, and three hours later consumed soup, lamb cutlets, sweetbreads, eggs, and ice cream. The patient had apparently been wired by Allan and was keen to answer. Thornton, meanwhile, had felt compelled to go back north to Mandalay, where he could do more sketching. Crowley was most upset he couldn't join his friend, but felt on tenterhooks because he wasn't sure when Eckenstein would turn up with his team for the K2 expedition in Kashmir, which Crowley had no intention of missing.

Crowley didn't hang about. On the twelfth he was aboard SS *Comilla*, bound for Akyab.*

AKYAB

On board ship, Crowley's thoughts were of Buddhism—mostly:

> Let me establish a portion of my mind and call it the Supreme God, and attribute powers of healing, protection, and other useful things to it: thus letting a Skanda mould Skandas. Dream—partly lascivious. Of the annoying kind where at the very last stroke something interferes.[10]

In Buddhism, a *skanda* can refer to a popular deity, whereas *skandhas* (Sanskrit) refers to inner aggregates that promote cravings—and suffering. Anyhow, it was probably the sea air that cleared up Crowley's health.

By 5:00 p.m. the next day, the ship was off Sandoway (now Thandwe), due west of Prome on Burma's west coast, an ancient town thought once to have been Arakan's capital (Arakan is now Rakhine State). Crowley alerted Allan to his imminent arrival, presumably by the latest ship's wireless. Still subject to intense dreams, Crowley now found them amusing and "singularly beautiful." He wondered if he wrote the dreams down, his waking memory of them might improve. Such interest in the ancient magic of dream interpretation chimed in with the latest psychological theories. Freud's *The Interpretation of Dreams* had appeared in 1899.

---

*Built in 1875, SS *Comilla* was run by the British India Steam Navigation Co. In 1905 she was sold to M. Ikeda of Japan and renamed *Chugoku Maru*.

The *Comilla* put in at Khyouk-pyu on the fourteenth, the place Crowley had vainly attempted to approach overland. Despite an attractive bay and beach, it was a "den of malaria." Besides, there was no chance to go ashore as the captain was anxious to race through the straits to Akyab. An estuarial island formed from the Kaladan, Mayu, and Lay Mro rivers all emptying into the Bay of Bengal, crosscurrents, tidal creeks, and the treacherous Oyster Reef, made timing, and a pilot, vital; the captain just made it, anchoring at Akyab's deep-water port at 8:00 p.m. The port consisted of an iron wharf, a small stone pier, and several smaller wooden jetties. The town, triangular in shape, covered about five square miles, with Europeans living on the southern side close to the coast. Known as the "white man's grave," Akyab suffered cholera, berri-berri, and malaria epidemics.

Coming ashore with the second officer, Crowley casually tried to find Allan in the dark. The first person he asked the way delighted in taking the new arrival in his own carriage to the monastery Crowley calls "Lamma Sayadaw Kyoung."* There, Crowley quickly found Allan in his Buddhist robe. He seemed the same, but for his height, which, when surrounded (as he often was) by diminutive Burmese, appeared gigantic! Crowley recognized Allan's familiar gentleness but was concerned his asthma had returned, a result, Crowley surmised, of the bhikkhu's having to be up before dawn, when the air was cold and damp. Commonsense Crowley regretted this incompatibility between sanity, sanitation, and sanctity. Many Buddhist rules, like most religious rules, were introduced after the founder's passing, as communities of followers encountered specific problems; rules then became solidified,

---

*If Crowley's "Kyoung" is a variant of *kyaung,* then the word is simply Burmese for monastery, while *sayadaw* means "royal teacher," and refers to a senior monk or abbot. If "Lamma" is a variant of the Tibetan Buddhist *lama,* meaning a teacher of the Buddhist rule, or venerated master of a monastery, then the "name" would mean something like the "Venerated Teacher Monastery." Alternatively, Crowley's "Kyoung" might be a person's name, as it is in Korea. Either way, while several monasteries are active in modern Sittwe, none bear this name; so Crowley either mistook its name, its name was changed, or the monastery was closed or amalgamated during the twentieth century. The Shwe Zedi Kyaung was founded in 1903 and may have absorbed Allan's monastery. Other existing Buddhist sites in modern Sittwe are the Dakkhoung Monastery, the Buddhay Pagoda, the Eastern Aye Zay Di Tayza Rama Monastery, the Ayadi Dham Monastery, and the Lawkananda Pagoda.

even dogmatized, often to the practical disadvantage of their essential, original purpose and sometimes distinct—even contrary—to the Buddha's original teaching. This was the way Crowley generally interpreted much, sometimes all, of the "morality" that Buddhist tradition itself held to be the very prerequisite of enlightenment.*

Having slept, and dreamed, in the temple, Crowley awoke next morning to return to the *Comilla* for breakfast with the ship's captain, to whom he bade farewell, expressing gratitude for the captain's manifest kindness displayed when Crowley was aboard. Gathering his luggage, Crowley went to the home of resident medical officer, Dr. Moung Tha Nu. The doctor heartily offered Crowley hospitality for his stay.

This was probably Allan's arrangement, for the doctor was Allan's chief *dayaka,* that is, benefactor (from the Pāli for donor, or supporter). In Theravāda Buddhism, the dayaka supports the Sangha by helping bhikkhus in their practice, study, and teaching of the dhamma. The dayaka may also help with lodging, food, clothes, or indeed anything that helps others come to know the dhamma. So helping Crowley was just part of the good doctor's obligations as a lay donor to the monks.

Having entered the Theravāda community, Allan's idea—and thus Crowley's idea—of Buddhism was shaped directly by the Pāli Canon: the *vinaya-pitaka,* or monastic rules, the Buddhist sermons (*sutta-pitaka*), and the philosophy and psychology of Buddhism (*abhidhamma-pitaka*).

Allan, or rather Bhikkhu Ananda Metteya—ordained novice on December 12, 1901—joined Crowley at the dayaka's house and, according to the diary, they discussed "A.P." and "P," which initials might stand for astral projection and, as they walked back to the temple, "Tried to discuss" might be more like it, for on the way, conversation was constantly interrupted by all sorts of people prostrating themselves at the European bhikkhu's feet, clinging to him, and giving varied presents, which, in a region whose staple crop was rice, doubtless included that offering, as well as buttered eggs, marmalade, brazil nuts, bicarbonate of

---

*When Bennett led the first Buddhist Sangha to England in 1908, his progress was greatly impaired both by his appalling health problems, and by the special rules he had to follow as part of his discipline, which made ordinary domestic conduct in London houses, and the provision of talks, a great trial for his hosts, contributing to the journey's poor results, in contrast to its great ambition.

potash, and works of Buddhism—such was the affection and reverence in which Ananda Metteya was already held in Akyab. Crowley's apparent distaste for some of the folk approaching his over-revered friend may be explained in part by a passage in the official *Burma Gazetteer* concerning pagoda slaves.* The *Gazetteer* relates a strange anomaly in Burma's Buddhist religion where temple servants were outcasts, shunned by the rest of the population: a practice going back to the days when the Arakan kings took from Bengal degraded castes as perpetual and hereditary pagoda slaves. To these were added pardoned convicts or people condemned to temple servitude on account of crimes. Whilst under British rule released from former compulsion and become farmers, they were still regarded with disgust by locals as low-caste Hindus were in India proper.[11] Ananda Metteya, however, was gracious to them.

One can certainly understand Crowley's frustration. He had gone through many an adventure to have the chance to discuss matters with the venerated bhikkhu, and, unlike the worshippers, had no motive for acquiring "merit" from the occasion. It seems likely the matters the two men attempted to discuss concerned the relation of magical powers to meditative states.

Passages within the Pāli Canon accepted that through ascetic, or meditative practices, followers could attain supernormal powers called *iddhi* or *iddhi-pāṭhāriya*. They are listed in the *Kevaddha Sutta* (*Dīgha Nikāya* 1.212) where the Buddha even asserts that a kind of magic (*vijjā*) can produce the same results, such as the ability to read other people's thoughts.[12] However, such things have, he insists, no religious value. Furthermore, the Pāli Canon elsewhere maintains that preoccupation with such powers constitutes fetters to be transcended or "blown out" in order to achieve complete *nibbana,* or enlightenment. Acquirement of supernormal powers may enslave one to desire, or attachment, or be used to attain desired objectives, whereas the bhikkhu's sole desire should be enlightenment, in attaining which even the desire to attain it should be extinguished, or become a selfless desire that others may likewise attain. Crowley seems already to have grasped in Ceylon that Allan was not even prepared to rest with attainments of the *jhānas* (such as dhyāna or the Buddhist samādhi, or concentration),

---

*Crowley's diary reads: "Fools dropped in incessantly to worship A[nanda] M[etteya]."

because there were higher, utterly *arūpa,* that is immaterial, states to be reached before ultimate release.

Bennett clearly felt that in order to embrace Buddhism for all its spiritual treasures, it was cardinal for him to lay down, or blow out the flame of his former mastery of magical techniques. It very soon became a point for him to consider magic, psychic powers, and esoteric knowledge as inadequate. He would thus have found Theosophy's conflation of these subjects with Buddhism a misleading source of confusion for others; hence he advocated Buddhism pure and unadorned as sole path to global enlightenment. He wanted Buddhism pristine from source, freed of all accretions. This is evident in the first issue of his Rangoon-published periodical *Buddhism,* published in 1903, a year after receiving *upasampadā*— higher ordination from the Venerable Sheve Baya Sayadaw, May 21, 1902—where Buddhism is specifically divorced from the esoteric,[13] while in *Buddhism's* fourth issue Ananda Metteya insisted on Buddhism's place at the first International Freethought Association because Buddhism was opposed to all supernaturalism.[14] Crowley may have found Bennett's views both interesting, and somewhat disconcerting.

That night, after reconstructing Book III of his poetic epic *Orpheus,* Crowley had two "lascivious" dreams, in one of which "the husband" appeared. He noted the two series as repeated phenomena, noting the "husband" theme as a specific dream type.[15] He was now carefully recording his dreams.

The next day, Crowley composed the "Great Complaint of Orpheus." Some verses in *Orpheus* Book III seem to have been touched by experiences on the Mindon Chaung, such as the thick mist on the cold river, which he may have translated to Orpheus traveling to Hades:

> So darker and colder
>> The stream as we float:
>>> Blacker and bleaker,
>>>> The mist on the river!
> Stronger the shoulder
>> Impels the sad boat.
>>> Sadder and weaker
>>>> Shudder and quiver
> The notes of the lyre.

Quenched is my fire
   In the fog of the air.
Dim my desire
   Cuts through the snare.
The cold confounds me;
The mist surrounds me;
   Life trembles and lowers;
Earth fades from my life.
The love of my wife,
   The light of the flowers,
   Earth's beautiful bowers.
Pass, and are not.
I am awed by the soul of the place, the hopeless,
   the desolate spot.

Published in 1905, Book III of *Orpheus* is dedicated "TO THE MEMORY OF IEHI AOUR, WITH WHOM I WALKED THROUGH HELL, AND COMPELLED IT." "Iehi Aour" is of course Bennett's Golden Dawn name, and there seems a hint of regret in Crowley's decision not to use his friend's now customary Buddhist name. The reference to walking through hell and compelling, or commanding it, may refer to his and Allan's evocation work in Chancery Lane in 1899, as well serving as an image for the "hell" of the material—but to the Buddhist, illusory—world whose fires of greed and lust bind body and mind.

Crowley's reference to Orpheus's "Complaint" may refer to a passage in *Orpheus* Book II ("Of Love"), described, tellingly, in the Contents as "[Orpheus] Complains of the antithesis of desire and power." The passage adds to a long lament for lost love (Eurydice in the poem, of course).

Let the far music of oblivious years
   Sound in the sea beneath!
Are not its waters one with all my tears?
Hath Atropos no comfort in her shears?
   No Muse for me one wreath?

❀

Were I now dead and free to travel far
    Whither I will, ah me!
As the old prophet on the child I fall
And breathe—but no breath answers me at all.
Not whither I must—were there no avatar
Drawn like my love from some close kindred star?
    No shape seen on the sea?

Were I now free of this intense desire,
    By swift magician power
I might fly westward shod with wings of fire
And find my love, and in her arms expire,
    Or wed her for an hour.

(Not for an hour as man, but even as God
    Whose day is like an æon.
Love hath nor station, stage, nor period:
But is at once in his inane abode
Beneath the spring Dircean.)

Alas, the will flies ere the power began.
    Lo, in the Idan grove
Invoking Zeus to swell the power of Pan,
The prayer discomfits the demented man!
    Lust lies as still as love.*

Therefore in memory only is there life,
    And in sweet shapes of art:
The same thought for the ointment and the knife—
Oh lightning! blast the image of my wife
    Out of my mind and heart!

---

*A footnote in the *Collected Works* edition (1905) of *Orpheus* says: "This obscure stanza means; that the invocation of high and pure forces cannot be diverted to low and impure ends; because the man becomes identified with what he invokes, of necessity." This caveat has a significant bearing on the question of the Buddhist critique that magic has no religious value.

While one might fancifully wonder if Crowley did not have past days with Allan Bennett in mind, as an image of unrequited love, Book II's dedication points us in another direction: "TO MARY BEATON WHOM I LAMENT." Mary Beaton was the married woman with whom Crowley enjoyed a love affair aboard ship between San Francisco and Yokohama now nearly a year ago, which liaison inspired his unfinished *Alice: An Adultery* poems, and which resonates perhaps with his repeated dreams of a husband discovering he and his amour, *en flagrant*. The verses' theme of the antithesis of desire and power resonates with debate on the value of magic. While Crowley desires Mary Beaton— as Orpheus does the dead Eurydice—he is powerless to change things. Furthermore, his desires bring him down (to Hades) in search of the lost, so diminishing his power to rise to higher things. *Does then the true source of superior power compel one to Buddhism?* This was the question that would obsess Crowley's mind for some time, and it was Ananda Metteya, and Crowley's bittersweet experience of love, that put the question there.

Allan showed up at the doctor's house after breakfast, hoping to avoid the throng of worshippers. He stayed all day "with only an occasional fool to worship."[16] Conversation was mainly devoted to Buddhism and, according to Crowley, plans shared to extend it to Europe.[17] The conversation continued over the next four days, and was probably quite intense. In the evening Crowley wrote Minos and fellow denizens of Hades's answer to Orpheus. Awaking, he noted he'd dreamed mostly of traveling, criticizing Buddhist art, and "trouble in hospitality."[18]

In his *Confessions,* Crowley reflected how the best thing in *Orpheus* Book III was the invocation of Hecate, goddess of magic and the night, and asserts that he used it "with full magical intention" at Akyab, obtaining thereby a vision of Bhavani.[19] While this magical rite is not referred to in his contemporary diaries, Crowley used the experience in his autohagiography to express his conviction in the essential identity of all religions. As an analogy he gave the example of a mountain, which viewed from three different countries received from each a different name, and perhaps different legends, but superior perspective revealed not only were they the same mountain viewed from different perspectives, but that the mountains were all joined and perceptible parts of unified flows of phenomena. A mountain is not "placed" on land as a separate object, but is the same earth raised through unseen forces.

He also commented revealingly that his natural poetic bent was toward magical invocation; that he was basically a lyric poet using verse to exalt his soul by "straightforward intoxication." His comments explain why he subtitled his Akyab-written "SABBÉ PI DUKKHAM" (Everything Is Sorrow) a "Lesson from Euripides." He'd bought a secondhand copy of the *Bacchae* in San Francisco and had realized that Euripides's work was fundamentally an invocation of Dionysus, god of intoxication, and that a poem could therefore, as a whole, serve essentially as subtle magical invocation through which the poet, having identified himself with the god, might raise the willing reader to similar sublimities. This does much to explain why Crowley's work has not found much of a modern audience, whose school-imbibed experience of poetry tends to be descriptive, nature based, or sociological and earthbound. Crowley's best verses are best *performed*. He would never escape the ravishment of magic; too deep it was within him.

He was again suffering from fever. The diary record shows that on the seventeenth he was "a shade feverish" at 98.6°; on the eighteenth a "rather bad go of fever" reached 102.8°, to hit a peak of 103° on the nineteenth. Interestingly, as the temperature increased, the vividness of dreams declined, from "slight dreams only" to "dreams of books (school prizes) and of going walks. Not as vivid as sometimes" to—on the highest temperature day—"Remember no dream."

On February 20 his temperature fell to 99° and by the evening, despite residual fever, had the feeling of being well again. He decided to write *Ahab* (see page 278)about Nature and God, and in the evening experienced dreams strange and striking. The next day, his temperature practically normal, he wrote a huge chunk of *Ahab* and talked to Allan about translating the Buddha sayings-collection, the *Dhammapada* (see page 222). Allan had the Pāli; Crowley had the poetic gift. It is likely Crowley was consulting a translation by Rhys Davids from the Pāli Text Society. He spent the whole of the next day with Allan also—"from morn to dewy eve" as his diary puts it—and felt very excited mentally. Allan's approval of *Ahab* was encouraging, and Crowley spent his last night at Akyab sleeping at the temple.

Aleister Crowley left Burma on February 23, 1902, and would not return for over three years. It was probably his only journey to a country where he enjoyed no intimate contact with women, and the effect of that can be discerned in his dream life, without recourse to Freud.

EIGHT

Across India

Operated by the British India Steam Navigation Co. Ltd., the SS *Kapurthala*—fifteen years old and named after a city of the Punjab—carried native passengers on deck and a few European passengers, including Crowley, in cabins. For those with accommodation, fares were a hefty £50 for Chittagong and Calcutta.* As she steamed into the open sea, Crowley dreamed vividly and repeatedly: a journey "through space," led him to England at the present time, where he was involved in an adulterous affair, with violent words and actions. He also met with old friends to discuss theology "and much besides."[1]

On the twenty-fourth the *Kapurthala* anchored outside Chittagong (now in Bangladesh), some 250 miles east of the mouth of the Hooghly. Considering the port unworthy of a visit, Crowley passed the next two days, when not writing the chorus of living creatures for *Orpheus,* reading about African travel, and in vivid dreaming about travel and sex. On the twenty-seventh he was back in Calcutta, collecting the mail awaiting him, and working on the *Tannhäuser* proofs, as well as *Ahab* and other unfinished writings. The Kashmir mountaineering expedition now uppermost in his mind, Crowley began shopping.

It had been agreed the party would assemble at Rawalpindi in the Punjab, some 250 miles southwest of Chogo Ri (K2), their destination.†

---

*SS *Kapurthala* was scrapped in Bombay in 1923.
†According to Crowley's "Agreement between Aleister Crowley and Oscar Eckenstein" (dated Kandy, October 12, 1901), Eckenstein agreed by letter of September 20, and cable of October 3, with Crowley's letter of August 23, 1901, that they together "climb a mountain higher than ever previously ascended by man." On August 23, Crowley

Preparations filled what time was left but for a day's snipe shooting at Sodepore (now Sodepur) in north Calcutta on March 2; the pintailed snipe being a winter frequenter of paddy land. Harry Lambe having gone to Australia on tea business, Crowley was staying with a friend of Thornton's, who joined him on the shoot. That night, Crowley dreamed Thornton reproached him over the expense of a punkah wallah, as well as for cavalier treatment of him. This was followed by a long, rational argument, and another dream scene where Crowley met up again with Allan "thus fulfilling my presentiment that we should meet again, and so making my death in N. India possible. This continued with varying incident."[2] This is, I think, the sole reference in any of Crowley's writings suggesting that climbing mountains could prove fatal for him.

Crowley worked hard on proofs, writing his poetic version of the *Dhammapada* (a scripture of the Buddha's sayings), while analyzing "Ascension Day" and "Pentecost,"[*] as well as arranging funding at the banks and letter writing. He continued recording his dreams—on the fourth he had a flash of insight: that Kelly and "one Fraser" were social performers. On March 7, he packed and caught a late (9:45 p.m.) train for Benares. Falling asleep on the train he dreamed of a train journey, and disgusting a woman who was kissing him by doing something objectionable. He seemed to love flirting with guilt, exhibiting a masochistic streak.

BENARES

Crowley's potential reflections on the holy city set on the Ganges's banks between Calcutta and Delhi were muted by meditations dismissing all wonders as illusions to fetter the soul. Borne by a native bearer, Crowley noted in cynical, blasé fashion the yogis, dancing girls, and temples, all reduced to a superficial cavalcade that, from a Buddhist perspective, had to be stopped in its tracks, its attractions blown out.

(*cont.*) placed £500 at Eckenstein's disposal for arrangements, and another £500 on October 10, for emergencies (*Confessions*, 278–79). Incidentally, "Chogo Ri" comes from two Balti words meaning "big" and "mountain" respectively.
[*]See chapter 12, page 250.

Fig. 8.1. Benares: Temple of the monkeys.
(Photo: Dr. Jules Jacot-Guillarmod, 1902)

8th.

Arrived at Benares. Hotel de Paris. Began Concentration. Considered: fear of future seems practically destroyed, the last six months having worked well. This removes all possible selfishness of incentive (after 4½ years.) Mitri-Bhavana is left, and that alone. Aum!!![3]

Crowley subjected himself and his motives over the years since leaving Cambridge to heavy criticism, and, to compensate, tried to extend a compassionate ray from himself to things and people he was naturally averse to. He was trying to conquer his nature, to get beyond crude appetite, to the soul of things, perhaps.

On Sunday March 9 he went to the Ganges to see the ghats (steps leading to the sacred river) and what he called the "Sex Temple," whose sculptures of physical union and sexual acts he would compare unfavorably to the more finished productions of Leonard Smithers.*

---

*Smithers published pornographic works in England, usually printed in Paris or Amsterdam, including some of Crowley's decadent writing, such as *White Stains*. The later reference to Smithers and the "Sex Temple" occurs in "Burmese River." (1909)

He is probably referring to the Pashupatinath Mahadev Temple, a terracotta-colored, part-wooden reproduction of the king of Nepal's favorite temple in Kathmandu, built when the king was exiled to Benares between 1800 and 1804. It contains sculptures celebrating erotic love compared to the more famous Khajuraho sculptures in central India. The Pashupatinath Mahadev Temple is situated by the Lalita Mandir and Lalita Ghat, by the Ganges.

Lalita, one would have thought, should have been very dear to Crowley, she being a *mahāvidyā* and highest aspect of goddess Adi Shakti. The goddess who embodies the natural creation as fertility, devotion, and love, Parvati, incarnates Lalita Maha Tripura Sundari. More pertinently, Lalita is the "Red Goddess," clothed in scarlet, and may be considered an image of the spiritual aspect of what Crowley would come to call the "Scarlet Woman," his partner in sexual, magical, and mystical rites. However, in Benares in 1902, Crowley had Buddhism, not Hinduism, most on his mind. Nevertheless, he found the Temple of Kali (presumably the Kasiraj Kali Temple), "very interesting."

Goddess of time, and death—for time devours life—Kali is, like Lalita, one of the ten mahāvidyās or principal goddesses of Hinduism, usually depicted as black, often carrying a necklace of skulls or severed heads, a belt of severed arms, a kukri dripping with blood, while

Fig. 8.2. Benares: An old temple fallen into the Ganges.
(Photo: Dr. Jules Jacot-Guillarmod, 1902)

brandishing in one of her several arms the bloody fruits of decapitation. Kali is often portrayed standing over Shiva, with Shiva presented as a corpse. Her devotees, including tantriks, may be seen at the temple nursing skulls in their laps, covered in red dye, or eating yoghurt from the skulls. In this sense, the Buddhist would see Kali as precisely that *from which* the Buddha attempted to save humankind. The special case of the Thuggee cult, bloodthirsty killers of some two million victims, operating chiefly in north India, and suppressed by William Sleeman between 1826 and 1848, demonstrates the extreme degrees to which devotees might traditionally go in serving, and identifying with, the favored deity.*

It is also interesting to see the basic approach to attainment the same *in dynamic* in both Hinduism and Buddhism. That is, in the cases of the tantrik and the yogi, the devotee attempts to identify himself fully with the god or goddess, by carrying weapons or accoutrements associated with the god or goddess, and in the case of the tantrik, going outside of conventions and covering himself with impurities, or doing impure things that the god, at any rate, has mastered and subjected. In Buddhism, the would-be enlightened follows the dhamma to imitate, and eventually become, the chosen state of being, or nonbeing: bodhisattva. The ultimate is to become a Buddha. Crowley will already have experienced, in the Golden Dawn, the magical idea of assuming god forms, to acquire the powers of a particular god, and would use such a practice shortly in Agra, as we shall see.

It may be presumed that beneath a devotion to Kali may lie, not a devotion to what Kali "does," as devourer, but to what Kali "is," that is, one who can lord it over death and devouring time, and therefore life itself. To embrace death is one way to conquer the fear of it. This may lie behind Crowley's "presentiment" adumbrated earlier to Allan that he might die in attempting Chogo Ri (K2). Is there an analogy between the embrace of death, or devotion to Kali, with the Buddhist embrace of the state of *anatta,* or no soul, *as a means of transcending*

---

*There is a notable story in the Pāli Canon in which the Buddha converts a devotee of, apparently, Kali and/or Shiva called Aṅgulimāla who wears a necklace of severed fingers, and kills all comers—the Buddha being the sole exception who "stops" him, extinguishing the fire that drives this haunting, murderous figure. Gombrich believes the story relates to primitive Hindu practices during the period of Buddhism's genesis, but garbled in later recensions of the legend. See Gombrich, *How Buddhism Began*, chapter 5, 134–54.

impermanence, change, and rebirth? Crowley would write that three months earlier he should certainly have sacrificed a goat at Kali's temple, but "I suppose by this time" considered himself "a pretty confirmed Buddhist, with merely a metaphysical hankering for the delusions of Vedanta."[4] *Vedanta* refers to philosophical speculation on late Vedic literature, principally, the Upanishads, combined especially with Advaita, which means "not two," that is, identity of essence exists between an individual soul (*ātman*) and Brahman (absolute deity). For most Hindus, the living world is everywhere ensouled by Brahman, accessible through his divine personifications, gods and goddesses. This for the Hindu is a living, intimate, colorful, daily reality, not simply a "philosophy" as Crowley tended to treat its thought-aspect, based on Vedantist literature. Buddhists denied continuity of essence, and this would generate problems in Crowley's mind.

Regardless of a discernible snobbery about Buddhism, Crowley's contemporary diary shows that he could not forebear an opportunity to interview "Sri Swami Swayam Prakashanand Maithila." Crowley asked about the expedition's fortunes, and was told: "At beginning of journey you will find a Swami who will find a yogin who will give you mantra etc." But "Your Guru is very far away." The swami promised to show Crowley a "yogin" the next day. So at 8:44 a.m. on March 10, Crowley approached the swami again, who told him that he was himself the promised yogin. As for the planned venture, Crowley was told it would "succeed after some trouble." In Crowley's 1909 *Vanity Fair* account of the meeting, where the swami is called "Sri Swami Swayan Prakashan Raithila, a Maharaja who has become Saunyasi," Crowley adds wryly: "The trouble turned up all right, I wish I could say as much for the success."* According to this account, the swami "made a curious prophecy on the spiritual plane which was in a certain sense fulfilled without the torturing language which he used too much; but the prophecy which he made on the physical plane went somewhat astray."[5] The contemporary diary records that Crowley promised to return and see him, if possible.

---

*It is likely that the swami's name in the diary account was mistranscribed and that the *Vanity Fair* article "On a Burmese River" is more accurate. Either way, I can find no further reference to this prophesying gentleman.

Crowley then attended a *nautch*, or traditional Indian dance performed by trained girls. Crowley complained of its dullness and lack of music, finding the girls overdressed, tuneless in voice, unexciting to watch, while the accompaniment sounded cacophonous. A curious diary reference: "Ginde becomes yogin," remains unexplained; Ginde is a rare Indian surname.

Crowley left for Agra on the twelfth, arriving at 1:00 a.m. the next day. He dreamed he traveled to nearby Delhi, by mistake, and also of social complications (a recurrent theme of his dreams), and of riding a white mule in Kashmir, which he took to be a good omen. Emerging into daylight in Agra, Crowley wrote a "National Anthem for Ireland," and more lyrics for *Orpheus,* complaining to himself: "How the thing drags on!" asking: "Will anyone ever try to read it through?" Not many, I should think. The published version carried Crowley's warning:

> May I who know so bitterly the tedium of this truly dreadful poem be permitted to warn all but the strongest and most desperate natures from the task of reading or of attempting to read it? I have spent more than three years in fits of alternate enthusiasm for, and disgust of, it. My best friends have turned weeping away when I introduced its name into conversation; my most obsequious sycophants (including myself) were revolted when I approached the subject, even from afar.[6]

Fig. 8.3. Jama Masjid Mosque, Agra, opposite Agra Fort.
(Photo: Dr. Jules Jacot-Guillarmod, 1902)

Forty-five years earlier, during the Indian Mutiny, rebellious sepoys had besieged Agra's fort—formerly the Mughal emperors' residence until they moved the capital to Delhi in 1638. Crowley inspected the fort's imposing, sandy-red crenellated battlements on the thirteenth.

> I went over Agra fort, which was very beautiful in places, but on the whole vulgar and depressing. There is too much of the thing altogether; and although it is well worth one visit, I cannot imagine anyone paying two.[7]

He then went to the Ganeshi Lall Emporium, jewellers since 1845. Another kind of jewel—the Taj Mahal—elicited mixed feelings the following day. Crowley felt this famous tourist magnet and statement of an emperor's extravagant affection for a much-adored wife extraordinarily beautiful at first sight, but discerned an absence of human qualities in it. Lacking therefore in fascination, he felt the design's exquisiteness out of proportion to the monument's scale. A sense that something loathsome and disgusting existed within it overtook him, and to cleanse his thoughts from rising nausea he again used the Hoor Paar Kraat formula. The Taj's central hall with its sarcophagus bore for him a "strained aura," like a magic circle after the banishing. He could be a most sensitive man.[8]

Fig. 8.4. Taj Mahal, Agra.
(Photo: Dr. Jules Jacot-Guillarmod, 1902)

In the evening, he observed another nautch, but found the dancing unbearable, inferior even to that of Benares. The morning of the fifteenth brought munshi (language teacher or secretary) Elahi Bux (or Bukhsh) to his door. Astrologer and geomancer Bux taught Crowley how to obtain a deadly hypnotic power: "Look hard at point on wall unwinking for many days, gradually increasing time. You will thus obtain hypnotic power even to D[eadly] and H[ostile] C[urrent] of W[ill]."[9] Bux also showed Crowley a peculiar method of geomancy:

> He obtained the "Mothers" not by points drawn in the sand or on paper, but by throwing little brass dice, four on a string, each side of which had one of the four possibilities of arranging points from two to four in number in two lines, one combination on each face. He had two such strings, and by putting them together, one obtained four figures, every possible variety being thus represented. He then proceeded in the ordinary way known to Westerns, though he gave different names to the figures, and attributed different qualities, though usually rather sympathetic: Puer, for example, he attributed to Saturn. Above I have spoken of the dice as brass, and that is what they looked like; but he told me they were composed of "electrum magicum" as described by Paracelsus, prepared correctly by mixing the seven metals during the conjunction of their corresponding planets.[10]*

Crowley caught the Delhi train at 9:50 p.m., falling asleep and dreaming of returning to Eastbourne, Sussex, where he used to live and chat up girls at nearby Beachy Head, and had yet another dream where he was correspondent in a divorce case. He also dreamed of his would-be artist friend in England, Gerald Kelly, of writing a book in archaic English about Sir Galahad, and had vivid, multiple dreams of *Orpheus,* opera, and eating. His train entered Delhi at 4:30 a.m., shrouded in high winds and a thunderstorm. Heading straight for Maiden's Metropolitan Hotel—widely considered the best hotel in Delhi—he set to as much outstanding literary work as was possible before Eckenstein's mountain-

---

*Khudah Bukhsh (or Bux) (1905–1981) was an internationally famous Kashmiri mystic, magician, and firewalker. One wonders if he was related to Elahi Bukhsh.

eering team arrived, after which he reckoned he'd have little time for composition or editing.

Spending most of the seventeenth in apathetic reveries, Crowley managed to pen Orpheus's invocation of the Erinyes, that is, the Furies: three goddesses of vengeance devoted to punishing men for crimes such as murder, offences against family and friends, lying, or offending the gods. Since the Erinyes sprang from Uranus's blood when castrated by son Cronus, a curse invoked from a parent on a child was deemed the strongest. Inspired at night, Crowley forced himself out of bed to write additional parts of *Orpheus*. He finally finished *Orpheus* Book III, the next day, having begun it on November 22, 1901. Glad to see the back of it, Crowley had many vivid dreams, one inspired by H. G. Wells's recently published *The First Men in the Moon*: "a moon-like darshana*—almost as bright and eternal. Suggested by Wells and my idea of possibilities of K2."[11]

I presume Crowley was thinking of what the night sky would look like from the peak of the highest mountain ever climbed, inspired by chapter 5 of Wells's farsighted novel, where the narrator opens a window onto outer space in Cavor's spacecraft:

> Those who have only seen the starry sky from the earth cannot imagine its appearance when the vague, half luminous veil of our air has been withdrawn. The stars we see on earth are the mere scattered survivors that penetrate our misty atmosphere. But now at last I could realise the meaning of the hosts of heaven!
>
> Stranger things we were presently to see, but that airless, star-dusted sky! Of all things, I think that will be one of the last I shall forget.
>
> The little window vanished with a click, another beside it snapped open and instantly closed, and then a third, and for a moment I had to close my eyes because of the blinding splendour of the waning moon.

It is fascinating that Crowley was not thinking, or dreaming, of the K2 climb in terms of the physical exercise required, or the art of mountaineering proper, but in terms of a new vantage point's relevance to perception, vision, science, the universe, and the mystical. It would

---

*An auspicious vision of a deity or something holy.

have been interesting to take Crowley into outer space with his note-book. Would he have found "elementals" there?

On the nineteenth he paid a visit to Delhi's famous Red Fort, whither the Mughal emperor Shah Jahan moved from Agra, and where the last Mughal emperor was tried in 1858 before exile in Rangoon. Crowley explored its mighty sandstone walls, enclosing some 256 acres, with a Major Graham, D.S.O. (Distinguished Service Order) who had, he said, been leading a convoy of Boer prisoners to Ambala (the Second Boer War was still raging in South Africa, the Boers having recently gained their last victory against the British Army). Crowley confided to his diary that the officer was a "prize fool," but soon revised the opinion when it transpired the "Major," with his fine and noble manner, had conned both the Maiden Hotel and a bank out of a significant sum.

Crowley enjoyed the restful ambience of the fort's Audience Hall but was annoyed to find a magnificent fresco on one wall whitewashed by a prudish Briton on account of its naturalistic depiction of the human body, which Crowley divined as having merely evoked fears of the las-civious contents of the whitewasher's own low mind. To add insult to injury, the hypocrite concerned had then realized the wall looked out of place amid the other frescos, so whitewashed *them* as well!—giving, as his reason, the need to "secure artistic conformity."[12] Constantly observing things of this kind made Crowley emphasize the idea that fearful suppression of the sex instinct breeds neurosis and social vandalism, if not worse. It was not himself, he held, that was "sex-obsessed" but society that suffered from a sex-abscess that needed lancing. Crowley was willing to oblige, and it did him no social good at all, not that he would ever cease from something that to him was a point of honor.

After visiting Delhi's fort, Crowley wrote feverishly, produc-ing "Crowleymas Day," a prose essay on the cosmos afterward called *Berashith,** then rewrote the introduction to "Ascension Day" and "Pentecost," a note about G. K. Chesterton,† and the "Exordium" to Book I of *Orpheus* dedicated to Oscar Eckenstein. The next day he began his accomplished essay "Science and Buddhism," inscribed to the

---

*For analysis of its contents, see chapter 11, page 228. My account of "Ascension Day" and "Pentecost" can be found in chapter 12.

†The note appeared in *The Sword of Song* collection, 1904.

revered memory of Thomas Henry Huxley, to whose observations on scientific method the exposition owes much.* He typed the essay up the next day, elaborating as he did so. Before the day's end, he received a wire from Eckenstein, on time for the planned meeting at Rawalpindi. For the second night running, Crowley had multiple sexual dreams, including one of "indecent Hindu pictures"—doubtless inspired by whatever lay under the Audience Hall's whitewash—as well as one or two about a doctor and a smallpox epidemic.†

On Saturday, March 22, Crowley spent his last full day in Delhi "magar shooting" with J. Maiden, proprietor of his hotel, and "one Schwaiger."‡

In 1902, J. Maiden took over from a joint hotel business run with his brother since 1894. *Murray's Indian Handbook* (1908) advertises "Maiden's Metropolitan Hotel" thus: "An experienced Englishman (the Proprietor) controls this Hotel. Specialities—*Cleanliness. Large Airy Rooms, comfortably furnished. Wholesome Food. Situation the best in Delhi; opposite the Club* (*Ludlow Castle*) J. MAIDEN, *Proprietor.*" Sir Edward Lutyens lived at the elegant, white, colonnaded hotel while designing New Delhi. It is one of the few fine buildings left involved with hosting the 1903 Delhi Durbar held by Lord Curzon to celebrate King Edward VII's coronation as emperor of India. The 1911 edition of *John Murray's Handbook to India, Burma and Ceylon* gives additional information. Room rates were 8 rupees a night. According to Maiden, "Electric Lights and Fans have been added, which convenience will be

---

*Included in *The Sword of Song* (*called by Christians the Book of the Beast*), and is discussed in chapter 11, p. 236.

†According to Sasha Tandon, in Delhi's neighboring territory of the Punjab, "smallpox accounted for 8,50,591 deaths in the region from 1868 to 1947. Smallpox broke out with maximum intensity from 1875 to 1919 when nine major epidemics of smallpox affected in twenty-seven districts, claiming almost 250,000 victims. One in every ten cases of smallpox turned out to be fatal, and of those who survived the attack, one-fourth were scarred." Sasha Tandon, Punjab University, Chandigarh: "Epidemics in Colonial Punjab," *Journal of Punjab Studies* 20, no. 1 & 2 (2013): 218.

‡This "Schwaiger" was probably Imre George Maria Schwaiger, born in Hungary in about 1868, who died in Delhi, June 24, 1940. Married to Nellie Saché (1876–1935), Imre Schwaiger was a prominent Hungarian art dealer and patron, with business bases in Delhi, Simla, and London. A colleague of Jacques Cartier, he was notable for his donations of Indian artifacts to the Metropolitan Museum of Art and British Museum.

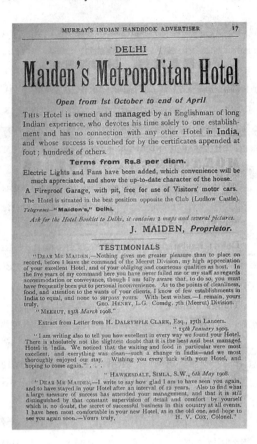

Fig. 8.5. Maiden's Metropolitan Hotel, advertised in Murray's Indian Handbook, *1911.*

much appreciated, and show the up-to-date character of the house." Electricity had entered Calcutta and Bombay in the late nineteenth century so Maiden's must have been one of the first buildings with the facility in Delhi.

The object of the day's shoot with Maiden and Schwaiger was the "mugger," or crocodile, whose nickname derived from *magar,* Hindi for "marsh." Much of Delhi is technically wetland, and notable marshes for shooting remained to the northeast and southeast of the old city, by the banks of the Jamna River. Crowley's reference to shooting at "Oakley" must refer to Okhla, about six miles southeast of Delhi Station at the confluence of the Jamna and Agra Canals, east of the Grand Trunk Road.*

---

*Today, the Okhla Bird Sanctuary, a mecca for nature lovers, is sited within what is now Okhla industrial suburb and industrial estate. How things change!

Crowley lent Maiden his Mauser rifle, and catering maestro Maiden provided admirable refreshments. The Canal Works' chief engineer granted permission for the party to take a small boat upstream. Eyeing a big crocodile warily slipping off the banks, Crowley crawled to the boat's bow and fired his .577 at 130 yards. Either by good luck or judgment, Crowley hit the beast in its heart. The dying animal's lashing about kept the natives from getting a boathook to the shore so they could secure the prize, so Maiden let loose fifteen Mauser cartridges which did little to help, so Crowley put his Express down the struggling crocodile's throat and fired off both barrels, the recoil from the second shot sending Crowley backwards and very nearly overboard: an unenviable place. Still unable to get a hook into the writhing crocodile, the party watched it slip from shallow into deep water where it sank. Twenty minutes were wasted on vainly hunting for the carcass.

The party rowed further upstream. A slightly smaller crocodile came into view. Crowley took very careful aim and hit the spine. Stone dead, the natives didn't believe it and feared approaching it. Gingerly they took its tail from the bank—and that was the day's prize, for the afternoon brought naught for pot or bag. The party took a pleasant tea and drove back to Delhi, whether by car or carriage Crowley does not say. If anyone would have a car in Delhi, save a maharaja, it would have been Maiden, but cars were extremely rare in India.*

Maiden invited Crowley to his house for an evening's fun with what was called the "willing game" whose rule required one to sit down, not to set about doing anything, but to wish it were done. This might have been a joke of Crowley's. Anyhow, he recalled conversation soon "degenerating" into a lecture on Buddhism—Crowley getting completely carried away, boring his hearers immensely as he preached "the Good Law," something he would still be doing the following year when on holiday in Nice. Crowley's contemporary diary simply notes, less modestly perhaps: "Lectured four hours on Buddhism in M[aiden]'s drawing-room."

---

*In 1911, Maiden's Hotel advertised its provision of a "fireproof" garage for motor cars. The maharaja of Patiala (Punjab) imported the first motorcar to India in 1892: a French De Dion Bouton steam-powered two-cylinder tricar. In about 1901 three Curved Dash Oldsmobile models were brought into India and sold to Jamshedji Tata, founder of the Tata Group of Industries, Rustam Cama, an attorney, and Kavasji Wadia of Bombay Garage.

On Sunday March 23, Crowley was borne to Delhi railway station, just west of the fort's north end, running east–west along Queen's Garden, about three-quarters of a mile south of Maiden's Hotel in the "Civil Station" district, outside Shahjahnabad (or what was then called "Modern Delhi" before "New Delhi" was built.) Planning to take the mail train to Rawalpindi to join up with his fellow climbers, the train, as luck would have it, already contained the expedition party. Crowley joined the carriage, where Eckenstein introduced Crowley—whom he had not seen for a nearly a year—to his chosen team: Heinrich Pfannl (an Austrian judge); Victor Wessely (also Austrian, a barrister); Dr. Jules Jacot-Guillarmod (a Swiss Alpinist); and the amiable Guy John Senton Knowles, twenty-two-year-old engineering graduate of Trinity College, Cambridge. Second-in-command Crowley espied problems looming almost at once. The Austrians he found somewhat small-minded, while Pfannl had overtrained, and would wear out in a scenario where *endurance* was key. Guillarmod had known only the Alps, and Crowley suspected he would be overwhelmed by the Himalayas, while Knowles was inexperienced in climbing and, being young, might lack endurance. Their quarry, K2, would require everything they could muster to conquer it. As it turned out, it wasn't only Crowley who was concerned at the preponderance of German speakers on the expedition.

NINE

K2

24th [March 1902].
My 13th year of anything like serious climbing.
At Rawal Pindi [*sic*]. Luggage not arrived. Slept in hotel tent. Think
no dreams.[1]

Eckenstein and Crowley's expedition aimed to conquer K (Karakoram) 2,
the second mountain in the Karakoram Range, the second highest
mountain in the world. From a plateau already 12,000 feet above sea
level, K2, or Chogo Ri as some natives knew it, then rose to a sublunary
height of 28,250 feet. Experienced climbers have said K2 is no less challenging a mountain than Everest herself.

Gathered at Delhi, the rather ill-assorted team immediately took
the train some 400 miles northwest to Rawalpindi, an important defen-
sive base for the troublesome border region with Afghanistan familiar
to legend as the North West Frontier. Rawalpindi's Lime Tree Hotel
being full, the management permitted the party to erect tents outside.

*Fig. 9.1. K2 Expedition tents
outside the Lime Tree Hotel,
Rawalpindi, March 1902.
(Photo: Dr. Jules Jacot-
Guillarmod, 1902)*

Fig. 9.2. Dak bungalow at Tret.
(Photo: Dr. Jules Jacot-Guillarmod, 1902)

Thence, everyone journeyed 150 miles northeast into the tapestry beauties of Kashmir, to Srinagar, that is to say, everyone but Eckenstein. An order from the viceroy of India, delivered by Rawalpindi's deputy commissioner to Crowley's dak bungalow at Tret, insisted that under no circumstances was Eckenstein to be permitted entry into Kashmir.

In his *Confessions,* Crowley does not appear very surprised by this frustration. Richard Spence* wonders whether it might not have been part of an intelligence plan.

The Karakoram Range was no tourist destination in 1902. The territory to be covered north of Srinagar included the Plains of Deosai in Baltistan and skirted the strategically significant Karakoram Pass, amongst other obscure routes to and from the north. In fact, K2 stood in uncomfortable terrain between Kashmir and Chinese Sinkiang: to the west, Afghanistan and the Russian Empire. To the east rose the plateau of Tibet. Intelligence assessed in Rawalpindi pointed to Russian agents in Tibet, tolerated by the Dalai Lama. Russia envisioned the possibility of Tibet as a client state, dangerously close to the British Empire. Heightening tension—Britain was still at war in South Africa—led to a decisive British military invasion

---

Secret Agent 666, Aleister Crowley, British Intelligence and the Occult, 2008.

of Tibet the following year, led by distinguished explorer Sir Francis Younghusband, and the eventual deaths of about four hundred Tibetan soldiers outside their capital of Lhasa in 1904.

The passes in the region about K2 were the means by which Russian agents and supplies could reach Tibet, so there was military value in a reconnaissance exercise to gather intelligence of unusual activity in the area, and to check the worth of maps made as long ago as 1861 during the Godwin-Austen survey of the area, should it be necessary to establish supplies for a military operation in the distant region. Crowley himself in his *Confessions* makes some criticisms of the accuracy of the Godwin-Austen mapping that was available to him. He made his own adjustments.

A parallel possibility is that Eckenstein had—or was suspected of having—recruited German-backed agents for the expedition with their own intelligence agendas (a mutual defense alliance would be signed by Russia's Tsar Nicholas II and Kaiser Wilhelm II in 1905). Giving Crowley time as leader of the expedition may have permitted an opportunity to assess the men's loyalties without Eckenstein's knowledge and to do some preliminary, unnoticed, intelligence work.

However, the most likely explanation is that Eckenstein's falling out with Martin Conway during the 1892 Baltoro-Muztagh expedition had festered in Conway's mind over the decade. Knighted in 1895 for his contribution to mapping the Karakorams, Conway became president of Eckenstein and Crowley's mountaineering bugbear, the Alpine Club, in 1901. Eckenstein's book about the 1892 expedition (see page 170) reveals Eckenstein's outspokenness in favoring indigenous peoples,* while Eckenstein's low opinion of Alpine Club attitudes was well known in mountaineering circles. A word in the right ear might have alerted Curzon to the fact that Eckenstein's father was German, Jewish, and a socialist, and questions of loyalty may then have been asked. Crowley for one was convinced the club was prejudiced against Eckenstein on account of his Jewish lineage, and in his *Confessions* insisted Alpine Club mores and rules prevented provision of British men fit to conquer Himalayan peaks.[2] Curzon had been extremely suspicious of Russian intentions in

---

*The Crowley-Eckenstein agreement that preceded the climb specifically stated that no offense whatsoever was to be given to native beliefs or customs.

Fig. 9.3. Street in Srinagar. (Photo: Dr. Jules Jacot-Guillarmod, 1902)

Fig. 9.4. Jhelum River, Srinagar.
(Photo: Dr. Jules Jacot-Guillarmod, 1902)

the area for many years; Eckenstein had brought three educated foreigners with him into sensitive British territory.

In the event, Eckenstein was permitted to rejoin the expedition after an interview with the viceroy—and an appeal by cable to Lord George Hamilton at the India Office in London—but not before valuable time was lost. Curzon insisted as a face-saver that Crowley and Knowles guarantee Eckenstein's good conduct.

Crowley had occupied his time after arriving at Srinagar, capital of Kashmir, on April 14 with big-game shooting while suppressing anxiety about rapidly melting snow and the potential loss of a narrow window of relative safety to climb the mountain. In the meantime, Crowley was grateful to the English residents' kindness and for government assistance.

Eckenstein arrived in Srinagar on April 22, and the expedition set off again on April 28, with 150 porters, fifty pack ponies, and some Pathans with cooking and livestock duties. The tallest of the group, Crowley was also the lightest, worn thin by illness. Above a now straggly beard, he wore a "pagri," a kind of small turban, excellent, he insisted, for all conditions, except rain.

On the fourth day, the ekka drivers gave trouble (ekkas were north Indian traps with big wooden wheels and little pram-like carriages with simple umbrella-style canopies, pulled by a horse or mule). Crowley observed the Europeans being tested by deliberate delays, such as wheels getting jammed into other wheels. Fathoming what he was wont to call "the native mind" he realized swift action was required. After another

Fig. 9.5. An ekka.
(Photo: Dr. Jules Jacot-Guillarmod, 1902)

delay, Crowley grabbed a driver by his beard (a great insult) and took his belt to him in front of everybody. This earned respect, for it was understood that wrong had been done. Crowley was convinced that if he'd let it pass, problems would have been endless. Instead he built a foundation of respect, which soon became devotion unto death if necessary. Had the act been unjust or mistaken, revenge may have been as fatal as it was certain.

> The first business of any traveller in any part of the world is to establish his moral superiority. He has to be uniformly calm, cheerful, just, perspicacious, indulgent and inexorable. He must decline to be swindled out of the fraction of a farthing. If he once gives way, he is done for.[3]

As the expedition made its way across the peaceful plateau of Kashmir, a territory mostly of Muslims, ruled by high-caste Hindus—which brought its own problems—Crowley was concerned about

Fig. 9.6. Basmai Sta (5,000 m), entrance to the Gorge of Sind, near Sonamarg. (Photo: Dr. Jules Jacot-Guillarmod, 1902)

Fig. 9.7. Salama Tantra Shikari.
(Photo Dr. Jules Jacot-Guillarmod, 1902)

rations, complaining that Eckenstein relied too much on a doctrine that a soldier's tinned ration was sufficient. Crowley saw great need for sugar, for the party would suffer from sugar starvation, especially after the Pathans stole extra sugar supplies to sell to villagers on the way.

Salama Tantra, Crowley's personal servant, so impressed him in managing subordinates that when in 1905 he set out for China, Crowley took Salama out of Kashmir as an indispensable asset. By contrast, the Pathan tribesmen—"fierce and handsome" as Crowley described these fighting men—tended to be overbearing toward the Kashmiris, and stole livestock. Crowley himself was still suffering from malaria and, worse, suffered itching in the groin and elsewhere of maddening intensity, finding release only when he experimented with an iodine bath on the affected areas.

Reaching Chogo Ri involved three main sections. Six marches to the Zoji La Pass that divided Kashmir and Baltistan; twenty-one marches to the foot of the Baltoro Glacier; and the rest: ice. Kashmir was grand and beautiful, fresh and exotic, and relatively easy going. The pass at Zoji La was only passable for a period, and Crowley thought it boded well that they made it as early as May 4; it would close again by snow in early autumn.

Crowley became increasingly irritated by the shortcomings of the Swiss and Austrians. On one occasion, as even Dr. Guillarmod reported in his *Six Mois dans l'Himalaya* (Neuchâtel: W. Sandoz, 1904): "Confident in the solidity of the ice, I adventured a little too far, when all a sudden, I plunged in, unpleasant early in the morning . . ." Crowley shook his head in disbelief at Guillarmod's naïveté and—by his and Eckenstein's standards—impractical nature. But Guillarmod's personal geniality did lighten things up, and he was popular with the porters.

The Austrians' survey of pass conditions was wildly inaccurate;

Fig. 9.8. Guillarmod referred to these expedition servants as "Our little Staff." (Photo: Dr. Jules Jacot-Guillarmod, 1902)

Fig. 9.9. The pass below Zoji La. (Photo: Dr. Jules Jacot-Guillarmod, 1902)

where they said it was steep, it was not; where free of snow, it was deep in snow.*

The far side of the Zoji showed a completely different face: from flowers and trees up to Baltal, suddenly it was desolation, all the way to Skardu. The ugly drabness of the mountainous lumps about them made the drudgery of the day's marching an ordeal of patience, exacerbated by sun glare and intermittent, biting winds. Distances were also highly misleading, with the rough and narrow track veering off to avoid the way that looked straight to start with. Crowley reckoned the Indian hill ponies distinctly inferior to those he and Eckenstein used in Mexico the previous year. But they kept going, and, after pointless meetings with local rajas at Hardas and Tolti, Skardu was reached on May 14.

---

*It is fascinating to read Guillarmod's French-language account of the whole expedition, replete with many of the author's photographs, not only because we see Crowley through the eyes of another (not that Guillarmod sees very deeply into things or people), and British India through the eyes of a Swiss, but perhaps above all because Guillarmod found so much more to record of the adventure than did Crowley. Guillarmod found a book's worth of adventure and relayed it for all it was worth. Crowley, as with so much he did in his life, had the more cavalier English attitude of taking it all in his stride, only noting things to him personally meaningful. He never had the tourist mentality, more of a passing creature who disdains unworthy prey, with his stealthy eye set on greater, spiritual, and philosophical prizes. Crowley was turned on by extremes.

Fig. 9.10. Dr Guillarmod's makeshift clinic under apricot trees at Hardas. (Photo: Dr. Jules Jacot-Guillarmod, 1902)

Fig. 9.11. Rajas at Tolti; Crowley in 1916 would compare their visits to that of the "kings" to worship Jesus in the Bible. (Photo: Dr. Jules Jacot-Guillarmod, 1902)

At Skardu, among its twenty thousand inhabitants living at 2,228 meters above sea level, Crowley was inspired by the spirit in which polo was played, with no interest in results, or any obvious rules, it was played for emotional and spiritual exhilaration, in a spirit of chivalry, unlike the bitterness and unmanliness that so frequently attends Western sports, or so Crowley observed. He believed enjoyment more

Fig. 9.12. Confluence of the
Indus and Shigar Rivers,
Skardu. (Photo: Dr. Jules
Jacot-Guillarmod, 1902)

Fig. 9.13. Plain of Skardu and valley of the Indus.
(Photo: Dr. Jules Jacot-Guillarmod, 1902)

important than what we persistently call "achievement," without thinking what it is we have *really* achieved. Crowley utterly despised what
Western materialism had done to virtue, a word he always stressed in its
original meaning of virility, inspiring a generous chivalry and personal
austerity.

After resting at Skardu—with some 150 miles yet to go between
there and the Baltoro Glacier—the serpentine party crossed the gushing
Indus River by ferry on May 19 and headed toward the attractive village
of Shigar, where they were received by another raja (or king) and where
Crowley spoke with various lumberdars before going pigeon shooting.
Not far from the village, three bas-relief Buddha-rupas had been carved

Fig. 9.14. The expedition is greeted by the wazir of Alchori, at Shigar.
(Photo: Dr. Jules Jacot-Guillarmod, 1902)

onto a big rock. Crowley spent the evening gently ribbing a missionary who had been living there comfortably for seven years, without a single convert, the locals calling him an idolater.

On the way to Askole they found Ghomboro, a delightful "nala" or valley of apricot orchards, below whose terraces roared the Bralduh, which jetted forth in the narrowness between cliffs. The character of the country seemed to change constantly; with no dak baghlas in the district, the men lived in tents, or under the trees. Crossing waterways was a constant challenge. In some, persistent throwing of rocks made a kind of path; crossing others relied on "rope bridges" made of twigs. Some places were of such beauty that Crowley felt, as he put it, the burden of the cynicism of his twenty-six years fall from him as he entered a natural paradise of crystalline deposits from a hot spring spread like a curtain on a hillside, to provide a bath fit for Venus. The basin that fed the gorgeous slope invited the highest aspects of Crowley's soul. He sank into the sulphurous waters as a pilgrim who had found his bliss at last. The bodies of himself, Guillarmod, and Knowles succumbed to its 35° centigrade caresses and delicious languor for an hour, warmed by the sun in a dry mountain air intoxicating in its clarity and freshness.

Fig. 9.15. Aleister Crowley in the sulphur spring. (Photo: Dr. Jules Jacot-Guillarmod, 1902)

Fig. 9.16. Relaxation; note Crowley's poncho, brought from Mexico. (Photo: Dr. Jules Jacot-Guillarmod, 1902)

From the spring to Askole was a gentle five-hour march. Entering the village, the party camped beneath poplar trees for ten days. A courier arrived from Skardu with mail from Europe, and Crowley scratched his beard trying to work out how best to station the supplies, since there would be none obtainable for the remainder of the trek. A man consuming two pounds a day, with thirty marches to undertake needs to carry sixty pounds, and that left no space for supplies, so porters had to be engaged while others carried their food. The valley was scoured for every available source of nourishment.

Eckenstein became exercised about the weight of bags and what the team should each carry. When Eckenstein told Crowley he must jettison his traveling library, Crowley shrugged his shoulders and said if he didn't take his Milton and other wise friends, he'd leave. Crowley got his way, and was sure that intellectual nourishment in extremes could save a man from madness. Guillarmod had his notes for his book, but the others would suffer, he observed, for lack of matter to occupy the mind and maintain balanced interiority.

Another of Eckenstein's points annoyed his friend, that is, that there might be competition between nations for honors, and that therefore Crowley was not to go farther than the main camp until everyone had arrived. Crowley would wish he'd remembered Nelson's blind eye and taken his opportunity when it later presented itself.

Crowley set off for Korophon—no more than a massive cubical block of granite 20 to 26 feet high—on June 5, a march of forty-eight hours, involving the crossing of the Biafo Glacier, where Crowley narrowly avoided being crushed by falling boulders bigger than a man. Shaped like a vast serrated arrowhead, the glacier was a formidable

Fig. 9.17. Guillarmod's portrait of "le bel [the fair] Abdullah," who looked after the mail. (Photo: Dr. Jules Jacot-Guillarmod, 1902)

Fig. 9.18. The expedition team: (left to right) *Pfannl, Eckenstein, Guillarmod, Crowley, Wessely, Knowles. (Photographer unknown, 1902)*

sight in itself, but before he could reach it, he had to cross a terrain of sharpened rocks with intense contrasts of temperature twixt night and day, with extremes of 40° centigrade in the daytime, and minus 30° at nights. In minutes, what looked like firm snow was transformed into sludge, with rocks rolling away from what had seemed fixed positions in fast-melting ice.

The Punmah stream on the way to Bardumal looked shallow, but packed incredible force. Knowles was nearly lost in it, saved by rope-tie to a colleague on the bank. Guillarmod described the sight of Crowley's man, Salama, and the "most handsome of our coolies" (according to

Fig. 9.19. Crossing the Punmah. (Photo: Dr. Jules Jacot-Guillarmod, 1902)

Guillarmod) struggling with staffs to cross it, even though the water barely covered their shins.[4]

The next day, a five-hour journey of depressing character took them to Paiyu, with the peaks still kept out of sight by the narrow valleys and steep spurs of the great range. Only the sight of a "giant"—the Muztagh (meaning "ice") Tower—relieved the day's monotony, appearing, as it did, directly before the goal, Chogo Ri.

Paiyu was no more than an open plateau skirted by mountain slopes with a handful of trees, but no shortage of stones to build a little square stockade for supplies. Here there was a contretemps with the Pathans, charged with looking after the traveling menagerie's livestock of fifteen sheep, thirty goats, and fowls. Despite claiming the fowls had died, it was clear they'd been stolen. The reserved sugar had also been purloined. Crowley's account of the Pathans' dismissal differs from Guillarmod's, in that the Swiss doctor credits Crowley with effective command of Hindustani:

> It was at Paiyu that, their conduct giving rise to new complaints, we got rid of these unfaithful servants. Assembling all the personnel, including the representatives of the authorities, Crowley, before everybody, addressed a short discourse in Hindustani to the chief [Abdullah Khan] and his two acolytes, reproaching them for undignified conduct and the bad example they set for the rest of the personnel; then, having settled with them what was owed, deducting the value of the stolen sugar, we ordered them to leave the area forthwith.[5]

Fig. 9.20. Porters waiting for their pay after Crowley's talk in Hindustani. (Photo: Dr. Jules Jacot-Guillarmod, 1902)

Crowley, in an article printed by *Vanity Fair* in summer 1908, makes no boast as to his linguistic skills, but shows him playing a fine joke of justice upon what was called in those days "the wily Pathan."

We held a summary court martial in the presence of the Chaprasi of the Tehsildar of Skardu, who had come with us, and of the Wazir of Alchori, who had also attached himself to so renowned a convoy as we of course appeared to native eyes; it being the first time in history that six white men had been at one time at Skardu; so Abdulla and his two partners in crime were packed off and sent back. By the coolies [porters] who accompanied them we sent warning to all whom it might concern that these men were scoundrels, and that they were to be on their guard against them.

As they were packing up for their departure Abdulla Baig, the second of the ruffians, complained that Hassan, a clever and useful little Balti boy whom we had picked up in the Leh Road, and attached to our corps of Naukars, owed him a rupee for a coat. This was Abdulla Baig's old coat, green with brass buttons, and very much worn; which he had discarded when we had provided him with a fine new coat against the cold. The Balti boy said he had paid the rupee; which I have no doubt was true, though probably not by his own will, as the coat was barely worth an anna. Abdulla Khan would, of course, have deducted the cash from his "talab." The whole of the "Arabian Nights" flashed through my mind in a single second, and I saw my way to an act of poetic and Oriental justice. I simply made the two change coats; the old coat was Abdulla Baig's, as Hassan had not paid for it; but the new coat was mine, and I had a perfect right to give it to Hassan. This arrangement greatly pleased the multitude.[6]

Crowley set out from Paiyu for Camp 10 on the Baltoro Glacier on June 9 with about twenty porters, while Eckenstein stayed to build a flour store. Reaching the glacier's snout was a staggering, disturbing experience, with moraines ten times the size of the highest in the Alps, and a blackness from which the Bralduh roared like gushing bile. Twenty tributary glaciers fed into the Baltoro, thirty miles long and some two miles wide. The rocks clinging to the moraines were unstable,

Fig. 9.21. Approaching the Baltoro Glacier. (Photo: Dr. Jules Jacot-Guillarmod, 1902)

Fig. 9.22. Godwin-Austen Glacier, a tributary of the Baltoro Glacier. (Photo: Dr. Jules Jacot-Guillarmod, 1902)

often exceptionally steep. Everything was of gargantuan, daunting scale. Great too was Crowley's admiration for the porters, who did not complain but showed great ingenuity. For example, they satisfied hunger on the glacier by heating a small stone over a campfire, round which they smeared a paste of flour and water, burying it into their shawls. By the time they reached camp, it had cooked and was still warm.

Fig. 9.23. Glacial lake,
temporarily empty.
(Photo: Dr. Jules Jacot-
Guillarmod, 1902)

Fig. 9.24. Camp 3 at
Rdokass; the Baltis
prepare their bread.
(Photo: Dr. Jules Jacot-
Guillarmod, 1902)

Fig. 9.25. At Rdokass,
waiting for sundown.
(Photo: Dr. Jules Jacot-
Guillarmod, 1902)

The atmosphere was so dry, washing was out of the question as the skin became brittle and water made it peel, leaving a wound. Grease was removed by the conditions. Rdokass—the last oasis—was reached after two days; with sufficient grass on its ledge for a few sheep, it offered restful views of wonders in all directions. From the next camp at Lhungka, Crowley could see the Masherbrum and the Gusherbrum, both over 22,600 feet, considered by Crowley the most spectacular of the range, "the one a stupendous wedge of brilliantly lighted rock and ice; the other a dim luminous cone."[7] When Guillarmod reached Lhungka, the doctor noted how the plants he was collecting were becoming rarer with every mile.

Though the porters did not moan about cold, Crowley built a wall behind which they could shelter from the sharp winds. Guillarmod's account informs us this was eventually monopolized by Pfannl and Wessely; Crowley would have been neither amused, nor surprised.

The highest temperature was 5° centigrade of frost. Surrounded by cliffs resembling vast frozen tidal waves, they went on, dots on the terrain, to Ghore—with Crowley building "stone men" on the way to guide the others—and there found a camping ground of fine level sand.

From Ghore to Biange is another long march, but less monotonous. The views are increasingly superb and the solitude was producing its beneficent results. The utterly disproportionate minuteness of man purges him of his smug belief in himself as the final cause of nature. The effect is to produce not humiliation but humility, and this feeling is only the threshold of a selfishness which restores the balance

Fig. 9.26. Avalanche debris on the Baltoro Glacier, between Biange and Doksam. (Photo: Dr. Jules Jacot-Guillarmod, 1902)

by identifying one with the universe of which one's physical basis is
so imperceptibly insignificant a fraction.[8]

From Biange, Crowley's vision was arrested by the "incomparable
architecture" of Mitre Peak, called so because its double horn suggested the bishop's hat. Crowley named another peak "Three Castles,"

Fig. 9.27. Mitre Peak from Doksam.
(Photo: Dr. Jules Jacot-Guillarmod, 1902)

Fig. 9.28. The "Three Castles."
(Photo: Dr. Jules Jacot-Guillarmod, 1902)

and Guillarmod recorded it in his book as such. At Biange, Crowley found a sheet of pure white marble, visible only as a blinding gleam. While Vienna's leading professor of geology Eduard Suess (1831–1914) had asked Pfannl to make geological notes on what the true Himalayan structure consisted of, and the marble was certainly a discovery he was proud to observe, it nonetheless caused great anguish to Eckenstein who found it impossible to bury his pick into it and make steps. One man's science is another man's misery.

A short march led Crowley and his men to a lake between the mountains and the glacier: Doksam, the glacier's head at 15,518 feet, close to the height of Mont Blanc, and yet they'd only ascended 400 feet in thirty miles! During the afternoon, the camp was briefly hit by a severe snowstorm. It cleared, but they'd received a small taste of what lay in store.

Four hours of marching on June 16 took Crowley over previously unexplored territory. There he sketched the mountain and pondered the best route: all were demanding. Crowley plumped for a walk up the snow slopes of the east-southeast to the shoulder below the final rock pyramid. He stopped at Camp 9 (17,332 feet) directly under the south face. The porters themselves were convinced they were being led onto Yarkand and certain death, which they accepted, as Crowley had been so nice to them. They could hardly believe it when reprieve from death came at Camp 10 at Chogo Ri's eastern foot when Crowley sent them back to alert the others! Crowley found the Baltis all innocence, loyalty,

Fig. 9.29. K2 or Chogo Ri or Dapsang, seen from Camp 8. (Photo: Dr. Jules Jacot-Guillarmod, 1902)

Fig. 9.30. Camp 8.
(Photo: Dr. Jules Jacot-
Guillarmod, 1902)

Fig. 9.31. Chogo Ri from
near Camp 8. (The Spirit
of Solitude, 1929; courtesy
of Ordo Templi Orientis)

human kindness, courage, and cheer, with warm faces framed by long
hair bristling in the icy breezes.

Concerned for their feet, wrapped in cloths (*pabu*) when ascending the 1,400 feet to Camp 10, Crowley cut large steps in the hard snow to help them. The Baltis avoided snow blindness by growing a fringe of long hair over their eyes; it sufficed where a European needed shades. Crowley was faced with hard choices over the site of Camp 10.

Eckenstein complained of insufficient shelter, but Crowley was anxious to avoid avalanches, close to the main climb. At the exceptional altitudes, snow does not melt unless pressured; it evaporates, and can disappear quickly in sunshine. An avalanche can evaporate en route downwards. Guillarmod wrote of the fatal crevasses on all sides, obscured by snow, and the inferior quality of the tents.

Crowley was disappointed to have to follow the instruction of sending down the men. He could have made it to the shoulder and established a camp from which the mountain could have been conquered "given one fine day."[9] He only wished he could have foreseen the volte-face in the weather.

Fig. 9.32. View of Camp 9 to the east. (Photo: Dr. Jules Jacot-Guillarmod, 1902)

Fig. 9.33. Porters below Camp 9. (Photo: Dr. Jules Jacot-Guillarmod, 1902)

Pfannl and Wessely arrived next day on June 19; Guillarmod and Knowles turned up at the huddled group of flapping tents amid a snowstorm on the twentieth. Poor as the weather was for the next three days, it got decidedly worse on the twenty-fourth when a blizzard hit the camp with full force. A corner of Crowley's tent broke loose, and all he could do was sit on it for a morning. The wind's ferocity was like nothing he had ever experienced. A poorly Eckenstein showed up on the twenty-seventh with some welcome provisions.

Fig. 9.34. Eckenstein's porters arrive.
(Photo: Dr. Jules Jacot-Guillarmod, 1902)

Fig. 9.35. Camp 10, at approximately 18,700 feet. (Photo: Dr. Jules Jacot-Guillarmod, 1902)

Fig. 9.36. Camp 10 after the storm.
(Photo: Dr. Jules Jacot-Guillarmod, 1902)

Fig. 9.37. Aleister Crowley and Guy Knowles (on right) *at Camp 10, looking southeast. (Photo: Dr. Jules Jacot-Guillarmod, 1902)*

On the twenty-eighth, Eckenstein's illness decided him in the direction of letting Crowley, Guillarmod, and Pfannl go on, keeping Wessely behind, which made the latter resentful, backed by Pfannl. Guillarmod observed it was both customary and right in such circumstances that all follow the group decision as a whole, and that should only one member—of whatever nation—reach the summit, everyone would share the honor. This clearly did not satisfy everyone.

Attempts to leave that day were obstructed by freezing winds. On the thirtieth, Crowley had snow blindness, like having red-hot sand at the back of the eyes. He'd only had his goggles off for a few minutes to adjust his tent; that was enough. From July 2 to July 6, it was unremitting snowstorm.

Crowley was glad to see the Austrians off on July 1 as they went to Camp 11 on Chogo Ri's northeast ridge. They duly reported the ridge climbable and it was decided to ascend by that route on Monday, July 7. Though ill, Crowley protested, finding their route absurd. It was even farther from the summit than where they were already, and the route involved a long, avalanche-ridden precipice. Crowley was overruled and had to go on with the doctor. One can understand the frustration of a

Fig. 9.38. Broad Peak (more than 27,887 feet) from Camp 10.
(Photo: Dr. Jules Jacot-Guillarmod, 1902)

Fig. 9.39. Broad Peak from Camp 11.
(Photo: Dr. Jules Jacot-Guillarmod, 1902)

man who knows his stuff dealing with people whom he doubts, and has reason to doubt. As Blake observed: "The eagle never wasted so much time as being taught by the sparrow how to fly."

On their way, a sleigh carrying supplies slipped into a crevasse from which Crowley and Guillarmod managed to extricate it, only for it to prove useless later, even when lightened by four of its seven loads, which were carried. They arrived at Camp 11 with all supplies on the men's backs. At Camp 11, on account of snow evaporation—except where protected by canvas tent—they had to move the tents because they could find themselves waking up on a ridge five feet above the glacier where the snow had been previously! He would dub it "Camp Despair." There he wrote *The Earl's Quest.*

There was some dispute about actual height reached, but Crowley erred on the side of caution out of respect for Eckenstein, who was fanatically against any sign of exaggeration of achievement. On July 9, Crowley, ascending the slopes beyond Camp 11, estimated he reached a conservative minimum of 21,500 feet—though he really thought it was something over 22,000 feet—where Camp 11 was at 20,000 feet or, in Crowley's estimate, a little higher. They had instruments to mea-

Fig. 9.40. Chogo Ri from above Camp Despair.
(The Spirit of Solitude)

sure but they all gave slightly different readings. He was, anyhow, over what he called "Windy Gap," as he could see over it. Guillarmod in his book gave his aneroid reading on July 10 in the company of Wessely as 21,800 feet.

Crowley began to suffer from fever, indigestion, and shivering. He found breathing impossible without muscular effort, and felt he would vomit all night, but could not. Ill, weak, and in pain he breathed better in the morning, when the weather cleared and he lay in the sunlight observing a bee, a fly, a butterfly, and some crows.

Eckenstein and Knowles came up on the eleventh. Crowley realized it was malaria that was plaguing him; the highest height reached by a man with malaria was now his record. He also wrote poetry (see chapter 11, "The Works"). The problem was that the longer they hung about not actually climbing, the sheer fact that they were not adapted by nature to living in such exteme conditions would create ever more problems, never mind the simple one that with a body temperature of 37° centigrade, and the outer temperature well below that, how much more food was required (and energy to digest it) to make up the difference. Little exercise was possible when cooped up in a tent all day with only very short trips out to try and get food, which became impossible to cook, before rushing back to the warmth (if not damp) of sleeping bag for some meager comfort. Crowley knew from old mountaineering colleague Norman Collie the way to deal with a serious mountain was to "rush" it and get away from the scene as quickly as possible. There was, he believed, no value in the idea of acclimatization, which took generations of adaption to have any validity in such conditions. Altitude sickness was not understood properly at the time.

On July 12, Pfannl and Wessely again went off to scout at about 21,000 feet. On the fourteenth it transpired the ever-training Pfannl was now ill, Wessely adding in his chit requests for all sorts of supplies. Eckenstein suffered from bronchial asthma. Crowley and Eckenstein felt better the next day, but Pfannl was worse. Guillarmod went up to Camp 12—"the highest ever established to this day"*—to attend to Pfannl, and brought him down with great difficulty. Overtraining had brought nemesis, in Crowley's view. The effort ended chances of reaching the summit by a dash. Heavy snow and storms persisted. Two fine days could have given Knowles and Crowley a chance, but for having to superintend "the caravan of invalids."[10] On July 19, a now delirious Pfannl called Crowley to his tent to tell him that as a poet, only he could understand his plight, which was that there were three of him; two were all right, but the third was a mountain with a dagger that

Fig. 9.41. Camp 12, described by Guillarmod as "the highest known to date." (Photo: Dr. Jules Jacot-Guillarmod, 1902)

---

*Guillarmod, *Six mois dans l'Himalaya*, 256.

Fig. 9.42. Wessely taken down on a sledge. (Photo: Dr. Jules Jacot-Guillarmod, 1902)

he feared would kill him. Guillarmod administered more morphine. Despite fine weather the next day, Pfannl was still under the opiate. On July 21, with Pfannl hinting at suicide, Wessely was asked to accompany him down to Rdokass by sledge with the doctor to provide sympathy. Guillarmod was to return for a chance at the summit.

Weather was grim again on the twenty-first and stayed that way till the arrival at dusk of a figure on the twenty-third: Guillarmod, steaming with sweat, in agony of fear. Eckenstein asked bluntly where his porter was. Guillarmod said he'd fallen into a crevasse. The doctor had left him; Crowley and Eckenstein put their boots on, seized a coil of rope and went to the rescue. Guillarmod's account is emphatic that he'd done everything he could to try to rescue the good Balti, but could not manage it alone, so came for help. Crowley, who forgot to take his goggles—giving him another two days of snow blindness—gave the impression that Guillarmod had thought first of himself. When they reached the porter, Eckenstein showed how it was possible to save a man with one hand. The man himself was calm, preparing to commit his soul to Allah. Guillarmod wrote that when he left him, he had begun singing, adding a footnote that he learned that such was the custom of Baltis when in great danger or when they expected to die. Guillarmod had wondered if the fellow was mad. They found the doctor had untied himself from his rope and left it in the snow. Crowley considered the evidence pointed to cowardice, imbecility, and incompetence on Guillarmod's part beyond Crowley's comprehension.

When the porter returned safe and sound, Guillarmod was alarmed the porter had left behind his tent. Everyone was afflicted by the conditions. Crowley found Wessely had taken most of the emergency rations. A storm began on the twenty-eighth and continued unabated for days.

On August 1, after a brief lull, the storm grew more violent than ever. A porter then brought news that cholera had hit the Bralduh Valley, ordered closed by the government. This had serious repercussions for their and their baggage's return to the Indus Valley. A long council ended with the conclusion that descent was unavoidable. Even had the weather cleared, the vast snow fields created in the storm would have needed a week to clear sufficiently for crossing. Provisions were sufficient only for a fortnight, and of that, some was required for the return. Food was life, on the edge.

Crowley had felt ever since it had been decided not to climb from Camp 10 that the operation was a failure. He had no wish to die trying to prove himself wrong. Claiming an instinct about weather, he felt he knew when a break was about to occur. They now lacked the required vital spirit, necessary even if they'd been sure of a fortnight's good weather.

Fig. 9.43. Last Farewell to Chogo Ri.
(Photo: Dr. Jules Jacot-Guillarmod, 1902)

Amid the raging storm, they broke camp on August 3 and descended from camp to camp, collecting sugar and anything worth over a half crown a pound. Climbing lower down was particularly tough because the snow had largely vanished from the ice, while they had to dodge deadly seracs up to fifteen feet high. Crowley was constantly ill with diarrhea, vomiting, and fever. Guillarmod had influenza.

On July 11, they got to Rdokass where the Austrians were waiting. Next day, a durbar was held in the rain at which Wessely was expelled from the expedition for taking provisions improperly. Pfannl went with him. Still reeling with fever and having to stop at short intervals, Crowley made it to Paiyu, amid chronic rainfall. The weather on the Baltoro continued casting the bad luck the higher mountain had incessantly scattered about them. Crowley was, he would note in his *Confessions,* always pursued by bad weather. Even when in Akyab, he noted, the rain had stopped only for twenty minutes during the nine days he'd been there. Still, Crowley could assert justly that he'd been on the glacier for sixty-eight days, two longer than any other member of the party. That was a world's record.

Surprised at Eckenstein and Knowles's reaction to the news of cholera, Crowley was a little skeptical. He passed through the Bralduh Nala without seeing any signs of mourning, nor were there any at Askole, though he insisted his men not contact villagers. Knowles and Eckenstein however, refused to enter the village at all. After that, Guillarmod and Crowley took a different route from Eckenstein and Knowles to Shigar. After eating apricots at Ghomboro and feeling much relieved, Crowley concluded problems on mountains were not atrributable to altitude sickness but to indigestion, such as returned to him when he ate fresh mulberries and melons at Shigar. Such was explorer Sir Richard Burton's view, and Crowley valued Burton's immense common sense, so rare.

Getting to Shigar entailed taking a *zak,* a bamboo raft bound by goatskins with a man at each corner with a stick to attempt to keep off rocks. Landing every twenty minutes was necessary because the goatskins got wet through. Nevertheless, Crowley adored the dizzying adventure of it all as the craft spun about deliriously amid eddies and splash. Meeting up again with Knowles and Eckenstein, who'd recovered equanimity, they got down the Shigar River to Skardu in two hours in a big zak, "with youth at the prow and pleasure at the helm!"[11]

Fig. 9.44. Rafting down the Shigar.
(Photo: Dr. Jules Jacot-Guillarmod, 1902)

Crowley decided to take a different route home—across the Plain of Deosai, rumored impassible. A table-plain from 14,000 to 17,000 feet it was crossed by four rivers whose ability to detain the hungry traveler was notorious. Eckenstein had bad memories of it from 1892, but eventually took Crowley's route. They had ponies, which made things easier, and Crowley enjoyed the bright details to be seen amid what was otherwise, but for the views behind them, a desolate scene. On one occasion, Crowley imitated the biblical Absalom in the manner of being restrained by a tree branch. Another remarkable meeting was with an old man returning to his village who'd gone to Skardu to sell dried apricots (a staple of the region) but could not quite get the price he wanted. He was resigned to dying at home. Crowley heard, and dug out four rupees to give to the despairing old man. The man's demeanor was instantaneously restored, as was his faith in a beneficent God who cared for his faithful. Crowley was delighted to play a part in this stark drama of providence.

The group descended from the plateau on the thirtieth in eight hours to Burzil where a dak bagla afforded shelter from the miserable rain. Inspecting the terrain, Crowley was highly amused by the

Fig. 9.45. The high plateaux of Deosai, from the col at Boorgi.
(Photo: Dr. Jules Jacot-Guillarmod, 1902)

Fig. 9.46. Crowley on
the Deosai Plain in his
Mexican poncho. (Photo:
Dr. Jules Jacot-Guillarmod,
1902)

Fig. 9.47. Heading home:
Jules Jacot-Guillarmod
in oriental headgear.
(Photographer unknown,
1902)

government's fears that a Russian invasion could be expected from the north. The road to Gilgit was absolutely packed with every kind of bullock and mule carrying stores to the Gilgit garrison. Crowley doubted whether the resources of Russia and Great Britain combined could afford to supply half a dozen regiments in such terrain. When people mentioned the invasion of Alexander the Great to Crowley as a precedent, Crowley was content to observe that climatic conditions had changed considerably from those times, as was evident from past civilizations, and what was currently in progress on this planet. He was convinced the terrain was far more fertile in antiquity.

Crowley was much impressed by beauties abounding the Burzil Valley. Cantering easily down a path, enjoying it all, Crowley was surprised to hear "Hat Jao!" that is, "Get out of the way!" behind him. It was a gigantic English major, and he, Crowley, was delighted to have been mistaken for a native.

At Gurais, Crowley again encountered Ernest Radcliffe, forest commissioner of Kashmir, who welcomed him with open arms, gave him a good bath and a hot dinner. Also dining that evening was the gigantic major who, failing to recognize Crowley as the chap obstructing passage earlier in the day, was greatly embarrassed when his error became apparent.

Fig. 9.48. The valley of Burzil, below Peshwari.
(Photo: Dr. Jules Jacot-Guillarmod, 1902)

Crowley journeyed on to Gurai and to Tragobal on August 3, through wild, rich forest and scenery of unsurpassable splendor. Joyfully he rode through a 10,000-foot pass with a feeling never recaptured in the city-civilization that twisted his true nature. Having crossed the pass, the distant Wular Lake and the Vale of Kashmir embraced delighted eyes. The path to Bandipura was bliss. There they chartered a *dunga* (a kind of traveling houseboat) and crossed the lake to a dak bagla at Baramula in a long twelve hours, its comforts marred only by malaria's return.

On August 6, a tonga took Crowley to Srinigar, 132 days after he had left it for Chogo Ri.

He had been amid the lovely wooden houses of Srinigar for a week when Radcliffe invited him to his Baramula headquarters for a shooting break. Crowley found the two days of bear tracking pure pleasure, now free of responsibility and in country that smiled upon him. The men had planned a more extensive trip but a telegram called Radcliffe away. Besides, Crowley was in need of pure rest, and he decided it was time to return as slowly as was reasonable, to England, which he had not seen for over two extraordinary years.

On September 21, 1902, Crowley left Baramula, first for Rawalpindi, then for Delhi and Ajmer. Drained of energy, he reached

Fig. 9.49. The new dak bungalow at Baramula.
(Photo: Dr. Jules Jacot-Guillarmod, 1902)

*Fig. 9.50. The Cashmere
Road near Murree.
(Photo: Dr. Jules Jacot-
Guillarmod, 1902)*

*Fig. 9.51. Dr. Guillarmod's
book on the 1902 K2
expedition, published in
1904.*

the port of Bombay on September 30. Something of the effects of his
expedition seemed to have affected his beard. When he shaved it for
Europe, it had been a mixture of black and red hairs, but when he let it
grow again, it was all white.

On October 4, Crowley sailed for Aden on the SS *Egypt*.* A curious
year would pass before a brief return to India in 1903.

---

*The P&O Liner SS *Egypt,* launched at Greenock, Scotland, in 1897, would famously sink
in the English Channel on May 19, 1922, in collision in thick fog with the French cargo
steamer *Seine*. With the loss of eighty-six souls, and gold and silver bullion worth over
£1 million (£200,000,000 at today's values), much of which was salvaged during the 1930s.

TEN

Return to Ceylon, via Boleskine

Before returning to India, Crowley had many adventures, not the least of which was a first try at marriage, which essay in the folly of romance led to a brief return to Ceylon in December 1903.

He had left India in 1902 very much in a state of spiritual lassitude. Arranging to meet friend Gerald Kelly in Paris—Kelly was learning to paint in the Rue Campagne Première, Montparnasse—Crowley first indulged in the fleshpots of Cairo, in the mood to let things drift. Even his Buddhism, which had inspired the soon-to-be-published *Berashith*, got lassoed into a general excuse for ennui and intermittent indifference to life. Crowley's restlessness was getting to him: "I want to enlarge my mind," he wrote in his *Confessions,* "This is the keynote of my life, the untrammelled delight in every possibility of existence, potential or actual."[1]

If "God" was in everything, as mystics had declared through the millennia, then there could be no harm in man's seeking wherever his angel led him, so long as the seeker stayed in equilibrium and took care not to violate his inner law, which itself pointed outward—to more experience. Crowley's phenomenal openness to new experiences ensured that his life was for sustained periods a nonstop adventure. Extraordinary things rushed into his life and purview—and he always seemed to be at the right place at the right time.

On March 24, 1903, for example, Crowley met Major General Sir Hector Archibald Macdonald, K.C.B., D.S.O., (1853–1903), commander in chief of British Forces in Ceylon—a popular hero in his native Scotland and the only senior general in the British Army to have come up through the ranks by merit alone. Born in a croft on the hillside facing Crowley's Boleskine house on Loch Ness, Macdonald recognized Crowley while lunching at Paris's Hotel Regina restaurant. Macdonald faced a summons to a court martial in Ceylon, where a large number of Ceylonese assembled to testify against him for alleged homosexual offences. The scandal reached the public the next day, courtesy of "an outrageously outspoken" account in the *New York Herald*'s French edition. Soon afterward, poor Macdonald was found dead in his hotel room. He had shot himself. Conversation with Crowley may have been his last. In December 1903, Crowley would encounter a deputation of Scots Kirk elders at the Grand Oriental Hotel, Colombo. Concerned to ascertain their beloved Macdonald's guilt or innocence, the anxious elders were visibly reassured by the Laird of Boleskine's insistence that the greater the number of native witnesses, the more likely it was that bribes had secured them.

There has been a longstanding tendency among biographers to underestimate in varying degrees Crowley's standing in Paris, even at this early point in his career. Two contemporary newspaper reports present a contrasting picture, even suggesting Crowley was rather self-denigrating about his status in the city's cultural milieu. More significantly perhaps, both sources have an important bearing on what his experiences in India meant to him at the time.* The first reference to Crowley appeared only eight days before Crowley's fateful meeting with Hector Macdonald, on page one of *L'Écho de Paris* (*Journal Littéraire et Politique du Matin*), Monday March 16, 1903, in the artistic society gossip column, "Lettres à Valmont."† The two columns give us an impression of habitués familiar to artistic Paris at the time.

---

*I am indebted to William Breeze, who found the original newspaper references, and kindly sent me copies. Translations are my own.

†Signed pseudonymously "Marquise de Merteuil," the "letters" conceit stood in ironic *hommage* to Freemason and protofeminist Pierre Choderlos de Laclos's *succès de scandale*, the epistolary novel *Les Liaisons dangereuses*, which revealed through a series of letters the callous plots of libertines the Marquise de Merteuil and the Vicomte de Valmont.

Delighting the columns' writer and kindred aficionados was Robert, Comte de Montesquiou-Fézensac (1855–1921),* wealthy and flamboyant Symbolist poet and art collector, considered a model for Jean des Esseintes in Joris-Karl Huysmans's *À Rebours* (1884)—a favorite novel of Crowley's. "Marquise de Merteuil" recounts the count's arousing artistic appreciation among the princes Sapieha and Troubetzkoï (of the Royal Duchy of Lithuania), the "Madames" Astor, Whitelaw Reid (former U.S. ambassador to France), Cornelius Vanderbilt III, Lady Bache Cunard (mother of Nancy, who would become Crowley's friend decades later), the "artists whom we love" French Symbolist painter Edmond Aman-Jean, American novelist Francis-Marion Crawford, and British novelist Richard Le Gallienne, at a poetic talk about "Mystery" and the beauties of France given at Louis Sherry's Restaurant, 5th Ave. and 44th St., New York City, where faces familiar to the Parisian cultural scene had recently gathered. The "Marquise" goes on to address Paris's openness to new, if disturbing, movements of art:

Our dear Paris remains always, you see, Valmont, despite her caprices for negro dances, the eternal home of Beauty. In the end, it is to her all these errant children come, as an indulgent mother to the worst excesses of art. Sometimes it is the "enfants terribles" that she adopts, terrible and charming, like Miss Barney [Natalie Clifford Barney, Paris-based, American novelist playwright, poet, 1876–1972] who simultaneously adores both the gods of Greece and the unknown god of Anarchy, or Miss Hannah Lynch [Irish born writer, 1859–1904], who strongly disconcerted Monsieur Bergeret,[†] last month, when speaking of his books with somewhat Irish license.

It is to Paris that the seekers of the infinite find their refuge. Is this not why Aleister Crowley comes to us, this English poet of Celtic blood, who has sung the glory of Rodin having descended from an audacious 7,000 meter ascent on K2 of the Himalayas? Aleister Crowley seems a fair brother to Maurice Maeterlinck, pale,

---

*For Montesquiou's place in the "French Occult Revival" in the 1890s, see my *Occult Paris.*

†Probably a reference to novelist Anatole France (1844–1924) whose 1901 novel *Monsieur Bergeret à Paris* dealt partly autobiographically with the notorious "Dreyfus Affair."

thin and firm as an arrow-shaft; his poems of a sensual metaphysic which exalt themselves to the peaks of the Earth and of Art; and, after having thought amongst us about some new drama, he departs again for India, to conquer Gaurisankar.*

Crowley's Rodin poems referred to by the "Marquise" would appear as *Auguste Rodin, Seven Lithographs by* [Auguste] *CLOT from the Water-Colours of Auguste Rodin, with a Chaplet of Verse by Aleister Crowley* (Chiswick Press, 1907), but the fine poems had long before earned appreciation from their subject. A letter from the great sculptor served as preface to the collection:

182, Rue de L'Université.
Mon Cher Crowley,
Vos poésies ont cette fleur violente, ce bon sens, et cette ironie qui en soit inattendue.
C'est d'un charme puissant et cela ressemble a une attaque bienfaisante.
Votre poésie est donc violente, et me plait par ce côté aussi.
Je suis honoré que vous m'ayiez pris mes dessins et ainsi honoré dans votre livre.

Votre,
AUG. RODIN.

The first poem, "Rodin," was translated into French by Marcel Schwob in Paris in February 1903. Distinguished Jewish French writer, sometimes regarded a precursor to the surrealists, Mayer André Marcel Schwob (1867–1905) wrote countless short stories, undertook much journalism, knew practically every literary and artistic luminary in Paris, and was influential on writers Jorge Luis Borges and Roberto Bolaño.

And it was Marcel Schwob who assisted when Aleister Crowley was interviewed by distinguished journalist and poet Fernand Hauser (1869–1941) for a long article that appeared on pages 1 and 3 of *La Presse*

---

*Himalayan mountain Gaurishankar, at 23,405 feet, is the second highest peak of the Rolwaling Himal, unconquered until May 8, 1979.

newspaper on Friday April 3, 1903, under the headline: "RETURN
FROM THE HIMALAYAS—A Poet Traveler—At the home of Monsieur
Marcel Schwob—The Irish poet Crowley—On the mountains—At a
height of 8,000 meters—Buddhist?"

An old mansion in the rue Saint-Louis-en-l'Île, one of those survivors from yesterday that once sheltered princes; today, it's a poet
who survives under this roof, Monsieur Marcel Schwob, author of
that beautiful translation of *Hamlet, Prince of Denmark,* which was
performed at Sarah's house.*

A Hindu, bearing of a lantern of red glass, opens the door and
introduces me in the drawing room, where the master of the house,
entirely clean shaven, making his brilliant, ascetic eyes shine all the
more, receives me; Monsieur Marcel Schwob interrupts a conversation with Monsieur Aleister Crowley to introduce us to one another.

Monsieur Aleister Crowley, with whom I was thus acquainted,
thanks to Monsieur Marcel Schwob, is a being somewhat apart, in
the world; an Irishman, glabrous, skinny and tall, who regards you
with dreamy eyes and who speaks in the soft voice of his race, when
they are poets; and Monsieur Crowley is a poet; he is also Buddhist;
he is, finally, a traveler; but what a traveler! Monsieur Crowley had
returned, quite simply, from seeing the Himalayas.

My conversation with Monsieur Crowley was fairly strained;
my interlocutor expressing himself in rudimentary French; but
Monsieur Marcel Schwob speaks admirable English, and he served
as interpreter.

A POET SCIENTIST

A poet, Monsieur Crowley, aged twenty-seven, first speaks with
detachment about his "youth," when, he said, he was a disciple of
Swinburne; he goes a lot further today; yesterday a symbolist, he
became a scientist; I mean to say that he dreams of works where his
poetry would be purged by scientific doctrines. He has already given

---

*Actress Sarah Bernhardt performed as Hamlet in Schwob and Paul Morand's trans-
lation in 1899, rapturously in Paris, but with poor notices at London's Adelphi on
June 12, 1899—there being prejudice against the idea of a female Hamlet.

us a *Tannhauser,* whose legendary hero he imagined very differently to Wagner; that was a nebulous work, among others.

Currently, Monsieur Crowley is preparing a work in which he'll try hard to project thoughts that evoke the works of Rodin; thus he has written verses on the celebrated "Balzac" [Rodin's sculpture], and here is Marcel Schwob's translation.*

˙ How had this poet, who, in these several verses appears to us, such as he is, a visionary, had the idea of climbing the very highest mountains? Is it love of the heights? The bird sings only when perched on high. . . . Must the poet wish to see the sky at its closest? Has he had the desire for altitudes, the obsession with summits; is this the "bitter science" which drives him towards the snowy peaks, where there is the "sad wisdom," or again, has he wished to feel "the air in a stupor shuddering on his flesh"?

"My father adored mountains," Monsieur Crowley told me. "I owe my love of peaks to him; as a child I climbed the summits of Ireland, then I went to the mountains of Scotland and Wales, of Switzerland and Austria and of Hungary; later I went to Mexico; I wanted, on the heights to see extraordinary things; the Mexican mountains are high; I climbed them very fast, I broke all the world's speed records. I wanted to do even more, that's why I left for the Himalayas."

—You are a sportsman, then?

IN THE HIMALAYAS

—"Perhaps, I don't know. I desire to do the things everybody doesn't do; with five men and 200 coolies, I climbed the massif of Mustach in the Himalayas, a group situated on the borders of Turkestan and Baltistan; the highest peak is K2, known to locals as Chogori; more than 8,000 meters high. I climbed there, the highest ascent possible in the world; in the Himalayas there's Gaurisankar which is 250 meters higher than Chogori, but it's inaccessible.

"To get to Chogori, you must get to Srinagar, the last town inhabited by Europeans; and to get to Srinagar you have seven days'

---

*I have omitted Schwob's French translation of Crowley's "Balzac," which may be found in *Rodin in Rime* (1907).

march; after that, you march twenty-seven days until you get to the last village, Askole. After that you march fourteen days and reach the foot of the mountain; then you make your way by paths you carve out yourself, in the midst of deserts strewn with stones, among rare plants, you come to the glacier; nothing to eat; to drink only snow-water; the only living beast, the ibex, a kind of goat the color of stone, ravens and birds that resemble the patridge; it was summer when I was there: we had twenty degrees below zero during the night, and forty above in the sunshine.

"We had to eat wretched tinned food and sleep in sleeping bags.

"To get to the summit required climbing a further fifteen days; a raven and a butterfly had followed us to a peak in Mexico, already, I had seen a butterfly at 5,000 meters, fluttering on the snows."

—Did you suffer altitude sickness?

—"No, when one climbs slowly one doesn't suffer from the rarefaction of the air."

—Were you a long time on the mountain?

—"Sixty-eight days, between 5,000 and 8,000 meters, and amid snowstorms; the vistas were terrific; it was fine; it was grandiose; you couldn't help but admire it all hugely; in life's miseries, in the midst of savage and uncultivated Nature, one loses the aesthetic sense; the absolute concentration of the brain is on the question of life and health; think about our expedition, so close to the Equator, was almost an Arctic expedition. We were fifteen days from life; one finds at the Pole the same physical conditions as the Himalayas."

—You had studied your itinerary?

—"I had no guide, but with our friends, we had organized the expedition methodically and scientifically. . . ."

—No one before you had seen Chogori?

—"Six years ago, an Englishman, Conway; but one had no idea how far he had climbed."

BUDDHIST

Now Monsieur Crowley talked to me of his determinism. He is persuaded that "life is decided in advance"; that's why he's become a fervent Buddhist; he went on pilgrimage to Anurādhapura in Ceylon; one of his friends, Allan Bennett, has done more, having entered as a monk in a monastery; Monsieur Crowley would like to introduce the Buddhist religion into the West in its real and pure form, as practiced in Burma and Ceylon, reliant on the Pāli Canon.

Monsieur Crowley's conversion is not only philosophical, it is religious and mystical. Perhaps even, one day, Monsieur Crowley might cease writing and become an apostle of the Buddha's doctrines.

And that Monsieur Crowley told me, with shuddering lips, and fevered eyes. Whilst Monsieur Crowley expressed his fervor for the Buddhist cult, I heard Monsieur Marcel Schwob insist on the sincerity of his conversion.

Has Monsieur Marcel Schwob, who returned to Ceylon, and who also went to Anurādhapura, returned to us, like Monsieur Crowley, a Buddhist?

I did not dare ask him, and I left, with curiosity unsatisfied, directed again to the street by the Hindu bearing a lantern, this time, with greenish hints.

—*Fernand Hauser*

Unpublished for 116 years, this article offers a privileged insight into the depth and color of Crowley's life in early 1903.

So, having struck up a friendship with sculptor Auguste Rodin, writer Marcel Schwob, and a distinguished coterie of painters, models (including Nina Oliver, to whom Crowley dedicated the poem "La Casque d'Or" in *Rodin in Rime*), and literary figures, he left Paris glowing in May to return to his old haunt, Boleskine, assailed by nihilistic abjection of unfathomable character. Perhaps it had something to do with the realization that had struck him again, but most forcibly in Paris, that Mathers was an ignoble man, hardly worth the sacrifices Crowley had made on his behalf. It might have been K2, or Buddhistic indifference, or sheer inner fatigue. Anyhow, aiming at objectivity, he attempted to assess coolly where he was intellectually. This he did in a preparatory note to his diary, beginning June 9, 1903:

In the year 1899 I came to Boleskine House, and put everything in order with the object of carrying out the Operation of Abramelin the Mage.

I had studied Ceremonial Magic for years, and obtained very remarkable success.

My Gods were those of Egypt, interpreted on lines closely akin to those of Greece.

In Philosophy I was a Realist of the Qabalistic School.

In 1900 I left England for Mexico, and later the Far East, Ceylon, India, Baltistan, Egypt and France. Idle here to detail the corresponding progress of my thought. Passing through a stage of Hinduism, I had discarded all Deities as unimportant and in Philosophy was an uncompromising nominalist. I may call myself an orthodox Buddhist.

With the reservations:

(i). I cannot deny that certain phenomena do accompany the use of certain rituals. I only deny the usefulness of such methods to the White Adept.

(ii). Hindu methods of meditation are possibly useful to the beginner and should not therefore be discarded at once (necessarily).

. . . [I] appear in the character of an Inquirer on strictly scientific lines.

This is unhappily calculated to damp enthusiasm: but as I so carefully of old, for the magical path, excluded all from my life all other interests, that life has now no particular meaning, and the Path of Research, on the only lines I can now approve of, remains the one Path possible for me to tread.[2]

Crowley's stance on his spiritual explorations would now proceed precisely in line with that word: *research,* patient, scientific, exhausting—and, ultimately, very surprising.

During the laird's long absence, Loch Ness, by which Boleskine stood, had become the focal point of curious disquiets. Abramelin demons appear to have been running amok in the environs and fantasies of locals. Crowley found it all very amusing—anything to shore up the rolling mist of boredom advancing toward him. Buddhism was indeed a possible cause; if nothing was real, then nothing really mattered. More Buddhism meant less life; but Crowley wanted more.

He began a second day at Boleskine reacquainting himself with the contents of the house, in the company of favorite aunt, Annie,* Crowley's Uncle Jonathan's second wife (and now widow), who agreed to be temporary housekeeper. On the eleventh her nephew moved his bed into the "temple." As his diary records, this "for convenience of more absolute retirement. This being outside the actual inner walls, I got dreams and visions of the most appalling Abramelin devils."[3]

The next day he performed a ritual banishing and cleansing operation: "Taking the familiar precautions, obtained the familiar immunity."[4]

On June 16 he experienced an impulse to begin "mahasatipattana." Perhaps he had with him a translation from the Pāli of the *Mahasatipatthana Sutta,* a sermon on the "Great Frames of Reference." *Sati* means "mindfulness," with the cognate idea of remembering or keeping in mind, and *satipatthana* refers to meditation aimed at establishing what may be described as: "being here now." The activity is best motivated by a desire for awakening as part of the progress to ending suffering. One is to keep attention on that goal in the here and now, to banish distraction or reaction. It makes good sense given Crowley's state of mind and the peculiar circumstances of his homelife at Boleskine at the time.

> It is easy to get into the way of it: as a mantra which does not interfere much with sense-impressions, but remains as an undercurrent. It was on breathing, and my nose is somehow wrong. Noticed some pain and some other phenomenon which I have now (17th) forgotten. A lesson to keep a note-book handy. N.B. There is a tremendous astral whir on in temple.†

Crowley's presence seems to have mysteriously galvanized the atmosphere of the house. He determined to restore equilibrium by applying what he'd learned of meditation in Ceylon with Allan, attempting to transmit the "Kandy" state of mind to the Scottish Highlands. He even tried the meditation in his boat the next day while out fishing, albeit in a "desultory sort of way."[6]

---

*née Anne Hegginbottam (1840–1921)

†A "whir" means something rapidly rotating, or moving to and fro, or something producing a low, continuous sound: a "whirring."[5]

He then spent a couple of days trying to get the house in order before returning to his pieties on Monday, June 22, when, after an attempt at mahasatipatthana while fishing, he returned to his rug in the temple, sitting down at 18 minutes and 20 seconds past 10 p.m. to perform mahasatipatthana on his breathing for half an hour before retiring to bed. He noted four results down. First, his breathing got deeper, and rather sleepier (he was tired). Second, he detected throbbing in the ājñā chakra and the front of his brain generally, accompanied by perspiration. Third: a tendency to forget what he was doing. He put this down to fatigue. Fourth, his concentration, though poor, was better than expected.

The next day he went for a walk, while practicing mahasatipatthana, and got the very clear intuition that "I breathe" was a lie. He regained his "delusion" with effort.*

11:30 Entered Temple. ["*I breathe*" definitely denied in consciousness. Making an effort for the sake of experiment, regained delusion, but not quite easily.]

11:33. P[rana]y[ama] 10.20.30. These figures express the duration in seconds of purakam, rekakam and kumbhakam respectively.†

Py 11:33–11:39. A good deal of pain etc.

11:40. M[ahasatipattana].

11:51 P[rana]y[ama]

10.20.30–11:56 I do seem bad! My left nostril is not at all [as] it should be.

11:57. Left Temple.

---

*In the following transcriptions of Crowley's unpublished diaries, the comments in brackets were added by Crowley later when writing up his notes—exceptions being when abbreviated words are given their full value by this author.
†Purakam = inhalation; rekakam = exhalation; kumbhakam = retention.

12:30. Began m[ahasatipattana] desultory. [12:30–1:30. Rapid degeneration to nothing.]

1:15 In t[emple] m[ahasatipattana]. Doing it very badly. Seem sleepy.

1:35. Went out.[7]

From that Wednesday until Sunday, June 28, he felt ill, suffering from glossitis, an inflammation of the tongue causing it to swell and change color. It might have been an allergic reaction, or low iron in his blood. On the Sunday night he meditated on the ājñā chakra with the mantra "Aum Tat Sat Aum," which aims to affirm the truth and reality of *Aum*, the word that manifests unmanifest reality. Taken together, the mantra concentrates the idea of "Supreme, Absolute Truth" as an offering to God, of goodness. He made similar but less involved efforts the next day, then, on June 30, aware that his concentration levels were low, decided to redo the kind of tests Oscar Eckenstein had enjoined upon him in Mexico in 1901 to reveal his capacity for concentration. Concentrating on the image of a red cross for two minutes, ten seconds, he had several breaks of the "Oh, how well I'm doing it" kind. He noted how he seemed to have forgotten the very long times he used to do. He held a white triangle in mind for ten minutes with twenty breaks. He reckoned twenty minutes with ten breaks was a "good performance."[8]

He then tried combining an *apas* symbol—a silver crescent or purple semicircle representing water—with an *ākāśa* symbol: a black or indigo vesica piscis, or egg shape. These were *tattva* symbols employed in Golden Dawn training as suitable "door" images to enter the astral plane. This proved difficult, finding even slight noises in the house very disturbing. He reminded himself to give "strictest orders" for silence when he was in the temple.

At 10:55 he held the image of a rose cross for six minutes with seven breaks. Breaks could be of varying length as they were unmeasurable as one could only "stop-watch" the exercise as a whole.

At 11:44 he managed twelve minutes on a triangle with ten breaks. He tried to find a way of counting the length of a break: "The only possible suggestion is to count the links in thought back to object. But not worth trouble, I think. I find myself close to identification of Subj[ect] and Obj[ect]. This is probably a (good) result of my philosophical studies."[9]

We see here Crowley definitely fulfilling his intent as to his overall approach: that of research, concluding on June 30: "It will perhaps be most scientific in these tests (and perhaps even in work) to stick to one or two objects and always go on to a special number of breaks—say 10. Then success varies as to time." The seriousness Crowley brought to bear on the exercises may easily be discerned from the following unpublished diary entries as he attempted to "up" his capacities for concentrated meditation. This was pioneering work.

July 2. [Thursday]
3:14. White triangle. 6½ m[inutes]. 6 b[reaks]. Disturbed by carpenter.
10:40 [White triangle] 29 [m[inutes].] 23 [b[reak]s.]
A "break" shall be defined as = a consciousness of the cessation of the object-consciousness. A simple outside thought arising shall not constitute a "break," since it may exist simultaneously with the object-consciousness. It shall be meritorious to perform a rosary upon the Rudraksha* beads at least once (at one time) daily; for why? Because 108 is a convenient number of breaks, and the large number will aid determination of rates of progress. [For the true "break," any thought not the object is never presented to consciousness until recognized as such. What I really count, then, is the number of pulls on the string (to take the old calf simile) and not the number of stones thrown into the lake (to take the lake simile).

Moreover an outside thought may exist, and be recognized, yet not divert the true thought. In particular sound impressions need not vitiate the sight-concentration. E.g., I hear a cow low; only if the image of the cow, or of some object following therefrom, be present in consciousness, and that to the exclusion of the primary, is it a break.

To determine the value of the fatigue factor, I will do a series of

---

*Rudrāksha: a seed from the Himalayan *Eliocarpus ganitrus* tree, used for beadmaking in Hinduism. *Aksha* means "eye," and the compound word means "the one who sees and can do anything," suggesting the third eye.

(a) 20 break (b) 40 break (c) 60 break . . . etc., and construct a table. Two objects △ and ajna with mantra shall be taken.]

If it be true, as I suppose, that fatigue to a great extent determines frequency, it will then be perhaps possible to predict a G[ood?].P[ranayama?]. (or mixed P[ranayama?].)

July 3. [Friday]
Returned from Inverness in afternoon.
10:58–11:10. Triangle. 3 mins. 5 breaks. In very bad state—nearly all break. A little p[rana]y[ama] to steady me.
11:10–11:15 ½. Triangle 5½ m. 4 br[eaks]. Remarks. Sneezed: totally forgot what I was doing. When I remembered, time as above.
Abandoned work for night; feel tired and dispersed. [Feeling tired and depressed. Gave up.]

July 4 [Saturday]
Short p[rana]y[ama] to begin.
9:45. Triangle. 13½ m[inutes]. 20 br[eaks].
11:34 [sic]. White Triangle. Called away.
10:25. Ajna. 32½ m[inutes]. 20 br[eaks]. With mantra. Throbbing at once. Invaders nearly all irrational. Strong sub-current of swift thought noticed. Quite like old times. *Near* neighbourhood concentration. Excellent: require less food and less literary work. Idea to do triangle with shorthand writer [with watch] to note times and nature of break: not with ajna, for I feel that *any* moment—(Try irritation of skin over ajna with Tincture of Iodene!?) [Observation: that ideas for doing it better, pictures of C[rowley?]'s body doing it here, there, and everywhere, are extremely common breaks.]

July 5. [Sunday]
[P[rana]y[ama] 5 m[inutes]. with great difficulty. A.M. 11:30 Aj[na]. 25 m[inutes]. 20 br[eaks]. V[ery].good.]
11:39. An[ahata chakra: the heart chakra]. 25 m[inutes]. 20 br[eaks]. As previous.
9:36. An[ahata] 15½ m[inutes]. 20 br[eaks]. Good notwithstanding.
[P.M. 1:36 d[itt]o 15 ½ m[inutes]. 20 br[eaks]. V[ery]. Good too. Indigestion and diarrhoea seem to start: some headache.]

July 6. [Monday]

[They continue—hence no work. Wrote this up about midnight.]

July 6–8. [Monday–Wednesday]

Diarrhoea etc. Inhibit work.

July 9 [Thursday]

10:57–11:04. P[rana]y[ama]. Better, nose not clear though. (There is no Purgative like pranayama.)

11:16. Ajna. 2 m[inutes]. 6 br[eaks]. Hyperaesthesia of sense. Sounds disturb much.

July 10 [Friday]

Again bed.

July 11. [Saturday]

3:37 ½–45 ½. P[rana]y[ama]. Going easier.

3:48. Triangle. 3 m[inutes]. 5 br[eaks]. Flabby.

5:51. An[ahata]. 19½ m[inutes]. 20 br[eaks]. Difficult to settle. Sound hyperaesthesia. Began to forget mantra.

10:12 ½–10:19. P[rana]y[ama]. 6 m[inutes]. V[ery]. hard. The smallest quantity of food injures power immensely.

10:21. Aj[na]. 23 m[inutes]. 20 [?] br[eaks]. (used cotton wool in ears). Thoughts of aj[na]. Go obliquely up (from opening of pharynx about) or direct horizontally forward. This gives idea to *chase* consciousness, i.e. to find by the obvious series of experiments the spot in which the thoughts dwell. Probably however this moves about. If so, it is a clear piece of evidence for the idealistic position. If not, by thinking of it—thinking of itself, and its falsity will become rapidly evident.

Consciousness. If ragged stream, we have no ground for reasoning. Think long of linga,* looking at it physically as V[*olo*].N[*oscere* = George Cecil Jones]., thought: This *may* be Vamacharya ["Left-hand path"] Yoga. *Namo Sivaya Namaha Aum!* [Adoration to Lord Shiva]

---

*Lingam, linga, Shiva linga, ling, or Shiva ling: image or object symbolizing Shiva and the main cultic object of devotion in Shaivism.

July 12. [Sunday]

12:08 to 12:19. Best so far. Incense going troubled somewhat.

12:27. 31 m[inutes]. 30 br[eaks]. Mantra got to *"tartsano"* [? *sic*]. Not in good form—suspect many breaks of long duration. Kept mantra going all day. Slept 2:30–4 about.

4:58. Pranayama 11 minutes. Perspiration.

5:14. P[rana]y[ama] 5:10.15 to try.

5:25. Quite a little holiday. [Wound up with a G[rand] P[rana] y[ama].]

5:28. 38 m[inutes]. 30 br[eaks]. V[ery]. tired towards end and difficult to get settled. To me it seems evident that the first 10 breaks or so are rapid.

6:10. P[rana]y[ama] 16 m[inutes].

8:15. Having continued mantra, ajna with m[antra]—8:47. 32 m[inutes]. 22 br[eaks]. Light coming a little—one very long without break. Some sound.

10:05. Aj[na] 12½ m[inutes]. 11 br[eaks]. Continuing mantra, save for short chat with Aunt.* Confused dreams—a bad night on the whole.

July 13. [Monday]

Casual mantring.†

10:44 P[rana]y[ama] Quite hopeless.

10:48. 32 m[inutes]. 30 br[eaks]. Rather frivolous.[10]

At this point Crowley's 1903 diary ended abruptly with a note added later that it was about this time that he went to Edinburgh "to meet Gerald &c." That "&c." covers quite a story, best told elsewhere.‡

The diary reopens seven months later with a retrospective summary, written in Helwan, Egypt, on February 22, 1904:

---

*Gerald Yorke noted on the transcript of the diary that on the opposite page Crowley had made several drawings, the first captioned "Devil seen behind Aunt's shoulder—her habitual companion," then one captioned "Another of Aunt's devils," and the last: "The lower part is 'Too Horrible.'"

†"Mantring": a neologism of Crowley; possibly "mantraing" but mistranscribed.

‡Concerning Crowley's marriage to Rose Edith, née Kelly, see my *Aleister Crowley: The Biography*.

On Aug. 6 [1903] (about)—my work had been interrupted by the arrival of Gerald Kelly the painter—I decided to go over to Strathpeffer [Spa, Scotland] and marry his sister Rose. This I did on Aug. 12, having been engaged 19 hours. Our acquaintance had begun in the Ideal Way, i.e. with more than "a little aversion" shown—A.C. kicked and so did R[ose] E[dith] S[kerrett]. Eros now took matters in hand pretty thoroughly and Hermes had a different office to that of Hierophant.

Crowley and Rose's sudden impulse to splice their destinies together caused consternation in the Kelly family, and elicited from Crowley a letter to distraught friend Gerald—Rose's brother—begging understanding for the fact he *had* tried to improve himself. For our purposes it is interesting because Crowley regards his "march to Buddhism" as part of his personal improvement program:

I have been trying since I joined the G∴D∴ [Golden Dawn] in '98 steadily and well to repress my nature in all ways. I have suffered much, but I have won, and you know it. . . . Did your sister [Rose] want to hear the true history of my past life, she should have it in detail; not from prejudiced persons, but the cold, drear stuff of lawyers. And English does not always fail me. If your worst wish came true, and we never met again, my remembrances of you, with or without a beard would, as you say, be good enough to go on. But I am ambitious. I hope one day to convince you that I am not only a clever (the 4^{tos} have "mentally deformed") man but a decent

Fig. 10.1. Portrait of Rose Kelly, by her brother, Gerald Kelly.

one and a good one. Why must 9/10ths of my life ie: the march to Buddhism, go for nothing; the atrophied 1/1,000,000[12] always spring up and choke me, and that in the house of my friends?

. . . All luck, and the greatest place in the new generation of artists be yours. So sayeth Aleister Crowley, always your friend whatever you may do or say. Vale! Till your Ave![11]

Crowley was in love, and nothing else mattered. Desiring to project that love before as many spectacular romantic backdrops as possible, the couple's initial honeymoon plan seems to have been to explore obscure parts of China, via Burma to visit Ananda Metteya—now in Rangoon, devoted to his enlightening new periodical, *Buddhism*. The plan would change, though it began conventionally enough, with a trip to Paris, to patch things up with Gerald. From Paris "love's light wings" whisked them southeast to Les Verrières in the Swiss Jura. Residing on family land by the French border, Dr Guillarmod was in good spirits, finalizing his ambitious *Six Mois dans l'Himalaya*, published in nearby Neuchâtel the following year. According to Charlie Buffet's *Jules Jacot-Guillarmod: Pionnier du K2* ("K2 Pioneer," Slatkine, 2012), Dr. Guillarmod gave Crowley a stereoscopic camera as a present during the brief stay from 7 to 8 November, describing Crowley as "rather greedy." Unrestrained love can provoke an appetite, and judging from photographs taken by Guillarmod of Crowley at the time, the Beast needed a good meal.*

From Les Verrières, Aleister and Rose headed south to Marseilles, Naples, then Cairo, where, on November 22, Crowley showed off his plumage, as he put it, by providing Rose with an "exhibition game" of

---

*I am grateful to "belmurru," contributor to the LAShTAL website (The Aleister Crowley Society) for information about Charlie Buffet's splendid paean to Guillarmod's achievements, and for indicating two rare photographs of Crowley at Les Verrières. Taken amid gentle slopes of Swiss farmland, one shows Guillarmod linking his arm with his slightly circumspect English guest. Rose, sadly, is not visible, but the images of Crowley at this moment of his life are strangely revelatory. In one he is seated, serious, and rather hunched up on a dry stone wall. In the other he stands, hands in his knickerbocker pockets (it's bright, but cold). His thinnish body is well-knit. Standing astride, his steely legs are determinedly straight, but not stiff, his woolen socks pulled tight above smart shoes. An ample double-breasted tweed coat, suitable for shooting, affords some insulation from

Magic, invoking the "Sylphs" (spirits of Air) in the King's Chamber of the Great Pyramid. Their presence, he insisted, manifested as a bluish light that lit the chamber till dawn.

In December 1903, "Lord and Lady Boleskine" left Port Said and sailed to Ceylon.

ALEISTER AND ROSE IN CEYLON

Crowley recalled that it was at Colombo where Rose became convinced she was pregnant, so the idea of going even farther east was held off. They decided that when it came time to leave Ceylon, it had better be in the general direction of Boleskine. However, they wanted to achieve *something* before returning, so for want of the—now rejected—alternative, Crowley and Rose considered a shooting expedition to Hambantota on the southeast coast of the island. They headed south to Galle on the southwestern tip, courted in the past by Helena Blavatsky and Col. Olcott, and now, in 1903, by Lord and Lady Boleskine.

At Galle, Crowley met "once more" a member of the Siamese royal family, Prince Jinawaravansa, who lived there for a time as a Buddhist monk.[12] Presumably having already encountered Jinawaravansa when in Ceylon with Allan, Crowley considered the prince a man of great spiritual attainments, co-dedicating his play *Why Jesus Wept* (begun on the island) to him, addressing the holy man as "you who esteemed the yellow robe more than your princedom."

From Galle, in mid-December, Crowley and Rose traveled to a base village from which they would enter the jungle by bullock carts. In his *Confessions,* Crowley speculated whether the act of changing into

---

(*cont.*) chill winds for his well-knit, thinnish body, while its broad, open lapels reveal a gentleman's white silk cravat and pin. Below a rather floppy, broad-brimmed, lived-in dark fedora of artistic or bohemian type, the poet's emphatic, man-boy face is sharpened like a flint arrow by a dark goatee beard, with fine, up-tweaked moustache. This is the game beard that adorns the famous photograph of "Prince Chioa Khan," that is, Crowley in costume, in Cairo, in Spring 1904, and you already feel that Crowley is fit to burst out of Edwardian constraint before a savage sun. Just below large ears what looks like a binoculars case swings diagonally like a Sam Browne belt across his front. Guillarmod, next to him with his very bushy moustache, resembles a genial patrician of his time; Crowley undoubtedly stands apart, a strange, compelling figure, inimitable and out of time.

shooting clothes somehow began a turn away from the "wholly lunatic rays of the honeymoon" toward his life's "ancient masters."[13]

The shooting did not go very well to begin with. He missed deer and hare. On January 7, 1904, Rose had a fever attack, so Crowley was spared from lovemaking long enough to write his poem of ecstatic love, *Rosa Mundi*. He remembered the date because he associated it with eating "buffalo steak"—though not one he'd shot; he only managed, according to his diary, "one little birdling." Eckenstein considered the poem sublime, and he did not normally take to poetry, though he did take to Rose, whom he adored, according to her husband.

Full of love, Crowley wrote his "Rose of the World"* as a voluptuous hymn to the divine yoni and the heavenly dew in which the poet loses himself:

> I have seen the eternal Gods
> Sit, star-wed, in old Egypt by the Nile;
> The same calm pose, the inscrutable, wan smile,
> On every lip alike.
> Time hath not had his will to strike
> At them; they abide, they pass through all.
> Though their most ancient names may fall,
> They stir not nor are weary of
> Life, for with them, even as with us, Life is but Love.
> They know, we know; let, then, the writing go!
> That, in the very deed, we do not know.

In retrospect, the poem feels something like a preparation for the epoch-marking *The Book of the Law*, received in Cairo just over three months later. There also, we see a reflection of the idea of Aleister and Rose as Egyptian deities: the celestial arch of stars, Nuit, embracing "Hadit."

The shooting Crowley liked was when he had no dependency on others, when he would enter a jungle and face the creature in lone combat. He liked big game for the same kind of reason he liked solitary climbing, and this is what would get him into society's bad books. One evening he

---

*Published in *Rosa Mundi, and other Love Songs,* 1905.

shot a sambar, or great stag, or thought he'd shot him, but the animal scarpered, and was only later discovered by Crowley twenty-five miles further on. Crowley had hit him all right, and everything pointed to a fatal shot, but the animal had a will to live, and Crowley understood the lesson nature was teaching him.

On another occasion, rumour of a fine buffalo bull that took his pleasure with a herd of tame cows raised interest. Sure he must end such shameful impropriety (!), Crowley assumed the moral stand, lay at the forest's edge by a clearing where the cows gathered, and shot the bull in the hoof. A far from amusing time followed. Tracking the wounded beast through the jungle, a bullet to the forehead finally felled the buffalo, and Crowley realized he'd emptied nineteen bullets in the beast's direction. *The will to live . . .*

Crowley hit numerous wild boar, but when it came to shooting an elephant, he felt, "much more like a murderer" than when killing a monkey. There was some sport in it, however. Elephants round Hambantota were adept at hiding, and even when visible, it was not easy finding the spot that would end their long days. The undergrowth was so thick he could have been standing next to one. It was more likely he'd be trampled than the elephant would fall from Crowley's double-barreled rifle. Crowley remembered one occasion when a Frenchman, taken to Ceylon by his wife as a cure for alcoholism ("out of the frying pan into the fire" opined Crowley), went out for a walk in the jungle. Well, the elephant got the Frenchman under his foot before Crowley did the elephant whose track he'd been following.

Crowley had fond memories of a camp about a kind of dak bagla by a lake. In the branches of stunning trees were legions of "flying foxes," that is, bats, and Crowley shot as many as he could, intending to make himself a waistcoat, and Rose a toque. Going out in a kind of punt into the lake, he fired at the trees, whereupon the sky was thick with the bats and he need only aim at the canopy above. One fell onto Rose, scaring her as it had its claws in her for half a minute before Crowley could free her. That night, Crowley was awakened by a bat squeal. On looking, it came from Rose, above him, hanging across the four posts of the bed that supported the mosquito net. Stark naked, she squealed like a bat. Scratching like a bat with claws deep, and oblivious to her husband's voice, Rose resisted attempts to get her down. It appeared she had become the dying bat in the boat, a phenomenon Crowley considered one of the oddest occurrences of "possession" he ever witnessed. Sure, it could be explained by her identifying herself with the bat in a dream, but as Crowley remarked, it was simpler to say the spirit of the bat had entered her.

One night in a bagla, Crowley got up to give Rose some medicine, but found the candle extinguished. Especially foolish of him, he thought, for he had left it far from the beds. Between them and him was an eighteen-inch krait, whose venomous bite could kill in minutes. Crowley mounted a table and yelled for the servants to bring a lamp. For all his learning from Allan, he had clearly not acquired what his friend had acquired where kraits were concerned.

On January 16, Crowley pursued a nineteen-foot rat snake, filled it with shot, or so he thought. Eventually his man hit it with a stick: not a mark on it! Testing the ammunition, he found the headman had swindled him with lousy pellets.

Crowley returned from Hambantota to Colombo intending to unload his wrath on the ammunition provisioner. He hated Colombo. He needed a dentist, felt weary, suffered with a sore throat, but there was worse. A diary entry from February 1924, lets a fascinating cat out of Crowley's bag of Ceylonese memories.

> Returned to Colombo from Hambantota January 1904: I got a lesion on my tongue—origin unknown—and a vision of Lady Scott & Countess Russell at the Galle Face Hotel.[14]

Fig. 10.2. The Galle Face Hotel, Colombo.

By his own admisision, the lesion, or morbid change to his tongue, put poison into his sensory faculties; he felt ill. One possible effect of this lesion would, as we shall see, have monumental effects on his life. As for the vision of Lady Scott and Countess Russell, we need first to disinter an old scandal from the cemetery of social history.

In 1890, Lady "Tina" Scott led daughter Mabel into marriage with "Frank," eccentric 2nd Earl Russell. A year later, Countess Russell sued for divorce. "Abominable libels" lost her the case. The libels continued. In 1896, Lady Scott accused her son in law of "immorality" with an Oxford don. She was imprisoned. In 1901 Earl Russell's bigamy with a Mrs. Somerville, whose husband had enjoyed an affair with the countess, became public; divorce was granted. As recently as April 1903, Countess Russell had hit the headlines by marrying a footman masquerading as "Prince Athrobald Stuart de Modena."

Now shift scene to Colombo's famous, luxurious, and still thriving Galle Face Hotel, then playing host to honeymooners Lord and Lady Boleskine. Enter notorious Lady Scott and Countess Russell; hideous mother, manipulated daughter.

Fig. 10.3. Mabel, Countess Russell.

Crowley takes up the story:

> They would have seemed extravagant at Monte Carlo; in Ceylon
> the heavily painted faces, the over-tended dyed false hair, the garish
> flashy dresses, the loud harsh foolish gabble, the insolent ogling were
> an outrage.[15]

After twenty-one years, Crowley's 1924 diary still resonated with his
experience of the gates of hell opening, snapping the remnant of his
honeymoon dream. Crowley wrote there of "the Genuine Ecstasy of
Loathing of the Evil Mother—magically seen for the first time in my
life." According to the *Confessions:*

> The daughter wore a brooch of what may have been diamonds. It
> was about five inches across, and the design was a coronet and the
> name Mabel. I have never seen anything in such abominable taste,
> and anyhow I wouldn't call a trained flea Mabel, if I respected it.
>
> The intensity of my repulsion makes me suspect that I wanted
> to make love to her and was annoyed that I was already in love.
> The gospels do not tell us whether the man who possessed the
> pearl of great price ever had moments of regret at having given
> up imitation jewellery. One always subconsciously connects noto-
> riously vile women who flaunt their heartless and sexless seduc-
> tion with the possibility of some supremely perverse pleasure in
> nastiness. However, my surface reaction was to shake the dust of
> Colombo from my feet and to spend my two days in Kandy in
> writing *Why Jesus Wept.*[16]

Dedicated to Christ, Lady Scott, Crowley's "friends" Prince
Jinawaravasa, his unborn child, and Mr. G. K. Chesterton, *Why Jesus
Wept*'s title alludes directly to Lady Scott and Countess Russell. One
look at them, and Jesus would have wept for everything he cared
for. Hypersensitized by Rose's beauty, the jungle, "plus the solitude,"
Crowley fled to Kandy to get the full horror of Lady Scott down into
a play. Kandy: the place where once he had experienced peace and illumination with Allan, now served as locus for a war cry against a society
of hypocrites. The play's "Minor Dedication" addressed "Tina" Scott as

My dear Lady S—

I quite agree with your expressed opinion that no true gentleman would (with or without reason) compare any portion of your ladyship's anatomy to a piece of wet chamois leather; the best I can do to repair his rudeness is to acknowledge the notable part your ladyship played in the conception of this masterpiece by the insertion of as much of your name as my lawyers will permit me.[17]

Crowley's idea for the play was to show a romantic boy and girl ambushed and ruined by male and female vampires: an allegory of society's corrupting influence. Its final passage offers its moral:

> I much prefer—that is, mere I—
> Solitude to society.
> And that is why I sit and spoil
> So much clean paper with such toil
> By Kandy Lake in far Ceylon.
> I have my old pyjamas on:
> I shake my soles from Britain's dust;
> I shall not go there till I must;
> And when I must!—I hold my nose.
> Farewell, you filthy-minded people!
> I know a stable from a steeple.
> Farewell, my decent-minded friends!
> I know arc lights from candle-ends.
> Farewell—a poet begs your alms,
> Will walk awhile among the palms,
> An honest love, a loyal kiss,
> Can show him better worlds than this;
> Nor will he come again to yours
> While he knows champak-stars from sewers.

Addressed to G. K. Chesterton—who had in 1901 expressed hope in the poet who sent him his *The Soul of Osiris*—*Why Jesus Wept*'s "Dedication Extraordinary" vented a volcano's worth of outraged energy, precipitated by an incendiary cocktail of acute social vision, broken bliss, and the nagging lesion of the tongue:

Arm! Arm, and out; for the young warrior of a new religion is upon thee; and his number is the number of a man.[18]

Crowley's name was then written in Hebrew, computed by gematria to 666.

Now we come to the crunch. *Why Jesus Wept* was the immediate literary predecessor to *The Book of the Law:* a declaration of war and license to live for Aleister Crowley and free men and women everywhere.

Young warrior of a new religion . . .

A new religion requires a fresh revelation, and Crowley was about to experience one in circumstances that combined the domestic-prosaic with the out of this world. To the end of his life, Crowley claimed he heard the voice of a more-than-human intelligence, for an hour a day on April 8, 9, and 10, 1904, in a Cairo apartment. The name of the intelligence, Rose announced, was "Aiwass," minister of the child Horus, the spiritual energy of the sun: force and fire; the "eye of God" at our solar system's center.

That experience was imminent, but at the end of January 1904, even though Rose was now convinced she was pregnant, Crowley still desired to visit Allan in Rangoon, but could not. Crowley does not explain precisely the details in his *Confessions,* but points out that when the gods want something, a strange compulsion prohibits doing what one might want personally. There was no way he could go to Rangoon. The couple left Colombo on January 28.

A damp winter in Scotland being too sullen a prospect, they returned to Cairo. During the ten days passage to to Suez, the couple cooked up a little fancy-dress game to add a bit of spice to their triumphal entry to Egypt's capital—at least that is how it looks on first acquaintance. He summarized the imposture in an article for a 1930s newspaper:

We landed at Port Said on February 8th. . . . It was part of the plan of the gods that my romantic passion and pride, the intoxicated infatuation of my hymeneal happiness, should have induced me to play a puerile part on the world's stage. . . . Now, however, for reasons that did not deceive myself, I proposed to pass myself off in Egypt for a Persian prince with a beautiful English wife!

I had never lost sight of the fact that I was in some sense or other the Beast 666. My poor mother, indeed, believed that I was actually the Anti-Christ of the Apocalypse and also her poor lost erring son who might yet repent and be redeemed by the precious blood. So I called myself Chioa Khan, being the Hebrew for the Beast, and my wife I named Ouarda, one of the many Arabic words for Rose.[19]

On February 9, Lord Beast and Lady Ouarda entered Cairo. In his *Confessions,* written years later, Crowley confessed that while it was all a great ruse to see how servile people could be when presented with an image of authority, the real joy lay in being whisked about the streets in a carriage with runners clearing the way while the sun-spangled jewels of their garments caused all to gaze in wonder. In other words, it was fantasy role playing—another way of becoming invisible!

There are aspects to the joyous pretense other than revealing the paradoxical character of himself and his richly ironic philosophy. If Nothing underlay the universe, then "What Ho!" couldst thou not "Do what thou wilt"? One was, after all, an aristocrat of life—an emperor of Nothing. In doing so, Crowley was challenging the lineaments of his time. He was "breaking time," cracking the inevitability of behavior: being (or trying to get) . . . free.

Apparently, what was trying to "get out" of Crowley was foreshadowed in his own chosen image, the "Lord Beast," an image of divine and earthly potency, an image of Horus, savage god—who is also a joke on the world. Crowley mocks the world and mocks himself; he has, as a Buddhist, wished himself a "swift termination of existence" and been granted a new, temporary identity. One must recall the profound abjection he was experiencing before Rose's appearance on the scene. Crowley's desire to "emancipate" her was just as much a projection of his own predicament; she had the power to emancipate him; he needed it. Did she know it?

This account of Crowley and India is not the place for details concerning the mysterious, momentous events that took place in Cairo, Egypt, that spring. Many readers will be acquainted with the salient import of Crowley's reception of *The Book of the Law.* The point I should wish to

---

*See my *Aleister Crowley: The Biography* for a detailed analysis of the evidence.

make here is that in his February 1924 diary, written at the Hôtel Blois, 50, rue Vavin, Paris, while suffering heroin withdrawal and a partial breakdown, assailed by daydreams so intense he wondered if he was not hallucinating, lost memories of *Ceylon* washed onto the shore of Crowley's consciousness:

> All these dialogues [he was experiencing in his mind] so vivid as to be practically audible: and I am reminded of writing down AL [*The Book of the Law*]. But at that time there were no circumstances soever at all likely to account for any hallucinations. Save this! Rose and I had on our programme, high up, a visit to Frater I.A. [Bennett] in his Kyoung at Rangoon (or Akyab—I had not seen him since he had formally joined the Sangha). Returned to Colombo from Hambantota January 1904: I got a lesion on my tongue—origin unknown—and a vision of Lady Scott & Countess Russell at the Galle Face Hotel.

According to this, Crowley's 1924 diary, it was the lesion on the tongue contracted in Ceylon that somehow affected his "sensorium," the brain's sensory apparatus:

> My idea was (in writing this note) that the poison which had attacked my tongue also attacked (later) my sensorium, thus causing hallucinations, similar to those of tonight, in March–April '04.
>
> [side note] This does no more than suggest the mechanism of hearing Aiwass. But then that point has always irked me, I being so free naturally from anything . . . of the kind.[20]

He meant he was not the sort of gullible type to "hear voices" and was highly skeptical of those who did. The effect on his brain's nerve centers sufficed to render Aiwass's voice audible to his physical ear. Crowley denied the *communication itself* was hallucinatory: *The Book of the Law*'s internally intelligible existence being its own proof; he heard, he wrote. It was not, he insisted, "automatic writing." The source was, as far as he was concerned, independent of himself. However, he is obviously suggesting that the means to hear the communication may likely have required some peculiar derangement of normal sensory function, caused, he surmised by the tongue lesion contracted in Hambantota.

Whatever may have been the objective case as to the phenomenon he described, it clearly had aspects of its seed in his experience of India, not only as regards *The Book of the Law*'s continuity of the spirit of revolt against existing norms of religion and behavior trumpeted in *Why Jesus Wept*, composed in Kandy, and *The Book of the Law*'s apparent provision as a text for the "new religion" the "young warrior" determined to promulgate against a rotten world, but also as a condensation, even explosion, of a deep-down resistance to the premises of a Buddhism he was otherwise consciously embracing as a cure for the world's ills: the "speedy termination of existence"!

More striking contemporary evidence underlines this important point. We had reason earlier to note how Crowley's 1903 meditation work at Boleskine was interrupted by Gerald Kelly's arrival in Scotland, and Crowley's subsequent marriage to Rose Kelly. Crowley's explanation for that interruption came from a summary of recent events made in his diary on February 22, 1904, when Crowley, dressed as "Oriental Despot" Chioa Khan was playing golf at Helwan, today part of Greater Cairo.

> We started for China via Burma. Arrived in Ceylon, the astral obstacles to a visit to Ananda Maitriya [Sanskrit for the Pāli Metteyya.] increased—became insuperable. In the Great Pyramid on Nov[ember]. 22 [1903] I performed a magical ceremony with remarkable results, the King's Chamber being filled with the glory of IAΩ [Greek: a Gnostic abbreviation for the Tetragrammaton, or Name of God]; and in the morning a practical work with Amoun result in my wife becoming pregnant. This, on the one hand: my own misfortunes on the other; drove us back disguised to Egypt.*
> I am here as Prince Chioa Khan, an ingenious and vastly amusing avatar; and more sceptical than ever. For, to say the truth, the follies of Buddhism, as represented by Allan [Bennett] and the "literary" school [I think Crowley means the Pāli Canon of Theravāda Buddhism], and the bestialities of Buddhism, as represented by the life of the people of Ceylon, have finished by disgusting me beyond all measure. I can no longer fight whole-heartedly for Gautama; I

---

*One may ask: What misfortunes? Why "disguised"?

am about to suck the Cosmic Egg of the camel-thief of Mecca;* but convinced in myself that to no great man can it ever be possible to work in any existing system. If he has followers, so much the worse for them.[21]

It is especially interesting in our context that the same section of the diary records conclusions from conversation enjoyed by Crowley on board ship from Colombo to Suez, when by remarkable chance he and Rose happened to share the voyage with Dr. Henry Maudsley (1835–1918), famed alienist and founder (1904) of the London psychiatric hospital that bears his name; in fact, Britain's leading brain specialist. Crowley had accepted that magical experiences might be expressed simply as neurological events, and that certain magical ceremonies stimulated specific neurological capacities. Such events could be further stimulated by use of drugs, which suggested neurological causes. He wanted Dr. Maudsley's views on whether yogic practices might also consist in alterations of brain chemistry (and might therefore be hazardous), and whether they could be achieved with chemical stimulants, without exhausting physical disciplines:

> Dr. Maudsley, the greatest of living authorities on the brain, explained to me the physiological aspect of dhyana (unity of subject and object) as extreme activity of one part of the brain; extreme lassitude of the rest. He refused to localize the part. Indulgence in the practice he regards as dangerous, but declined to call the single experience pathological. This is perhaps to be regarded as a complete victory for me; since I would always admit so much. No doubt the

---

*Old accounts of Muhammad include stories of how, when ejected from Mecca by the Quraish, he sent his men to attack Meccan caravans of hostile "polytheists." According to an early nineteenth-century edition of the French *Encyclopédie Larousse:* "Muhammad remained in his moral corruption and debauchery a camel thief, a cardinal who failed to reach the throne of the papacy and win it for himself. He therefore invented a new religion with which to avenge himself against his colleagues." This quotation is cited in *The Life of Muhammad,* by Muḥammad Ḥusayn Haykal, preface, xxxvii, when dealing with Christian scholarship's past historical attitudes to Muhammad. An admirer of Islam, Crowley praised it on many occasions throughout his life. When in Cairo, he started learning Arabic, the Qur'an, Arabic Qabalah, and skills known to the Sufi Sidi Aissawa, and contemplated a journey to Mecca in imitation of his hero, Sir Richard Burton.

over-fatigue is indicated as the danger; but has not Eckenstein—who again shines!—too often urged this very danger? After fatigue, said he, rest altogether for 24 hours. Well! And I doubt not that follies of so many enthusiasts, the terrible warnings of Blavatsky and others, are explained (the one) and justified (the other) by this circumstance. Let me therefore warily proceed! (not merely—proceed warily!).[22]

Crowley proceeded, and what he may not have realized at the time—or maybe he did—was that his sensory apparatus was already being affected by a stimulant: poison from the tongue lesion, which, apparently, was about to permit extraordinary access to dimensions of expression hitherto beyond his experience, an experience that he would later confess generated the sole event that made his life worthwhile, having experienced, he believed, communication with intelligence independent of sinew and nerve, inaccessible to ordinary consciousness. If we accept his testimony, we may say from this moment, that the seed was sown that would flower in Crowley's developed view that mysticism took the mind to levels where "magick" of a high order became possible, and this was the core of why yogic practices remained central to his practical and theoretical system.

Crowley's Buddhism didn't die all at once with the Cairo revelation's denial of Buddhism's cherished premises. Indeed, he apparently contrived to mislay the manuscript of *The Book of the Law* in Boleskine's attic, and engaged in family life, an unaccustomed domesticity disturbed only by a magical attack allegedly launched against his estate by an irate Mathers, angry at Crowley's having renounced loyalty to him. In summer 1904, Crowley did some precautionary magical work "with Beelzebub" and demon servitors to counterattack, and to protect his nearest and dearest—even so, Crowley was convinced black magic emanating from Mathers in Paris was responsible for the sudden deaths of his pack of hunting dogs, and other outrages, including an apparently unprovoked attack on his wife by a builder renovating the estate.

Other than that, things seemed contented enough! For this was no ordinary estate. Crowley and Rose now had a new daughter, Lilith, born on July 28, 1904. While occasional squealing would send Crowley out rabbit shooting, such occasions provided welcome respite from the laborious task of book publishing. *The Sword of Song (Called by Christians the Book of the Beast)*—a digest of Indian experiences in prose and poetry—went for review in the second week of August 1904. It was listed in the "books received" column of Ananda Metteya's impressive *Buddhism* periodical, published in Rangoon. As we shall now see, "Sword"—as Rose called it—reveals in no small measure the depth of perception Crowley brought to bear on his experience of India.

BOOKS RECEIVED.

WE BEG TO ACKNOWLEDGE, with many thanks, the receipt of the following works, since March, 1904 :—

BOOKS IN EUROPEAN LANGUAGES.—The Sword of Song, by Aleister Crowley, from the Author ; The Hearts of Men, by H. Fielding, from the Author: Precis de Grammaire pâlie, par Victor Henry (Bibliotheque de l'Ecole francaise d'Extreme-Orient, Tome II) from the Publishers. *These works will be reviewed in future issues of Buddhism.* The Legends and Miracles of Buddha Sakya Sinha, by Nobin Chandra Das, M. A., from the Author ; Primavera d'Idee, Arnaldo Cervesato, from the Author ; The Law of Evolution, by J. Scouller, from the Author.

PERIODICALS. The Journal of the Royal Asiatic Society; The Hibbert Journal; The Open Court ; The Buddhist ; The Mahâ-bodhi Journal ; The Light of Dharma ; The Light of Reason ; The Theosophist ; The Theosophical Review ; Theosophy in Australasia ; The New Zealand Theosophical Magazine ; The Malabar Quarterly ; Industrial India ; The Interpreter ; Bulletin de l'Ecole francaise d'Extreme-Orient ; Neue Metaphysische Rundschau ; Ost-Asien ; La Nuova Parola ;— all current numbers between above-mentioned dates.

Also, The Whim, for January 1904 ; The Monist, for July 1904 and the Journal of the Buddhist Text Society, for September 1904.

Fig. 10.4. The Sword of Song *listed in "Books Received" column in* Buddhism, *Allan Bennett's periodical published in Rangoon, Burma, in 1904.*

ELEVEN

The Works: 1901–1904

And the history of our Science is the history of all Science. If you choose to ape Christendom and put the *pioneers of rational investigation into the nature of consciousness* on the rack (i.e. into lunatic asylums) I doubt not we shall find our Bruno.* But it will add an additional pang that persecution should come from the house of our friends.[1] (my italics)

A recent reissue of the Beatles' album *Sgt. Pepper's Lonely Hearts Club Band* included a booklet describing the personalities depicted on the celebrated album cover. Aleister Crowley is there described as one who "dabbled in black magic." A cursory inspection of volume 2 of Crowley's *Collected Works* (1906) should arrest even the meanest intelligence by the depth of its learning, mastery of subject, concern for science, and serious artistic and intellectual ambition. Neither "dabbling" nor "black magic" may anywhere be discerned, though the publisher's name might guide us: "Foyers, The Society for the Propagation of Religious Truth." It would be better to describe Crowley as "a propagator"—or at least scientific investigator—"of religious truth."

In India, Crowley lived, lived fully, and as he lived, he wrote. The poems, plays, and essays that poured from sweaty palm and pen in that

---

*"Bruno" refers to Giordano Bruno (1548–1600), Dominican monk and natural philosopher, burnt in Rome in 1600 as an "impenitent heretic," having insisted on heliocentrcity and on the universe's infinitude, while attempting a "return" of the Church Catholic to Hermetic solar-Egyptianism. Bruno would probably have understood Crowley.

period have received scant critical and biographical attention: a pity, since much of Crowley's mature position stems from consideration of his Indian experiences, years formative of his mind and flowering persona. In future years, he would take for granted that readers or hearers of his word were familiar with the depth of what he had himself assimilated long before. Crowley built the empire of his mind on sure foundations, and ignorance of those foundations renders much of his later perspectives on subjects magical, metaphysical, and scientific, vulnerable to serious misunderstanding.

It is not difficult to see why past writers have eschewed Crowley's early works. Prose essays, for example, despite characteristic good humoredness and occasional bathos, are yet written in a self-consciously university style, as if to goad the dons of Trinity, but then, Crowley was aware that he was, in contributing expositions poetic and prosaic on subjects as apparently diverse as Brahmin philosophy (Advaita and Dvaita), Buddhism, Christianity, psychology, physiology, formal logic, and scientific method, assuming ingress to superior dens of academic thought. Mentally equipped for the task, determined to impress, he may appear a bit fresh. Ambitious to build a reputation, if not a career, he is as keen to be noticed as to entertain. Here, he tells us, is a new, indeed leading, voice. Beneath the scholarly pundit's upholstery, however, beats the heart of a prophet with a message (his reference in the quotation above to Giordano Bruno is telling), mediated unto a number of entrenched scientific attitudes inherited from a century of materialist rationalism. Crowley approaches them with fire of poetic passion and cool steel of analytic scalpel. In a tradition illuminated by Erasmus Darwin (1731–1802) and Samuel Taylor Coleridge (1772–1834), Crowley viewed it as a flourish of a gentleman's intellectual genius to handle intricate philosophical paradoxes, scientific propositions, and metaphysical conundra through a medium of cleverly contrived verse. We are in the presence of an anticonformist classicist.

Not all is intellectual play, however. The first poem stemming from his Indian experience to appear in his collection of early poems, *Oracles, the Autobiography of an Art* (1905), is one of devotional rapture, written at the house of Sri Parānanda Swami, shortly after Crowley's arrival in Ceylon in 1901. A footnote informs us: "The manuscript of this Hymn most mysteriously (for I am very careful) disappeared two days after being written. I can remember no more of it than the above; nor will inspiration return."[2]

Surviving fragments of "The Dance of Shiva" begin thus:

> With feet set terribly dancing,
>   With eyelids filled of flame,
> Wild lightnings from Him glancing,
>   Lord Shiva went and came.
> The dancing of his feet was heard
> And was the final word.

"Sonnet for a Picture" was written "in the woods above Kandy" and inscribed to one T. Davidson. The setting appears to be a Ceylonese brothel, and the sardonic "picture" illustrating the sonnet would consist of a man in sudden shock of realization, having been "Lured by the loud big-breasted courtesan" to a dirty prostitute's bed where it appears two sluts have attempted to satisfy him. Alas, for the victim, the poem concludes: "This night thy soul shall be required of thee!"—a dreadful premonition, quite likely, of syphilis![3]

"The House: A Nightmare" was composed amid Anurādhapura's ruins (see page 86), and its horror story based on one of the regular dreams of "Allan Bennett Macgregor" wherein the dreamer finds himself expecting a much loved friend, long since parted, to come to the door, only to realize with a shock that he is stuck in a house from which he had once fled, remote on marshy moor in depth of night: the house of his deadliest enemy. At last:

> Now—in the central core
> Of my own room what accent of keen hate,
> Triumphant malice, mockery satiate,
>   Rings in the voice above the storm's wild roar?
>   It cries "Open the door! Open the door!"[4]

Some thirty-one miles southeast of Anurādhapura stands the extraordinary rock outcrop some 660 feet high called Sigiraya, or "Lion Rock." Crowley was "under" the great serrated, ruddy rock of Sigiraya when he began his poem *Anima Lunae* ("Soul of the Moon"), to be completed near Aden en route for Cairo in late 1902. Little, if anything, of Sigiraya seems to enter Crowley's poem of vexed renunciation, save perhaps the setting of an ancient palace. Crowley sets his rumination on life's futility and Nature's yoke of fate in some "oriental" fastness, perhaps Persia, Afghanistan, or within India's Mughal Empire where a king, Zōhra by name, finds satisfaction neither in thought, love, nor flesh, but longs instead for a cessation final and absolute (nibbana). Perhaps Crowley was inspired by the sight of more ruins, and their vanishing beneath the branches of Nature's incessant creeping, obscuring the pride of the past, leaving only Nature behind, immovable (the rock). Nature is fatal to man's presumptions, pride, and vain desires. Whither ambition? In the poem, death comes in the form of a beautiful girl, whose kiss, like lunar dew, is final and carries the poem's subject with her from life as we know it to a state that is "Not heaven and not hell" but Nature triumphant: "no longer mother, but a bride! Ay! There is none beside." The ashes of his life are the remnants of the poem that "brothers" in future might breathe life into, enliven "embers dull / Of these poor rhymes and leave them beautiful."

Graceful logic ensures the next poem in *Oracles* is titled from the Buddhist's first noble truth: *Sabbé Pi Dukkham* ("Everything Is Sorrow"). Written in Lamma Sayadaw Kyoung, Akyab, in February 1902, Crowley had discovered Bhikkhu Bennett, after the abandoned attempt to approach his friend via the jungles and hills of central Burma. Crowley decides in the poem to join the Greek myth of Pentheus, made famous in Euripides's play *The Bacchae,* to Buddhist doctrine. According to blind seer Tiresias, *Pentheus* means the "man of sorrows." Pentheus's sorrow comes from his grandfather the king of Thebes's abdicating in his favor, a move followed by Pentheus's outlawing worship of Dionysus. Dionysus, taken as a worshipper, is imprisoned, but easily breaks his bonds and lures Pentheus, dressed as a woman, to Bacchic rites, expecting to witness sexual scenes. Instead, his mother Agave and his aunts set upon him, mistaking Pentheus for a wild animal. Mother Agave assists in tearing her son asunder. In Crowley's poem, Pentheus is guilty of a blasphemy that has deluded him. He is "caught already in the meshes / Of the fate that means to catch and crush him." The "maddened mother" Agave is described as "Nature's self" and effects the consummation that is in the poem clearly equated with the process of dissolution of subject and object implicit in the trance dhyāna:

> So the wise, enlightened by compassion,
> Seeks that bliss for all the world of sorrow,
> Swears the bitter oath of Vajrapani:*
> "Ere the cycle rush to utter darkness
> Work I so that every living being
> Pass beyond this constant chain of causes.
> If I fail may all my being shatter
> Into millions of far-whirling pieces!"

The aim is cessation.

> All hath past beyond the soul's delusion.
> All hath changed to the ever changeless.
> Name and form in nameless and in formless
> Vanish, vanish and are lost for ever.[5]

Crowley has an elusive nirvana on, and beyond, his mind.

THE ARGONAUTS

Crowley's underlying quest for an elusive, compelling spiritual goal may have influenced his decision to turn the classical search of Jason and the Argonauts for the fabled Golden Fleece into a play. According to chapter 26 of his *Confessions,* the idea emerged as part of an attempt to celebrate in lyrical verse "everything in the world in detail." This spectacular overambition would eventually manifest as the enormous *Orpheus,* into which Crowley originally intended to insert his five-act play as but an incident in Orpheus's wooing of Eurydice! Crowley jocularly surmised in retrospect that the conception's grandiosity resulted from visiting San Francisco in April 1901, where American "vanity and vulgarity" directed at the "big" stimulated a like passion in himself for straining the limits of the possible. Jason enjoyed attractive attributes other than lust for

---

*Protector of the Buddha and early bodhisattva.

adventure directed at the Golden Fleece's miraculous powers. Jason was also husband to jealous sorceress Medea, and great-grandson to messenger god, Hermes: like Crowley, Jason's destiny was wrapped in magic.

Published separately as a play by his Society for the Propagation of Religious Truth in 1904, Crowley worked on *The Argonauts* during a week's break from meditative exercises in Ceylon in August 1901, continuing at Akyab, Burma, where "Sabbé Pi Dukkham" was composed in February 1902. The play became a kind of analogue to Crowley's journeyings of 1900 to 1904, Orpheus's songs in act 4 drawing descriptive material from observations of the harbor at Vera Cruz (the "Colchian harbor-song"),* the breakers on Waikiki Beach, near Honolulu,† and Hong Kong's harbor entrance,‡ while each of the five acts was autobiographically prefaced by extraordinary dedications included in the original publication, though mysteriously omitted from the play's commonly known version in *Collected Works,* vol. 2 (1906).

Crowley's dedications are curiously telling. The first act—"Jason"—is dedicated "affectionately to the author of ION." *Ion* was a play by Euripides (circa 413 BCE), whose *The Bacchae* inspired "Sabbé Pi Dukkham." *The Argonauts'* first act is also dedicated "admiringly" to Euripides specialist Dr. A. W. Verrall (Arthur Wollgar Verrall, 1851–1912), whose translation *The Ion of Euripides* was published by Cambridge University Press in 1895 when Crowley went up to Trinity College, Cambridge, where the play was performed.

Ion concerns orphan Ion, whose mother Creusa, seduced by the god Apollo, abandoned Ion (like Moses) in a basket. Ion grows to be a temple attendant at Delphi, grace of Hermes's providence. The arrival of Creusa and husband Xuthus in Delphi for oracular guidance as to whether they might yet produce an heir initiates a series of events ultimately leading to Ion's reunion with his mother—who thus comes to worship Apollo—while Ion himself becomes ruler of Athens. Goddess Athena appears at the dénouement to reassure humankind that the gods may be slow to act, but in the end, their strength is manifest: a favorite theme of the mature Crowley.

Collected Works 2:106 (1906).
†*Collected Works* 2:105 (1906).
‡*Collected Works* 2:111 (1906).

Translator Verrall was one of Crowley's tutors at Trinity. Appointed Fellow in 1874, Verrall encouraged Crowley's respect for the Greek and Latin classics, reflected in his choice of poetic and theatrical subject matter, and in later visions of former incarnations.

Verrall was a member of the highly secretive, and exclusive, Cambridge fraternal society "The Apostles," and his *Euripides, the Rationalist* appeared in Cambridge in 1895, and may still reward study by persons concerned with Crowley's intellectual development. Interestingly, Crowley's tutor's strong interest in psychic research was shared with his wife, Margaret, herself a classics lecturer at Newnham College. Margaret Verrall—a medium—belonged to a Cambridge group investigating "spiritualism" and automatic writing. Daughter Helen was also a medium, and would marry William Henry Salter, who became president of the Society for Psychical Research the year Crowley died.

The Argonauts' first act was also dedicated to the Rev. F. F. Kelly "on the occasion of my voyage of 1904." Frederic Festus Kelly (1838–1918), father of Crowley's close friend, Gerald Festus Kelly (1879–1972), and of Crowley's wife, Rose Edith Kelly (1874–1932), was vicar of Camberwell. The "voyage" dated to 1904 may refer to the couple's entire honeymoon (or marriage)—perhaps blessed by Camberwell's vicar—beginning in November 1903 in Paris, Marseilles, Naples, Cairo, and, from December, Ceylon, or more specifically, to the voyage from Colombo on January 28, 1904, to Port Said, Egypt (February 8, 1904), whose ensuing sojourn saw reception of *The Book of the Law,* before the couple returned to Britain in early summer, 1904.

The second act "Argo" (after the vessel in which the Argonauts sailed to Colchis) is dedicated, perhaps strangely, first to "the Hon. P. Ramanathan," Bennett's tutor in Ceylon, and then to British poet and storyteller Rudyard Kipling (1865–1935) "on the occasion of Sunrise." Famed for his books set in the British Raj, Kipling—who was born in Bombay—included a "Morning Song in the Jungle" in the tale "Letting in the Jungle" from his *The Second Jungle Book.* First appearing in the *Pall Mall Gazette* in December 1894, we see Kipling's young hero Mowgli anxious his adoptive mother is to be condemned as a witch by charcoal burners. Coming to Mowgli's aid, sympathetic gray wolves sing a magnificent "Morning Song in the Jungle" to prevent tragedy. Crowley's reference to "Sunrise" may then represent a conflation of

Kipling's dawn song with Crowley's personal experience of the "golden dawn" of dhyāna—that came to him after prolonged meditation in Ceylon on October 1, 1901.

The third act "Medea" is cheekily dedicated "to Whomsoever and the British Army on the Occasion of reading *Man and Superman*." First published as a book in 1903 by Constable & Co. Ltd., George Bernard Shaw's play *Man and Superman* was first performed (with omissions) in 1905. Partly toying with a story more familiarly known as *Don Juan,* Shaw's play blends a Nietzschean theme of evolution toward a "superman" able to take the full burden of existence alone, with Shaw's own ideas that woman represents the "Life-Force" without which the "creative genius," proper to the male, cannot contribute to humanity's spiritual evolution. In the play, it is the *woman* who conquers, and the male Don Juan cannot resist the conquest. Crowley may have been thinking of the character of "sorceress" Medea who takes Jason by storm from the vessel of male heroes he leads. In the play, Ann Whitefield becomes the hunter of the slightly mad anarchist Tanner: her quarry, whom she will marry. One wonders if Crowley saw himself in this position when recognizing his newly married status: *who really willed the bond, and to what end?* Crowley's probably cynical reference to the British Army may imply realization that the conqueror and defender of the future would be as likely female as male, and a hope that British power may yet serve the higher cause of spiritual evolution via spiritual revolution. Needless to say, *The Book of the Law* would in the fullness of time provide textual force to Crowley's long-held instinct for female sexual emancipation.* At the play's end, Medea is triumphant, but violent consequences will ensue at some unknown time in the future, for, as Crowley understands the myth, the constellation of the Ram (Aries,) whose grove Jason has violated, becomes "golden" when the sun enters it, marking spring, and releasing "Madness," who personified becomes instrumental in the karma—or "curse"—of the drama.

The fourth act bears the title "Sirenae." Perhaps the Sirens, whom Greek legend asserted lured hapless seamen to the rocks of fate by beautiful song, are embodied in the names of those to whom Crowley

---

*Crowley would return to Shaw's work in 1915 with an extended, critical response to the equation of Jesus's message with socialism, as adumbrated in Shaw's preface to *Androcles and the Lion.*

dedicates it. Below the name of Councillor von Eckartshausen (the message of whose *Cloud upon the Sanctuary* of 1804 "lured" Crowley into the Hermetic Order of the Golden Dawn, and thereby, much dramatic stress) we find "Laura Graeme, Lucile Hill, Mary Beaton on the Occasion of Homecoming." Several layers of ironic suggestion appear to be at work here, given the ambiguous reference to "homecoming," which one might imagine referred to Jason's return, *and* that of Mr. and Mrs. Crowley to the Boleskine estate in 1904. The ladies named in the dedication were all married women with whom Crowley had enjoyed passionate liaisons between 1899 and 1901.

The fifth act—"Ares" (referring to the grove in which the ram's Golden Fleece is secreted)—is first dedicated to "Common Sense," and then to the "Qabalists, Clergymen, Peers, Alchemists, Subalterns, Sorcerers, Thieves, Necromancers, Missionaries, Lunatics, Doctors and Rosicrucians Among Whom I have Lived (Being in England) on the Occasion of My Going Away." Since *The Argonauts* was published in 1904, the "Going Away" may refer less to Crowley's developing plans to return to India to climb a suitable mountain in 1905, than to a general intention to be out of the country again as soon as possible, since the tone of the dedication suggests he finds the company of his native land a distracting Babel of deceptive promises, stupidity, superstition, and hostile opposition. Crowley takes the "Ares" of Jason's adventure as referring equally to the Greek god Ares of intemperate, passionate, and bloodthirsty war, called "Black Ares" at the start of the fifth act. Black Ares calls blind "Madness" from the deep to effect judgment.

While the version of *The Argonauts* appearing in Crowley's *Collected Works* omits the dedications, the latter publication does include a significant editor's footnote (probably by Crowley) absent from the play's first printing:

> This play, written when Crowley was studying Hindu religion, derives much of its colour and philosophical import from Patanjali, the Upanishads and Sankarakariya's commentary, Shaivite mysticism, the Bhagavata Purana, Bhagavad Gita, and Vedantist literature in general.*

Collected Works 2:86 (1906). Śaṅkarācārya—also known as Adi Shankara (among other spellings)—was a religious philosopher, who in the early eighth century CE attempted

A similar itinerary of learned Hindu sources was enunciated by Crowley in a letter written to a pupil some forty years later:

> I also studied all the varieties of Asiatic philosophy, especially with regard to the practical question of spiritual development, the Sufi doctrines, the *Upanishads*, the *Samkhya*, *Veda* and *Vedanta*, the *Bhagavad-gita* and *Puraṇas*, the *Dhammapada*, and many other classics, together with numerous writings on the tantra and Yoga of such men as Patanjali, Vivekananda, etc. etc.*

Careful reading of *The Argonauts* bears out Crowley's account in his *Confessions* (chapter 33) that the work "introduced a number of Hindu ideas, both about Magick and about philosophy." In a footnote to the *Collected Works* version of the play,† Crowley confesses to eschewing the myth's astrological implications‡ in favor of a maturer treatment influenced by Indian thought. This is most apparent in Jason and his comrades' mind-struggle with sirens Parthenope, Ligia, and Leucosia's

---

(*cont. from p. 215*) a far-reaching "summa" of Hindu thought centered in the Vedanta Advaita traditions. Probably largely composed between the eighth and tenth centuries (CE), the Bhagavata Purana—a purana is a history—incorporates both Advaita and Dvaita traditions among many educative sources to expound a philosophy where *bhakti* or correct devotional attendance to Krishna will lead to liberation. It is a text dear to Vaishnavites. For Crowley's use of Patañjali's yoga sūtras, see pages 52, 63, 390–91, 411, and 418.

Magick without Tears (Hampton, N.J.: Thelema Publishing Company, 1954), 157. This being Karl Germer's edition of the Crowley letter transcripts, William Breeze has suggested to the author that the text may be corrupted partly due to possible misreading of Crowley's original letters. For example, reference to "the *Samkhya, Veda*" above may not have originally referred to the *Sāṃkhya* school of rationalist, enumerative philosophical interpretation of the Vedas and Upanishads—dedicated to freeing the mind from multifarious errors of thought—but may represent a corruption of "Śaṅkarācārya," whose name appeared intact in the *Collected Works* footnote regarding *The Argonauts*. The isolated singular "Veda" after *Sāṃkhya* does not seem to hang right in context.

†*Collected Works* 2:90 (1906).

‡Crowley recognized a link between the serpentine dragon guarding the fleece, and Scorpio. Tradition holds Mars rules constellations Aries and Scorpio, while opposite signs, Libra and Taurus, are ruled by Venus.

intensely erotic, dreamy, lyrical songs in Act 4. As Jason is heavily attracted by siren calls for eternal, sleepy, sensual balm of lust and love, Medea calls on Orpheus to raise his voice and golden lyre to counter-attack the Sirens' proffered delights.

While on one level the juxtaposition of competing voices may be seen as a joke of Crowley's that he was himself most impervious to tempting calls of lovers' siren needs when a persistent traveler (!), none-theless, with that wisdom went the caveat that what would save him (and humanity) was to attend to a higher song than that offered by the ordinary, material world of home and hearth, however attractive these comforts might appear. Such doubtful consolation is powerfully and dramatically revealed as the Sirens' ultimately illusory, false promises. Beneath this realization is the philosophy of material illusion favored by sages Crowley regarded as guides.

In the third act, Medea opines: "Love is itself enchantment!" and quickly replies to Chorus's reflection that: "Some kind god whispers from this a little light of hope," with the emphatic retort: "Only the hope-less are the happy ones." A footnote in the *Collected Works* (page 100) gives the intended sense: "'The hopeless are happy like the girl Pingala' (Buddhist Proverb). Pingala waited for her lover, and mourned because he came not. But, giving up hope at last, she regained her cheerfulness. Cf. 2 Samuel XII, 15–23." One thinks of the conclusion to Crowley's affair with Mary Beaton in his poem *Alice: An Adultery* (1903): "Thank God I've finished with that foolishness!" Here is the Crowley for whom the sole ground for attachment is love, and the sole motivator, a will higher than love alone.

Siren Parthenope has a perverse answer to the unstable quality of earthly life:

> O mortal, tossed on life's unceasing ocean,
>   Whose waves of joy and sorrow never cease,
> Eternal change—one changeless thing, commotion!
>   Even in death no hint of calm and peace!—
> Here is the charm, the life-assuaging potion
>   Here is a better home for thee than Greece!
> Come, love, to my deep, soft, sleepy breast!
>   Here is thy rest!

But Orpheus has a counterargument to the Buddhistic lulling of Parthenope, such as to stir the heart of the Greek heroes:

> Why take one pleasure, put aside
>   The myriad bliss of life diverse?
> Unchanging joy will soon divide
>   Into the likeness of a curse.
> Have we no maidens, slender, strong,
> Daughters of tender-throated song?

Siren Leucosia then sings an invitation to a deathless oblivion of love and release from time and care so seductive that Medea feels the men will be lost in a swoon of forgetfulness, a perfected death in life and love in death. Even Orpheus fears Jason is being punished by Madness, but Medea insists his song must be even sweeter. Inspired by the gods, Orpheus's retaliatory song appeals directly to the presence of the divine in man—"the Star":

> I rather will exalt the soul
>   Of man to loftier height,
> And kindle at a livelier coal
>   The subtler soul of Light.
> From these soft splendours of a dream
> I turn, and seek the Self supreme.
>
> This world is shadow-shapen of
>   The bitterness of pain.
> Vain are the little lamps of love!
>   The light of life is vain!
> Life, death, joy, sorrow, age and youth
> Are phantoms of a further truth.
>
> Beyond the splendour of the world,*
>   False glittering of the gold,

---

*A footnote in *Collected Works* here informs us: "The theory of these verses is that of certain esoteric schools among the Hindus."

A Serpent is in slumber curled
   In wisdom's sacred cold.
Life is the flaming of that flame.
Death is the naming of that name.

The forehead of the snake is bright
   With one immortal star,
Lighting her coils with living light
   To where the nenuphar [water lily]
Sleeps for her couch. All darkness dreams
The thing that is not, only seems.

That star upon the serpent's head
   Is called the soul of man;
That light in shadows subtly shed
   The glamour of life's plan.
The sea whereon that lotus grows
Is thought's abyss of tears and woes.

Leave Sirenusa! Even Greece
   Forget! they are not there!
By worship cometh not the Peace,
   The Silence not by prayer!
Leave the illusions, life and time
And death, and seek that star sublime—

Until the lotus and the sea
   And snake no longer are,
And single through eternity
   Exists alone the Star,
And utter Knowledge rise and cease
In that which is beyond the Peace!

Orpheus's appeal to the "Self supreme"—which is none other than
the Advaitist identity of individual ātman with Brahman—does the
trick, breaking the spell of the Sirens' appeal to the heroes' lower nature.
Crowley's appeal to "One Star in Sight" will last for the rest of his life

and become the inspirational goal of his Thelemic system to this day: an individual revelation.

On a less exalted plane perhaps comes Crowley's use of a Hindu "trick" in the play's fifth act. Medea cunningly entices Alcestis, daughter of Pelias, Iolchus's usurper king—whom Jason aims to replace—to dismember him in a magic ritual the sorceress promises will renew Pelias's youthful being. There is only one caveat: that uttering the spell "let no thought arise in any of your minds!" Crowley explained in a footnote to the passage:

> It is a common jest among the Hindus to play this trick on a pupil, i.e., to promise him magical powers on condition that during a given ceremonial that he abstains from thinking about a certain object (e.g., a horse.). He fails, because only the training of years can enable a student so to control his mind as to accomplish the feat of suppressing involuntary thought.*

Since so much of Crowley's meditative efforts were directed to the "slaying" of *thought,* accomplishing perfect stillness of mind akin to a sublimely calm lake, we need not be surprised at Crowley's import, dramatized here, that *Thought slays the King,* that is: rupture of the highest trance, or true will enacted, thwarts highest attainment; assertion of ego into consciousness destroys progress to the "Self supreme."

The relatively few who have troubled to read *The Argonauts* may well have been perplexed by the play's dénouement where "Chorus" reflects upon "Madness," let loose upon Jason's destiny by his violation of the sacred grove of Ares.

> So fearful is the wrath divine,
>   That once aroused it shall not sleep,
> Though prostrate slaves before the shrine
>   Pray, praise, do sacrifice, and weep.
> Ten generations following past
> Shall not exhaust the curse at last.

Collected Works 2:115 (1906).

This "wrath divine" Crowley clearly interprets not in the sense of Judaeo-Christian "judgment," or even Hellenistic machinery of "fate" but as enactment of *karma:* actions have consequences that reverberate beyond the rupture that caused them—a natural, ineluctable law, not a caprice or inciting of revenge. The "true will" is considered consistent with the best response to circumstances in line with the highest, or least troubled, karma possible. Insofar as consequences may extend through generations, it is poetic license to describe such consequences as a "curse."

> From father unto son it flees,
> An awful heritage of woe.
> Wives feel its cancerous prodigies
> Invade their wombs; the children know
> The inexpiable word, exhaust
> Not by a tenfold holocaust.

The "golden fleece" of earthly motivation is not worth having; it involves sacrilege, in Crowley's telling of the myth, and the sacrilege, in the economy of nature, does not go without consequence. This is directed, in mythic terms, by "wild" or "black" Ares, whose description chimes in very well with the revelation of the karma-recompensing god of *The Book of the Law,* where he appears as god of vengeance, "Ra Hoor Khuit," bringing dire consequences to those not heedful of the book's message. As this god appears at the final chapter of *The Book of the Law,* so Ares has the last word in *The Argonauts:* a mythic marriage of Eastern with Western conceptions of the heroic life:

> Hail to wild Ares! Men, rejoice
> That He can thus avenge his shrine!
> One solemn cadence of that voice
> Peal through the ages, shake the spine
> Of very Time, and plunge success
> False-winged into sure-foot distress!

❀

Hail to black Ares! Warrior, hail!*
   Thou glory of the shining sword!
What proven armour may avail
   Against the vengeance of the Lord?
Athena's favour must withdraw
Before the justice of thy law!

Hail to the Lord of glittering spears,
   The monarch of the mighty name,
The Master of ten thousand Fears
   Whose sword is as a scarlet flame!
Hail to black Ares! Wild and pale
The echo answers me: All Hail!

THE DHAMMAPADA

From the *Khudakka Nikāya,* part of the Pāli Canon of Theravāda Buddhism, Crowley extracted verses from the Buddha's sayings collected in the *Dhammapada.* According to a footnote, he attempted to "translate the noblest of the Buddhist books into the original meters. The task soon tired." Still, he managed fifty-nine verses, no mean feat, and accomplished with admirable grace, clarity, and economy of word and form. The moral aspect of Buddhist psychology is precisely drawn out in Crowley's version, as clear as plainsong.

All that we are from mind results, on mind is founded, built of mind.
   Who acts or speaks with evil thought, him doth pain follow sure and blind:†
   So the ox plants his foot and so the cart-wheel follows hard behind.[6]

---

*Compare with line 71 of the third chapter of *The Book of the Law* 3:71: "Hail! Ye twin warriors about the pillars of the world! For your time is nigh at hand." And also: "Now let it be first understood that I am a god of War and of Vengeance. I shall deal hardly with them." (*The Book of the Law* 3:3).
†*Blind*: that is by law, not deity's caprice.

Crowley's footnote is telling of a distinctive attitude to his Indian sources. He is clear that since everything we perceive takes place in the mind, then the mind is the principal object of our interest, and by gaining knowledge of it we may better control it. The aim is to maximize the mind's potential. This is Crowley's conception of "Magick," a theoretically unlimited development of intelligence. The first obstacles the yogi (one who aspires to "union") must contend with are the characteristic qualities of Nature, mediated to mind via bodily sensations. These the mind must accommodate, that is, understand, and thus master in mind to achieve liberation from Nature's fatality, which fatality, in Buddhism at least, renders ordinary human effort ultimately futile, unless that effort be directed beyond the conditions of existence, the which conditions include in Buddhism the allegedly illusory idea of an eternal self, soul, or subject.

It was perhaps through such painstaking exercises as translating the *Dhammapada* into modern English verse that led Crowley to take a distinctly dim view of the plethora of moral and ethical perorations in the numerous Hindu and Buddhist shastras and guides available to him. Crowley became convinced that ethical proscriptions began as simple practical observations on matters that distracted right attention upon the aims of meditation. For example, while a full stomach may inhibit concentration, that did not mean that certain foods or drinks were "wrong." Likewise, the footnote above, emphasizing that consequences follow actions as a "law," does not mean a god has decreed certain things as being absolutely right or wrong in the totality of possible circumstances, and therefore warrant for punishment when practiced, according to a reactionary deity's "caprice." It simply means that the processes of Nature are incessant, inexorably following a path of least resistance; a wise person observes this. The original aim of proscriptions as regards behavior were intended, Crowley believes, as simple practicality, as one would clear a breadboard before rolling dough, or secure a clean sheet of paper before making a drawing, but priestcraft, and common ignorance, elevated meditative guidelines into a means to control, ascribing virtue to conformity and willingness to be so conformed. For Crowley, the aim of initiation is knowledge of the "star," acquiring thereby spiritual freedom, while the enemy of initiation is inappropriate restraint on freedom. Passions are not "wrong" in the high moral sense, but, since they may inhibit concentration, preventing results, they should better be spent before engagement with yoga. That is how we must understand such verses as these:

> A well-thatched house is proof against the fury of
> the rain and wind.
> So passion hath no power to break into a rightly-
> ordered mind.

> The virtuous man rejoices here, hereafter doth he
> take delight,
> Both ways rejoices, both delights, as seeing that his
> work was right.

> Who little of the Law can cite, yet knows and walk
> therein aright, and shuns the snare
> Of passion, folly, hate entwined: Right Effort
> liberates the mind, he doth not care
> For this course done or that to run: surely in
> Priesthood such an one hath earned a share.[7]

Crowley's scientific, experimental—and skeptical—approach to the question is evinced in his essay "Time—A Dialogue Between a British Sceptic and an Indian Mystic," published in *Collected Works* in 1906 (probably written in 1903). The protagonists are discussing the relation of subject and object in the experience of dhyāna. The Indian Mystic explains something he's said to the Sceptic about courage, single-heartedness, and holiness. *What*, asks the Sceptic, *did he mean?*—to which the Mystic replies confidently: "That extreme virtue is a necessary condition for one who is desirous of attaining this state of bliss." The Sceptic will have none of it: "There, my friend, you generalize from three. Let me stand forth (like Ananias) and tell you that after many vain attempts while virtuous, I achieved my first great result only a week after a serious lapse from the condition of a Brahmacharyi." Astonished, the Mystic cries: "You?"—answered in a word by the Sceptic: "The result of despair." "This," says the Mystic piously, "may serve you as excuse before Shiva." The Sceptic interjects: "Quit not the scientific ground we walk on!"[8]

A footnote to the word *brahmacharya* informs us: "Chastity is probably referred to, though Brahmacharya involves many other virtues." Crowley's developed idea of "chastity" meant disciplined behavior appropriate to the operation in question—purity of intent; it did not necessarily mean, "avoid sex at all costs." In fact, Crowley was alluding to the fact that before his breakthrough trance of dhyāna in Sri Lanka, he had been driven by tense exhaustion to liven himself amid Colombo's whorehouses, a vacation from meditation that probably inspired the earlier poem "Sonnet for a Picture." In his case, the breakthrough followed a voluntary release of pent-up sexual energy. This behavior may have in itself meant nothing at all to success in meditation, but its exercise certainly contradicted the moral gloss of traditional yoga that sexual continence, suppression of lusts, was a vital virtue *in itself,* and that otherwise spiritual results would be impossible to achieve by what missionaries would simply condemn as "sin." Crowley's scientific attitude is that an act's virtue consists in its appropriateness to an aim. If the aim be true, the act is too.

Almost to illustrate this point even further about what in any particular case may constitute "right action," the next poem in *Oracles* gives us a very contrasting picture of the consequences of past actions (karma), resulting inevitably in what is apparently justifiable violence and killing, though with how much conviction the passion is intended to be promulgated, remains a testing question.

"St Patrick's Day, 1902," written at Delhi on March 17 of that year, while waiting for the arrival of his K2 expedition team, is a no-holds-barred hymn to freedom in Ireland (at the time a possession of the British Crown).

> Our weapons—be they fire and cord,
> The shell, the rifle, and the sword!
> Without a helper or a friend
> All means be righteous to the End!

The chorus is even more direct:

> Death to the Saxon! Slay nor spare!
> O God of Justice, hear us swear!

One would be right to question whether meditation alone would free Ireland—a cause dear to Crowley's imagination—but that is not the purpose of the yogic exercise. The principle, however, applies: iron will is required to crush inhibiting and distracting forces, and to restore harmony. It's little use thinking about meditating if someone is about to knock down your house, or knock off your head. Crowley was scornful of the many apparently pious Buddhist and Hindu proscriptions regarding harmlessness and killing. For Crowley, the Hindu religious principle of *ahiṃsā,* or harmlessness, was simply a practical means of generally getting by in a violent and foolish world. You are less likely to invite obstruction in your aims from a potential opponent if you present a harmless and nonreactive face to interference—no great virtue there, other than the will to maintain practicality and to ensure the will be not thwarted. Apply the principle of nonkilling to its fullest extent, however, and breathing and walking—never mind eating—become impossible, for as we now know our every breath kills or maims some aspect of living organism, and it was simply ignorance of the microscopic world that made past pundits imagine absolute "harmlessness" was physically possible, let alone desirable. Everything in Nature eats off something within the system; interfere at one's peril: there is no sentiment in Nature. As I long ago concluded: "Nature eats herself for breakfast."

Of course, interfering directly in the harmless will of another to the deliberate and possibly fatal detriment of that being may not be contrary to the law of survival, but if one does so, one simply opens oneself up to the same possibility being perpetrated on oneself. The inertia of the system overall insists actions accrue consequences, and the yogi should avoid where possible collision with consequences negative to success. Human morals in general should, according to Crowley, be a means to ensure the greatest practical freedom to those who know what they are doing, and who understand like necessities in others. Crowley is in no doubt as to what to do to ensure contrary forces do not threaten freedom; capable as he was of "loving his enemies" he was no pacifist, foreseeing the near inevitable violent overthrow of outmoded authorities.

Oracles informs us that the poem "The Earl's Quest" was written "at Camp Despair, 20,000 ft., Chogo Ri Lungma [K2], Baltistan."[9] The poem recounts a romantic quest undertaken by an idealistic earl who rides out into the howlings of dark Nature in search of something beyond early preoccupations with black magic and horror:

> The demon spiders, and the shapeless toads
> Fed by their lovers duly on the draught
> That bloats and blisters, blackens and corrodes.

He is given a weapon, blessed by a mage that will serve so long as he is "clothed in silver mail of purity, and iron-helmeted with ignorance of fear." Thus protected, he would pass through distractions of women and be immune to "fear, hatred, envy" and "self-conceit." Having reached the limits of wild forest, he comes to an inn by a seashore where he must confront past follies and be tempted with "power, knowledge, and love" via "the symbolic drink of ale and the cherry cheeks of the maid." "The Earl's Quest" is unfinished, but would, the poet informs us, had he been willing to continue, have recounted the maid's coming to him to warn him he must "destroy the three vices, faith, hope and charity. This he does easily, save the love of the figure of the Crucified; but at last conquering this, he attains."[10] The quest's ultimate end is beyond adherence to the conditions of a conventional religious ethic. One might dismiss it as an "impossible dream" but Crowley held greatness meant attempting the impossible; he must conquer himself utterly. The juxtaposition of Crowley's imagination and the physical circumstances of composition would make a poignant sequence in a movie.

"The Earl's Quest" was not the poet's sole literary endeavor while stuck on K2 amid appalling conditions. Before leaving Delhi with the expedition, Crowley began two significant essays. In both he wrestled with complexities of thought regarding what he had learned of Hindu Advaita philosophy and of Buddhism, and how what he had learned related both to science and to the theory and practice of "Magick." Work commenced March 20–21, 1902.

"Berashith"—Hebrew for the opening of Genesis, "In the beginning"—was originally entitled "Crowleymas Day" (following satirical poems "Pentecost" and "Ascension Day" begun some six months earlier) and was printed in Paris by Clarke & Bishop, 338, rue St. Honoré, to be issued privately in January 1903, after returning from the East to Paris on November 5 the previous year. As "Berashith,

An Essay in Ontology, with some Remarks on Ceremonial Magic," it would join his important essay "Science and Buddhism" in *The Sword of Song* (*Called by Christians the Book of the Beast*), published in Foyers, Scotland, August 1904. Both essays had been revised "while the weary hours of the summer (save the mark!) of 1902 rolled over Camp Misery and Camp Despair on the Chogo Ri Glacier, in those rare intervals when one's preoccupation with lice, tinned food, malaria, insoaking water, general soreness, mental misery, and the everlasting snowstorm gave place to a momentary glimmer of any higher form of intelligence than that ever necessarily concentrated on the actual business of camp life. The rest, and the final revision, occupied a good deal of my time during the winter of 1902–1903."[11]

BERASHITH

In his *Confessions*, Crowley rather suspected himself of a "swelled head" when, on the strength of his adventures in India, he arrived in Paris seeing himself as something of a "lion." Being so accepted by the "big people" of the capital's artistic world may have exacerbated his egoism: compensation, he suggests, for what was in fact his "enfeebled" spiritual state at the time.[12] The powers of Nature, and what he saw as human weakness, had thwarted his and Eckenstein's aim for K2's summit. But he had learned a lot, and presumably wanted the world to see it.

And so Crowley changed the name of "Crowleymas Day" to the portentous "theory of the universe" that is *Berashith, An Essay in Ontology*, and signed it as the work of "Abhāvānanda." This special name has its own interest. The word *abhāva* is Sanskrit for "nonexistence" or "negation," while the suffix comes from the Sanskrit ānanda, which is "bliss" or "joy." The name, or motto, thus refers to one whose joy (ānanda) is in nonexistence (abhāva). This special name rather explains why in his introduction to "The Writings of Truth" Crowley stated: "I exist not: there is no God: no time: no place" (see page 44). By analyzing the idea of creation from an *absolute* Zero, or nothingness, Crowley's essay *Berashith* daringly undertook to "eliminate the idea of infinity from our conception of the cosmos."[13]

Ontology is that branch of philosophy analyzing the nature of being and becoming, their reality or otherwise, as well as the study of the categories of being and their relations to one another. While Crowley's title might sound pretentious, his essay conforms to ontology's proper requirements; indeed he composes an original approach through comparing, in philosophical and mathematical terms, the implicit ontologies of Hinduism, Christianity, and Buddhism. His trump card turns out to be the kabbalistic "zero."

Crowley opens his essay with the statement that his attempt at adapting to ontology, in terms mathematical rather than mystical, the divergences between the "three great forms of religion now existing in the world" is the chief claim his "theory of the Universe" possesses for serious attention. He does not include "Mohammedanism" since whichever school of that faith is referred to, "it must fall under the one of the three heads of Nihilism, Advaitism, and Dvaitism."

Crowley views Nihilism as the ontological basis of Buddhism, Advaitism of Hinduism, and Dvaitism of Christianity. Advaitism, meaning "not two," means that divine being is the same whether posited for the supreme Brahman beyond creation or the individual ātman, or soul. Dvaitism supposes a difference in kind between the individual soul and absolute being or divine spirit. Nihilism Crowley regards as the ontological base and ultimate of Buddhism since Buddhism denies infinity to any individual soul, ego, or God.

Christianity, he writes, includes Man, God, and Satan and his angels as being in the category of existent, and while antagonistic, nonetheless real. Hindus see "Brahm" as infinite in all dimensions and directions, a conception identical to the Gnostics' "Pleroma," or fullness. Maya, illusion, is also existent, and Vedantist distinction between Brahm and Maya corresponds to the Western distinction of noumenon (thing in itself) and phenomenon (thing as perceived).

Crowley then looks at the "force quality" of the existences in question, and observes that if, as in Christianity, God is infinite, the other forces (Man, and Satan) can have no effect on "it." If, God is finite, then the reasons for worshipping "him" are diminished severely. "In our mechanical system, if one of the forces be infinite, the others, however great, are both relatively and absolutely nothing."[14]

He then looks at space as a hypothetical category of existing things. Space has come to be regarded as infinite. Now, either space is filled with matter, or it is not. If it is filled with matter, matter is infinite. If matter does not fill it, matter is infinitely small; its smallness persists ad infinitum. Whether the matter-universe be ten to the ten-thousand light years in diameter, Crowley insists, makes no difference. It is infinitely small, and in effect, is Nothing, its existence an "unmathematical illusion" corresponding to the Hindu "Maya." It is not "God," nor infinity, with no claim to absolute existence (this would dispense with pantheism). To reverse the proposition somewhat, and assert that the matter-universe is infinite, then "Brahm and God are crowded out, and the possibility of religion is equally excluded."[15] Crowley sees the ontological basis of Advaitism as the real reason why Hinduism cannot intelligibly account for Maya, which is seen as the cause of suffering. In Christianity, there is a reluctance to distinguish between the nature of the human soul as distinct from divine soul or spirit. Christianity would not permit the Manichaean assumption that Satan is an equally positive force in the creation to that of God, but since Man is regarded as Satan's dupe, not the source of evil, the status of *his* existence is not defined much further than he is a "created thing," but one nonetheless whose very life (according to Genesis) comes from divine spirit, or "breath."

Crowley then seizes the idea that if God *is* infinite, Christianity's ontological status of Man is effectively disproved, and so "God the Person disappears for ever, and becomes Ātman, Pleroma, Ain Soph [or "En Sof," the kabbalistic "Not End," or God as infinite, before manifestation], what name you will, infinite in all directions and in all categories." This line however has been pursued only on the basis that space is infinite, and would seem to favor the Advaitists, leaving Christianity with sufficient inconsistencies as to characterize its faith as that of a willingness to be convinced on insufficient grounds.

"What," Crowley then asks, "is the sum total of the Vedantist position?"

"'I' am an illusion, externally. In reality the true 'I' am the Infinite, and if the illusionary 'I' could only realize Who 'I' really am, how very happy we should all be!" And here we have Karma, rebirth, all the mighty laws of nature operating nowhere in nothing!

There is no room for worship or morality in the Advaitist system. All the specious pleas of the Bhagavad-Gita, and the ethical works of

Western Advaitist philosophers, are more or less consciously confusion of thought. But no subtlety can turn the practical argument; the grinning mouths of the Dvaitist guns keep the fort of Ethics, and warn metaphysics to keep off the rather green grass of religion.

That its apologists should have devoted so much time, thought, scholarship, and ingenuity to this question is the best proof of the fatuity of the Advaitist position.[16]

Crowley now reaches into his bag of Hebrew mysticism and comes out with the kabbalistic understanding whereby the origin of divine self-disclosure—and by extension all phenomena—may be expressed as from 0 (zero) to 1, as a circle opens into a line. This is consistent with Christianity where God exists before the creation. Crowley takes the "En" (Not) of "En Sof" as indicating the fundamental, untarnished conception:

I am bound to express my view that when the Qabalists said Not, they meant Not, and nothing else. In fact, I really do claim to have re-discovered the long-lost and central Arcanum of those divine philosophers.

I have no serious objection to a finite god, or gods, distinct from men and things. In fact, personally, I believe in them all, and admit them to possess inconceivable though not infinite power.[17]

One can see the appropriateness of the idea to the demands of ontology: being starts with not being. Crowley exclaims what the Buddha never dared, nor wished to promulgate as the origin of the universe of sorrow: "I ASSERT THE ABSOLUTENESS OF THE QABALISTIC ZERO." Nothingness, Crowley maintains logically, is that about which no positive proposition is valid. Zero properly indicates "absence of extension in any of the categories."

Crowley then compares the zero with the unity at the basis of Advaita, and deduces from its expression in algebraic terms that Man-in-the-world is extended into numerous categories, such as time (a), space (b), being (c), heaviness (d), and so on. He is $X + a + b + c + d$ (etc.). If man ceases to occupy space or to exist, his formula is X^0. Whatever X may represent, if raised to the power of 0 (i.e., extended in no dimension or category), the result is Unity, and the unknown factor

X eliminated. This, Crowley asserts, expresses the Advaitist conception of man's future: the personality bereft of all qualities is lost, as the impersonal Unity of Brahm arises in its place. (The same conception is to be found among Sufis with the "al fana" or passing away of the only relatively existent self in the mystical Allah, or Unity.) Also, we find the same dynamic in Christian gnosis where the pneuma ("spirit") departs from the hylē-psychē realms and returns to the pleroma: the Light of Man or "living Jesus" is a heavenly being the world cannot ultimately "hold" or contain.

Going back a step from Unity, we may posit a zero absolutely not extended in any categories, for there could have been no categories in which to extend, zero being true zero. Ordinary, or mathematical zero requires for its definition categories, otherwise one could not speak of zero not extending into categories. Crowley wants an absolute zero, with neither subjects nor predicates: 0^0. By the following equation Crowley uncovers its value:

$$0^0 = 0^{1-1} = \frac{0^1}{0^1} \quad [\text{Multiply by } 1 = \frac{n}{n}\,].$$

$$\text{Then } \frac{0^1}{n} \times \frac{n}{0^1} = 0 \times \infty.$$

From this Crowley deduces the origin of something other than nothing:

> Now the multiplying of the infinitely great by the infinitely small results in SOME UNKNOWN FINITE NUMBER EXTENDED IN AN UNKNOWN NUMBER OF CATEGORIES. It happened, when this our Great inversion took place, from the essence of all nothingness to finity extended in innumerable categories, that an incalculably vast system was produced. Merely by chance, chance in the truest sense of the term, we are found with gods, men, stars, planets, devils, colors, forces, and all the materials of the Cosmos: and with time, space, and causality, the conditions limiting and involving them all.[18]

It should, Crowley explains, not be thought that "our 0^0" existed; neither would it be true to say it did not exist. Existence was not a formulated idea.

But 0^0 is a finite expression, or has a finite phase, and our universe is a finite universe; its categories are themselves finite, and the expression "infinite space" is a contradiction in terms. The idea of an absolute and of an infinite God is relegated to the limbo of all similar idle and pernicious perversions of truth. Infinity remains, but only as a mathematical conception as impossible in nature as the square root of −1. Against all this mathematical, or semi-mathematical, reasoning, it may doubtless be objected that our whole system of numbers, and of manipulating them is merely a series of conventions. When I say that the square root of three is unreal, I know quite well that it is only so in relation to the series 1, 2, 3, &c., and that this series is equally unreal if I make $\sqrt[3]{50}$ the members of the ternary scale. But this, theoretically true, is practically absurd. If I mean "the number of a, b, and c," it does not matter if I write 3 or $\sqrt[3]{50}$ the idea is a definite one; and it is the fundamental ideas of consciousness of which we are treating, and to which we are compelled to refer everything, whether proximately or ultimately.[19]

To anyone who should ask how such a change from absolute zero came to be, Crowley insists that his explanation of the universe avoids having to explain its cause. *How did nothing come to be?*—a question requiring no answer. Absolute Nothing is not in any category, including existence, so has not come to be. "Had 0^0 been extended in causality, no change could have taken place."

Here, then, are we, finite beings in a finite universe, time, space, and causality themselves finite (inconceivable as it may seem) with our individuality, and all the "illusions" of the Advaitists, just as real as they practically are to our normal consciousness.[20]

Crowley then adumbrates numerous conclusions that may be drawn if his explanation is accepted. First, there is no a priori reason for supposing the resultant universe's inertia will permit return to the primary state, so one might still be justified in thinking free will, though if existent, finite like everything else, may assist one to find and adopt a path, with the possibility that it doesn't matter anyway, if Herbert Spencer's "First Principles" be accepted. Crowley then leaps to the interesting observation that one can now see what morals and religion are really all about; they are methods "good or bad" to extricate oneself from the universe!

Crowley sees no sign of an infinite intelligence working in the universe; all goes according to development along the least line of resistance. All laws may be generalized into one: the law of inertia, which may be identified with destiny. Free will is doubtful. Those who see infinite intelligence operating with an ethical imperative might recognize what philosophers have concluded, that all-love and all-power are not compatible, and the universe itself demonstrates this. Sorrow is an inescapable aspect of the universe. As Crowley observes, the Deist needs the Optimist for company, and all is well by the cozy fireside, "but it is a sad shipwreck they suffer on emerging into the cold world."[21] All this explains, he writes, why defenders of religion are at pains to emphasize that the universe has no real or ultimate existence. This results in the Advaitist "muddle." One might conclude in terms of Christianity that God so loved the world that he created it in order to destroy it, and bad men and women and children with it. Crowley's philosophical objection to Christian ontology is identical with his moral objection: one supports the other.

Nevertheless, Crowley recognizes the practicality of morality and religion in restraining the more violent forces in man and nature. Law and order are vital so we can investigate and bring under control the powers that imprison us, and approach the freedom we largely dream of. Mysticism is for advanced students; for the general well-being, we need, and should support, soldiers, lawyers, and "all forms of government."

Of the speculative forms of mysticism, Crowley favors the kabbalistic, and the Buddhist, which, unlike Hinduism, does not create an absolute to deny and abolish his own finitude. The Buddhist aims at extinction. "The esoteric Christian or Hindu adopts a middle path. Having projected the Absolute from his mind, he endeavors to unite his consciousness with that of his Absolute, and of course his personality is destroyed in the process." As far as thought is concerned, Buddhist nirvana is extinction, but is considered an extinction the nature of which cannot be thought, and it would be folly to define the unthinkable, so nirvana may be considered to retain an undisclosed and inexpressible virtue, though of no conceivable kind.

Crowley concludes his study by praising true meditation as the preferred means for analyzing one's being, if, that is, it is possible for the individual concerned. Crowley is in no doubt that the highest meditations involve disciplines tough indeed, and therefore not suitable in practice for all persons. For those seeking another way, he suggests that true magical ceremonial aims at much of what is aspired to in meditation: the absolute restraint of the mind for the contemplation of a single object, be it gross, fine, or altogether spiritual. In magical ceremonial, every act, word, and thought serves to focus the aspirant on the object of the ceremony. Fumigation, purification, banishing, invocation, evocation, are acts chiefly to make vivid the single purpose so that at the supreme moment, the entire being is gathered in one overwhelming "rush of the Will" directed at the object desired. The whole process is training for the mind, and once the knowledge and experience has been assimilated, the practitioner may move on to "not thinking" and thereby "destroy the Universe," which, as Bishop Berkeley maintained, only exists by virtue of the thinker's thought!

Crowley speaks from experience when he asserts that the Buddhist arahat might also usefully perform magical rituals, for true symbols really do awaken the macrocosmic forces of which the symbols are eidola, and practice increases magical potential. Crowley recognized there are magical processes that disperse or overexcite "mind-stuff" rather than control it, and these are to be discarded (I think he refers to addictions to goetic evocation or black magic). Yoga's eight limbs of morality, virtue, body-control, thought-control, force-control, concentration, meditation, and finally, rapture, prepare the mind for the understanding of the mind that annihilates its categories toward utter extinction, while anticipation of nirvana is itself adequate to bathe the aspirant in something corresponding to bliss ultimate, inconceivable. Crowley appropriately concludes *Berashith* with a regular mantra: *Aum* [sacred symbol of sound, consciousness, being] *Mani* [jewel] *Padme* [lotus flower] *Houm* [spirit of enlightenment].

If there be no infinity absolute, then truly all things must pass, in that passing that leaveth neither trace nor thing.

Twenty years later, Crowley summed up *Berashith* thus for his *Confessions:*

The twentieth and twenty-first [of March 1902] were great days in my life. I wrote an essay which I originally gave the title "Crowleymas Day" and published under the title "Berashith" in Paris by itself, incorporating it subsequently in *The Sword of Song*. The general idea is to eliminate the idea of infinity from our conception of the cosmos. It also shows the essential identity of Manichaeism (Christianity), Vedantism and Buddhism. Instead of explaining the universe as modifications of a unity, which itself needs explaining, I regard it as NOTHING, conceived as (illusory) pairs of contradictories. What we call a thought does not really exist at all by itself. It is merely half of nothing. I know that there are practical difficulties in accepting this, though it gets rid so nicely of a priori obstacles. However, the essay is packed with ideas, nearly all of which have proved extremely fertile, and it represents fairly enough the criticism of my genius upon the varied ideas which I had gathered since I first came to Asia.[22]

SCIENCE AND BUDDHISM

It is no accident that Crowley's essay "Science and Buddhism" is dedicated to Thomas Henry Huxley (1825–1895), progenitor of "Agnosticism," celebrated comparative anatomist, and famous supporter of Darwin's theories of evolution against the religious objections of Bishop Wilberforce of Oxford. Crowley draws on Huxley's Romanes Lecture "Evolution and Ethics," delivered at Oxford in 1893, a landmark in the philosophy of science less than a decade old when Crowley composed his essay in India. Picking up on Huxley's lecture references to Buddhist sutras in showing discomfiting problems of evolution for man's evolving sensibilities, Crowley's thesis goes further to state that, with incidentals removed, Buddhism itself conforms to scientific principle, rendering it a proper path of inquiry for any science concerned with mind. Buddhism is therefore, according to Crowley, as much, in its essential principles, science as it is religion, and as such compels respect.

Behind the towering arguments employed may be discerned what will be an abiding principle of Crowley's, namely, that the most ancient science was identical to the most ancient religion, and that ancient science, or quest for truth, could be distinguished by the word *Magick,* to the extent that Crowley's *Equinox* magazine series beginning in 1909 could take as its rubric: "The Method of Science. The Aim of Religion." More importantly, Crowley's conception is not simply a romantic search for a "lost science"—as if everything worth knowing had already been discovered—but a statement of commitment to science's future, with the caveat that science must bring within its purview the furthest reaches of mind, even when data passed beyond what was currently regarded as rationally intelligible. Crowley's experience of dhyāna in October 1901 was, for him, a profound challenge to the empire of reason since reason's fundamental dualism of subject and object, was apparently obliterated, and the experience's accompanying bliss absolutely real to sense. Furthermore, the experience in Kandy conformed to Huxley's requirement of Agnosticism, that one must go with reason as far as possible, and not pretend that a thing was certain until a statement was proved and proved repeatable by demonstration. Crowley had reached dhyāna by following ancient instruction; where he walked, many had walked before, and many would yet walk. As religion would need to adopt the boon of science, so science must be prepared to investigate suprarational categories of being, when such could be demonstrated. Somewhere in the back of Crowley's mind was the vision of a kind of "mega-science" to come, born from the pangs of a decaying, materialistic era, whose midwives were science and magic both.

Crowley states his aim at the outset: "to show that Buddhism, alike in theory and practice, is a scientific religion; a logical superstructure on a basis of experimentally verifiable truth; and that its method is identical with that of science."[23] Crowley is at pains to distance himself from Theosophical notions of an "Esoteric Buddhism,"* or from misinformed romantic associations of Buddhist Nirvana with Christian Heaven† or again with those who consider modern science to be the automatic friend of atheism and materialism. Crowley also insists on disregarding "incidentals" such as oriental legends and stories that have been accompaniments to essentials, to be regarded as modern theologians regard

---

*"Esoteric Buddhism" by A. P. Sinnett, 1883.
†See Sir Edwin Arnold, *The Light of Asia* (1879), or Dr. Paul Carus's *Gospel of Buddha* (1894).

ancient myths of the Hebrews in the Bible. Where pure thought is demonstrated, there are the essentials. These essentials Crowley finds in the Four Noble Truths, the Three Characteristics, and the Ten Fetters, as well as in the "definite theory" involved in "karma."

As to the Four Noble Truths, Crowley finds the first—existence is sorrow—in Huxley's "Evolution and Ethics" where Huxley states that "suffering is the badge of sentient things; that it is no accidental accompaniment, but an essential constituent of the Cosmic Process," with pain varying in relation to consciousness. Thus, the more civilized man has become, the more pain troubles him.

The Second Noble Truth—that the cause of sorrow is desire—is demonstrable insofar as desire means change, and change is the cause of pain. The fundamental desire of man is for "continued consciousness" and it is consciousness that is responsible for both desire and its concomitant unpleasantness. This leads to the Third Noble Truth, that cessation of sorrow is obtained by cessation of desire, the logical inference of the Second Truth. How such cessation is to be effected may be found via the Noble Eightfold Path.

Crowley moves on to the Buddhist's tenets of the cosmos and of man known as the Three Characteristics: change (*anikka*), sorrow (*dukkha*), and absence of an ego (*anatta*). Again, Huxley directly supports the idea that nothing is at rest in the cosmos, everything is involved in ceaseless activity and change, perceptible or not: stability through instability, so to speak, while permanence is relative to inevitable change. Hence, Huxley refers to the "Cosmic Process" whose end is not in sight, and therefore may appear, or be, purposeless.

The third characteristic is the dart the Buddha aimed at Hindu philosophy: *anatta*—no soul. There is no eternal identity, nothing of a permanent self or center of being, only finite conglomerations of what appears to be stable identity: no essence. This may be proved by asking a being what it remembers of itself and its actions: vagueness soon creeps in, characters change, the light dims. Identity is forever subject to change, and therefore sorrow and loss. This may be observed "objectively." The existence of Brahman reflected in the soul of Advaitism is then to the Buddhist no kind of hope, for the existence of a conscious ego simply exacerbates desire. Thus, Nietzsche (whom Crowley read) could talk of Buddhism as "passive nihilism." Even a post-mortem continuity, or reincarnation of a soul, or ātman, is in Buddhism merely the waning of something whose constituents must eventually dissolve to reconvene in other forms since change is the condition of everything, and losing consciousness, and the fear of it, part of sorrow's inevitable course. If, as Nietzsche opined, the "cross" (of Christianity) is a curse on life, Buddhism regards existence itself as a curse. Is not a desire for nirvana as fatal a desire as any other, one might ask? But the theory of anatta ultimately demolishes mind and leaves nothing but an illusory flux in its wake, a position not far from that of the pre-Socratics in Greece, contemporaries of the Buddha, but who spoke, as it were, from within the "flux," whereas Buddhist theory appears to speak from outside of it, insofar as it makes judgments about the process itself. Crowley, passing through the arguments in support of the Buddhist theory does not ultimately commit himself to them. He sees the theory as a probability, rather than a certainty. The approach, however, of the anatta theory is, however, scientific, being based on observing such of the phenomenon as may be observed—the latter caveat may form the basis of agnosticism with regard to the theory.

Crowley moves on to karma and handles it swiftly: "The law of causation is formally identical with this."[24] He removes all threats of heaven and hell, and reincarnation theory, and sees the doctrine as a simple observation of the inevitability in Nature of cause and effect. All actions tend to results. "We reap what we sow." Motion continues until interrupted by a counterforce. Crowley adds that the doctrine of karma is ultimately identical with determinism. Readers of Crowley's early plays and narrative poetry will note how haunted he was by the idea that free will may count in the first chain of causes but proves powerless to alter results, and that is what the ancients meant by "fate" (or Nature), and the principle makes folly of men's desire. The question would then remain whether a human being could ever initiate a first cause. Again, Crowley thinks a truly free will looks improbable, but its nonexistence may not be certain, and man has only the chance to make the best of what he has, illusory or not. Eventually, Crowley's Thelema system will identify free will with determinism: "Thou hast no right but to do thy will."

Crowley next considers the Ten Fetters or "Sanyoganas." These "fetters" are aspects of thinking and behavior that keep man in the grip of sorrow. The first is the Buddha's *petitio principii:* belief in a soul (*sakkaya-dithi*). The second—doubt (*vikikikkha*)—appears anathema to the scientist, as Crowley observes, before suggesting that what is meant is principally that the mind needs to be settled before work may commence, giving the example of a scientist testing the boiling point of a substance. He does not stop midway to worry whether the thermometer is working. If he is settled, he has tested it already. Research is based on fixed principles. The third fetter should appear obvious to the scientist: reliance on the efficacy of rites and ceremonies (*silabbata-parāmāsa*). The fourth fetter: bodily desires (kama). Crowley remarks we should not wish to combine Newton with Caligula! Hatred (*patigha*) is fifth. Concentration of mind without brooding on dislikes is essential to scientific work, though a controversy may stimulate research. Numbers six and seven—the desire for bodily and spiritual immortality (*ruparaga* and *aruparaga* respectively)—are contingent on having perceived the suffering of all forms of existence. That pride (*mano*) is the eighth fetter, requires, writes Crowley, no comment, for it and its opposite humility are likewise forms of delusion. Self-righteousness (*udhakka,* the ninth fetter) is like the former two, but on the moral plane. The great enemy, writes Crowley, is the tenth fetter: ignorance (*avigga*), which science aims to dispel. Crowley's comment is typical: "Theists alone have found the infamous audacity to extol the merits of this badge of servitude."[25] Crowley adds that scientists could doubtless add to the list, which, though perhaps not complete, is as far as it goes, accurate.

Crowley moves on to discuss "the relative reality of certain states of consciousness." He begins with an analysis of the dream state compared to the waking state and concludes the waking man is justified, on a number of grounds, for according primacy to the waking condition as being better fitted to judge the matter. Crowley then posits a state of mind that might from the standpoint of ordinary consciousness be thought of as a "dream" but that stands in the mind of the one experiencing it as infinitely more satisfying than any waking state experienced. He refers to dhyāna: "The method of attaining it is sane, healthy, and scientific." He expresses it thus: "The mind is compelled to fix its attention on a single thought; while the controlling power is exercised and a profound watchfulness kept up lest the thought should for a moment stray."[26] Crowley compares the process to an electrician experimenting with very delicate equipment, requiring acute concentration and sensitivity, but where the instruments are the will and the mind. As to the ascetic preparations for the trance, Crowley jests: "How would the electrician do his work after a Guildhall Banquet?" *How* the process works is a matter for investigation, not ridicule. He recalls a shallow wit saying his achievement could not take place in a laboratory, to which Crowley replies: "You have your own laboratory and apparatus, your mind; and if the room is dirty and the apparatus ill put together, you have certainly not me to blame for it."[27] Crowley concludes that arguments employed to deny the dhyāna state are equally and indeed more forcefully arrayed against the "normal state," and to persist therefrom would mark one as "unserious." Crowley admits that the trance might appear differently from the standpoint of one who had attained samādhi, but since he has not yet had the experience, he refrains from comment, but moves on anyway to discuss "the most famous of the Buddhist meditations," Mahasatipatthana.

Crowley informs us that Mahasatipatthana differs from Hindu methods in that it is basically an observation practice, not dependent on changes to body functions (as in prāṇāyāma) nor constrained to a single object. The simple question that begins the practice is: "What is it that is really observed?" The "catch" is that the ego-idea is resolutely removed from the beginning, in a matter that would be approved of by Herbert Spencer's *Principles of Psychology* (1855, 2:404—dealing with "Compound Quantitative Reasoning"). Behavior is recorded without the "I" factor, so that a motion of sitting down may be rendered: "There is an in-drawing of the breath" (I, me, and mine are excluded). As for walking: "there is a raising of the right foot." So it begins, but one may go on, from, say "I raise" to "There is a raising," progress with it must soon undermine Descartes's famous *Cogito ergo sum*, for the first person singular is excluded. But what is this raising? Well, there is a *sensation* (*vedana*) of raising. We then move to perception (*sañña*): there is a perception of a (pleasant or unpleasant) sensation of raising. Once this has become intuitive consciousness, one will find that emotions of pain and pleasure have vanished, having been "subincluded in the lesser skandha of Vedana; Sañña is free of them. And whoever can live in this third stage forever is in no more pain, only motivated by the kind of intense interest that enables a scientist to watch and note accurately his own death-agony.

Beyond Sañña, Sankhara and Viññanam take analysis to its ultimation: *There is a consciousness of a tendency to perceive the (pleasant or unpleasant) sensation of a raising of a right foot.*" A psychologist such as Spencer would hardly disagree and could reach the point by reasoning, but, notes Crowley, "the Buddhist goes further' only so far as he may be said to knock down the scaffolding of reasoning processes, and to assimilate the actual truth of the matter."[28] "What," asks Crowley, "will occur when one reaches the final stage of Viññanam, and finds no Ātman behind it?" Crowley speculates that the state will soon seem as unreal as those passed before it, and such a person must be very close to "nirvana." Crowley feels sure that the bliss of dhyāna will occur before even passing up to sankhara. Crowley imagines achievements of this kind will enable one to throw Voltaire's jibe at the mystery mongers of *his* day back at the materialists of Crowley's own: "Ils nient ce qui est, et expliquent ce qui n'est pas": "They nullify that which is, and explain that which is not."

As a note to the foregoing section, Crowley makes some points with regard to Herbert Spencer's critique of idealists in his phrase "Transfigured Realism." Crowley says as far as reason goes, Spencer is sound in concluding that idealism is "but verbally intelligible" but wrong that idealists are bewildered by their own terminology; "the fact is that idealist conclusions are presented directly to consciousness, when that consciousness is Dhyanic." And further: "Nothing is clearer to my mind than that the great difficulty habitually experienced by the normal mind in the assimilation of metaphysics is due to the actual lack of experience in the mind of the reader of the phenomena discussed."[29] Idealism here denotes that facts are primarily facts of mind, and the appearance of matter is dependent on the mind's perception of matter. As for the necessity of experiencing the ideal: *being is seeing.* Mystical experience is a primary fact, not the disease of a secondary one. Crowley asserts that his experience and progress marks an empirically indicated path, not a result of some dissipation of mind, and invites scientists to investigate for themselves. There is a great deal more to discover in the field and it requires further experiment, increase of knowledge, and a gathering together and classification of data to erect a sure foundation for a science of mind in its potential fullness.

Crowley does not say that T. H. Huxley found his agnosticism in the teachings of the Buddha, but he is clear that the Buddha's nondogmatic, proof-by-experience method does in fact constitute "agnosticism" according to Huxley's scientific meaning. As Galileo could not rely on echoing Tycho Brahe, so Buddha could not have progressed had he relied on faith in the Vedas alone. The most cherished hypotheses must be thrown to the dogs if new facts come forth that deny them. Even the First Noble Truth may be dumped if proof may be delivered of a reasonable (intelligent) existence not liable to sorrow. He quotes *Mahāparinibbāna Sutta* (ii, 33): "Therefore, O Ananda, be ye lamps unto yourselves. Be ye a refuge to yourselves. Betake yourselves to no external refuge. Hold fast to the truth as a lamp. Look not for refuge to any one besides yourselves." The "topmost height" is reserved for those who show such anxiety to learn. How can scientists not concur when they look back on the burning of Bruno, persecution of Galileo, the obscurantism of the schoolmen of the Middle Ages, and all the many and vicious weapons by which science was distorted and stunted in the contrary interest?

Crowley calls on scientists to embrace Buddhism rather than the indifferentism of the present.

> Are we never to go forward, moreover? Are our children still to be taught as facts the stupid and indecent fables of the Old Testament, fables that the Archbishop of Canterbury himself would indignantly repudiate? Are minds to be warped early, the scientific method and imagination checked, the logical faculty thwarted—thousands of workers lost each year to Science?
>
> And the way to do this is not only through the negative commonsense of indifference; organize, organize, organize! For a flag we offer you the stainless lotus-banner of the Buddha, in defence of which no drop of blood has ever been, nor will ever be shed, a banner under which you will join forces with five hundred million of your fellow-men. And you will not be privates in the army; for you the highest place, the place of leaders waits; as far as the triumphs of the intellect are concerned, it is to Western Science that we look. Your achievements have shattered the battle-array of dogma and despotism; your columns roll in triumphant power through the breaches of false metaphysic and baseless logic; you have fought that

battle, and the laurels are on your brows. The battle was fought by us more than two thousand years ago; the authority of the Vedas, the restrictions of caste, were shattered by the invulnerable sword of truth in Buddha's hands; we are your brothers. But in the race of intellect we have fallen behind a little; will you take no interest in us, who have been your comrades? To Science Buddhism cries: Lead us, reform us, give us clear ideas of Nature and her laws; give us that basis of irrefragable logic and wide knowledge that we need, and march with us into the Unknown![30]

Crowley presents himself here as a man in spiritual league with friend Allan Bennett's International Buddhist Society, the Buddhasanana Samagama, established in Rangoon in 1903, with whose publications, edited and contributed to by Bennett, Crowley is in close touch and

Fig. 11.1. Buddhism, *quarterly review of November 1904, edited by Bennett (Ananda Metteya). It contained articles by C.A.F. Rhys Davids, A. W. Perera, Dr. Paul Carus, and "Ananda M.," including an obituary of Sir Edward Arnold, and essays on Ceylonese antiquities, Buddhist philosophy, pre-existence and "The New Civilisation," (by the editor) wherein Buddhism would, he asserted, find a dominant place.*

sympathy. Indeed, Crowley recommends Bennett's "able and luminous" exposition on the Four Noble Truths in a pamphlet by Bhikkhu Ananda Maitriya, published by the Buddhasasana Samagama, 1 Pagoda Road, Rangoon. Crowley calls for a global reform of Buddhism on scientific lines as a way of uniting East and West, science and spirituality: "And if, in the West, a great Buddhist society is built up of men of intellect, of the men in whose hands the future lies, there is then an awakening, a true redemption, of the weary and forgetful Empires of the East."

Crowley returns from "our little digression" to the main course, that is, the Fourth Noble Truth that is the Noble Eightfold Path.

The goal of the path is nirvana. All things that exist are subject to change. In nirvana is no change. Therefore nirvana cannot contain an existing thing. Buddhist nirvana means absolute cessation. This may be compared to Hindu conceptions where nirvana means cessation of existence only. One is reminded of Crowley's favoring the "Qabalistic Zero Absolute." The cold blade of nihilism is never far from Crowley's heart. Nothing. Nothing. Nothing. Nevertheless, Crowley understands enough of Buddhism to assert: "Nirvana is a state belonging to a different plane, to a higher dimension than anything we can at present conceive of. It has perhaps its analogies and correspondences on the normal planes, and so shall we find of the steps as well as of the Goal. Even the simple first step, which every true Buddhist has taken, Sammaditthi, is a very different thing from the point of view of an Arahat [Buddhist saint]. The Buddha stated expressly that none but an Arahat could really comprehend the Dhamma." Crowley proceeds to enunciate the stages from Bhikkhu Ananda Maitriya's aforementioned pamphlet.

First step is Sammaditthi, Pāli for holding the Right Views, which views are the Three Characteristics, which entail abandoning false beliefs and entering on what Bennett calls "the Holy Way."

Second is Sammasankappo, or Right Aspiration. While all things suffer, the Buddhist must not add to the suffering, so renunciation of sensual pleasure is vital lest desire be enflamed, and compassion may be offered to all that lives. Once the speech indicates no malice for anyone, one is in sight of the third stage, Sammavāca, that is, Right Speech. This person speaks the truth. The next stage follows logically, Right Conduct, or Sammakammanto, for the one who is truthful in thought and word sees the pitiful nature of things and feels mercy of loving and pure motivation. When such conduct evinces progress toward holiness, the fifth stage becomes real: Sammājivo, or the Living of the Life that's Right. This might later have meant to Crowley something like his conception of the "True Will." As it stood, and not surprisingly from what we know of Crowleyan ethics, Crowley took issue with his friend's sentence: "Abstaining from all that can cause pain, he has become blameless, and can live only by such occupations as can bring no sorrow in their train."[31] In a footnote, Crowley reiterates the point that from his point of view, such conduct is impossible in the nature of things. "If willful infliction of pain only is meant, our state becomes moral, or even worse!—mystical. I should prefer to cancel this sentence."

Crowley's view of morality here is one where people assume that what is customary in certain situations is right, and right on all planes in all places. Crowley sees the Eightfold Path rather as a scientifically valid adjustment of consciousness, with the proper conduct in a situation reflecting the state of consciousness attained. One man's meat is another man's poison. We get a sense of Crowley's incipient rebellion against passivity. When he was a boy he was subject to pain inflicted on him by others; when he revolted, he began the active life and it made him stronger and more in touch with his being; that's how his mountaineering began, and to join him on a climb, for example, was to undergo pain, and perhaps death, arguably caused by the motivation of the expedition leader. Likewise, Crowley was prepared to suffer in a good cause, and surely, renunciation entailed some suffering somewhere.

Crowley is in full agreement with Bennett's next point that a life of voluntary restraint gives powers extraordinary to ordinary men, for the extraordinary man is he who has conquered his mind. The ability to focus the powers of the will is the sixth stage, Sammāvayamo, "Right Effort." "Right Will-power" or even "Right Energy" are, Bennett thinks, nearer to the essence of it. He had long shown himself able to accomplish this and had taught Crowley "a thing or two" about the power of the will. The aspirant may now focus on the goal, day and night. Constant recollection and keeping in mind holy things is the seventh stage, Sammasati. Sammasati may also involve profound introspection into the causes of tendencies and actions in oneself, tracing karma back, even through previous lives. Bennett calls it a "transcendent faculty" and by the power of it, the Buddhist may rise "through the Eight High Trances to the very threshold of Nirvana," where "he at last, in the Trance called Nirodha Samapatti, attains, even in this life, to the deathless shore of Nirvana, by the power of Sammasamādhi, Right Concentration (the Eighth Path). Such a one has, by destroying the cause of all his chain of lives, "become Arahan, a Saint, a Buddha himself."[32]

Crowley makes the point that, as their author knows, Bennett's interpretations are but reflections of those on a higher plane, the "scientific plane." Crowley is convinced they are mnemonic keys to whole classes of phenomena anciently regarded as magical. "It is to establish such a method; to record in the language, not of the temple but of the laboratory, its results, that I make this appeal; that I seek to enlist genuine, not pseudo-scientific men in the Research; so that our children may be as far in advance of us in the study of the supernormal phenomena of mind as we are in advance of our fathers in the sciences of the physical world."[33] Alas, Crowley's call went largely unheeded, so we have perhaps lost a century of possible development, while modern science continues to teeter between the materialism of most biologists and the spiritual indifferentism of most mainstream scientific orthodoxies. Crowley concludes: "What I require is advance in the Knowledge of the Great problem, derived no longer from hearsay revelation, from exalted fanaticism, from hysteria and intoxication; but from method and research. Shut the temple; open the laboratory!" Nevertheless, Crowley kept his temple open, in his mind.*

---

*Thelemite Joseph Thiebes has drawn attention to proof of Crowley's assertions of the relation between religious experience and neurology in the article "Science and Religion" on his website "AC 2012," citing the work of Dr. Andrew Newberg. Newberg found the brain's "Orientation Association Area" (O.A.A.) goes dark when people have religious experiences: "Dr. Newberg found this to be true in widely diverse practices such as: Pentecostal Christians feeling the presence of the Holy Ghost during glossolalia; Carmelite nuns feeling united with God through ecstatic prayer; and Tibetan monks' experience of annihilation in Samādhi after prolonged periods of meditation. Newberg has demonstrated that meditation works by quieting the mind & body, resulting in the O.A.A. shutting down. Once the experience of Samādhi occurs, the O.A.A. is almost completely dark." Thiebes quotes Crowley in Magick without Tears that magick works by inflaming the mind: "Magick explores and learns to control those regions of Nature which lie beyond the objects of sense. Reaching the highest parts of these regions, called the divine, one proceeds by the exaltation . . . of the consciousness to identify oneself with those 'celestial' Beings.'" Dr. Newberg's experiments suggest that when the

Before his last words on the subject, Crowley emphasizes the Three Refuges of Buddhism avail themselves of strictly scientific application. "I take my refuge in the Buddha." That there was one who found the Way is encouragement for all who take the Way. "I take my refuge in the Dhamma [law.]" Crowley writes: "The Law underlying phenomena and its unchanging certainty; the Law given by the Buddha to show us the Way, the inevitable tendency to Persistence in Motion or Rest—and Persistence, even in Motion, negates changes in consciousness—these observed orders of fact are our bases." "I take my refuge in the Sangha [brotherhood]." The seeker of the goal is not wholly isolated. Crowley observes that one-third of humanity is Buddhist; add to these men of science and they are a majority. The compassion of, and for, the whole of humanity necessitates the taking of the path of research. Compassion binds together those who take the Way. "Ay, in joy and in sorrow, in weakness and in strength, do I take my refuge in the Sangha."[34]

Crowley concludes that he has shown the identity of science and Buddhism in respect of their fact, their theory, their method, their enemies, and that while thus admitting Buddhism to be a branch of science, he has shown it to be the most important branch "since its promise is to break down the wall at which all Science stops."[35] "If Science is never to go beyond its present limits; if the barriers which metaphysical speculation shows to exist are never to be transcended, then indeed we are thrown back on faith, and all the rest of the nauseous mess of medieval superstition. . . . And the history of our Science is the history of all Science. If you choose to ape Christendom and put the pioneers of rational investigation into the nature of consciousness on the rack (i.e. into lunatic asylums) I doubt not we shall find our Bruno. But it

---

(*cont. from p. 247*) O.A.A. "shuts down," the brain has to experience itself as timeless and boundless, and experience of that follows the form of the cultural paradigm familiar to the individual. Crowley drew attention to relativity of spiritual perception repeatedly: Catholics get Catholic visions; Hindus get Hindu visions; Muslims get Muslim visions, and so on.

Neuroscientist Andrew Newberg, M.D., is Director of Research at the Myrna Brind Center for Integrative Medicine at Thomas Jefferson University Hospital, an adjunct professor of Religious Studies, and an associate professor of Radiology at the University of Pennsylvania. See his *Principles of Neurotheology* (Farnham, Surrey, England: Ashgate Publishing, 2010).

will add an additional pang that persecution should come from the house of our friends."[36]

Crowley's final imperative: *Research!* He did so, and in the course of it, was as surprised as anybody that it led him to *The Book of the Law,* and a rebuke to Buddhism's First Noble Truth. Twenty years after writing "Science and Buddhism," Crowley was still entertaining private, internal arguments with Gautama; Crowley usually won, coining the jibe, "Buddha the hypochondriac." In 1920 he would write: "The Universal Sorrow was cured when he went out for a drink with the Universal Joke." In the end, the active would not submit to the passive.

TWELVE

The Works II: "Ascension Day" and "Pentecost"

"Science and Buddhism" first appeared as the penultimate inclusion to Crowley's *The Sword of Song,* printed by Philippe Renouard, 19, rue des Saints-Pères, Paris, and published in August 1904 by Crowley's S.P.R.T. (Society for the Propagation of Religious Truth), a punning anagram on "spirit" and "spurt," and pointed skit on British religion-for-export's chief publishing wing, the Society for the Promotion of Christian Knowledge, or S.P.C.K., founded in 1698. *The Sword of Song*'s title page gives its provenance as Benares, but this is a blind in keeping with the remarkable qualities of the published volume. The bulk of "Sword"—as Crowley's wife Rose referred to the publication—is dedicated to two poems, written, Crowley tells us, in reaction to aspects of Robert Browning's poems, "Christmas Eve" and "Easter Day" (1850) where Browning considered his position regarding mythologies, theologies, and behavior accreted over time to the Christian message, as the poet understood it.

According to *Confessions,* Crowley was reading these poems in a vellum edition at Tuticorin (now Thoothukudi, Tamil Nadu state) on the southeastern Coromandel coast of India some 105 miles across the Gulf of Mannar from Ceylon, the which island Crowley had just departed, having found Christian missionary attitudes to native Buddhism annoying. Crowley considered Browning had backed off from the force of his own insights, and asked what kind of "good faith" could be expected from defenders of a religion who plainly picked only the bits they liked from Christianity's uneven hold. Crowley, as is well known, had received his religion in a fundamentalist, uncompromising, but by no means unreasoned form, the sum of which tended to torture mind and body. For Crowley's benign-spirited father, Edward, acceptance of Christian salvation was simply implicit to the logic of the Christian case; it would be bad manners to refuse resurrection. Crowley felt that at the core of the Christian faith was a kind of blackmail, with a bloody atonement doctrine inherited from Judaism, and that so long as Satan and Judas Iscariot were cast out from the redemptive scheme, then unlimited love could hardly be seen as Christianity's keynote message. Certainly, Browning finds little love to be shared when he takes shelter in a chapel at the start of his "Christmas Eve." Like John Lennon in times to come, who would say that when a boy he was sure God had been inside his local church, but preferred it outside, Browning makes his escape from the gathered flock to the wilds of wintry nature:

> My head grew lighter, my limbs more supple,
>   As I walked on, glad to have slipt the fetter.
> My mind was full of the scene I had left,
>   That placid flock, that pastor vociferant,
> —How this outside was pure and different!

In Nature, Browning had long ago found his God, a God who gave his creature, man, freedom to find himself. Crowley simply wondered why someone of this romantic awareness should bother to call himself "Christian" at all, likewise many mystics and gnostics of Christian history. Browning's poem opens thus:

> Out of the little chapel I burst
>   Into the fresh night-air again.
> Five minutes full, I waited first
>   In the doorway, to escape the rain
> That drove in gusts down the common's centre
>   At the edge of which the chapel stands,
> Before I plucked up heart to enter.

Crowley's response came as "an elaborate parody on Browning's" conceived on Friday, November 15, 1901, when, as explained in his notes to the poems, "I left Ceylon, where I had been for several months, practicing Hindu meditations, and exposing the dishonesty of the missionaries, in the intervals of big game shooting. The following day I wrote 'Ascension Day' and 'Pentecost' on the Sunday, sitting outside the dak-bungalow at Madura. These original drafts were small as compared to the present poems."[1]

"Ascension Day" opens with a spurt in riposte to Browning:

> I FLUNG out of chapel and church,
> Temple and hall and meeting-room,
> Venus' Bower and Osiris' Tomb,
> And left the devil in the lurch,
> While God got lost in the crowd of gods,
> And soul went down in the turbid tide
> Of the metaphysical lotus-eyed,
> And I was—anyhow, what's the odds?

Crowley maintains he had "got the message" early in life and dispensed with the Christians' God summarily. He wrote in his *Confessions*:

> I was criticizing it [Christianity] in the light of my experience in Dhyana [which had abolished Duality], and the result was to give me the idea of answering Browning's apology for Christianity by what was essentially a parody of his title and his style. My poem was to be called "Ascension Day and Pentecost." I wrote "Ascension Day" at Madura on November 16th and "Pentecost" the day after; but my original idea gradually expanded. I elaborated the two poems from time to time, added "Berashith"—of which more anon—and finally "Science and Buddhism," an essay on these subjects inspired by a comparative study of what I had learned from Allan Bennett and the writings of Thomas Henry Huxley. These four elements made up the volume finally published under the title *The Sword of Song*.[2]

Sword's subtitle *Called by Christians the Book of the Beast* introduces the arch-humorous tack followed throughout the volume. The book may parody aspects of Christian apologetics, but it also takes care to parody its author and, indeed, the book itself, which opens with "Alice" asking searching questions about the book's many possible titles and subtitles in the manner of Lewis Carroll's Alice obtaining cryptic "answers" from the hookah-smoking caterpillar on the mushroom in Wonderland! Read in the right spirit, the book, while often abrasive, is also charming, exceedingly quick witted, and enlightening: a worthy, and friendly, opponent to Crowley's admired poet, Robert Browning, whom we may be certain would have been amused.

Crowley takes on in advance the arguments of those who are bound to attack him for "such petty spites as these you strew throughout your verse." He puts it down to the "chance of birth" that made Christianity the object of his scorn. Had he been born in Tibet, then Christ would have had "Peace" and he'd have attacked Buddha instead! He addresses "the yoke of faith that tortures English folk" because he's a poet and a poet must address the culture he is a part of, even if he might wish he wasn't!

PANSIL

Nevertheless, in the interests of balance, and as an example of what he might have to say to annoy a Buddhist, Crowley included in the notes to "Ascension Day" a brief treatise on "taking Pansil," that is, the Buddhist vowing of obedience to five precepts (or "virtues"), the which are examined seriatim by the Beast.[3] While an admirer of Gautama's scientific methods of thought, Crowley regards Pansil's precepts as "mere nonsense," on a par with the moralistic ethics that he believed distorted with dogma what he considered an ancient path of spiritual attainment. Nonsense, as they stand, but Crowley is convinced they rather represent a cynical and ironic comment on the First Noble Truth, the *impossibility* of strict adherence to them proof that existence is so permeated with sorrow that its annihilation must be the aim!

The first precept forbids taking of life in any form. It being impossible so to do, Crowley wonders if the Buddha was not in mind to be rhetorical. For even in speaking the words "living protoplasm was changed into dead matter," as he breathed in millions of living organisms and killed them. Eating and breathing are fatal to something. He recalls Huxley's citation of the biologist who stunned a Brahmin proud of being "ahiṃsā" (harmless) by showing through a microscope the countless creatures alive in a drop of water. Ethical principle is no respecter of scale!

Crowley then reveals a cause of tension between himself and Allan Bennett: "How such a fiend incarnate, my dear brother Ananda Maitreya, can call him 'cruel and cowardly' who only kills a tiger, is a study in the philosophy of the mote and the beam." This tension will be further exhibited when we come to Crowley's story around "The Three Characteristics." The subject was clearly a bone of contention. Crowley concludes that a mind such as Gautama's must have viewed the precept rather as "a bitter commentary on the foul evil of this aimless, hopeless, universe, this compact of misery, meanness, and cruelty."

Crowley's dispensing with the second precept—the forbidding of theft—is another comment more in tune with Crowleyan irony than the Buddha's, one suspects. Defining theft as the appropriation of something that is another's by right, Crowley cleverly accuses the Buddha of theft on the grounds that by giving a command, he denies the one commanded proper and rightful exercise of his free will. "Further, all voluntary action limits in some degree, however minute, the volition of others. If I breathe I diminish the stock of oxygen on the planet." When the earth becomes as dead as the moon, one's breathing will have deprived another being of "the dearest necessity of life." Crowley is now on a roll. Moreover, all theft is, he says, temporary, for even a millionaire must die, and theft is anyhow universal, for even a Buddha must breathe!

The third precept against adultery is one Crowley would touch on "but lightly." Not that the subject is unpleasant—"far from it!" The Buddha was guilty of adultery on the principle that to think a thing is to commit it (so says Jesus anyway, according to the gospel), but not only in mind, as it were, but "since A and not-A are mutually limiting, therefore interdependent, therefore identical, he who forbids an act commits it." Crowley, however, presumed the Buddha did not refer to adultery in the divorce court sense—which "assumes too much proprietary right of a man over a woman, that root of all abomination!"—but to incontinence. We know, he writes, that Buddha had left his home, "but Nature has to be reckoned with." Anyhow, the "error in question" resolves itself into a mixture of murder, theft, and intoxication, as Crowley has defined them (intoxication to come), showing them all inevitable concomitants of the existence the Buddha wishes all to be free of.

Considering the fourth precept leads Crowley to conviction that they constitute "a species of savage practical joke." The proscription on lying, Crowley regards as laughable since "we all lie all the time; we are compelled to it by the nature of things themselves—paradoxical as that seems—and the Buddha knew it!" This conclusion follows the reasoning that in giving a command to another, the Buddha denies his own doctrine: that a personality did not exist (anatta). That one could be expected to to be addressed, or even commanded, presumed the existence of a "one," which must be a delusion, according to Buddhist text *Sabbasava Sutta* (par. 10), where personality is a delusion and therefore belief in it a lie! By exercise of the high Buddhist meditations, the furthest to admitting some kind of being might be only to say: "Something called consciousness appears to itself to exist." Dhyānic consciousness includes such an assumption, and denies it too.

The fifth precept forbids intoxication. Crowley's comment: "At last we arrive at the end of our weary journey—surely in this weather we may have a drink!" For east of Suez a man may raise a thirst, to quote Macaulay. "No!" shrieks the Blessed One. Now if intoxication is "the loss of power to use perfectly a truth-telling set of faculties," why, such faculties are forever hindered by the exigencies of existence. Food may intoxicate, pictures too: *living* may be intoxicating! Besides, if everything is sorrow, which poisons joy, and if the toxicity be the key to the word, then life is toxic, and death is surely proof of that, the failure of faculties presaged in all by illnesses many and fearsome, afflicting body and mind so mind depends on body and the reverse too. No, says Crowley, all our faculties are intoxicated by Nature and by their individual limitations. What the eye sees as flat, the fingers feel as round. And by Buddha's own token, what *is* this delusion of personality but a profound and centrally seated intoxication of the consciousness, which is itself an intoxication, release from which is devoutly to be wished. Crowley's ironic genius enables him to attribute to the Blessed One kindred intellectual and spiritual perspicacity. Buddha, he says, knew exactly what he was saying! He knew the universe was continually "rotting our very bones with poisonous drunkenness, And so his cutting irony—drink no intoxicating drinks!" Buddha saw Truth, asserts Crowley. "Do not believe that the sorrow of existence is so trivial that easy rules easily interpreted (as all Buddhists do interpret the precepts) can avail against them; do not mop up the Ganges with a duster; nor stop the revolution of the stars with a lever of lath." Oh, what folly is man's! "Awake, awake only!" Sorrow is here by the inherent necessity of the way the universe is made, not by malice, nor volition, but nude nature. If the cure is the uprooting of desire, do not imagine it can be achieved like salvation for a threepenny bit in a collection plate. The Path is one of "austere self-mastery, of arduous scientific research, which constitute the Noble Eightfold Path."

So, Crowley can apply his scalpel to the practice of Buddhism with equal force to that applied to the missionary religion he encountered in India and at home, and no doubt a zealous Buddhist might call him a "devil" for so apparently demolishing the taking of Pansil! But to master oneself, one must know oneself, and Crowley knew what he was, for his mother had told him, and he would later add to the first draft of "Ascension Day" his now-familiar self-designation as the "Beast," but it should be noted, it appears as self-parody, in the spirit of, "If you insist on Easter day, then I'll give you Beaster Day!":

> Yet by-and-by I hope to weave
> A song of Anti-Christmas Eve
> And First—and Second—Beast-er Day.
> There's one who loves me dearly (vrai!)*
> Who yet believes me sprung from Tophet,
> Either the Beast or the False Prophet;
> And by all sorts of monkey tricks
> Adds up my name to Six Six Six.
> Retire, good Gallup!†

---

*French for "true."

†This is a reference to Elizabeth Wells Gallup (born New York, 1848) who caused controversy in a book published in 1898 by drawing attention to Francis Bacon's alleged "Biliteral Cipher" and enthusiasm for cryptography in business she believed evident in Bacon's *De Augmentis* (Paris, 1624) and other works by contemporaries such as Spenser, Marlowe, and Shakespeare. In 1902, a Mr. Sydney Lee attacked her theories in a letter to the *Times;* Mrs. Gallup defended herself in a pamphlet published that same year (*Replies to Criticisms*). Crowley is remarking on the heated controversy by suggesting hidden "ciphers" in his own literary conceits!

In such strife her
Superior skill makes you a cipher!
Ho! I adopt the number. Look
At the quaint wrapper of this book!
I will deserve it if I can:
It is the number of a Man.

The one who dearly loves him but calls him the "Beast" or false prophet from Tophet—where, according to 2 Kings 23:10, Canaanites in Jerusalem sacrificed children to Moloch—is of course mother: Emily Bertha Crowley. As to the "quaint wrapper" of the book, the book's design included a Hebrew glyph of his name roughly spelt in Hebrew so as to compute by kabbalistic gematria to 666. Crowley very well knew it was more to amuse or shock than convince. Crowley's mother was not amused. Her son's 1904 S.P.R.T. publications included *Why Jesus Wept*, his satirical play written after encountering British upper-class hypocrisy at the Galle Face Hotel, Colombo, during a Sri Lankan honeymoon with the former Rose Edith Kelly in late 1903. *Why Jesus Wept* was issued with an outrageously funny—and doubtless to Christian sensibilities—blasphemous advertisement, a copy of which Rose Crowley dispatched to her husband's mother in Eastbourne, Sussex, eliciting the following letter, itself published, astonishingly, as part of the introductory section to *Why Jesus Wept*:

WEST CLIFF MANSION
ST JOHN'S ROAD
EASTBOURNE

April 25th 1904

My dear, dear boy,

How I grieve over you—*You, my only child,* yet never writing anything to me but what you know must grieve me and now sending me through the medium of your wife that horrible advertisement which I do not trust you will keep from all eyes that have not seen it—it is unworthy of a man—all is truly sad and yet surely beneath all the extravagant irreligion and blasphemy there must be deep down in your soul a need which only Christ can fill. You want *Power*. Well "Power belongeth unto God" and man cannot use God's power except in weakness. St. Paul said "When I am weak then am I strong." There is another power and this you have taken up with—you have got hold of the *wrong* power—Satan is strong and can energize his agents, but thank God, there is a stronger than he! You will have to bow to Him one day. Why not now?

Oh, Alec, my dearly beloved son, do turn from the arch enemy of your soul—You have tried most of the religions, now try something new—Try "a Friend that sticketh closer than a brother," you know as well as I do, that you must take Him as your Savior first—Oh do come now—"without money and without price" see what easy terms—much better than your advertisement—Don't make fun of this, Alec my dear, dear son—I am in dead earnest—may God forgive the past, may He snatch you out of the jaws of death and hell—Oh, may He bring you to Himself, so that you may see your awful sins in their true light—I have had some sight of my own sins in the past and oh what horror!

> "Behold One hanging on the tree
>   In agonies and blood
> He cast His languid eyes on me
>   As near His cross I stood
> Sure never till my dying day
>   Shall I forget that look.
> It seemed to charge me with His death
>   Tho' not a word He spoke"

I feel I have not been half in earnest with you, though I have indeed looked to God for you again and again, and how often have I thought you were really coming to Christ and have been disappointed. Not that God has not heard—He has heard and is ready to bless you! Only, when is it to be? I cannot but say "Lord how long?"

Satan is keeping you away from the only One who can befriend you and I do entreat you to come now. If you only act on the terms of God's Agreement "Now is the accepted time. *Now* is the day of

Salvation," Satan and all his hosts will have to flee "Resist the devil and he will flee from you." You know the way so well. Then come ere the day of grace passes away.

God forgive and bless you,

My poor dear Alec,

Y' loving mother
EMILY B. CROWLEY

"Ascension Day" deals within itself with the criticism of impiety and the use of hatred to make a point:

> "But why revile"
> (You urge me) "in that vicious style
> The very faith whose truths you seem
> (Elsewhere) to hold, to hymn supreme
> In your own soul?" Perhaps you know
> How mystic doctrines melt the snow
> Of any faith: redeem it to
> A fountain of reviving dew.
> So I with Christ: but few receive
> The Qabalistic Balm, believe
> Nothing—and choose to know instead.
> But, to that terror vague and dread,
> External worship; all my life—
> War to the knife! War to the knife!

Next, Buddha speaks and asks how one who adhered to his law could use hatred to defend truth. All right! Says Crowley, he's no Cain smashing Abel. He'll adopt gentler words. In another later addition to the poem, written in early 1903, Crowley gives poetic voice to the kind of liberal theologian that, fully aware of the uncertainty surrounding authorship of parts of the New Testament nevertheless expects to impress or convert the interlocutor by sweet reason, that is, that despite the best efforts of scholars to diminish the credibility of the text, there is yet a full Christian religion that compels assent "behind it." In fact the conversation adumbrated took place in artist Gerald Kelly's studio in Montparnasse, Paris, with the Rev. J. Bowley, who introduced

Crowley to his Parisian Masonic Lodge (Anglo-Saxon Lodge No. 343) not long after Crowley's return to Europe from India.

> I met a Christian clergyman,
> The nicest man I ever met.
> We argued of the Cosmic plan.
> I was Lord Roberts, he De Wet.*
> He tells me when I cite the "Fall"
> "But those are legends after all."
> He has a hundred hills to lie in,
> But finds no final ditch to die in.
> "Samuel was man; the Holy Spook
> Did not dictate the Pentateuch."
> With cunning feint he lures me on
> To loose my pompoms†
> on Saint John;
> And, that hill being shelled, doth swear
> His forces never had been there.
> I got disgusted, called a parley,
> (Here comes a white-flag treachery!)
> Asked: "Is there anything you value,
> Will hold to?" He laughed, "Chase me, Charlie!"
> But seeing in his mind that I
> Would not be so converted, "Shall you,"
> He added, "grope in utter dark?
> The Book of Acts and that of Mark
> Are now considered genuine."
> I snatch a Testament, begin
> Reading at random the first page;—
> He stops me with a gesture sage:
> "You must not think, because I say

---

*British and Boer generals on opposite sides in the Boer War.
†Nickname for the Vickers, Sons & Maxim (VSM) autocannon used on both sides in the Second Boer War, called a "pom pom" gun from the sound of its firing. The reference to the ditch to die in concerns the awful slaughter by Boer artillery of British soldiers in shallow trenches, "choked with dead and wounded" as Winston Churchill reported, at the Battle of Spion Kop in January 1900.

St. Mark is genuine, I would lay
Such stress unjust upon its text,
As base thereon opinion. Next?"
I gave it up. He escaped. Ah me!
But so did Christianity.

Crowley draws on his Indian experience for an—arguably facetious—assessment of the story of Christ's "ascension." In the East, he asserts, large legends are built on small surprises. In athletic verses, Crowley takes the case of what sustained prāṇāyāma might achieve: a curious buoyancy that Bennett and Crowley witnessed of each other, in that the upturned but stiff positions in which they were on occasion discovered, could only have obtained had the body risen or "hopped" in a startling manner, *apparently* defying gravity and unbeknownst to the one so moved.*

No tithe of the immense amounts
Of powers demanded by the wise
From Chela ere the Chela rise
To knowledge. Fairy-tales? Well, first,
Sit down a week and hold your breath
As masters teach—until you burst,
Or nearly—in a week, one saith,
A month, perchance a year for you,
Hard practice, and yourself may fly—
Yes! I have done it! you may too!

There is a serious implication: the "rising" to the Godhead or to "sit on God's right-hand" indicates to Crowley's esoteric vision that the yogi has accomplished *moksha*, or liberation, by his consciousness rising through the chakras to the highest in the upper part of the skull, which in the jñāna yoga scheme opens unto heavens above, and

---

*Some years ago, something of the kind was observed among practitioners of that "Transcendental Meditation" favored by followers of Maharishi Mahesh Yogi who formed a "Natural Law Party" assisted not only by support from George Harrison, but by stories and video clips of the curious feat of "yogic flying." Seems Crowley was ahead of the game on that one!

in the Advaita system generally is home of the true "I" or *parātman* above illusion. In other words, the original figure known as Jesus (or a component of that perhaps collective identity) was a yogi, but followers unacquainted with yogic methods took the language of "rising" quite literally, as in the case of failing to see that the phrase attributed to Jesus in Saint John's Gospel "I and my Father are one" is a perfect description of yoga (union) itself, when the individual *jīvātman* realizes its identity with parātman or Brahman, a bliss sure to make for a nimbus radiant.

It is nonetheless curious that Crowley's swipes at Christianity consist almost entirely of moral objections, whereas we find consistently in his treatment of Hinduism and Buddhism an attitude that is eager to dispense with a priori moral content. In other words, Crowley will not give to Christianity a like leverage of tolerance for what he regards as incidentals. He does not say, well, what of the Christian nature? What of the Christian man and woman who has practiced honestly the love of God and the love of one's neighbor as oneself? We can only surmise that Crowley did not regard the moral scheme of Christianity as incidental, but axiomatic. The book of Revelation—staple text of obsessive sectarianism, with its Last Judgment and mass condemnation/extermination—was never far from Crowley's childhood universe. That is how he had been taught, and when it came to judging the religion from the figure of the virtuous Christian, he may have been as hard-pressed to locate one as Browning was in his chapel on Christmas Eve. He recognizes great figures of the faith but suggests they were overgenerous to practices and beliefs they deviated from; why call themselves Christian? If Jesus is the heretic of Christianity, so much the worse for Christianity!

And which of the logia attributed to Christ should one stress? After ascending to heaven, as the story goes, what does Jesus leave behind? Crowley thinks the dominant prophecy of the last 1870 years is "I bring not peace; I bring a sword."

> Which of his sayings prove the true,
> Lightning-bescrawled athwart the blue?
> I say not, Which in hearts aright

Are treasured? but, What after ages
Engrave on history's iron pages?
This is the one word of "Our Lord";
"I bring not peace; I bring a sword."
In this the history of the West
Bears him out well. How stands the test?
One-third a century's life of pain—
He lives, he dies, he lives again,
And rises to eternal rest
Of bliss with Saints—an endless reign!
Leaving the world to centuries torn
By every agony and scorn,
And every wickedness and shame
Taking their refuge in his Name.

Furthermore, what bothers Crowley, he says, is evident lack of charity in the essentials. Following his preacher father's injunction, he picks on John 3:16: "For God so loved the world, that he gave his only begotten Son, that whosoever believeth in him should not perish, but have everlasting life." At first sight, it may seem generous, but see its amplification: "He that believeth not is condemned already." If you don't believe, you perish, and "perish" throughout the gospel means hell, and with the grisly threat of that, the Church has ruled. Crowley finds more latitude for the individual in Buddhism where, as it were, "go to hell!" is better expressed "get well soon!" His point, as he says, is that "the world lies bleeding," not for want of judgment but of understanding, love, and science.

I must obey my mind's own laws
Accept its limits, seek its cause:
My meat may be your poison! I
Hope to convert you by-and-by?
Never! I cannot trace the chain
That brought us here, shall part again
Our lives—perhance for aye! I bring
My hand down on this table-thing,
And that commotion widens thus
And shakes the nerves of Sirius!

> To calculate one hour's result
> I find surpassing difficult;
> One year's effect, one moment's cause;
> What mind could estimate such laws?
> Who then (much more!) may act aright
> Judged by and in ten centuries' sight?
> (Yet I believe, whate'er we do
> Is best for me and best for you
> And best for all: I line no brow
> With wrinkles, meditating how.)

Crowley believes his exalted moments recognize divine truth as well as any or the best man, but that very capacity makes him sure that the accepted cosmogony of Christianity is fundamentally the inherited work of man in his pettiness, and hatefulness and fear, who has then heaped his life-warped estimations of wishfully thought rights and wrongs upon the Almighty he has created:

> Ay! Let him rise and answer me
> That false creative Deity,
> Whence came his right to rack the Earth
> With pangs of death, disease, and birth:
> No joy unmarred by pain and grief:
> Insult on injury heaped high
> In that quack-doctor infamy
> The Panacea of—Belief!
> Only the selfish soul of man
> Could ever have conceived a plan
> Man only of all life to embrace,
> One planet of all stars to place
> Alone before the Father's face;
> Forgetful of creation's stain,
> Forgetful of creation's pain
> Not dumb!—forgetful of the pangs
> Whereby each life laments and hangs . . .

This God is man-made, he declares; better the shoreless sea of "nibbana," and if, on these terms there exists free choice between Christian heaven and Christian hell, then 666 would rather seek refuge in hell than nuzzle down with hypocrisy amid those who "believe" for fear of the consequences of not doing so.

Crowley next dispenses with the jibe that come imminent death or illness, he will seek refuge with the salvation taught him as a child. "You won't be so proud then!" Crowley agrees: absolutely! In such wretchedness he will find no recourse in "cursing," rather in "my mother's nursing," and will lean on the nearest help, whether God, doctor, or mother. But, he says, should "the brainish fancies of a man hovering on delirium's brink," should they be "classed his utmost span?" Are such states of mind as these all he can, or ought, to think?

> No! the strong man and self-reliant
> Is the true spiritual giant.
> I blame no weaklings, but decline
> To take their maunderings for mine.

In the end, and on consideration of the "futility of the whole discussion," Crowley says he'll take the *symbol* of "Ascension Day" and leave the fact. His "Christhood-soul" in himself has risen lately above the "smallest taint of Earth" and its God, has transcended the ordinary sphere and flies toward the "fourth dimension." He approaches "Jeheshuah": name of the symbolic "Flaming Star" of the Kabbalah, in particular, the *Zohar*. Having done so, the religion he knew as Christianity fizzles to nothing, so to attack it is to attack nothing. He then takes refuge in affirming a true Nothing, the Qabalistic Zero apparently identified with the cessation absolute of the Buddha's nibbana, the which recognition has brought him back down to earth, but at peace in his soul at least, dedicating his life to "liberation of the soul." The world may stay earthbound; the star in Crowley has arisen!

PENTECOST

Crowley's poem "Pentecost" is very different from "Ascension Day." Perhaps it takes its initial tack from Browning's "Easter Day." "Easter Day" deals with problems involved in believing:

HOW very hard it is to be
A Christian! Hard for you and me,
—Not the mere task of making real
That duty up to its ideal,
Effecting thus complete and whole,
A purpose or the human soul—
For that is always hard to do;
But hard, I mean, for me and you
To realise it, more or less,
With even the moderate success
Which commonly repays our strife
To carry out the aims of life.

Like Browning's poem, Crowley's "Pentecost" also deals with problems of belief, the scope of philosophy, the validity of thinking about religion, but above all, it is a poem filled with introspection, rumination on what he has learned from MacGregor Mathers and the Golden Dawn,* or what he has learned and understood from Allan Bennett and his studies and practice of rāja and jñāna yoga.

---

*The Notes to "Pentecost" include in this regard a superb short essay: "The Initiated Interpretation of Ceremonial Magic." This lucid text is a "must" for anyone who wishes to understand what Crowley understood of the practice of traditional ceremonial magic at this time, or by anyone today who believes such practices are fanciful, impractical, or absurd. Crowley indicates succinctly how magical practices stimulate the senses, and thus focus parts of the brain, bringing those parts under control of will, so finally they may be fused in a single-minded exercise of controlled, sanctified will. Thus, sight is stimulated by the circle, the square, the triangle of conjuration, the vessels, lamps, robes, and implements. The sense of sound is stimulated and focused by the invocations; smell by perfumes; the sense of taste by the Sacraments; touch by contact with the objects of the ceremony; and finally Mind itself, in which all the above are combined, reflected on in their significance, and directed according to will. Magic is revealed rationally as the power to bring forth from subconsciousness in recognizable symbols hitherto unknown faculties or powers of the brain, for the general and specific welfare of the "magician." However, for the time being, Crowley is content to leave behind the practices, as Allan Bennett did when he embraced the bhikkhu's robe; Crowley is finding the practices of yoga and the paths of Buddhism as stimulating and useful, and has come to see ceremonial magic as a form of mind control and discipline, perhaps more suited to some natures than the meditative paths he has now embraced.

"How very hard it is to be"
A Yogi! Let our spirits see
At least what primal need of thought
This end to its career has brought:
Why, in a word, I seek to gain
A different knowledge. Why retain
The husk of flesh, yet seek to merit
The influx of the Holy Spirit?
And, swift as caddies pat and cap a tee,
Gain the great prize all mortals snap at,
heroic guerdon* of Srotapatti?†

Having long since banished the fear of hell, Crowley has now through dhyāna experienced the abolition of duality, if only temporarily, and cannot see any absolute division between "natural" and "supernatural," earthly or divine realms. "So I must claim Spirit and matter are the same." The soul is a "mere phantom of the thought." While there may be an element changeless through all eternity, "compounds ever fluctuate" with time or space in various states: chemistry so testifies. And with that Crowley is off on a poetic run of dazzling brilliance as he announces his weariness with endless thoughts on all the different systems he has encountered that say the same things, their contraries, and that say nothing, in phases of dualistic speculation dizzying, denying and damning. Even his own peroration comes under scrutiny:

The metaphysics of these verses
Is perfectly absurd. My curse is
No sooner in an iron word
I formulate my thought than I
Perceive the same to be absurd
(Tannhäuser). So for this, Sir, why!
Your metaphysics in your teeth!
Confer A. Crowley, "Berashith."
But hear! The Christian is a Dualist;

---

*Reward.
†One who has "entered the stream" of nirvana.

Such view our normal consciousness
Tells us. I'll quote now if you list
From Tennyson. It isn't much;
(Skip this and 't'will be even less)
He says: "I am not what I see,
And other than the things I touch."*
How lucid is our Alfred T.!
The Hindu, an Advaitist,
Crosses off Maya from the list;
Believes in one—exactly so,
Dhyana-consciousness, you know!
May it not be that one step further
"This lotused Buddha roaring murther!"?
Nibbana is the state above you
Christians and them Hindus—Lord love you!—
Where Nothing is perceived as such.
This clever thought doth please me much.

He looks again at Buddhism and to the schools of Advaita, and
still cannot wonder at why any kind of being should permit the world
of sorrow we know. Some of the arguments might carry the mind so
far, but then the troubling doubt is there. Crowley does not look to
the cosmos and see the "wonders" of the TV scientist's magnificent
cosmos (just add synthesizer music in cod-Wagnerian mode), but sees
"this disgusting drear system of stars." He sees the dismalness of the
exercise, as William Blake did, its endless (apparently) imprisoning
quality. Faced with it, "all conceptions fail and fall." Facts is facts
and nonfacts is nonfacts—and still the world on waking! Why do
Advaitists try to account for the universe as "maya," rendering their
essential cry "not one, but two"? Does a fact plus a nonfact equal a
fact? But then comes the resistance to sense. While the pundit will
say ultimately human reasoning cannot "comprehend the infinite" so
the Western philosopher will say it's all a game of language, and our
metaphysical words denote only limitations of thought, not "realities."
They can then argue endlessly about what is "real." And so on: the

---

*From Alfred Tennyson's "In Memoriam."

world wagging on, and the pain continuing. A university education for many brings despair, and if that is the universe of universality, then Buddha is right, and to flee is best. But then again, Crowley has found there is a faculty, if that's the right word, in the brain, that transcends rationality and seems to indicate a transcending reality in which subject and object cease their separation, so that subject and object are paradoxically one. The mind can achieve this through concentration, and in "a lightning flash, solve doubt and turn all Nature inside out"! One feels at this point Crowley is close to the Universal Joke he later laid so much stress upon.

Then suddenly, through the mire and mirk of thought appears amid the verses . . . *poetry.*

> There is a lake* amid the snows
> Wherein five glaciers merge and break.
> Oh! the deep brilliance of the lake!
> The roar of ice that cracks and goes
> Crashing within the water! Glows
> The pale pure water, shakes and slides
> The glittering sun through emerald tides,
> So that faint ripples of young light
> Laugh on the green. Is there a night
> So still and cold, a frost so chill,
> That all the glaciers be still?
> Yet in its peace no frost.
> Arise!
> Over the mountains steady stand,
> O sun of glory, in the skies
> Alone, above, unmoving! Brand
> Thy sigil, thy resistless might,
> The abundant imminence of light!
> Ah!
> O in the silence, in the dark,

---

*A.C.'s note: "This simile for the mind and its impressions, which must be stilled before the sun of the soul can be reflected, is common in Hindu literature. The five glaciers are, of course, the senses."

In the intangible, unperfumed,
Ingust abyss, abide and mark
The mind's magnificence assumed
In the soul's splendour! Here is peace;
Here earnest of assured release.
Here is the formless all-pervading
Spirit of the World, rising, fading
Into a glory subtler still.
Here the intense abode of Will
Closes its gates, and in the hall
Is solemn sleep of festival.
Peace! Peace! Silence of peace!
O visionless abode! Cease! Cease!
Through the dark veil press on! The veil
Is rent asunder, the stars pale,
The suns vanish, the moon drops,
The chorus of the spirit stops,
But one note swells. Mightiest souls
Of bard and music maker, rolls
Over your loftiest crowns the wheel
Of that abiding bliss. Life flees
Down corridors of centuries
Pillar by pillar, and is lost.
Life after life in wild appeal
Cries to the master; he remains
And thinks not.
The polluting tides
Of sense roll shoreward. Arid plains
Of wave-swept sea confront me. Nay!
Looms yet the glory through the grey,
And in the darkest hours of youth
I yet perceive the essential truth,
Known as I know my consciousness,
That all divisons hosts confess
A master, for I know and see
The absolute identity
Of the beholder and the vision.

Here is poetry, sublimity, or as Crowley parodies of himself, the poet, "the Browning manqué." It is as though he has said: we can talk, we can be clever, but poetry says what reason cannot grasp that only spirit encompasses. Here is "the sword of song" to cut through the jungle of thought and lead to the shoreless sea. And he continues, and says he's as capable as anyone of dismissing this fabric of his own. How "true and deep" he says, is Lewis Carroll when Alice cries: "It's nothing but a pack of cards!" He then paraphrases Saint Paul, to the effect that "The mere terrestrial minded man knows not the things of God, nor can their subtle meaning understand." Then he adds: "A sage, I say, although he mentions / Perhaps the best of his inventions, God." Unlike Browning, Crowley goes to the limit.

He invokes the goddess Sāvitrī, wife of Brahma, that she may illumine his mind, and recalls how literary giant of the time, G. K. Chesterton, had castigated Crowley's *The Soul of Osiris* in 1901 for its worshipping of Egyptian or Hindu deities as inauthentic religious tourism. Crowley says he never worshipped them. He "merely wished to chant in verse / Some aspects of the universe, / Summed up these subtle forces finely, / And sang of them (I think divinely)." For, he adds: "Gods, and devils too, I find / Are merely modes of my own mind! / The poet needs enthusiasm!"

He then takes on critics that all the "meditation stuff" is just "self-hypnosis." Well, says Crowley, the same could be said of following any religious practice, but more's to the point, does this self-hypnosis lead to a better state of mind than normal? He says, if you are an artist, take me to your studio, show me your best work and when you point to this or that stroke of genius, can you not say that at the moment you executed that stroke, or portion of work, that the mind was apart from the world for a moment at least, and wholly concentrated in itself on the object of its vision? Did you not "lose yourself" at that moment, when time and space were as nothing to your hint of "superconsciousness." Then, likewise in meditation, which Crowley has realized is key to realizing "genius" or authentic being on high, that is, above the normal. Do we not call such moments "inspiration?" And when there is none, how vainly we try to copy Nature and fail, not being inspired, to inspire? There is a mind beyond the day, a mountain high not far away. The essence of meditation is to cast aside systematically the accidentals, then the incidentals, to focus until the seer and the seen are one. Yes, the opposition says, but when the brush is down, and the work is done, the world goes on, the sun is sun, for that is real and all we feel cannot surpass it. Hard to argue with, says the poet. But let us judge by the end; what achieves in the end, what fruits are gained, what bliss delivered? Was this not the mark of the Christian "Pentecost": ecstasy—the apostles accused of drunkenness, or "self-hypnosis," and what did *that* achieve? It changed a world so made it real by dreams gleaned from another plane, the Ascended One. So might again the Word be spoken, and all our darkest heavens open. Once more to the breach, with meditations hard to teach. Crowley goes, his flag unfurled, his verses writ for all the world!

And Crowley comes to see "perchance I am Myself a Christian after all!" For he at least recognizes that Christ may have attained by methods similar to those he has studied, tasted heavenly "Amrita," food of the gods that makes the wine of the world like water and in his ascendant sees a world above he calls "Love." Crowley speculates whether the "Holy Ghost" received at Pentecost, according to the story, was not the very "superconsciousness" of which he now himself speaks. He then suggests that while such consciousness may be followed by what the ignorant term "miracles," that the followers of Jesus lost the "Spirit" "in the act." That is, they tried to bring the heavenly down to earth and confused the planes, so broke the oneness they had at their highest moments experienced. So Crowley attributes the follies of man to duality, the consciousness of the earthly, which having its place, is not to be confounded with the consciousness of the one, and the None.

He concludes that so long as people believe matter is "pure clay" and spirit "pure ether," they shall err and fail to see: "The plain fact is: materialize / What spiritual fact you choose, / And all such turn to folly— lose / The subtle splendor, and the wise Love and dear bliss of truth."

And now he closes, having talked too long, but leaves one parting thought. If you cannot bring God into the compass of human thought, "Let human thought itself expand—Bright Sun of Knowledge in me rise!"

Aum! let us meditate aright
On that adorable One Light,
Divine Savitri! So may She
Illume our minds! So mote it be!

After which magnificent climax, it is something of a comedown to read G. K. Chesterton's review of *The Sword of Song*, which appeared on its publication in the *Daily News*. Readers may judge for themselves the appropriateness of Chesterton's comments on Crowley's work:

Mr. Crowley has always been, in my opinion, a good poet; his "Soul of Osiris," written during an Egyptian mood, was better poetry than his Browningesque rhapsody in a Buddhistic mood; but this also, though very affected, is very interesting. But the main fact about it is, that it is the expression of a man who has really found Buddhism more satisfactory than Christianity. Mr. Crowley begins his poem, I believe, with an earnest intention to explain the beauty of the Buddhistic philosophy: he knows a great deal about it; he believes in it. . . . But Mr. Crowley has got something into his soul stronger even than the beautiful passion of the man who believes in Buddhism; he has the passion of the man who does not believe in Christianity. He adds one more testimony to the endless series of testimonials to the fascination and vitality of the faith. For some mysterious reason no man can contrive to be agnostic about Christianity. He always tries to prove something about it—that it is unphilosophical or immoral or disastrous—which is not true. . . . A casual carpenter wandered about a string of villages; and suddenly a horde of rich men and sceptics and Sadducees and respectable persons rushed at him and nailed him up like vermin; then people saw that he was a god. He had provided that he was not a common man, for he was murdered. And ever since his creed has proved that it is not a common hypothesis; for it is hated. Next week I hope to make a fuller study of Mr. Crowley's interpretation of Buddhism [he didn't] . . . suffice for the moment to say that if this be indeed a true interpretation of the creed, as it is certainly a capable one, I need go no further than its pages for example of how a change of abstract belief may break a civilization to pieces. Under the influence of this book earnest modern philosophers may, I think, begin to perceive the outlines of two vast and mystical philosophies, which if they were subtly and slowly worked out in two continents through many centuries, might possibly, under special circumstances, make the East and West almost as different as they really are.

Returned from India to the comforts of a Montparnasse studio at the beginning of November 1902, distressed inwardly over the failure of the K2 expedition to reach the mountain's summit, Crowley took the annihilating core of Buddhism to anarchically hedonistic conclusions in his lament "Summa Spes" ("The Sum of Hope" or "Summit Hope") published in Paris as winter melted into spring, 1903. Having recently emerged from Camp Despair its tone does not surprise, but the wound did not altogether heal, and "Summa Spes" would constitute an attitude and refuge that would remain with Crowley, at sundry times, for the remainder of his life.

I.

Existence being sorrow,
The cause of it desire,
A merry tune I borrow
To light upon the lyre:
If death destroy me quite,
Then, I cannot lament it;
I've lived, kept life alight,
And—damned if I repent it!
Let me die in a ditch,
Damnably drunk,
Or lipping a punk,
Or in bed with a bitch!
I was ever a hog;
Muck? I am one with it!
Let me die like a dog;
Die, and be done with it!

II.

As far as reason goes,
There's hope for mortals yet:
When nothing is that knows,
What is there to regret?
Our consciousness depends
On matter in the brain;
When that rots out, and ends,
There ends the hour of pain.

III.

If we can trust to this,
Why, dance and drink and revel!
Great scarlet mouths to kiss,
And sorrow to the devil!
If pangs ataxic creep,
Or gout, or stone, annoy us,
Queen Morphia, grant thy sleep!
Let worms, the dears, enjoy us!

IV.

But since a chance remains
That "I" survives the body
(So talk the men whose brains
Are made of smut and shoddy),
I'll stop it if I can.
(Ah Jesus, if Thou couldest!)
I'll go to Martaban
To make myself a Buddhist.

V.

And yet: the bigger chance
Lies with annihilation.
Follow the lead of France,
Freedom's enlightened nation!
Off! sacredotal stealth
Of faith and fraud and gnosis!
Come, drink me: Here's thy health,
Arterio-sclerosis!
Let me die in a ditch,
Damnably drunk,
Or lipping a punk,
Or in bed with a bitch!
I was ever a hog;
Muck? I am one with it!
Let me die like a dog;
Die, and be done with it!

It might be argued that Crowley employed something of a double standard when it came to the worth of relative religions in dealing with experience of flat despair behind the "sum of hope." That is to say, was the common notion of the Christian hell really any worse than the estimation of Life in this world he had absorbed from Buddhism, from bitter personal experience, and from plain observation? The Buddhist estimation of life's impermanence and sorrow was, as he expressed it, so bad that only annihilation would do, and naught else! Crowley clearly needed *some kind* of redemption from a life-prospect of sorrow, pain, then back again.

Nevertheless, Crowley in 1903, whilst wracked with despair in the world yet clung to the idea that in Buddhism there was at least a path, if only to Nothing. That this did not alter fundamentally his view of life is evident in "Rondels (at Monte Carlo)," written in the casino there in 1903 and published in *Oracles* in 1905.

> THERE is no hell but earth: O coil of fate
> Binding us surely in the Halls of Birth,
> The unsubstantial, the dissolving state!
> There is no hell but earth.
>
> Vain are the falsehoods that subserve to mirth.
> Dust is to dust, create or uncreate.
> The wheel is bounded by the world's great girth.
>
> By prayer and penance unregenerate,
> Redeemed by no man's sacrifice or worth,
> We swing: no mortal knows his ultimate.
> There is no hell but earth.
>
> . . . .
>
> It is a path where tears are ever shed.
> There is no joy—is that a path for me?
> Yea! though I track the ways of utmost dread,
> One way sets free.

"There is no hell but earth," but "one way sets free." Crowley needed the active verb; he could not be content with a passive or resigned position on life. The signs of an inner fight-back through assertion of an active principle are evident in his poem "New Year 1903," appended to *Ahab, and Other Poems,* published in the fall of 1903, shortly after meeting, and falling in love with, Gerald Kelly's sister Rose. Perhaps it took abandonment to the love of Rose to help to release something of the overpowering counterassertion to Buddhism that permeates *The Book of the Law,* received by Crowley in Cairo some seven months after publication of *Ahab,* following a return trip, in honeymoon style, to the Ceylon, not of the spiritual seeker, but of the upper-class English tourist.

> Path of the eightfold star! Be thou revealed!
> Isle of Nirvana, be the currents curled
> About thee, that the swimmer touch thy shore!
> Thought be your sword, and virtue be your shield!
> Press on! Who conquers shall for evermore
> Pass from the fatal mischief of the world.

Marriage worked wonders for the lonely sage, though it could be argued that marriage is endemic to, and inseparable from, the world's fatal mischief.

DONE, AT AKYAB

As the Beatles, some sixty-five years later, employed their leisure hours at the Maharishi Mahesh Yogi's ashram at Rishikesh, Uttarakhand, composing a quiverful of poetic songs for their *White Album,* so the monastery at Akyab's sultry, damp tranquility encouraged Crowley to initiate a bevy of literary works. Several Akyab poems would appear in *Ahab, and Other Poems* in autumn 1903, while Crowley's short story "The Three Characteristics" illuminated *The Sword of Song* in 1904.

Following a mysterious dedication dated December 9, 1902, to "pilgrim of the sun" George Cecil Jones, *Ahab* opens effectively with a beautiful three verse "Rondel" that begins:

> By palm and pagoda enchaunted o'er
>   shadowed, I lie in the light
> Of stars that are bright beyond suns that

all poets have vaunted
In the deep-breathing amorous bosom of
forests of amazon might
By palm and pagoda enchaunted.

"Rondel" is followed by the bulk of the collection, "Ahab," a fairly effective verse-telling of the biblical story of Old Testament "bad boy" Ahab, and how he comes to slay Naboth for his vineyard under the influence of biblical bad girl, Jezebel.

Why the presence of Prome's and Akyab's enchanting pagodas should have conjured to Crowley's perhaps bored imagination this particular tale of childhood memory—the poet seems to identify with a forgivably human Israelite King Ahab—is no more clear than why, in the first published version, the whole poem was printed quite deliberately in almost unreadable heavy, black gothic script redolent of the bygone days of Caxton's first type-shop, even down to the archaic use of ſ for an s that had become typographically obsolete over half a century before. One feels Crowley liked the idea of playing William Morris and the Kelmscott aesthetic, at his own expense, and more, that he did not value the poem very much anyway.

"Ahab" does not lack wit; Crowley rarely did. Ahab's reflection on Elijah's showdown with the god Baal on Carmel is particularly amusing. Crowley looks at the famous contest from the informed eye of one that suspects Elijah knew some "magic" tricks. The flame that ignites the bullocks on the funeral pyre Crowley-Ahab attributes to "Greek fire," that is, a contrived incendiary weapon used by the Byzantines to defend Constantinople, and that was thought to have ancient precedents. Thus, Ahab noted how Elijah urged the assembled to gaze heavenwards for "Water," and while their eye was cunningly distracted, Elijah uses craft to ignite artificially the pyre by chemical means. Crowley-Ahab reflects then in Buddhistic vein concerning the Elijah v. Baal contest intended to show the Hebrew Jahveh's superiority:

In my inmost heart I feel,
Deep as pearl in seas of Ind,
A vision, keen as tempered steel,
Lofty and holy as the wind,

And brighter than the living sun:
If these be gods, then there is none!

Old Ahab's a new skeptic! By the poem's end, identification of seer and subject is all but complete, as the poet has made us see what magic made Jezebel so irresistible, and what made poor Naboth architect of his own demise, and in the end we may ask, *what of the mote in thy brother Ahab's eye compared to the beam in your own?* In the end, the bitterness of life's false promises coats even the king with the robes of existential futility:

I see him, a fantastic ghost,
　The vineyard smiling white and plain,
And hiding ever innermost
　The little shadows on his brain;
I laugh again with mirthless glee,
As knowing also I am he.

A fool in gorgeous attire!
　An ox decked bravely for his doom!
So step I to the great desire.
　Sweet winds upon the gathering gloom
Bend like a mother, as I go,
Foreknowing, to my overthrow.

The year 1902 would not mark the end of Crowley's personal relationship with Allan Bennett, but there are perhaps signs of some significant variance of fundamental attitude and perhaps growing conflict in orientation in Crowley's humorous-but-serious story, "The Three Characteristics"—the three characteristics of Buddhist world assessment being of course, sorrow, impermanence, and absence of an ego or personal soul, or eternal essence.

"The Three Characteristics" is Crowley having intelligent fun with Buddhist tradition, a friendly parody-with-an-edge in the style of a *jātaka,* or traditional tale of an incarnation of the Buddha. Typically, Crowley's intuitive empathy gives him command of a formal style as idiosyncratic as Kipling's tales from *The Jungle Book.*

"LISTEN to the Jataka!" said the Buddha. And all gave ear. "Long ago, when King Brahmadatta reigned in Burma, it came to pass that there lived under his admirable government a weaver named Suraj Ju [the Sun] and his wife Chandi [the Moon]." His celestial parents' mutuality begets "Perdu' R Abu," in whom we may recognize *Perdurabo*, Crowley's spiritual motto "I shall endure," that is, (pointedly in the tale) to *the End*.

Perdu' R Abu's burgeoning happiness in youth is struck to naught by the three characteristics: "Sorrow, Absence of ego, and impermanence!"

Enter "Jehjaour," a "mighty magician" whose soul was "dark and evil" whose "lust was of life and power and of the wreaking of hatred upon the innocent." This is none other than a transposition of "Iehi Aour"—motto of Allan Bennett in the Golden Dawn: "Let there be Light," now manifest as Ananda Metteya.

It is likely that Crowley was thinking, not only of Allan's, that is, Bhikkhu Ananda Metteya's, dark countenance and frail health, but also ruminating on the possible effects of his friend's now-total immersion in Buddhism on the "innocent" (those not formerly acquainted with its message), a doctrine that, from the West's point of view, would undoubtedly be viewed by many as dark, and evil, insofar as it denied lasting spiritual (or any other) value to this life, and if carried into Western civilization (as Bennett would soon enterprise) would make Bennett as spiritually powerful a transformer of Western progressive optimism as could be imagined. Crowley sees the irony perfectly, I think, on lines similar to that understood by those who correctly diagnosed the "nonviolence" of the later Mahatma Gandhi as being more destructive of Western power than violent terrorism. Gandhi's political method (or "magic") was to generate *shame* in the resistor to passive resistance; Buddhism likewise may shame any who have adapted to the conditions of natural life on earth, who accept the just war with its principle of necessity that life be taken by force from those deemed hostile to the march of Life. It should also be noted that Crowley had a lifelong suspicion of, and distaste for, the "Gentle Jesus, meek and mild" image and pattern of spiritual attainment (or resignation). Bennett's Buddhist absolutism put a mantrap into Crowley's fundamental nature, which beforetime had accommodated life's realities, pleasant and unpleasant. Note too Crowley's lifelong maintenance that he was happy to have pursued a career in the diplomatic service of his country until he underwent an overwhelming sense of the futility of nonspiritual endeavor when at Cambridge, described, after his Buddhist education, as the "Trance of Sorrow," which like the "Three Characteristics" robbed his youth of deep satisfaction, despite his guiltless, if personally qualified, embrace of wine, women, and song, in principled opposition to his mother and her conception of religion.

Returning to the story, the magician Jehjaour gazes into a crystal ball to see all the "fears as yet unborn on earth." There is the hint here of Crowley ribbing his asthmatic friend for a kind of spiritual hypochondria, an obsession with the negativities and life-threatening potential of so much we pass through in life, and that he, blissed-out, wished to avoid. Crowley knew, for example, that knowledge of the facts of human reproduction came late in life to Allan Bennett, and on learning the facts, the young man was personally horrified, temperamentally disgusted at the "base" means by which human life was propagated; it simply made normal life untenable for him. The darkness in the magician is likely that of Bennett's melancholy outlook. As regards the facts of sexual reproduction that so disturbed him, to Crowley such was only one side of a handy and necessary coin; the other side was also there to be enjoyed.

Perdu' R Abu had, we are told, "been his friend," but the crystal ball always showed "that sensual and frivolous youth" (Crowley) "as a Fear to him: even to him the Mighty One." One thinks immediately of Bennett's horror of Crowley's big-game hunting in Ceylon while he, pious bhikkhu-to-be himself luxuriated in the warm balm of ancient Buddhist history at Dambulla and elsewhere on the island of Lanka. We receive here, I believe, a glimpse of a shard fallen from the broken mirror of the men's relationship. Bennett, after all, had taught Crowley all he knew about Magic, and much about narcotics. They had evoked demons together, in Chancery Lane, London, under the noses of a police watch in 1899–1900. A declivity had, in short time, opened up between Aleister and the renunciate bhikkhu, though it's likely the root fissures existed from the start of their unusual relationship.

"But the selfish and evil are cowards; they fear shadows, and Jehjaour scorned not his art." When the crystal ball—or its dark, animating spirit—cannot see the Fear implicit in Perdu' R Abu it is because its source comes from a source far higher than the scope of an evil spirit. The resulting frustration manifested in the magician as red rage: "his whole force went out into a mighty current of hate towards his former friend." Was Crowley here entertaining a premonition of future break-down in understanding between Bennett and himself, to a time when Bennett would dismiss the religion of apostate Crowley?

The magician Jehjaour goes to elephant god Ganesha, telling the god—forsaken already by Perdu' R Abu and by the magician—that his enemy had already become "Srotapatti" (one who had entered the stream of nirvana) and in only seven births! At his current rate of prog-ress he'd cease to be reborn! So, if Ganesha wants Perdu' R Abu's wor-ship, he'll know what to do! The magician advises the unintelligent god that each subsequent birth must perforce be as long as possible. Only if Perdu' R Abu attained arahatship would he be a serious danger to Jehjaour.

First idea: let the enemy Perdu' R Abu be an elephant, longest liv-ing of all the beasts. But Perdu' R Abu as an elephant was not as other elephants, and when Ganesha paid call on the lonely "tusker" he was found meditating solitarily on the Three Characteristics, showing lit-tle sign of elephantness. Unseen (and undreamed of by Buddhists), a *Bacillus* entered the jungle and took the elephant out of it at the prema-ture age of seventeen. Jehjaour's plan was foiled.

The evil one arranges Perdu' R Abu's next incarnation as a parrot, for a parrot, we are told "may live 500 years and never feel it." However, a Tibetan lama enters the jungle with his prayer wheel, muttering "Aum Mani Padme Hum" ("O the Jewel in the Lotus! Aum!"). The atten-tive parrot picks up the mantra and repeats it continually. The words had their effect and soon the parrot is meditating on the conditions of existence.

Scene switches to a home in "Inglistan" (England) where an old lady is sitting with a gray parrot in a cage. The parrot suddenly grasps the spiritual meaning of the Four Noble Truths and Three Characteristics, and blurts out the mantra in a moment of enlightenment, and does not cease blurting. The old lady calls her maid and insists she do some-thing about the filthy talking parrot. *What?* "Wring its neck!" The par-rot, we are told, was only eight years old. Foiled again by the Three Characteristics!

Ganesha accuses Jehjaour of being a "muddler and an idiot." Surely, Perdu' R Abu should be made into a spiritual thing. A "Nat" (elemental spirit) lives for 10,000 years: ideal! So Perdu' R Abu manifested among a family of Nats in a big tree at Anurādhapura close to a holy dagoba (Buddhist stupa or moundlike sacred structure). One day a Siamese holy bhikkhu came and made the tree his abode and Perdu' R Abu used his gossamer wings to keep the mosquitoes from disturbing the bhikkhu's peace. But the British Government didn't like such a thing, what with him living in a tree as the locals brought him rice, onions, and gramophones! And Perdu' R Abu heard them talk and learned the great secret of Impermanence, of Sorrow and the mystery of Unsubstantiality, as the government evicted the holy man and cut down the tree, so all the Nats perished. And Perdu' R Abu was only three years old.

Near to despair Jehajaour called on Ganesha to make Perdu' R Abu a flute girl before Indra's throne. And the beautiful flute girl played and sang sweetly, for she knew the mystery of love and death and dimly remembered a world beyond, and one day she perceived the Noble Truths, at which moment a mosquito got trapped in her flute, and rather than endure the buzzing of it any longer, Indra cast one of his lightning discs in her direction and ended an existence of only eight months.

Rescue to the scheme came when Indra was guillotined for the murder, whereupon the magus yelled that his place should be taken by Perdu' R Abu! His virtue would save him practically indefinitely. So Perdu' R Abu became Indra and found himself amazed at the improvement of his memory. He remembered lots of changes, and all recent. And Indra recalled reading "Crowley's Dhammapada" that virtue would keep him steady. He contentedly chewed betel with Lady Bhavani in Arcadian bliss. But Bhavani found him so pious and so concentrated on applying the Three Characteristics to the recent banking scandal, the Affaire Humbert, that he would not make love to her, even when she pleaded—so Bhavani gulped him down in one swallow! As Indra, Perdu' R Abu endured seven days.

"Only one more birth" groaned the magician. Ganesha insisted he cheer up. Help was in his gift. There was no change in the Arupa-Brahma-Loka! (the Hindu's highest heaven). Perdu' R Abu would be elected Mahabrahma. Through aeon after aeon, Mahabrahma will endure on his lotus throne. But something troubled Jehjaour. The picture unfolding all seemed a bit touched by Edwin Arnold's *Light of Asia*. He asked Ganesha if he had read it. Constantly, said Ganesha. It was the only way the gods knew of finding out clearly who they were! Perdu' R Abu wouldn't have to *do* anything now, for he knew the Bible lesson that nothing good for mankind could follow an ill-timed action on the part of the deity!

Yet the formless abstraction that he was, was troubled. His identity. What was it? Here he was now and presumably forever, above all change, but only an hour before he'd been Indra, and before that a flute-girl, and then, was he not a Nat, a parrot, a Hathi, and how could they connect? Mahabrahma saw to ask a holy man near a Bo-Tree, whereas, if he'd remembered that bit more, he would have known about Jehjaour and that as a Srotapatti he had only one more birth and might have well put in the billions of aeons that would "elapse before lunch in rejoicing over his imminent annihilation."

Assuming the appearance of a cowherd, Mahabrahma addressed the holy man, who was in fact, Gautama, the Buddha. How had Perdu' R Abu passed from change and death to the unchangeable? The holy man rebuked him. His facts were wrong so he could not make correct deductions. All things, be it you "O Mahabrahma" or a grain of dust, "possess Three Characteristics." Gautama goes on: "The truth is that you're a very spiritual sort of being and a prey to longevity. Men's lives are so short that yours seems eternal in comparison." Nonetheless, Gautama assures him he'll yet be dead in a week.

Then, a paper by Huxlananda Swami appeared (Thomas Henry Huxley): "Mahabrahma had never been much more than an idea. He had only lived six days."

The Buddha continued his jataka. In his wickedness, Jehjaour had joined himself to Mara (the evil principle) to prevent discovery of the truth, and when Mara fell, as his hatred recoiled upon him, he fell too: into the Lowest Hell—"he became a clergyman of the Church of England, further than he had ever been before from Truth and Light and Peace and Love; deeper and deeper emmeshed in the net of Circumstance," as false Vichi-Kichi (Ignorance) caught him at last!

Perdu' R Abu was reincarnated as a child of Western parents ignorant of his wonderful past. "But a strange fate," Buddha announces, "has brought him to this village." Among the listeners was a white man. "Brother Abhavananda,* little friend," said the Buddha. "Lord!" responded the white man, "they are unstable, everything is sorrow, in them is no inward Principle, as some pretend, that can avoid, that can hold itself aloof from, the forces of decay." *How did he know that?* Brother Abhavananda had considered the Universe. Besides, the consciousness of the Three Characteristics was ingrained in his deepest sense of being, perhaps due to his past incarnations. The Buddha bids him rise: "I dub thee Arahat!" And lo, "he perceived." Buddha then explained his tale. Brother Abhavananda was the Perdu' R Abu of the story. While Buddha was the *Bacillus* in the forest of Lanka, as he was also the old lady, and even (he shuddered) was he the British Government, as he was also the mosquito that buzzed into the flute, and he was Bhavani, and "I was Huxlananda Swami" and now, at the last, at this blessed hour: "I am—that I am."

And the arahats are scandalized. For is he not therefore guilty of six violent deaths? What of the Buddha's first precept? Here we see the grain that would split Crowley from orthodox Buddhism. *How could the Perfect One kill?*

And the Glorious One addressed them as "Children." Do not think, he instructed them, that death is necessarily an evil. "I have not come to found a Hundred Years Club, and to include mosquitoes in the membership." *In this case,* keeping Perdu' R Abu alive would have been to play into the hands of his enemies. "My First Precept is merely a general rule." In most cases one should abstain from destroying life, wantonly or willfully, "but I cannot drink a glass of water without killing countless myriads of living beings." All forms of life are at odds with one another for survival. It is deadly and it is inevitable. If you understood, you would conceive the First Noble Truth, that no existence can be free from sorrow. Second, that the desire for existence only leads to sorrow, and that ceasing from existence is the ceasing of sorrow, and then you would seek the Way that is the Noble Eightfold Path.

As arahats of course, Buddha politely, but ironically, suggested they did not need this instruction, but the words of Buddha must go on to illuminate the whole system of ten thousand worlds, "where Arahats do

---

*"Bliss of nonexistence": one of Crowley's pen names.

not grow on every tree. Little brothers, the night is fallen: it were well to sleep."

And one may conclude that it was through earnest meditation on the Three Characteristics that ensure that eventually, in the fullness of the blessed hour, Aleister Crowley did not remain a Buddhist, though perhaps he became a Buddha, if only for a moment. But a moment in Brahma is as . . . the three characteristics.

THIRTEEN

1905: Jñāna Yoga

With *Sword* safely delivered to a disinterested public, autumn 1904 was devoted to Paris, where Crowley's Buddhist enthusiasm, though relatively understated, was still in evidence. Following Masonic initiation into Anglo-Saxon Lodge No. 343,* Gerald Kelly received a letter from his friend sent from the Langham Hotel, 24, rue Boccador, on attractive blue paper embossed with an orange crest *B* for Boleskine, with the embossed motto (also in orange): SRIOCHAL NO DHREAM: Gaelic for "E'en Do and Spare Not," followed prominently by the Theravāda bhikkhu's Buddhist salutation: *Namo Tassa Bhagavato Arahato Sammasam buddhasa.*†† No sign here of ditching Buddhism for *The Book of the Law*'s spiritual-warrior creed.

As Crowley subsequently admitted, he even forewent an opportunity to advance the Cairo revelation's cause in late spring 1904 when providence provided Theosophical Society leader Annie Besant's presence on the ship from Egypt to France. A remarkable pair, Besant and Crowley doubtless conversed on spiritual matters, but it is unlikely in the extreme that Besant would have opened herself to *The Book of the Law*'s denunciation of pity as damnable, its acclamation of war as admirable, or its maintenance that sorrows are shadows, and pass, whereas

---

*Chartered in 1899 by the Grande Loge de France, unrecognized, at the time, by the United Grand Lodge of England, but subsequently recognized, shortly after Crowley demitted from it, in 1913.

†*Namo* = "I pay homage"; *tassa* = "to him"; *Bhagavato* = "to the Exalted One"; *Arahato* = "to the Worthy One"; *Sammasam buddhassa* = "to the Fully Enlightened One."

existence is "pure joy." Crowley himself, at this period, did not seem convinced by much of this either; he resisted the book, not really knowing how he was supposed to "take it," and in due course would find his way back to Ananda Metteya for advice on spiritual progress (or his lack of it). Spiritual initiation at the level Crowley aspired to can prove mightily inconvenient; though one might justifiably say that Crowley asked for it.

While in Bern, Switzerland, twenty-six-year-old Albert Einstein was about to commit to paper his general theory of relativity, Aleister Crowley waved off a prolonged, somewhat decadent house party at Boleskine and reentered his temple to renew his rāja ("royal") yoga meditations. Crowley needed no hints from Einstein that the perceptible state of phenomena was relative to the conditions and position of the observer. Crowley, too, was dedicated to consciousness revolution.

The date: Wednesday, March 29, 1905:

> 11:00A.M. Entered Temple.
>
> 11:04–11:22. [mantra] Aum Tat Sat Aum and ajna [chakra]. 30 breaks—whole direction of thought very weak. It is of course nearly two years since I did a serious test.
>
> Walk with mahasatipattana on breath.
>
> 12:06–12:13. Aum Tat Sat Aum and ajna. 10 br[eaks]. The anaesthesia of ajna is so marked that I am going to try some other cakra. It is rather curious that the strange dullness of brain that I have been suffering from of late should be accompanied by this lack of feeling in ajna.
>
> 12:22–12:42. Anahata and Om Mani Padme Hum. 30 br[eaks]. Slight subjective disturbance on right jaw—made me think of the Plattner Story.* This I thought kept on and on—probably 12 or more breaks to its own check. Some 4 or 5 breaks were due to attendant tramping about. Got headache.
>
> 4:14 A[um] M[ani] H[um] anahata [heart chakra]. Got the sleep effect.
>
> 4:57. 16 min. Not quite 30 br[eaks]. Sleep again.
>
> 6:34. Svadistthana. Aum. 15 m. 22 br[eaks.][2]

---

*H. G. Wells, *The Plattner Story and Others,* London: Macmillan, 1904.

The *svādhiṣṭhāna* ("one's base") is the second or sacral chakra (below the navel), sometimes illustrated as a white lotus with six vermilion petals that represent *vrittis,* or states of mind, such as affection, destructiveness, delusion, and suspicion: all emotional states, and thus expressive of deeper changes. Meditation on the svādhiṣṭhāna traditionally may provide special powers (*siddhis*) such as freedom from enemies, eloquence, clarity, and awareness of astral beings.

At 9:19, Crowley repeated the Shaivite mantra *Namo Śivaya Namaha Aum* for fifteen minutes, sustaining twenty-two breaks, with his eyes open.

> Will experiment twirling a vibration on desired cakra with O[m] M[ani] P[adme] H[um]. This latter seems a good mantra for me just now. Of the various things I have tried it with anahata seems best— most effective, apart from break-considerations.
>
> Made this experiment—worth repeating.
>
> Am very thirsty for water all day—why? Change of diet?[3]

The next day's effort (Thursday, March 30) Crowley recorded as being a bit slack, with prāṇāyāma and *Om Mani Padme Hum* mantraing on the heart chakra (anahata) in the afternoon. He counted sixteen breaks in ten minutes shortly before 4:00 p.m., but didn't believe his count as he got so deeply into the mantra washing around the lotus in the heart like a wave that he thought he may have gone on counting beads "without a break automatically"—he was using the beads in his fingers to register breaks, writing down the number passed at the end of a sequence.

He then tried five minutes of prāṇāyāma and wondered if five minutes was all he could do, questioning whether "the air" was foul, which he decided it was. At 6:21 he tried prāṇāyāma without a pause for retention, as a way of getting practice, then did ten seconds breathing in and twenty out, with twenty seconds of "khumbhakam" (holding his breath). It was harder to hold breath after breathing out than after breathing in. He noted afterward he should do some meditation daily without counting the breaks at all.

He then adopted the "accomplished" āsana; in Sanskrit: *siddhāsana* at 8:28 p.m. and meditated on the ājñā chakra to the *Aum Tat Sat Aum* mantra until 8:46 p.m. He realized that counting breaks was really a "meditation in itself" and "therefore quite inimical to doing true meditation." At 10:58 he managed eleven minutes of prāṇāyāma, reckoning it would be all right in another two or three days. He also continued doing occasional ājñā meditations to the *Aum Tat Sat Aum* mantra day and night.

On Friday March 31, moving outside for a change, he could only manage thirteen minutes of prāṇāyāma. One suspects he was the sole being performing this practice outside in Scotland, or probably inside, that morning. He continued through the day at intervals with cycles of ten seconds breathing in, twenty of pause, and twenty breathing out, complaining that belching had become a problem, though he was finding the āsana less painful. In Tangier, Morocco, meanwhile, the German kaiser—to Morrocco's ally France's anger—met Sultan Abdulaziz, provoking the "First Morroccan Crisis," challenging Britain's *entente* with France and giving a harbinger of world war to come.

At 8:47 Crowley notes applying what he calls "Sabhapaty's second method" for twenty-six minutes. Readers may recall Crowley's first introduction to the work of Sabhapaty Swami came via the exceedingly kind but unnamed authority on yoga from the village by Madura who

Fig. 13.1. "Gnyana Guru Yogi Sabapathi Swamy" from his Om, A Treatise on Vedantic Raj Yoga Philosophy. *(Courtesy of Henry S. Olcott Memorial Library, Wheaton, Illinois)*

facilitated entry to restricted shrines within Madura's great Meenakshi Temple (see page 89). In order to grasp what Crowley had embarked upon, and the thinking behind it, we need to look carefully at this remarkable swami and the work that formed the marrow of Crowley's understanding of a gnostic Vedanta, a conception he would reverence profoundly all of his life.*

THE MAHATMA GURU YOGI SABHAPATY SWAMI AND HIS VEDANTIC RAJ YOGA PHILOSOPHY

In March 1905, Crowley paraphrased the "second method" from pages 35, 36, and 38 of part two of Sabhapaty's book thus:

> Draw the light of your two eyes internally to *kundali* by *idā* and *pingalā* respectively.† Imagine the mind as a straight pole *brahmarandhra-kundali*‡ and the consciousness at the bottom of this pole. Take hold of the consciousness by the two keennesses of your eyes and pull it slowly up (? by *kumbhaka*). This process must take at least twenty minutes. (The citta [consciousness of perceptible things; thoughts] must be slowed considerably before this is possible.—A.C.) Keep consciousness in *brahmarandhra* for 20 min. more.
>
> Then drop and lift it through suṣumnā so fast that it takes less than 1 sec[ond]. Practice this for a few minutes. Then let your mind stand steady on the pole (? As before). In calm silence void

---

*The practice taught by Crowley in his "Liber HHH" is derived from Sabhapaty's teachings. See *Magick,* 598–603.

†In yogic anatomy, the *idā* and the *pingalā* are the left and right channels, or *nadīs,* of prāna energy, associated with the left and right sides of the spine, while the central nadī is called the *sushumnā.* The idā and pingalā may also represent the basic duality in existence, corresponding to Shiva and Shakti.

‡*Brahmarandhra* or "aperture" of Brahman, the passage by which life enters the body, and associated with a spot at the top of the head: a threshold between this world and the higher spiritual world, as can be seen in Sabhapaty's illustration. It is where the sushumnā nadī terminates. *Kundali* means in Hindi literally a "coil," as in rope or a snake. It refers to the energy coiled at the *mūlādhāra* chakra that may extend through the spine to the crown of the head. *Kundali* is then "the Mother" who at the crown of the head (*sahasrāra*) may unite individual with cosmic consciousness: a "union with the Lord."

and without motion, free from all thoughts and fickleness—so be it. Then join the "conscious sight of the two eyes" (which have gone back to their usual place?) with the top of the mind in *bramarandhra,* forming a triangle. Having got success in this practice, imagine your head to be removed and that the whole space (? of the head) is filled up by the Universal Consciousness which now becomes the holy *ākāśa* [ether; space; origin of mind; atmosphere] itself. This is neither dark nor bright coloured nor formed. Consider this as infinite—take it [as the] centre; Earth floats below centre, sun to right above, moon to left above, stars etc. At top. Then expand your universally diffused consciousness (*sic!*) till it fills and permeates all space and matter. It is perfect vacuum; cancel luminous or dark *ākāśas* wh[i]ch may appear. Be very careful to cancel the true one. You become *bhāvāna brahma-jñāni brahmacarya*—Hurra! (All this is obscure and often nonsensical.)[4]

Crowley noted the results of attempting this method. His eyes seemed to "excite" the chakras "as they passed." At svādistthāna, there were nervous movements in the lower limbs. There was stirring in the anāhata and manipūra* chakras.

Crowley goes on:

Visuddhi[†] swallowing movement, above in brain peculiar throbbings.

Nothing much followed the "Middle Pillar" rush,[‡] but on enlarging the head I got almost complete loss of surface. Shooting-

---

*Manipūra is the third primary chakra between the navel and solar plexus, associated with the element of fire.

†The vishudda chakra, the fifth, is situated in the throat; from *visha* = impurity, poison, and *suddhi* = purify. Its corresponding element is ākāśha or space, and is associated with dedication to purify prāna.

‡Crowley is referring to the "Middle Pillar" exercise he learned in the Golden Dawn, which is akin to the chakra meditations of Sabhapaty. In the G.∴.D.∴. exercise, the five energy centers in the body are associated with the sephiroth, seen as colored light, over which, so to speak, one vibrates the appropriate God names (cf: the mantras), so cleansing the aura in a powerful self-performed ritual. This is a kabbalistic exercise and is what Crowley means when he adds later that Sabhapaty's method seems like the "Western formula," which itself points to a profound link between jñāna (knowledge) yoga and Gnostic practices of Egypt in late antiquity. See my book *Gnostic Mysteries of Sex.*

star effects pretty natural; here seems the difficulty: for I may have *thought* this. The whole thing was rather like a Western formula than an Eastern; but very remarkable and persistent. In spite of H.P.K. [Hoor-Paar-Kraat] formula (repeated) and cognac to intensify ego the vague feeling of head still persists (10 min[utes]. later). During hydrocephalus I did lose ego more or less; there was no definite ananda [bliss].

N.B. Apart from the short time, there were several errors in the practice which I will read up properly.[5]

I was fortunate to obtain a copy of the original English-language publication of Sabhapaty Swami's *Om, A Treatise on Vedantic Raj Yoga Philosophy** through the good offices of staff at the Henry S. Olcott Memorial Library, Wheaton, Illinois. Brought from Adyar, the copy was formerly Col. Olcott's own and bears marks of much use and travel!

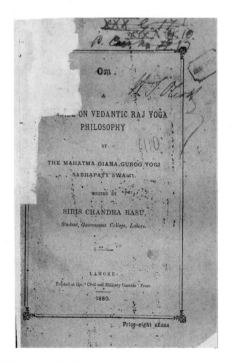

Fig. 13.2. Col. H. S. Olcott's copy of Om, A Treatise on Vedantic Raj Yoga Philosophy. *(Courtesy of Henry S. Olcott Memorial Library, Wheaton, Illinois)*

---

*"By The Mahatma Giana, Guroo Yogi Sabhapaty Swami; Edited by Siris Chandra Basu, Student, Government College, Lahore: Printed at the "Civil and Military Gazette" Press. 1880. Price: eight annas." The dedication page bears the stamp of the T.S. "ADYAR LIBRARY 1110." The cover bears H. S. Olcott's personal signature.

It contains Sabhapaty's original colored illustrations, which show in graphic form the passage of nadīs through the chakras from mūlādhāra to brahmarandhra (see fig. 13.3 on page 298).

Prefaced by a life of the guru, vouchsafed to us by "An Admirer,"* it contains legendary elements traditionally associated with great gurus, that is, incredible feats, but despite these elements, it is all we have.[6]

Sabhapaty's synthetic approach to his jñāna yoga seems to owe much to his travels. Born in Madras (now Chennai) in about 1840, he first traveled to Burma on family textile business, having received boyhood education at a Christian missionary school. Discourse with Buddhist monks ensued, following which he ventured to Nagore, a port near Nagappatinam on India's east coast (now Tamil Nadu state), about 230 miles northeast of Madura. There he conversed with Sufi followers of Pir Saiyid Abd al-Qadir Shahul Hamid Nagore (1502–1570).† Three years spent absorbing alien ideas on top of Christian ones did not, however, bring him to the "brahma-jñāna" he craved.

He then, we are told, spent seven years studying the classics of Hinduism: the Vedas and the Darshanas, the latter being the six philosophical schools based on the Vedas: the Nyāya, the Vaisheshika (these two being the Indian system of logic), the Sānkhya (the exercise of reason and observation), the Yoga (mastery of *vrittis,* or thought waves, systematized by Patañjali), the Mīmāmsā (ritual knowledge, or right action, based on the Vedas), and the Vedanta. The first three schools would correspond in a general way to what Westerners know as empiricism, or sense-knowledge. All together, the Darshanas aim at banishing *mithya jñāna,* or false knowledge, or *aviveka* (inability to discriminate between real and unreal), which is regarded as the source of disorder and suffering.

This, we may say, was—even when added to Sabhapaty's charitable works—"all very well," but, however grand the knowledge vista, it was still learning, or external knowledge, things of memory, not absolute realization or *gnosis.* Being told one's soul is of the same substance

---

*The account also appeared as "The Madras Yogi Sabhapaty Swami" in the *Theosophist,* vol. 1, March 1880. "Life" signed: "AN ADMIRER, LAHORE, January 3rd, 1880."
†Nagore's Muslim dargah minaret is still a striking monument, all white and resembling a stately and ancient lighthouse.

as God is not the same as *knowing* it as such without having to be reminded.

Relief for Sabhapaty commenced with a vision, aged twenty-nine, of holy man Agastya, whose name is given as author of several hymns in the *Rig Veda* (circa 1500–1200 BCE). The sage of vision told Sabhapaty to go to Vedaśreṇi, a temple in what used to be rural Madras, where the twenty-nine-year-old experienced *śiva-darśana* or the samādhi of Shiva. Agastya now appeared again and told Sabhapaty to hasten to Nīlagiri, the "Blue Mountains" on the borders of what are now Kerala and Tamil Nadu states, where he found his guru and joined an initiated group, after which he returned to Madras with a mission. He began writing books, becoming a pilgrim to temples throughout the country, before settling in the Punjab at Lahore.

Sanskritist and civil servant Sriṣa Chandra Vasu (Besu in Bengali; 1861–1918) edited Sabhapaty's book on Vedantic rāja yoga and brought it into the Theosophical circles he frequented, subsequently achieving prominence in Hindu revivalism. Thanks to Besu, publication of Sabhapaty's yoga book came a good sixteen years before Vivekānanda's *Rāja Yoga*—usually regarded as the initiator of modern yoga. Noted as a source in Max Müller's *Six Systems of Indian Philosophy* (1899), Sabhapaty's yoga text was also taken up by O.T.O. co-founder Franz Hartmann who, in 1909, published *Die Philosophie und Wissenschaft des Vedanta und Rāja-Yoga, oder Das Eingehen in Gottheit von Mahātma Ināna Guru Yogi Sabhapatti Svāmī aus dem Englischen übersetzt von Franz Hartmann* (Leipzig: Jaeger).

Scholar Keith E. Cantú has drawn attention[*] to Sabhapaty's relations with Col. Olcott and Madame Blavatsky. Initially enthusiastic about the swami, an apparent claim of Sabhapaty's to have actually flown in his physical body from Lake Manasarovara in modern Tibet two hundred miles to Mount Kailāsa to commune with Mahādeva[†] brought skepticism even from broad-minded, sympathetic Col. Olcott, who opined that if the guru had specified a journey undertaken in his

---

[*]See 2016 paper by Keith E. Cantú, "Śrī Sabhāpaty Swami: The Forgotten Yogi of Western Esotericism."
[†]Meaning "supreme God," a title sometimes accorded Shiva, among other figures in Hinduism and Buddhism.

astral body or clairvoyant vision, then he would have been receptive. As it was, the story even had the guru joined by two rishis from the *Mahābhārata!* In this case, the vaunted Theosophical aim of bringing spiritual matters into scientific purview seems to have won out. The story's rejection obviously had some embarrassing consequences for Besu, if not for Sabhapaty, for it was probably Besu who composed the following footnote to the 1895 reprint of *Om:*

> This need not have been in the physical body of the Rishis; they might have flown towards the holy mountain in their Mayavi Rupa Kama Rupa (astral body), which to our author (who certainly is not an Adept in the sense the Theosophists use the word) must have been as real as if he had travelled through air in his physical body.[7]

To persons familiar with Simonian and Sethian Gnostic itineraries of the second and third centuries, albeit distorted by patristic authors Hippolytus and Tertullian, Sabhapaty's system bears a familiar ring. The meditator's consciousness is to flow with the prāṇa that runs up and down the occult body, rather like the Gnostic Sophia moving up and down the "tree" that extends from the divine pleroma above, to the physical body below, to restore pneumatic union (Gnostic "resurrection"). The process also has a typologically sexual subtext, both for Sabhapaty and for the ancient Gnostics. This implication would not be lost on Aleister Crowley, who, as Keith E. Cantú observes, was "particularly interested in Sabhāpati's rich visual meditations (dhyāna) on the spinal cord as a phallus (liṅga) and the cranial vault as the *kteis* (yoni), which Crowley published in modified form as an instruction for his students."* A link at a deeper level between ancient Gnostic ideas and Sabhapaty's system may also explain why Crowley in his March 31, 1905, diary note refers to the meditation having a "Western" feel to it, for kabbalistic

---

*In Crowley's *Liber HHH: SSS* in the *Equinox,* vol. 1, no. 5 (London: Simpkin Marshall, 1911). According to Cantú, "Sabhāpati's subtle physiology is situated around twelve tantric cakras and four transcendent states, which in part may also explain Crowley's willingness to entertain notions of additional cakra to the commonly known system of seven (or 'six plus one') as usually found in Western 'New Age' systems of the cakra that follow the pattern laid out by Charles W. Leadbeater (1854–1934) and John Woodroffe/Arthur Avalon (1865–1936)."[8]

ideas of the *sephiroth* appear at the very least influenced by Gnostic and Neoplatonist speculation regarding the pleroma's extension as "aions" or emanations, often as pairs (compare the dualism of nadīs). There is also of course the kabbalistic speculation that "Adam Kadmon" held within him the universe; thus we may see the Gnostic aions internalized as both chakra and *sephira* (emanation) in the potential *universal man,* who is light.

SABHAPATY'S SYSTEM

Sabhapaty's system proceeds from the conception that man as he ordinarily knows himself is deluded regarding the essential being that makes him alive, and is what he is in reality. A mystery to himself, man is veiled in delusion (*bhrānti*). The meditations are designed to pierce these veils to restore jñāna (knowledge). Delusion is attributed to the limitations of sense perceptions, or deceiving impressions (*vāsana*), which must be transcended to reach liberation (*mukti*).

Delusions melt away with the awakening of *kuṇḍalinī* ("kuṇḍali" in Sabhapaty's work) and *jñānākāśa* ("ether of gnosis") or *prāṇākāśa* ("ether of vitality") along the spine and head's twelve chakras, which are regarded as providing ingress for delusionary senses of identity from the illusory nature of sense experience with the world. It is fascinating to note that the kuṇḍalinī is known as the "Mother," for that is the same epithet granted to the heavenly Sophia in Gnostic systems, to whom repose comes only when reabsorbed in union or complete reflection, with the "Father."

Sabhapaty also advocates Patañjali's established *ashtāṇga* (or eight-limbed path), giving the traditional yama, niyama, āsana, prāṇāyāma, dhāraṇā, dhyāna, samādhi, and saṃyama, a collective description of "nine states of practice." The practices in Sabhapaty's view all assist in the attaining of spiritual states whereby powerful visualizations may be achieved, or "spiritual states of God," as he calls them, that require processes of *bhāvana,* which he defines as "meditative formulation." This means creative visualization, and comes very close indeed to practices with which Crowley was familiar in magic, including the assumption of god forms in the Golden Dawn. So, for example, in the "second method" Crowley paraphrased above, the mind is to imagine the process

Fig. 13.3. "The Posture of Samathy or Trance," showing the
"nadee" from the crown ("Brahmarantar") to the "kundlee," in
Sabhapaty's Om, A Treatise on Vedantic Raj Yoga Philosophy.
(Courtesy of Henry S. Olcott Memorial Library, Wheaton, Illinois)

described (the "pole," and so forth) to the extent of its becoming, to a
progressively cleansed consciousness, a spiritual reality. The important
thing is, by yoga, to exclude any thing, image, or thought that might
obstruct and impede the flow of prāṇa to where one wills it. Part of this
process involves a kind of chakra "cleaning," even destruction, a banishing of the sense of "self" (jīvātmā) given by each energy center, to be
replaced by infusion of spiritual brahman that enters via the crown of
the head, when the system is purified and thus able to accommodate
what is axiomatically true, divine Paramātman.

The above conclusion serves to introduce Sabhapaty's treatise: "The purpose of this treatise is to show the method by which the human soul is sure to gain success in holding communion with the Universal Infinite Spirit, and thereby to become the very Infinite Spirit itself." It does not take much imagination to imagine what was likely to have crossed Crowley's mind when he read this. Was this not another way of expressing the aim of the "Sacred Magic of Abramelin the Mage"?—that is, the "Knowledge and Conversation of the Holy Guardian Angel"?

Sabhapaty begins his treatise with a peroration on the importance of acquaintance with the Vedic shastras, meditation on which scripture permits communion with infinite spirit, which communion enables a life of wasted resources and ignorance of the infinite in worldly pleasures to contemplate instead the purification of the jīvātma or soul, by itself, and therefore the "true reality" of Brahman.

It is a wayward mind that has led the jīvātma into vain sins, and the jīvātma longs for *moksha,* "salvation." God the Infinite Spirit exists in the form of every soul or created thing, though in their *bhranti,* or deluded state, they dream themselves in separate existence "from me." Rather, "I am the eternal delight, the giver of everlasting happiness to all souls . . . every soul is I the Infinite Spirit." This becomes true for all "who forsake the world and its pleasures, who have brought under subjection all the wandering thoughts of their mind, who are anxious and true-hearted, resolute in their search after Vedantism and are dauntless and brave."[9]

Crowley would probably have sniffed somewhat at some of Sabhapaty's "Holy commandments of voidness and purification by Parmatma," such as: "1. You must consider all females from five to hundred years of age, however beautiful and attractive they may be, as mothers without the least idea of loving them as wives." He may have found common purpose with: "10. You must consider gold, and precious stones, as toys, and pebbles, and spurn them away with the feet of your mind."[10] Crowley often complained at the way Hindu gurus filled their technical advice with moral exhortations that were, in his opinion, beside the point. You can clear the mind of distractions, he might think (because they distract), without having to moan about how "dirty" the distractions were. The objection lies in their presence, not their character. The swami was trying to banish obsession by emphasizing its characteristics to be impure, and harmful, therefore encouraging the good path he advocates to the minds of his readers. On page 8, Sabhapaty says there are 1,008 specific doubts that have to be banished to cleanse the soul of Maya (illusion), so that knowledge of spirit may occur. And further:

> The main part is the emancipation of Jivatma from this earthly bondage. . . . Consider the soul to be a reflection of the Parmatma. But by the interposition of the curtain of Maya the Jivatma considers itself distinct from Parmatma. But if this curtain be removed Jivatma attains the true knowledge of its identity with Parmatma.

Thought creates separation. This principle seems very close to Saint Paul's maxim that "the carnal mind is enmity against God" (Romans 8:7). Yoga stops this thinking.

In rather peculiar English, with abundance of obscure terms, Sabhapaty basically gets the meditator to take his Parmatma, or Universal Spirit, from the top of his brain right down through the nadī to the kuṇḍli, then up through the linga and through the spinal column back to the crown.

> I now bring down my Universal Spirit in its fullness into the chamber of your brain calling it the Spirit of Spirit or Parmatma. From the Brahmarantar it drops down or descends through the Sukhmana Nadee (a hollow vessel through which Atma Pran akas runs) down to the *Kundlee* . . . it comes to the Kundlee (No. 18; 19) where joining with the Lingam and taking a bent upwards and ascending through the spinal cord or the back-bone it ends again in the Brahmantar (No. 30). This part of Sukhmana vasi from the Kundlee along the back-bone up to the Brahmarantar is called the *Kumbhak*.[11]

The Spirit is to inspect twelve descending "faculties" (chakras), which may be compared to Gnostic emanations. First, the Spirit sees "my first reflection or appearance" in the first "kingdom" in the center of the skull. Sabhapaty wants it to be understood that each faculty changes the *appearance* of the Universal Spirit according to its limitations, illusory state, or nature. The first faculty, however, we find in the brain is,

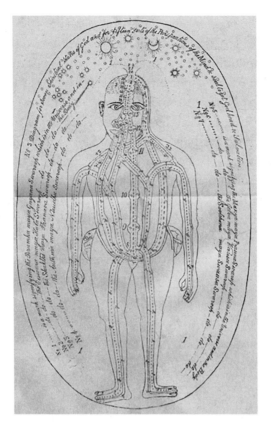

Fig. 13.4. Diagram of svarūpa *("inherent forms") that
communicate the divine, spiritual cosmos via prāṇa
through the human anatomy, in Sabhapaty's*
Om, A Treatise on Vedantic Raj Yoga Philosophy.
(Courtesy of Henry S. Olcott Memorial Library, Wheaton, Illinois)

appropriately, called "Wisdom." Now this is a near-perfect parallel with
the Gnostic system where the feminine Sophia (= Wisdom!) is described
at the head of the pleroma as the *reflection* of the "unknowable Father."*

---

*When I first encountered the Gnostic systems in Irenaeus's work in Pusey House Library,
Oxford, aged eighteen, I recall the moment when I read the curious account Irenaeus
dismissed as "madness," and thinking, "This is a kind of map of the spiritual aspect of the
brain." Page 19 of Sabhapaty's book refers directly to "Self Emanation" and "the seem-
ing emanation of wit or Intelligence." "Intelligence" is one of the aions in Valentinus's
emanationary system circa 160 CE.

Parallels with the famous sephirotic Tree of Hebrew Kabbalah are also striking, from the correspondence of the first sephira, Kether (the crown) with the aperture of Brahma at the crown of the head, then going down in balanced pairs, with Tiphareth (the heart), down to Malkuth (kingdom), or manifest Nature, corresponding to svādishthana and mūlādhāra in the chakra system. Beyond the Crown of Kabbalah is the unknowable, limitless Ain Soph, corresponding to Brahman, the unmanifest principle. Of such, we may say, is made the microcosm that is man.

In the second kingdom of Sabhapaty's system, in the top of the brain, the Spirit finds wit, or intelligence. And here, Sabhapaty tells us, begins the consciousness of the difference between Spirit of Spirit, and the Human Spirit, and from this place Maya begins to spread her net of temptation.* Here commences the duality of "Jivatma" and "Parmatma." The wit or intelligence, properly purified, we are informed, has responsibility to guard against doubt and unbelief.

The third kingdom, in the middle of the brain, "my [the Spirit's] third reflection or appearance," is the faculty of knowledge. "It introduces unbelief and sins, because it is here that the emotions of love suddenly burst forth. The Human Spirit here is changed into Triune soul or here the faculties of thoughts are first evolved. . . ."[12]

The fourth faculty, at the bottom of the brain, is called Prudence. Here springs up the love of momentary pleasures, vainly taking them for eternal delights. The fifth, at the center of the forehead is Memory, the sixth: Muse, powers of false imaginations, poetical conceptions, and inventions of themes of all kinds. All these faculties invite laws to counter their tendencies.

The seventh kingdom is the tip of the nose: self-esteem, self-love, self-delusion, against which ambitiousness stand patience, meekness, and contentment. The eighth, the center of the tongue: irritation, dullness, mildness; things that lead one to hasty action. The ninth is the center of the throat, called Intellect, with four subdivisions (the remaining faculties have numerous subdivisions also). Tenth is the center of the heart: passions, notions, states of mind. Eleventh: the navel, the senses.

---

*One may compare the activity of Maya, or *bhranti* here with the Gnostic false god, or demiurge, Ialdabaoth who does not recognize the divine spirit but wishes to possess it, being jealous that there is a god higher than itself.

Twelfth: the Kundlee, faculty of nature and the elements—elements of matter and elements of the senses.

Sabhapaty's conclusion from this tour through the occult, or subtle body: "Therefore O Jivatma you are a combination of my twelve deeming emanations or reflections in a human shape. I will now prove that I am not *you*—the twelve faculties."[13]

Sabhapaty's next section sets out to prove not only Jivatma's "false existence," as done already, but to prove Jivatmas's nonexistence. The Jivatma can only think of his existence when he thinks himself separate from the Parmatma. Hearing this, the Jivatma begs humbly to be shown the methods whereby he can void himself of the twelve faculties by entirely destroying, forgetting, and dropping them. This, by the way, explains what Crowley means by such hazardous phrases as "destroying the ego." The "ego" is the Jivatma that thinks it exists only when separate from Guru Parmatma. To paraphrase Jesus, he who "loses" this sense of self is saved. This also explains the Gnostic distinction between the "psychic" and the "pneumatic," the one Jivatma, the other in Sabhapaty's terms, *Parmatma,* not separate or two, but advaita: one with God.

It is vital to distinguish between the everlasting and transitory things of the world. The claims of the twelve reflections of the Parmatma are then systematically denied, starting with Kundlee and working back up. They are derivations of the second principle and not the Infinite Spirit itself.

On page 24, Jivatma, humbled, says: "It is through false wisdom that I created the eleven subordinate faculties whom I have just now conquered. I must not have the slightest difference between me and the Infinite Spirit"—to which the Infinite Spirit replies: "You are not yet cleansed of all your impurities, so you cannot now become the IS [Infinite Spirit]. But now I will tell you the practice of Yoga Samādhi which will take away your remaining sins, and give you final absorption."

Paramatma (*sic;* variant spelling) tells the Jivatma what he must next do. Note the suggestion that "Koondli" (*sic*) is a snake, by the language of "taking hold":

Then the Paramatma said "Now again go down to the Koondli O Jivatma, and take hold of the Soul of Nature [serpentine suggestion], and purging it from all its powers, bless it by saying: "Be purified Soul of Nature, and become a holy spirit." Then bring it up through Idakala, pingala and sushumana Vasees (No. 1, 3, 2 respectively); making the Gyana akasha to utter the following mantras: *Om Namashivaya, namaha.* This is the holy, divine mantra for the purification (or Bhuta Shuddi) of the physical organs of your body. Thus bring it up to the navel and make the Soul of Nature be absorbed in the Soul of Senses. Now you are no longer the Soul of Nature, because you have lost that existence, by its absorption in the Soul of Senses, where it loses its identity and attributes. There contemplate on the consciousness or (giyana sarup) of your being the Infinite Spirit, for a short time.[14]

There follow respective mantras for purification of the Soul of Nature, passions, senses, intellect, conscience, ambition and ideas, memory, muse, prudence, knowledge, wit or intelligence, and so on, all done in meditation with creative visualization.* The reclamation of fallen nature continues with successive descents into Nature ("Kundlee") and ascents—"like a serpent with its tail in the Kundli, to devour the Brahma Chaitanyam and be absorbed in the Infinite Spirit"[15]—uttering the mantras with force until absorption in the Infinite Spirit is achieved. The descent is specifically indicated as purifying yourself, the ascent as giving absorption. One, as it were, dies and rises again. The seed goes into Nature where it emerges to flower. We see a perennial typology of ascent and descent, birth, death, and rebirth. The false "I" must be willing to die, to rise again.

The twelve faculties must be dead and buried, not to rise and distract and make you their victim:

If in this state you have any consciousness of seeing the Infinite Spirit, cancel that consciousness also. For who is it that sees and

---

*Again, it may be noted in the Gnostic *Second Treatise of the Great Seth* the distinction between the man who is nailed "to their death" and the "living Jesus," who says: "For my death, which they think happened, [happened] to them in their error and blindness, since they nailed their man unto their death. For their Ennoias did not see me, for they were deaf and blind. But in doing these things, they condemn themselves. . . . But I was rejoicing in the height over all the wealth of the archons and the offspring of their error, of their empty glory. And I was laughing at their ignorance."

what is that, that is seen? In fact empty yourself from the conscious-ness of wisdom and duality. *You must become the Infinite Spirit with-out the idea of becoming the Infinite Spirit.*[16]

The "secret state of Samādhi or Vedantic Raj Yogue [*sic;* Sabhapaty's spelling for 'yoga'] or Shiva Yogue," successfully attained, is then described:

You are like a tree universally spread. Your stem represents all the souls of all the creations, your larger branches are natural pow-ers, your smaller branches are senses . . . your flowers are muse and memory, and your fruit is knowledge and wit, and your seed is wisdom. But in this spiritual state you will entirely forget what you are? Who you are? Whence you are? You will not have the least idea of the existence of your body and your twelve faculties. You will be the universal IS, the eternal holy divine sight, witness-ing all internal thoughts, and external actions of all the creatures.*

Then you become the Infinite Spiritual, universal Linga Sorup, embracing the sun, moon, stars, the earth, and all their creation within the universal circle of your Linga Sorup. . . . You become a perfect moral God, perfect social God, a Yogi full of God. . . .

You become witness to all the notions of every soul, yea the spirit of the universe. You raise yourself from personal to impersonal, from sensuous to supersensuous, from finite to Infinite, and arrive at the shore of Nirvana or Jivanmukt:—it is the only spiritual state, the perfection of Samādhi. You become the one with all things, yet the one separate from all things. You become the mind diffused throughout the universe. You will be out of the world of phenom-ena, which is but an unreal phantom, to the world of absolute reality which is the only true substance. . . .

You will not be the ignorance that fetters the spirit, but the wis-dom that liberates it. You will be same in pleasure and pain, hope and despair, have the same regard for rich and poor.[17]

---

*In terms of the Golden Dawn system, this would correspond to the grade of *Ipsissimus,* "his own very self," corresponding to Kether, the Crown.

That "I am (that I am)" is with us always.

Sabhapaty's remarkable book ends with a "Poem of Blessing":

> Blessed be they that aim
>   This truth in them to gain
> With faith and without shame
>   His grace on them to rain.
> His grace in them will shine.
>   An Infinite Spirit
> With this the world must shine
>   What needs then this merit
> This truth the world must search
>   Universal Creed it's
> Universal Church it's
> Universal truth it's
>   END

"Every man and every woman is a star." (*AL* I:3)

Crowley tried doubtless to take all Sabhapaty's mystic piety with a pinch of salt, unwilling to see samādhi as a unique thing, independent of natural sequence. That would simply bring back the whole train of the supernatural, and Crowley was, like Henry Maudsley—whose T. H. Huxley–influenced scientific philosophy lent toward mechanical automatism—determined to subject prescientific mentalities to higher knowledge. That is to say, the great mystics and magicians of old were *right* as to significant subject matter, but wrong, or inadequate, as to *causes* and the objective nature of the means. Crowley's conversation with Henry Maudsley after leaving Colombo on January 28, 1904, had confirmed in him the idea that the state of samādhi must be like any other spiritual or mental state insofar as it could be induced by attendant, consciously applied physiological changes, just as cocaine anesthetized inhibitions creating "courage," or whisky made men happy, or veronal made them sleep. It was simply a matter of perfecting the means. *Interpreting* the phenomenon would depend solely on the religious, mythological, or ideological predilections of the practitioner. Crowley's study of comparative religion recognized these interpretations were all relative, with an underlying core of experiential truth, which Crowley would come to call "Magick" out of respect for what he saw as a great, misunderstood tradition from the past: that of the ancient Magi.

Crowley was convinced experiences of the order of dhyāna and samādhi could release the latent genius ("true will") of an individual. He envisaged a future where this might be achieved at will. Seeing a world where this latent genius was almost everywhere repressed, with attendant deformation, *this* was what he meant when he later adopted the rubric for his magazine, the *Equinox:* "The Method of Science. The Aim of Religion." The obvious and almost universal repression of the sex instinct he saw as emblematic, symptomatic, of the repression of genius, or "God" in Man, whose source may be accessed at the highest potentiality of the brain, beyond the strictly rational faculties. Genius confounds the wits.

While he seems by spring 1905 to have had an instinct for these mature conclusions, he was still "on his way." He had, anyhow, not yet experienced the flower of Vedanta—samādhi—himself, nor was he yet able to, as it were, enjoy knowledge and conversation with his "Angel," or genius—though he would realize fully later, his Angel had already had conversation and knowledge *of him,* a phenomenon, note, apparently linked to a physiological abnormality, or adjustment: the lesion of the tongue affecting the sensorium (see page 202).

And so he worked, worked hard, on mastering the physiological apparatus: hence the overriding concern with "breaks," for a break meant temporary loss of control. This was how he interpreted Sabhapaty's emphasis on purifying the chakras of thoughts. The mantra was intended to interfere with the normal thought process (mental excreta) and wash thoughts away by a continual, unbroken rhythm that doubled as an invocation of "higher power."[18] Rationally speaking this was what was really intended by the inherited phrase of magical lore: "the word of power."

Some time during or after August 1905, Crowley systematized what he'd learned in this regard in a summary entitled "The Character of Breaks" (see p. 77, for the scheme's appearance in *Book 4,* Part 1):

1. *Primary Centers.* The Senses.
2. *Secondary.* These seem to assume a morbid activity as soon as the primaries are stilled. Their character is that of the shorter kind of memory. Events of the day, etc.

3. *Tertiary*. Partake of the character of "reverie." Very tempting and insidious.

4. *Quaternary*. Are closely connected with the control center itself. Their nature is "How well I'm doing it!" or "Wouldn't it be a good idea to____?" These are probably emanations from the control, not messages to it. We might call them "Aberrations of control." Of a similar depth are the reflections which discover a break; but these are healthy warnings and assist.

5. *Quinary*. Never rise into consciousness at all, being held down by the now almost perfect control. Hence the blank of thought, the forgetfulness of all things, including the object. (Neighbourhood conc[entratio]n. Not partaking of any character at all, are the "meteor" thoughts which seem to be quite independent of anything the brain could think, or had ever thought. Probably this kind of thought is the root of irrational hallucinations. E.g., "And if you're passing, won't you?"

6. Perhaps as a result of the intense control, a nervous storm breaks. This we call dhyana. Its character is probably not determined by the immediate antecedents in consciousness. Its essential characteristic being the unity of Subject and Object, in a new world is revealed [*sic*]. Samādhi is but an expansion of this, so far as I can see.

   The slaying of any of these thoughts often leaves their echoes gradually dying away.

7. Marriage! The biggest break of all, lasted 2 years!

On Saturday April 1, 1905, Crowley wrote up his analysis of Sabhapaty's practice regarding the mind as a "pole." He admitted the difficulty in understanding and applying directly some of what the guru was getting at. He then spent most of the day in grueling prāṇāyāma exercises, resuming his practice from Sabhapaty's book (part 2) for fifty-five minutes, but occasionally forgetting the mantra provided, and using the salutation to Shiva with which he was familiar. He complained of being worried physically by the birds singing at dusk and the sound of his wife "messing about."[19] He resumed prāṇāyāma at 9:35 p.m. for twenty minutes and felt he could have gone on well for another hour; he hadn't eaten since 3:00 p.m.

He did fifteen minutes around midday on Sunday, before going for a long wander, and playing billiards while saying his mantra. Finally getting himself comfortable at 2:30 p.m. he meditated on the mūlādhāra chakra, the root and foundation supporting physical energies and consciousness. The chakra is sited around the perineum. Crowley uses the phrase "muladhara or bhuta." According to Patañjali, whose works Crowley referenced, *bhūta* is Sanskrit for "element," (the five elements = matter) and *bhūta shuddhi* is the purification of the elements, which practice chimes in exactly with Sabhapaty's recommendations. The lowest sephira of the Sephirotic Tree, Malkuth, the kingdom, corresponds to "earth." Interestingly, *bhūta* can also mean a malignant spirit, spirits that delude or devour human beings, and one wonders whether Crowley might also have had thoughts of his ubiquitous "Abramelin demons" breaking into his mind when performing the mantra *Aum Namo Sivaya Aum,* which he continued outside for an hour. He recorded that his left leg had gone completely numb, with no pain in his āsana, wondering if the effect was due to the mantra on the mūlādhāra. He took up his mantra again at 5:54 for forty minutes with similar effects on his leg. At 9:20 he continued his mantra with prāṇāyāma, working very hard, reaching his limit at 9:48: "Sweating like a pig." He'd only eaten a small cake since 10:00 a.m.

> Mantra dropped from sheer necessity of concentration on watch and breath.
> Continued mantra (and bhuta as much as possible) from 10:40 till sleep, perhaps 12:30 or 1 o'clock. Began again 8:30 this Monday A.M.[20]

On Monday, he recommenced his mantra while having the bath filled at 10:20 a.m., and in the afternoon had another attempt at Sabhapaty's "pole" practice, but was disturbed by a fly in the room. He often forgot his mantra or mispronounced it, or forgot altogether what the object of the work was. After forty-six minutes, his head "seemed fairly unreal."[21]—hardly surprising considering the visualization Sabhapaty recommended! Crowley wrote he was "disgusted" by this, and furthermore was "very worried by wife's negligence in not putting things ready for tea."[22] He decided to take a "holiday," that is, have a day of rest, so did nothing on Tuesday (the fourth).

On Wednesday, he woke up saying his mantra, having gone to bed with it at 3:00 a.m. He had a lot of business to attend to and wasn't feeling well, managing fifteen minutes of prāṇāyāma in the afternoon. Then he had more diarrhea, for which he took opium. It was snowing incessantly, and he couldn't get the temple warm. At 7:17 p.m., he managed thirty-one minutes of the Sabhapaty practice. Results were "rather mixed and No Good," perhaps affected by a cough and other "silly worries."[23] The cold in the temple made dhāraṇā next to impossible.

He left his yoga for a few days, resuming for only eighteen minutes on Saturday, simply saying "Aum" in relation to the top of his head, which seemed to him to contain a black ball the size of a pea, which then burst showing kaleidoscopic streaky light effects, a vision disturbed by "tramping of myriads of armed men, herds of wild cattle in panic flight etc., or else Rose."[24] The brief snippets in which his wife, Rose, is mentioned suggest that the marriage was going through a dull patch, a thought that is reinforced by a piece of observation we shall soon note, as the yoga, despite Sabhapaty's insistence that he sacrifice all to it, wound down amid a plethora of domestic and social distractions, of which the greatest was the arrival on April 27 of Jules Jacot-Guillarmod.

FOURTEEN

Kangchenjunga

As Crowley contemplated Dr. Guillarmod making his way from Foyers railway station to Boleskine on April 27, 1905, he found that intense meditation had heightened his perception that ordinary human life, deprived of a spiritual referent, was a complete joke. Thus, he could do no more than take pleasure in Guillarmod's earnestness and naïveté. It did not take much for joker Crowley to convince Guillarmod that a haggis is not a Scottish dainty but a terrific animal of fearsome nature. Crowley had his gillie dress up a ram to make it look bigger. The gillie then burst in to declare that the beast had been sighted on the hills. Straight-faced, Crowley reached for his .577 Express cartridges and rushed Guillarmod into the chase. After due time stalking the ferocious haggis in pouring rain, crawling at earth level, with Guillarmod's more than ample backside wobbling irritatingly in front of his dripping wet face, the laird offered his excited guest first shot at the monster. The animal's hindquarters were duly blasted to smithereens and Guillarmod thought himself a very fine fellow. In the evening, Crowley had the remains piped in to a banquet and Guillarmod returned home to Switzerland with a trophy skull—of a sheep. Its whereabouts is today unknown, but Guillarmod's family have assured researcher Clint Warren that they still possess the taxidermist's bill for mounting the "haggis."[*]

There was bigger game to bag. Eckenstein and Crowley now

---

[*]Jules Jacot-Guillarmod receipt dated June 27, 1905, "Tête du Haggis 25.40."; information via email from William Breeze to the author, November 2, 2018.

discussed plans for the conquest of Kangchenjunga on the Sikkim-Nepalese border. At 26,208 feet, it was only 42 feet less than K2. To Crowley's great disappointment, Eckenstein declined. Crowley says his disinclination to go was "for one reason or another."[1] He may have disapproved of Crowley's leading the expedition, as he was too individual, but then, could they not have arranged to co-lead it, as before? Eckenstein did advise against taking Guillarmod on what he regarded as a "foolhardy" enterprise. The Swiss doctor had proved incompetent on Chogo Ri; he would be again. An excited Crowley ignored Eckenstein's advice, revealing a perpetual weakness in his personal armory: "In face of the plainest evidence, I cannot believe in the existence of dishonesty and malice, and I always try to build with rotten material." This self-criticism would prove true time and time again. He considered it an attribute of genius to be able to make a silk purse out of a sow's ear. He had watched his father convert people, and was convinced he could do it too. However, the usual thing was that the converted either turned against the converter or became pathetically dependent on him; neurotic people were attracted to Crowley. When the teacher got fed up and headed off, it always looked like malice rather than the endgame of a progressive exasperation. And we should not forget that Crowley had a broad masochistic streak. He should have taken Eckenstein's withdrawal from the project as an omen, but he was forever attracted to the impossible; it was, he said, natural for the greatest artists to commit the most atrocious failures, since only they attempted impossibilities, the sole game fit for mastery. But Kangchenjunga was not art, and besides, Crowley, attracted to the idea of seizing the world's highest climbing record, regarded the challenge as far from impossible. And Crowley insisted on the one rule he regarded as personal insurance. Whoever Guillarmod picked to join the expedition, all members were to obey Crowley as to all matters regarding mountaineering conduct on the mountain. This taking on the mantle of responsibility would also, in his own mind, absolve him from responsibility as regards conduct independent of his orders. A specific clause of the agreement that bound the members stated: "No one will be obliged to risk his life, on account of cold, lack of food, perilous ascension, leading to a fall."[2] In other words, if risks were taken without Crowley's orders, they were responsible for themselves.

We gain a few details of Guillarmod's approach from his own diary, now held in his home town of Lignières, Switzerland, as well as some hints as to why Crowley was ready to take leave of his wife:

27.4 [April]. Arrival at Inverfarigaig where I find Crowley and his wife waiting for me at the landing. Go on foot with them to their home. A nice, comfortable house, beautiful pictures but a little too erotic for most people. Testing rifles in case a wild sheep is seen in the area.

28.4. A Haggis spotted in the briar . . . which I got at the first shot. . . . Congratulations from Crowley.

29.4. Regarding Kangchinjunga [*sic*]; calculation of budgets. After a game of chess, Crowley suddenly asks me to make a contract similar to the one I signed on our first trip to the Himalayas; I'm beginning to believe that he has decided to join us and supply the funds we lack. We discuss a few details beside the general conditions of this contract and finally it is decided to follow it up and sign it tomorrow.

30.4. Operate on a dog of Crowley's under chloroform, which has a tumor in its mouth and on another with papillomas all over its body. Signed the contract with Crowley who made 5 machine copies.

1.5 [May]. After supper Gillis [*sic:* Hugh Gillies, Crowley's gillie] played the Bag Pipes (Pibrock) for us, and played handsomely well in his beautiful Scottish attire.

2.5. We wanted to do some rock-climbing, but some guests arrived. Mrs. Crowley is definitely a peculiar woman whom her husband has finally convinced is a complete idiot; she tries to put on airs, is critical and even abusive with the servants, and I understand Crowley who cannot wait to leave for the Indies and to stay there for several months!

4 May. Leave for the landing at Inverfarigaig. Train for Edinburgh.[3]

Fig. 14.1. HMS Marmora

Crowley left two days later. On May 12 he took the P&O SS *Marmora,* arriving in Cairo on May 23. Either at Port Said or Cairo, Crowley picked up a man. The pair went sailing on the Nile, a tryst celebrated in Crowley's poem "Said" (dated May 1905), published in *Gargoyles–Being Strangely Wrought Images of Life and Death* (1907):

> The spears of the night at her onset
> Are lords of the day for a while,
> The magical green of the sunset,
> The magical blue of the Nile
>   Afloat are the gales
>   In our slumberous sails
> On the beautiful breast of the Nile.

>   . . .

> Sweet sleep is perfection of love.
> To die into dreams of my lover,
> To wake with his mouth like a dove
> Kissing me over and over!
>   Better sleep so
>   Than be conscious, and know
> How death hath a charm to discover.

Perhaps this brief affair may explain the recent discovery that when at Port Said, Crowley opted to postpone the expedition. We learn this significant detail from an entry for June 1, 1905, in Guillarmod's diary when, having only just got an agreement for the climb from Swiss army officer Alexis Pache, Guillarmod dined at his mother's house at Saint-Blaise:

1.6. St Blaise. Received a letter from Crowley who is ill at Port Said; he would like to send the expedition back to next year, I do not want to; and telegraphed him that we will leave anyway this year. Made my accounts, I have already spent 2.700 francs on the expedition.[4]

One wonders whether it was really illness, or a competing passion that made Crowley try to avoid an expedition that was Guillarmod's, not his own, brainchild. Crowley obviously felt that having already committed 5,000 francs to it, he had better go along, for he sailed from Port Said on May 31. On June 15, Guillarmod received a letter from Crowley, posted from Aden. Crowley was on his way to Darjeeling where Guillarmod could telegraph him. On the same day, Guillarmod heard from Charles Adolphe Reymond who said he'd come, but on several unspecified conditions.

Crowley reached Bombay on June 9, his first taste of India's low country in the hot season, but discomfort was compensated for by the region's superior mango, better than any other he'd known. He soon departed for Calcutta by train, taking a room with an exceptionally scalding shower, the coach having been at a siding in the sun too long. Arriving at Calcutta at four in the morning of the eleventh, he breakfasted and dined with old friend Edward Thornton, and left for Darjeeling the next day. Kangchenjunga is on the Sikkim-Nepal border so the journey took him to new territory, which Crowley found enchanting, once he'd crossed Bengal's acrid plains. At Sara Ghat, the burgeoning Ganges advanced like a queen across desolation. At sunset, her waters glowed with Martian reds and orange flecks, glittering in her train. Crowley wrote of an "evil coppery sheen upon its waveless turmoil." It was "like a river of hell." It seemed, he wrote, as if the whole earth were decaying, and he found it, and enjoyed it, as a frightful and fantastic sight. He crossed it on a steamer, on which dinner was served, which gives an idea of the river's breadth.[5]

Night on the train, whose funerary march was now resumed, was stifling, his tormented skin finding nothing cool to relieve him. Dawn brought a slight coolness to the air, and alighting from the carriage he was captivated to find in the distance, rising above wooded hills, the faint blue, rose, and whiteness of Kangchenjunga. The name meant the "Five Treasures of the Snow," and its god would not surrender those treasures willingly.

Reaching the foothills, where Blavatsky had once trod half a century before, Crowley took the famous narrow-gauge railway, completed in 1881, known as the "Toy Train" that wound its way up amid tropical vegetation, shrouded in cold mist, before emerging at an exposed ridge at Ghum, to begin a downhill slope to the destination. Relieved to arrive, Crowley watched amazed as a young girl took his massive trunk on her back and up steep narrow paths to the Woodlands Hotel, a three-story Alpine-style chalet perched on a steep hill above what is still Darjeeling's Mall, though the hotel has gone.

Crowley remarked that only official ineptitude could have picked Darjeeling as an official station. Chumbi was a better site, but was forty miles further than Darjeeling. But Chumbi had forty inches of rainfall a year, whereas Darjeeling had some two hundred! It was so steep, the stairs from one house to another were, he wrote, more like ladders. And the town stank, he insisted, of mildew. Regarding Darjeeling as the last hope for the shabby-genteel, it pullulated with ladies whose sole hope of finding a marriage was to learn piano, though the climate made keeping a piano in tune for longer than five minutes impossible! Crowley found the food awful; exorbitant prices justified by menu descriptions in bad French! Crowley suffered sore throat, arthritis, and all kinds of irritants. He did not, he wrote, like Darjeeling!

But Crowley found the "heaven-born" British officials and soldiers cordial and eager to extend comradeship. Happily, a Masonic lodge was installing a new Worshipful Master, so he went to the *Jadugar-Khana* (known to Indians as "magic houses") and enjoyed ceremony and banquet, meeting Bengal's lieutenant governor, Sir Andrew Fraser,* as well as

---

*Fraser was at the time involved with Curzon's plans for the highly controversial partition of east and west Bengal, which divided Muslims from Hindus, heavily opposed by Hindu Bengalis.

Darjeeling's commissioner, deputy commissioner, the maharaja of Kuch Behar, and many other delightful people who wished to aid his expedition.

Crowley had for guidance excellent photos of the mountain by Signor Vittorio Sella, and Professor Garwood's map that was fanciful regarding the Yalung Glacier, including a peak where no peak could be seen. The exercise would be very different to Chogo Ri. No villages stood between Darjeeling and the mountain from which men and supplies might be drawn, so eight thousand pounds of food required dispatch to a depot as close to the glacier as possible. Government transport officer, Major White, offered assistance, but had trouble with the Tibetan Buddhist porters, who were not, Crowley believed, in the same league as the Kashmiri and Balti porters he was familiar with. Many dumped their loads where they felt like it, or stole them. Crowley got some measure of control through rehiring three of the best men from 1902: Salama, Subhana, and Ramzana. He had, meanwhile, moved to the Woodlands' sister hotel, the Drum Druid, where he persuaded the Italian hotel manager Alcesto C. Rigo de Righi to handle the bandobast, accepting his offer of joining the expedition as transport manager. Crowley would regret the decision, finding De Righi by turns servile, insolent, and very heavy on the natives, and Crowley felt he should have foreseen what would happen beyond the confines of the Raj catering industry.

On July 9, Crowley inspected the mountain with binoculars, reckoning the highest peak easily accessible by the col west of it. The weather in the mountain's vicinity, unlike Darjeeling, had been fine. It was only forty-five miles away. Fed up with sore throats and the climate, Crowley left for a few days in Calcutta to stock up.

Guillarmod reached Port Said on the tenth, but on the fifteenth Crowley received a telegram: the Swiss doctor had been shipwrecked in the Red Sea. It seemed typical. Still, Guillarmod made it to Aden on the eighteenth, arriving in Bombay on July 25. On July 31, Guillarmod took what he called the "Lilliputian" railway and was met at Ghum by Crowley and Salama. Finding Guillarmod fussy and self-conscious, Crowley piled up the latest provisions in two rooms, and assessed Reymond and Pache generously. Pache admitted inexperience, but was charming, unaffected, and would learn. Reymond was a bit dour for Crowley's taste but at least had his feet on the ground, which could help when there was no ground to be found.

Guillarmod's diary reveals problems already appearing: Crowley had juggled "a little too easily" with other people's money, and, the doctor complained, had done things "too luxuriously."[6] Guillarmod felt it incumbent on himself to "moderate it a little." He also mistrusted Righi's motives as being self-centered and too inclined to assume authority. All this explains what Crowley referred to in his *Confessions* as Guillarmod's "fussiness." Having now committed all his money (over 8,000 francs) and more, Guillarmod would need yet more for his return. On August 4, Crowley obtained signatures from the three Swiss and the Italian that they would accept his orders as final. Two days later, Guillarmod complained to his diary that Crowley had the bank pay out large sums on the expedition's account for his own personal use.

On August 8, the expedition, including six servants and seventy-nine porters left Darjeeling in a downpour. They arrived at a dak bungalow at Jorpokri—eight and a half miles from Ghum—the first of five stages, followed by Tonglu (eighteen and a half miles), Sandakphu (thirty-three miles), Falut (forty-five miles), Chabanjong (fifty-one miles), with the first four stages each having dak bungalows for shelter. It sounded straightforward enough, but the rain on the ridge was unlike anything in Crowley's experience. Wet through after only eight and a half minutes of leaving the warm fire of the baghla, the air was all water, and swept up in sheets from the valley in all directions. Twelve days offered scant respite, while the last five days offered none at all. Leeches were another serious problem. Once a leech worked its way up a pony's nose, the poor animal bled to death amid the downpour.

When mists cleared momentarily, views were stunning, but the vegetation, largely consisting of fifteen-foot-high rhododendrons with stalks as thick as a thigh, was a devil to cut through. And there was trouble with the porters. At Jorpakri, the police caught up and arrested one for petty crime; six deserted early on. On August 17, Crowley went ahead, leaving Pache in charge. Five deserted; Pache couldn't communicate with them and allay superstitious fears. But Crowley himself, out ahead, learned, according to Guillarmod's notebook, that forty of Major White's bearers had also "escaped," leading the doctor to ask himself: "Would this be the beginning of a debacle?"[7]

There was still no sign of the official permit to allow the expedition into Nepal. Guillarmod had visited Darjeeling's deputy commissioner, but he had not the power to issue it. Permission arrived while Crowley was waiting at an "abominable place" called Nego Cave, where, to his dismay, there was no cave shelter to be had. On the eighteenth, a long eight-hour march took them down three thousand feet from the ridge into a valley and camp at Gamotang. Gamotang he found as magical as Sonamarg in the Kashmir, and could only account for its unearthly, soft brilliance by supposing creatures imperceptible to gross sense took as much pride in it as might some people who cared for their row of cottages while others left them to fester. The weather beat Darjeeling's: rain only started mid-morning!

Crowley kept his men by prizes: the first three men on duty received a prize (probably cigarettes), and those who did it three times had their pay raised. Sitting round the fire with the porters and exchanging stories and songs, he never allowed them to get the better of him, but was calm in authority.

> The secret is that I am really unconscious of superiority and treat all alike with absolute respect and affection; at the same time I maintain the practical relations between myself and others very strictly indeed.
>
> It is the fable of the belly and the members. It is absurd for one speck of protoplasm to insist on its social superiority to another speck, but equally absurd for one cell to want to do the work of another.[8]

As he put it, Crowley identified his purpose with destiny, remaining imperturbable. Such could not be said, Crowley wrote, of Guillarmod and Righi. Righi was particularly noisome, on one occasion threatening a porter with a kukri and a revolver. The porter laughed at him, knowing he wouldn't dare use them. Thus Righi lost the porters' respect, and that could have proved fatal. Crowley was regarded with affection; Guillarmod was not. "He was fussy and helpless,"[9] wrote Crowley, even on one occasion trying to bribe a man with boots and crampons for doing what was his duty. Crowley had his porters working like a machine, their fears stilled. Guillarmod's diary for August 22 reads: "Continued disputes and disagreements with Crowley."[10]

Crowley climbed four hours to the Chumbab La, then skirted the Kang La slopes to descend into the Yalung Chu branch valley, pitching camp by a great block of quartz three and a half hours beyond the pass. Having had trouble with his porters, Guillarmod arrived late. The day following, Crowley had to cross another pass before descending into the valley to a group of huts near Tseram on the main stream, just a few miles below the snout of the Yalung Glacier. The dewan of Nepal was sending an officer to superintend, for Britain's treaty with Nepal ensured no foreigners could enter without the dewan's leave. Crowley understood the dewan's concern:

He knew that the most harmless of Europeans is the herald of disaster to any independent country. Where the white man sets his foot, the grass of freedom and the flower of good faith are trampled into the mire of vice and commercialism.

But in the present instance our route touched only this one tiny outlying hamlet of Tseram and permission had been obtained without difficulty for us to pass. At the same time, the Dewan was going to have a man on the spot to see that we did not maltreat and corrupt the natives as we have done in every other part of the globe in which our impulses of greed and tyranny have seen a possibility of satisfaction.[11]

As the dewan's man had not yet appeared, Crowley left a man with a message for him, pressing on with a small party, leaving Pache in command to wait for the main body of porters. Crowley went to reconnoiter the glacier stream. Was it passable? Wanting to establish a camp as high as possible, Crowley was struck by the mountainous valley's extraordinary beauty, peppered with stunning roses and primroses. Now at about fifteen thousand feet, with his body in excellent shape, his soul sang. Weather was good and there were only five miles to the mountain to go. Crowley espied the possibility of a second camp by a sheer precipice, above the glacier on a rock resembling slabs of the Eiger. Though perilous-looking, Crowley reckoned the rock secure, and the level space of snow at the end of the climb free from avalanche. From there he envisaged working a way west, avoiding seracs, ascending steep slopes of ice, covered in snow, on to a great snow basin.

On August 22, Guillarmod's notebook informs us he arrived at the Yalung Glacier. Rain having started again, he couldn't leave his pitched tent at Camp 1 all morning. There he wrote how disputes and disagreements with Crowley continued.

Crowley's account speaks of "perversity" on Guillarmod and Reymond's part. It was arranged he find a way to Camp 3, chosen by binoculars, leaving Guillarmod and Reymond in charge of most of the porters. Though tricky, ascending the glacier was considerably easier than what they'd traversed on the Baltoro in 1902. Though Crowley's prediction of Camp 3's suitability proved accurate, Professor Garwood's map was seriously wrong on many points, and Crowley had to go on what he could discern himself.

Crowley sent a man down from Camp 3 to alert the others it was

Fig. 14.2. Sherpas cooking beneath an overhang at Camp 3, Kangchenjunga. (Photo: Dr. Jules Jacot-Guillarmod)

Fig. 14.3. Daunting scale of Camp 3: note the tent lower center. (Photo: Dr. Jules Jacot-Guillarmod)

all right to join him. Then, he became aware of porters coming in a long circular route round the head of the glacier, for, as far as Crowley could see, no reason at all. Toward evening, clearer weather enabled Crowley to see them within three quarters of an hour's comfortable climb up firm rock, and couldn't believe Guillarmod was pitching camp where he was, on bare ice. Crowley had to go down; having done so, there was no time now to pack up again. Why had Guillarmod done it? Crowley maintained Guillarmod had received a report that Crowley had broken his leg on a moraine. Nothing of this appears in Guillarmod's diary, which passes by this stage of the expedition—six days between August 22 and 28—without entries, but for the aforesaid statement (in brackets) about continued disputes. Crowley, in his account, began to think something was seriously wrong with Guillarmod.

Righi, meanwhile, sent quarrelsome messages from the rear, while porters—responding to his "antics,"—were in open revolt, quelled only by Pache's good humor. Unfortunately, Pache took it on himself to come up, and Righi, in Crowley's view, went "insane;" the "grandeur of nature" having got to his small mind. It is not unusual for normally level-headed people to "lose it" on mountains, and it is doubtful if Righi was very level-headed to begin with. One senses a certain sadistic delight in Crowley for putting such types "through it." Crowley in his *Confessions,* reproached himself for not seeing the nature of the problem, or else he says he would have descended and packed Righi off back to his kitchen.[12]

Crowley says Guillarmod, claiming he'd pitched camp because the porters had refused to go further, was astonished that Crowley's bearers behaved themselves when Crowley was on the spot. Crowley reckoned Guillarmod, not sensing the source of his power, "imagined that I must be terrorizing the men by threats and beatings. In point of fact, I never struck a man during the entire expedition, save on one occasion to be described presently."[13]

At about 18,000 feet, Camp 3 proved pleasant with sun, shade, and magnificent vistas. The march to Camp 4 had to be started early, as ahead lay passages of snow that would melt as the sun rose. Guillarmod suggested the porters warm themselves first in the sun!—words of "sheer insanity" to Crowley's recollection. The march went well, but there was a problem at a slope in the direction of the great precipice. Crowley

Fig. 14.4. Camp 4. (Photo: Dr. Jules Jacot-Guillarmod)

showed them glissading, head first, as the way to make short work of the snow. The men, he said would have grasped the idea, had not Guillarmod and Reymond gesticulated and made scared noises, fearful for their skins. After getting the men across, Crowley hit what to him was a difficult series of passages requiring little more than scrambling. He arranged a fixed rope as some protection, so porters could go up and down to bring supplies.

Camp 4 was pitched atop this rocky slope on a level ridge, "not as broad," Crowley wrote in his *Confessions,* as he'd have wished: an understatement. Suffering from sun glare, Crowley administered atropine to the men, and the dizziness passed. He sent down for Pache to come up to Camp 3. Asking Guillarmod and Reymond if they had anything to convey, they were too tired to speak. Crowley was astonished.

In the morning, Guillarmod started cursing the expedition chief. Crowley thought he must have been ill mentally or physically, perhaps from heat stroke, as Kangchenjunga was extremely hot at midday. Then Pache arrived. Pache was supposed to wait at Camp 3 until Crowley had found a better camp at the snow basin above. Camp 4 was now overcrowded. Crowley could not understand why his instructions were not being followed precisely; his whole plan relied on them doing their part. Only he could grasp the whole picture. Deviation would lead to disaster. Crowley considered disobedience always led to blaming things on the person disobeyed. Righi refused to send up either supplies, or Nanga, the sirdar in charge of Righi's porters, as Crowley requested. Camp 4 was short of petrol and food, as a result.

Pache reported some of his men had deserted. Crowley never found out why. One, disobeying orders, had left by himself, and fallen to his death, apparently bearing Pache's sleeping valise.

Guillarmod's notes record on August 28: "We learn that men have slipped in the corridor where Crowley had cut the steps. One had been thrown down by rocks and must have died."[14] Next morning, Crowley sent the doctor down to investigate, and to get food that Pache reported Righi was deliberately withholding. Guillarmod noted on August 29 that he descended with five men, discovered the corpse, and buried it with prayers. Meanwhile, Crowley went up with Reymond to inspect what lay ahead. Pleasantly surprised, prudence, Crowley believed, would get them through comfortably. Nevertheless, there were severely treacherous passages of what looked like snow, but in fact covered very loosely composed ice, which, when struck with an axe, shattered everything about it. Crowley was also suffering from severe sunburn: every reason to start early and finish climbs by midday.

Fig. 14.5. The Expedition team: (left to right) Jules Jacot-Guillarmod, Charles-Adolphe Reymond, and Alcesti C. Rigo De Righi at base camp. (Photograph taken with a remote cord [see lower left] by Jules Jacot-Guillarmod)

Here the two accounts go awry. Crowley says that on the "19th" with the doctor sent to the rear, he, Pache, and Reymond took their party in three hours to Camp 5 at 21,000 feet. Guillarmod's notes are clear that he descended on the twenty-ninth. It is likely Crowley's error, or his typist's, to mistake *2* for *1* as his next date mentioned is Thursday August 31.[15]

Pache's valise did not arrive that night, nor did petrol or rations. Crowley lent Pache his own eiderdown sleeping bag, and with no rations they were obliged to stay put next day. Pache was anxious about his lost boots, clothes, papers, and sleeping kit. Some provisions turned up during the day, but no food for the men, or petrol. Crowley sent men down with urgent orders and extra men—who couldn't be fed where they were—to carry supplies. Though petrol arrived later, Crowley sent a letter to the doctor in which he and Pache (who signed it) blamed bandobast failure on Righi. Crowley insisted Righi send all stores to Camp 3 while Guillarmod join them as soon as possible with ten loads of *sattu* (a stuffing for parathas) and Nanga to help.

On Thursday, August 31, Crowley and six men started up the slopes. Salama was sent ahead to cut big steps for the porters, and put his gang of four with axes and shovels on a rope to clear loose snow and enlarge Salama's steps. Crowley stayed close to the gang's leader, Gali, in case he fell. All seemed well. They reached a narrow corridor, with Reymond and Salama ahead of the others. Chips were sliding down from their efforts, picking up surface material. Crowley could tell the ice was about to move. Gali was frightened by the "little avalanche" and fell out of his steps. Crowley caught him, and quickly anchored the rope to a wedged axe. But the man's nerve had gone and he mindlessly began untying the rope, deaf to pleas to cease. Crowley realized the man's only chance was to make him more scared of Crowley than he was of the mountain, so Crowley hit him with his axe; Gali then pulled himself together without alarming the others. After that, it went well enough. Returning to Camp 5, wary of what lay ahead, Crowley found the men's morale shaken by the avalanche experience. They began babbling about the demons of the mountain and amplified Gali's slip and the "wallop" he'd received into "the wildest fantasies."[16] During the night, some slipped away, down to Camp 3.

Next morning, Reymond, Pache, Salama, and Crowley renewed

Fig. 14.6. Camp 5. (Photo: Dr. Jules Jacot-Guillarmod)

their efforts. Contrary to instructions, the three got out of Crowley's hearing when he needed them to help the porters over a bad patch they had themselves delighted in overcoming. Heavily burdened, the porters couldn't be helped by Crowley alone, so Crowley awaited the three men's return. He saw below the arrival of a large party at Camp 5: a "new muddle," observed Crowley, resulting, he surmised, from Guillarmod's "hysteria" and Righi's "malignant stupidity."

Guillarmod's notes may be interpreted, if you choose to see it that way, as confirming Crowley's assessment of the doctor's state of mind. On September 1, Guillarmod, down with Righi, had got up at 8:00 a.m. and decided with Righi to "go and see the others."

We decide with Righi to go see the others, that is Pache, Reymond and Crowley. We eat a little and we take with us all men of good will. We leave at 10am for the camp above. We take men with us without loads for several reasons. It's first of all to help us make and mark the way, with their bad Tibetan shoes that are not made for snow and glaciers and make it firm for the following days in case this fresh snow melts and adheres to the underlying ice. Then yesterday these men came back from the upper camp saying that Crowley had beaten them and hit them with his ice axe when they did not go as he pleased. These men refused to walk with him anymore and preferred not to receive any more treatment and even asked to return without anything; they must be pushed to the limit! There is better than that: these men argue that the chosen route is too dangerous and we could pass by the left with much less risk. Crowley too proud not only take into account these very fair observations, but still taunts them and is obstinate that none should ever say he had listened to the common opinion of the natives expressed by Nanga's sensible words; finally, we hope to return and defend them against Crowley to preserve their assistance, if necessary, by eliminating Crowley.

Besides, so far, Crowley has not done anything useful whatever, from a mountaineering ["Alpiniste"] point of view for the ascent itself. All he has managed to do is advance the steps thanks to Pache and Righi who have done miracles to get up to the upper camp the many and disparate things which Crowley still thinks he needs. Still did he want to advance much too quickly in the last days above all has not measured that we are ourselves at the supply base, nor make him understand that it's necessary to wait two then three then four days before renewing communication with the base.[17]

Guillarmod's notes tell us how he saw his advance to Camp 5. He left the supply camp at ten o'clock, climbing quickly to the bottom of the great slope, remaking steps because of avalanche. Righi was useless, but Guillarmod forgave him as a novice. At the top they found two loads abandoned by the sherpas who'd fled from Crowley's alleged misdemeanors. They couldn't find Pache's suitcase. They easily reached Camp 4 to find two or three porters unable to sleep any higher. Half an hour later they were at Camp 5 where Crowley saw them arrive.

Guillarmod says he perceived Crowley lying on a bag with three porters who could not catch up with Reymond and Pache. He found it asinine of Crowley constantly to want to advance without proper tactics, pushing into the chase men without assuring them of a shelter to sleep. The men had been there since nine in the morning and it was now 2:30 p.m.

He then says Crowley "abandoned" his men and came down to them, where Righi emptied his heart of all he had to say to Crowley, leaving Crowley flattened. Guillarmod, for his part, said he no longer recognized Crowley's authority and was going to descend.

Crowley's account is that the party had brought nothing required and their behavior was unintelligible. The doctor didn't seem to know

Fig. 14.7. Pioneers, perched on a crest at 6,150 meters (20,177 feet), dwarfed by Kangchenjunga's inhuman scale. (Photo: Dr. Jules Jacot-Guillarmod)

what he was saying, his one idea being to hold a durbar and have himself elected as leader. Their agreement allowed no such possibility, in Crowley's view. Guillarmod said the agreement was a scrap of paper. Crowley attributed Guillarmod's sour grapes to the feeling of "foreigners being bossed by an Englishman," something he'd encountered with Pfannl in 1902.[18] When Pache and Reymond turned up, they had nothing to complain about, Reymond being actively friendly. Crowley said he was concerned about the porters brought up by Guillarmod and Righi, with no supplies or shelter for them at Camp 5. The snow was unsafe. The porters would have to go down to Camp 4 and shelter behind rocks. They could probably manage the conditions, but Crowley knew Guillarmod and Righi—"the mutineers"—would be bound to come unstuck if they insisted on descending. Pache then said he wanted to go down with them; Crowley put this down to the fact his suitcase had not been recovered. Crowley implored he wait till morning; he could have Crowley's sleeping kit. Crowley tried, but Pache may have

doubted Crowley's view that Guillarmod had developed into a dangerous maniac. Shaking hands, Crowley said: "Don't go; I shall never see
you again. You'll be a dead man in ten minutes."[19]

Guillarmod noted Crowley's having to watch his men abandon him
and go over to "us." Shouting a little, he was able to talk with Pache and
Reymond, and after a moment they decided to descend, so he and Righi
agreed to wait for them. Pache said he wanted to join Guillarmod and
Righi on a rope, and descend with them because it would be less cold.
He was proud to have reached 6,500 meters (21,325 feet), and seemed
content with that. Guillarmod and Pache took summary leave of
Crowley who was left with Reymond, Salama, and two or three porters.

The first steps went well though there was some slipping in the steps
redone on the way up by the men at the front. Some steps ahead were fast.
Guillarmod and Righi took them well but two porterss at the back slipped.
Unable to regain their footing, they dragged Pache, and Guillarmod's
"nanka" holding his bag, from the ice. The snow below their feet came
away and they were thrown down a forty-five-degree slope, Guillarmod
soon losing sight of his comrades in a swirl of snow. Having lost his ice
axe, he stopped with a blow to the kidneys, tried to get up and saw Righi
on his back behind him, held flat by the rope. Righi and Guillarmod
called for help. Reymond responded immediately but Crowley only said
(according to Guillarmod): "They fell in an avalanche and there's nothing
you can do!"—without even putting his nose out of his tent.[20]

Crowley's prediction of ten minutes proved in the event to be less
than half an hour. Hearing Guillarmod and Righi's frantic cries, Crowley
recalled Reymond wanting to rescue at once, but Crowley saw it was
nearly dark and—thanks to Righi—they had no men to send. He remembered there was no indication *why* they were yelling; they'd been yelling
all day. Reymond still had his boots on, and said he'd go, and would call
Crowley if he needed his help. Reymond went off and neither returned
nor called. Crowley says he went to sleep and rose at dawn to investigate.

Guillarmod's account confirms Reymond's joining him and Righi as
soon as he could, on the basis that avalanches, once having descended,
were no longer a danger: an optimistic assumption, perhaps. Righi and the
doctor tried to dig in the snow, but it was like cement and they could only
manage half a meter. Reymond picked up three ice axes and joined them.
It proved impossible to dig further. The night had come. Exhausted, they

didn't know how to return to camp, but would have to move or die. It was no good risking their lives in further searching. Undoubtedly, their friends were lost, so Guillarmod concluded, and they would return with tools to find them the next day or in days ahead. They descended.

Guillarmod's next entry is for September 3: "Crowley announces that he's going. He leaves at 11am as a deserter and takes with him the best coolies [porters]. Dirty egoist. Soon after their departure, I take with me fifteen coolies to show them the location where the corpses are. Reymond comes with us, and ever dedicated, makes most of the steps."[21] They start digging, but without benefit of a shovel, Guillarmod decides they don't want to get caught by the dark like last time, and go down to Camp 3. Next day, under Nanga's leadership, the porters take the necessary tools and, around 10:00 a.m., they return with Pache's corpse, having entombed their three comrades, arms crossed on the chest, in a crevice, leaving them as high as possible in the hands of the god of Kangchenjunga. Guillarmod and Reymond dug a grave into which Pache's body was placed at midday. Pache had the swollen face of a drowned man; there was blood on his right arm and in his nose. The body was photographed then covered, with the coolies find-

Fig. 14.8. Inspecting the fatal avalanche.
(Photo: Dr. Jules Jacot-Guillarmod)

ing stones to make a fine "mausoleum." On the stone are inscribed the words: "ALEXIS A. PACHE + 1.IX.1905 +" Guillarmod left Camp 3 on September 6, and arrived in Darjeeling on September 20, having picked up a lot of plants of scientific interest on the way.

Crowley's inspection of the death scene, the morning after, revealed that the deaths could have been avoided—in what he considered a relatively trivial avalanche—had Guillarmod not insisted on roping the men together, and not keeping at the back, seeing the rope was kept taut all the time. They had obviously been on each other's heels, and so while a falling man would easily have survived the fall onto the slope, it was impossible to guarantee survival when there was the combined weight of other men dragging them down. Instead, Guillarmod was in front, as was evident from Righi's written account, which Crowley reproduced in his *Confessions*. Crowley remarked that seventeen porters—without Guillarmod—had crossed the fatal spot safely. These were the ones who had taken Crowley's advice, gone down to Camp 4 and slept under the rocks there. Crowley's view was that by breaking the agreement, and renouncing his authority, Righi and Guillarmod were themselves responsible for the disaster. Crowley's account states that it was he who, having descended to Camp 3, made arrangements with the porters for digging out the lost men and the erection of the cairn.

Now back in Darjeeling, Crowley obtained some relief from a brief, intense passion with one Tenguft, a Nepali girl, a passing joy he celebrated in a rondel, "Nepali Love Song":

> O kissable Tarshitering! The wild bird calls its mate—
> and I?
> Come to my tent this night in May, and cuddle close and
> crown me king!
> Drink, drink our fill of love at last—a little while and we
> shall die,
> O kissable Tarshitering!

Readers familiar with old Nepali names will note "Tarshitering" is a boy's name. In his *Confessions,* Crowley said that he was simply observing oriental modesty in a poet's not mentioning a woman's name, as in Elizabethan times, women did not appear on stage. Anyway, he loved the sound of Tarshitering. Astute readers may also note a melodious imperative—"Drink, drink our fill of love at last"—reminiscent of *The Book of the Law*'s first chapter, received in Cairo eighteen months earlier:

> Come forth, o children, under the stars, & take your fill of love! (*AL* I:12)

> Also, take your fill and will of love as ye will, when, where and with whom ye will! (*AL* I:51)

This he was doing, as ever. The phrase has another antecedent, one surely familiar to Crowley:

> Come, let us take our fill of love until the morning: let us solace ourselves with loves.

That gem comes from Proverbs 7:18, in the Bible, where Solomon quotes the "loud and stubborn" harlot seductress whose "house is the way to hell, going down to the chambers of death." Hence Crowley on his path of redemption by sin celebrates this Darjeeling-Tarshitering passion in Catullus-like abandonment of the very physical kind the Latin poet enjoyed with the woman he dubbed "Lesbia," in full knowledge that in "a little while we shall die." We know this moral from Crowley's return from K2 to Paris, when in "Summa Spes" he made it clear he was ready to "die and be done with it." Perhaps a similar mood struck again after the catastrophe of Kangchenjunga, comparing his Nepali lover to beetle, to butterfly—and to scorpion!

> Droop the long lashes: close the eyes with eyelids like a
>   beetle's wing!
> Light the slow smile, ephemeral as ever a painted
>   butterfly,
> Certain to close into a kiss, certain to fasten on me and
>   sting!

Nay? Are you coy? Then I will catch your hips and hold
   you wild and shy
Until your very struggles set your velvet buttocks all
   a-swing,
Until their music lulls you to unfathomable ecstasy,
        O kissable Tarshitering!

The feeling is undoubtedly close to Catullus's fifth poem to Lesbia:

> Lesbia, come, let us live and love, and not
> listen to the vile jabber of ugly old fools,
> for when our brief light has set,
> night is one long everlasting sleep.
> Give me a thousand kisses and a hundred more
> a thousand more again, and another hundred,
> another thousand, and again a hundred more,
> as we kiss these passionate thousands let
> us lose track; in our oblivion, we will avoid
> the watchful eyes of stupid, evil peasants
> hungry to figure out
> how many kisses we have kissed.

Dr. Guillarmod had no comparable feeling for poetry, or for Crowley as a poet. His entry for September 21 at Darjeeling states that he found Crowley there paying off the native bearers, or as he says, stealing money from the expedition account for personal expenses incurred. This does seem to have been a, if not *the,* major issue for the doctor, judging from repeated references to anxiety over costs (including securing money from Pache and Reymond, as well as Crowley) in his notebooks, from the very beginning. Crowley recorded his perception of events at Darjeeling in different terms, asserting that expedition costs were banked against Guillarmod's or his own signature.

    The doctor had written to the bank manager demanding he refuse to honor Crowley's signature. The manager, according to Crowley, thought the Swiss must be out of his mind, advising Crowley to draw out the whole account to be sure to pay the bearers what was owed them, lest Guillarmod take the money. This Crowley did. When Guillarmod and the others arrived on the twentieth, he had all the accounts in order and paid the men what was their due, with a reasonable amount of backsheesh (*that* would have upset Guillarmod). Crowley states Guillarmod was anxious not to come to a settlement. Crowley having no further business in Darjeeling asked for an accounts release, which he duly signed; it is reproduced in the *Confessions*. The release specifically says all claims were now void, the accounts being definitively settled on September 20, 1905. Compensation to the parents of the dead would be paid from the expedition chest. After which, Crowley reports, Guillarmod became very friendly and asked if he'd lend him money!

Guillarmod's notebook records he and Righi giving their account of the accident to the deputy commissioner and the chief of police on September 22. Crowley states his account of the accident had been "frank," and might necessitate an enquiry if Guillarmod and Righi were criminally responsible for the deaths. Guillarmod then went to the bank to withdraw the little he had left. The deputy commissioner advised the giving of 100 rupees to the parents of the three porters, and their pay. Righi and Reymond offered to make contributions to the indemnity for the dead.

Crowley wrote accounts of the expedition for the *Pioneer* of India, and London's *Daily Mail*. According to Crowley, Guillarmod visited him on the twenty-third and asked Crowley to say no more to the papers. The matter was discussed fully the next day, Guillarmod apparently admitting he'd been in the wrong, excusing himself on the grounds of ill-health and nerves. On the twenty-fifth he and Righi violently attacked Crowley in a newspaper, piling blame on the porters. Crowley concluded Guillarmod's overtures had just been buying time, and replied to the paper saying their comments about the native bearers simply reflected incompetence in managing them; the porters' conduct had been admirable. Guillarmod had in his own mind dismissed any idea of Crowley's integrity, accusing him of "bad faith," in his notebook. Crowley hit back and cut Guillarmod publicly on the twenty-sixth. Guillarmod sent Crowley a letter the next day, demanding Crowley send him an owed cheque for 300 rupees by 10:00 a.m. the next day or he would put a copy of Crowley's decadent *Snowdrops from a Curate's Garden* in a place where he would prefer not to see it. Crowley took the letter to a lawyer who warned the Swiss doctor that by the Indian penal code he was rendering himself liable to a long prison term for blackmail. Crowley did not press the charge, accepting Guillarmod was insane. In the event, Crowley says he did pay him a small sum for some items overlooked, despite the earlier written agreement that all accounts were now settled.

On September 28, Crowley left for Calcutta. As regards the mountain, Crowley felt he'd established a good way up, and was sure of establishing a camp within striking distance of the summit. He had reached a height, he claimed, of approximately 25,000 feet and found it possible to live and work at that altitude. He proposed "Kangchenjunga II" to Eckenstein for 1906, on condition no foreigners took part, and went to New York to promote the idea. Unable to raise backing for a return match, Kangchenjunga would remain unclimbed for another half century, finally succumbing to the skills of Sir Charles Evans who made the first wholly successful assault in 1955.

The *Confessions* inform us that Crowley used his journalistic expedition accounts to rap the British Alpine Club for alleged restrictive practices and attitudes, and for what he insisted was its virtual ignorance of Himalayan climbing.* Crowley's barbs obviously stung, for in February 1906 the club's *Alpine Journal* launched an exceedingly harsh attack on Crowley, a rabid assault whose evident bias was camouflaged by a faux-modest claim to have been giving the "other side of the story."

> Crowley's account of the disaster that, on September 1, put a stop to the expedition has been widely circulated in this country in the "Daily Mail" and in India in the "Pioneer." It is strongly objected

---

*For example, *Daily Mail,* London, August 29, 1905, "A Great Climb Ready to Ascend Kinchinjunga; The Food Supplies": ". . . Mr. White, of the Political Department, was kind enough to supply the coolies for this purpose; and I have also specially to thank him for the trouble he took in sending for his photographs from Gantok and Calcutta for my examination.

Mr. White 'makes no claim to be a mountaineer,'—perhaps just as well, if one takes his fine mountaineering record, and contrasts it with the much-advertised achievements (if it is an achievement to be pulled up a mountain by an overpaid peasant) of the pusillanimous braggarts of Savile Row [the Alpine Club], whose policy has brought the sport into such contempt that England, once its leader, can now produce no three climbers of the first rank to set against the 80 or 100 experts of Austria or Germany."

to by the remaining European members of the party, and in justice to them we think it right to reproduce in an abbreviated form a portion of the narrative published by Dr. Jacot-Guillarmod in the "Gazette de Lausanne" (November 11, 1905).

. . . The cries of the survivors soon summoned Reymond, who found apparently no difficulty in descending alone from the upper camp. Crowley, however, by his own avowal, remained in the tent in bed, drinking tea, and on the same evening wrote a long letter, printed in the "Pioneer" of September 11, from which the following sentences are culled: "As it was I could do nothing more than send out Reymond on the forlorn hope. Not that I was over anxious in the circumstances to render help. A mountain 'accident' of this sort is one of the things for which I have no sympathy whatever. Tomorrow I hope to go down and find out how things stand." In another letter, written three days later and published on the 15th, he explains that it would have taken him ten minutes to dress, and that he had told Reymond to call him if more help was wanted, which he did not do. The first search for the bodies was in vain. They were not found until three days later (after Crowley had left the party), buried under 10 ft. of snow.

Into the internal dissensions of the travelers, discussed at lamentable length in the newspaper correspondence, we must decline to enter. In the conditions described, and with for a leader a man capable of writing the extraordinary letters printed in the "Pioneer," trouble in camp and disaster on the mountain were to be looked for. We will only add for the sake of foreign members and readers who have not seen these letters that the "Special Commissioner" [Crowley] of the "Daily Mail" has never had any connection with the Alpine Club. To these who have seen the letters in question this statement will be altogether superfluous.

In another and more important respect we trust that this disastrous expedition may have results which will, to some extent, compensate for the temporary discredit it has brought upon mountaineering in India. All who are seriously interested in Himalayan exploration must join with us in the hope that the authorities at Calcutta may recognize the expediency of exercising in future the same caution they have, as a rule, exercised in the past before facilitating the entrance of travelers into the native States or territories on the northern frontiers of India. . . .

The Indian Government gave, it will have been noticed, the expedition commanded by the "Special Commissioner" of the "Daily Mail" [Crowley] very unusual assistance. Mr. White and Mr. Dover, the local officers in Sikhim, procured coolies for it; permission was even applied for and obtained from the Nepalese authorities for it to enter their territory. The travelers, as was to be expected, had trouble with the coolies, and then blamed the Government in place of themselves and the nature of the coolies. Fortunately they did not penetrate far into Nepal, for we tremble to think what complications might have been produced by a leader who has apparently not only succeeded to the post but also inherited the methods of Mr. Savage Landor.

Clearly, seniors in the Alpine Club had been deeply stung by Eckenstein, and especially Crowley. After all, *how dared these reckless, maverick non-Club members enter Nepal with government assistance!*— had they not consulted the club's very own published guide on "How to Climb Kangchenjunga" (*Alpine Journal* 22, no. 164)?

It may be observed that Crowley's article, reproduced below, which appeared on September 11, 1905, in London's *Daily Mail,* makes no self-serving reference to Guillarmod's determination, confirmed by Guillarmod's notebooks, to "eliminate" Crowley from command of the expedition:

THE GREAT CLIMB

Four Men Killed on Kinchinjunga Expedition Abandoned at 21,000 Feet

We have received the following cablegram from Mr. Allister [sic] Crowley, recording the abandonment of the expedition up Kinchinjunga the third highest mountain in the world, after an altitude of 21,000 ft. had been reached.

Darjeeling, Saturday, Sept 9.

Our advance guard attacked the south-west face of the mountain, and reached easily an altitude of 21,000 ft. Unfortunately, at this stage some members of the party decided to return. I solemnly warned them against the folly of descending late in the evening over "avalanchy" snow. However, a party of six, closely roped together, started, set going an avalanche of snow, and all fell.

Pache, who commanded the rear guard, and three natives were killed, the doctor and De Righi slightly injured, and Reymond was rescued. The latter had to cut the rope to release themselves. The bodies of the dead are buried under many feet of snow and are being searched for. As the avalanche was neither large nor steep, I am of opinion that if a rope had not been employed the accident would not have happened.

In consequence of this loss of life, I declined to assume further responsibility and returned with the remainder of the expedition. I am not altogether disappointed with the present results. I know enough to make certain of success another year with a properly equipped and disciplined expedition.

Notable features of the climb have been the warmth, persistent fog after 8 o'clock in the morning, a total absence of wind, flowers growing at 20,000 ft., the excellence of properly treated coolies, the comparative infrequency of large earthquakes, and the unseemly reluctance of nature to correspond to the published maps of Kinchinjunga.

The only trouble I experienced was in the form of headaches, caused possibly by the glare. The height of 21,000 ft. represents a minimum estimate. It might have been more.

ALEISTER CROWLEY

M. Pache was a lieutenant in the Swiss Calvary, he was thirty-one years of age, and joined the expedition chiefly in order to hunt in the Himalayas. His love of adventure, says Reuter, led him to fight among the Boers in the late war in the Transvaal.

It is curious how in later years Crowley would describe persistent bouts of near-annihilating asthma attacks as those of the "Storm fiend" and the condition in general as "Kangchenjunga Phobia" when, as we have seen, those conditions, meteorologically speaking, more properly belonged to the agonies of K2 with its howling isolation in Camp

Despair. Obviously, Kangchenjunga caused a lifelong anxiety, from which, arguably, Crowley never quite recovered. Its precise cause may still be pondered.

It was not, I think, fear of death; he was about to flirt with *her* once more.

FIFTEEN

Moharbhanj

Knocking about Calcutta in an agitated mood after September 28, Crowley saw a lot of friendly architect Edward Thornton. They'd jig about the city in Thornton's "tum-tum," a single-horsed, two-wheeled carriage used for shooting; a box for retrievers at the rear doubled as a passenger seat. Friendship with Thornton almost certainly explains Crowley's invitation from the maharaja of Moharbhanj, Sriram Chandra Bhanj Deo (1870–1912), to go shooting in the kingdom of Orissa,* thirteen hours from Calcutta.

In 1905, Moharbhanj (now Mayurbhanj) was a princely state in the British Raj, and Thornton and Martin & Co. were renovating the maharaja's 126-room Greek-Victorian-style palace at Baripada, some one hundred miles southwest of Calcutta. By 1908, the palace facade would resemble a bijou Buckingham Palace. Like Thornton, the maharaja's son was a member of the Asiatic Society of Bengal, which Crowley had visited in January 1902. Crowley notes in his *Confessions* that the enlightened benefactor to his people—promoted to maharaja status with a gold medal at the Delhi Durbar of 1903—was away for the day when he arrived at Baripada, so his "Minister of Public Works" was deputed to welcome and entertain Crowley until the ruler's return.

Crowley's comments about the minister he calls "Martin" demonstrate Crowley's conviction that ancient racial characteristics in the subconscious persist, often in a determinative way, despite education, which Crowley regarded as frequently of superficial impact on the psyche. One

---

*Today the state of Odisha.

could acquire the "form" quite easily, but not necessarily the "spirit" of a thing. For example, Crowley maintained that despite having taken a high degree at Oxford, and having studied engineering and science very thoroughly, Martin revealed within twenty-four hours a belief "in the most primitive superstitions, from ghosts and witches to mysterious medicines."[1] Crowley observed that no one would have suspected from the man's outward appearance his having a Bengali grandmother. It all proved the aphorism, "Blood will tell," Crowley concluded.*

Not that Crowley had anything against authentic traditions in

---

*It is still unclear who precisely this "Martin" was. It seems rather a coincidence that he was minister of Public Works and named *Martin,* at the very time the famous Martin & Co. was involved with the maharaja's palace. One might think "Martin" was Thomas Acquin Martin's younger brother Francis Ambrose John Martin, sometime chief engineer for Afghanistan's emir Nasrullah Khan, but *his* parents were from Birmingham, and his mother's parents came from Herefordshire of Welsh stock. Crowley's Martin was not of an age to qualify as one of Sir Thomas Acquin Martin's sons' sons. The possibility is that Frank Martin had married a woman who had a Bengali mother and that "Martin" was Frank's son. William Breeze's endnotes for his unpublished unexpurgated *Confessions,* refers to note 319 of the MS notebook of Crowley's *The Scented Garden* (Austin: University of Texas, Ransom Center), which has: "Morbhanj—J. A. Martin Esq.; North of Balasur [Odisha]," an identity confirmed in *Thacker's Indian Directory* for 1905: "Martin, J. A. L.C.E., State eng[inee]r p[ublic] w[orks] d[epartment] Morbhanj Raj, Balasore." *Thacker's* 1910 adds: "in ch[ar]ge Mourbhanj State light railway, Mourbhanj," the railway discussed by Crowley above in connection with Orissa's mining interests. L.C.E. may be "Licentiate in Civil Engineering," not a credential of the Institute of Civil Engineers in London (usual abbreviation: L.E.Civ.). There is no record of this man at Oxford or Cambridge (despite Crowley's assertion), and he was not one of Sir Thomas Martin's four sons employed in his company. The 1899 *Thacker's Directory* has him attached to C. A. Martin & Sons of Lucknow, which also employed a C. H. Martin; a firm possibly founded by a relative of Sir Thomas Acquin Martin. It is possible that J. A. Martin was an illegitimate son of either Thomas or Frank Martin. Or, he might yet have been Sir Thomas's brother, Francis Ambrose *John* Martin, using initials from Ambrose and John. "Frank" Martin, described as a "Mechanical and Civil Engineer" on the Institute of Mechanical Engineer's registry (accessed through ancestry.com) was proposed a member of the Institute of Mechanical Engineers on September 27, 1905, proposed by James D. Roots and received October 6, 1905, signing himself as "Frank A. Marti," between 1892–1894 contractor on the Cawnpore Water Works, where he became a Freemason, passed aged twenty-six in Lodge of Harmony 438, Cawnpore, described as "Comml Assist" (folio no. 293, records of United Grand Lodge of England). Frank had ceased working for the emir of Afghanistan in 1904. However, he may have had nothing more in common with "J. A. Martin" than his surname.

Fig. 15.1. Maharaja of Moharbhanj, Sriram Chandra Bhanj Deo (1870–1912).

Orissa—quite the opposite. He had arrived in time for October's Durga Puja, the great West Bengali season of vibrant festivities and worship in honor of Shakti goddess, Durga, and Crowley very much liked what he saw, preferring the natives' natural enthusiasm to the corrosion of their civilization he encountered in Calcutta. The problem, as Crowley saw it, was not the unscientific character of traditional beliefs, but the too-hasty fastening of native minds into Western thought. He saw a case of his principle on the maharaja's return the day after his arrival. Crowley found Sriram Chandra Bhanj Deo extremely interesting and delightful. How could he not enjoy, as he put it, meeting a man descended from a peacock! Crowley regretted the ruler did not take his ancestral myths seriously, in that the maharaja, in Crowley's laconic view, had exchanged one set of illusions for others equally absurd, but less inspiring. The maharaja had taken on Herbert Spencer and John Stuart Mill(!), and had brought representative administration to his ancient state in a recent reorganization of conciliar government, in a manner most satisfying to the Raj, and, of course, as the ruler saw it, to the benefit of his people's progress, efforts for which he would be remembered with affection to this day.

Crowley found certain of such efforts illustrative of his view that "principles" of economics, politics, and suchlike were "balderdash." Furthermore, to apply theories from "the Thames Valley" to the

Coromandel coast was "damnable heresy and a dangerous delusion"![2] A strong example of mismatch became apparent once Crowley took advantage of his presence in the attractive province to take stock of his past and assess what he might best do next, before Rose and Lilith arrived on October 29. Exploring the beauties of Orissa, he encountered a range of hills three thousand feet in height, whose exposed parts revealed rounded "bosses" of almost solid iron pyrites or "fool's gold." He described the wonder of seeing them at sunset: a red like bull's blood in sunlight. Aware of the commercial value of the hills' mineral content, the maharaja desired to exploit them. All he lacked was a line to the coast. He presumably consulted Martin & Company's expertise in specialized railways. Only one problem dogged the scheme. In the maharaja's enthusiasm to bring the benefits of Western liberal principles to his subjects, he decided the farmers would be better off as independent freeholders, without himself as zemindar or landlord. Realizing it would be no good simply giving the land to the peasantry, he had made a rule that farmers who cultivated their portion of soil consistently for fifteen years could keep it; well and good, one might think. However, the family custom in the region was to take enormous pride in impressive weddings for their daughters. It happened that the Marwaris, originally from the Marwar region of Rajasthan, had been attracted to Calcutta for trading opportunities developed by the British, for the Marwaris were traders before anything else, with an eye on opportunity. The maharaja provided an unforeseen one, and Marwari moneylenders descended on Moharbhanj where there was a ready market of freeholders willing to mortgage their prospects of owning land for vast advance sums to finance dream weddings. The result was the farmers' ruin and—though he could not see it—the maharaja's too, ever convinced he had done great service to his people. Another unfortunate effect of his liberality was that the Marwaris now refused to grant the maharaja a concession so he could build the light railway and get on with melting his mountains down! Crowley found the ruler's distress at this predicament comical. His people were now poorer than previously, though British administration of the maharaja's revenues had secured an increase from three to eighteen lakhs in under twenty years—one lakh meaning 100,000 rupees (with a value of about 13 rupees to the pound).

The maharaja had less painful tales to tell his celebrity guest. One concerned inhabitants of the province's unexplored jungles, where lived a people of much darker skin who went about naked, or in a bare loin-cloth. They had their own language, apparently unrelated to any other, with a vocabulary of some three hundred words of which 250 were regarded as obscene. Skillful in metallurgy, as well as with bows and arrows, the people had strong instincts for beauty. Crowley remarked on the women's breasts, which were small and pointed upwards, a marked improvement in his view, to the average breasts of Indians or any Europeans. He described their skin as a "superb velvety black" that was more like purple, noting with approval they had far less inhibitions than ordinary Indian women he'd met, loved beautiful things, and were amorous with refinement and skill.* Crowley found the primitive Austroasiatic tribe he described as "Jewans," (Juangs) fascinating, thought of locally as "the wild men of the woods," rarely seen, and some said, never by a white man. They lived in jungles and carried on a trade, with white stones marking the edges of villages, where rice and other cultivated products were left, replaced in the mornings by things found, killed, or made in the jungle, such as woven baskets. No one had seen the exchange, the "Jewans" being so wary. Of about thirteen primitive tribes in Orissa, the Juangs say they are the original people, having emerged out of the earth of the Gonasika Hills, Keonijhar region, Odisha. In Crowley's day, they had migrated to the Dhenkanal district.

When it came to Crowley's preferred sport of shooting, the maharaja abstained, appointing one d'Elbroux as forest officer to assist.† Mauled by a bear when young, d'Elbroux's features were patched together with metal plates. D'Elbroux prepared a *machan* or tree platform from which

---

*William Breeze, in his endnotes to the unexpurgated *Confessions*, suggests the tribe may have been the indigenous "Adivasis."

†William Breeze reckons this was probably Francis John d'Elboux. He appears in 1899 as F. d'Elboux in *Thacker's Indian Directory* as "treas[ur]y off[ice]r., Morbhanj Raj, Balasore" and as Francis John d'Elboux in the contemporary edition of the British Board of Trade Directory. The *International Code of Signals for the Use of all Nations* (London: Commerce of Lloyds, Spottiswoode, 1899) has him born in London in 1833 to an English family of Huguenots. In his early seventies in 1905, he worked in treasury, not forestry. He may have held a forestry post through the maharaja. It's possible Crowley met the son of Francis John d'Elboux; he had at least two wives and several recorded children, some educated in England. As he was severely disfigured, he might have remained in India and found a forestry position in Balasore with help from his father.

Crowley could take his aim at anything but the elephant. Tigers and bears were fair game, but *hāthī* was reserved for viceroys and royalty. Seven hundred beaters began their noisy work. A bear encountered the first barrel of Crowley's 10-bore, but the second went off unexpectedly, hurling Crowley onto his back while a bullet shattered a thick tree. The tree fell toward the machan, narrowly missing one of the men. Another machan was built near a salt lick (or *bhul*) where animals came to satisfy a mineral craving, that is, to get a lick of salt. The expected beast was a fine tiger, a regular at the lick. After dinner, Crowley mounted the machan to sit dead tight as a three-quarter moon rose. Preferring to stalk, this wasn't really Crowley's idea of a shoot. As the moon rose, the noisy jungle fell silent. The creatures that had visited the bhul in the dark vanished. Crowley, lying flat, was alerted by a mysterious disturbance. Lifting his head, he saw gigantic shapes, then, looking again, he counted twenty-four elephants. The shikari warned him that no other animal would threaten the habits of the jungle master, but Crowley was now in danger, for if an elephant took a dislike to the machan, it could snap the tree trunk in an instant, and its height was no protection. Despite this, Crowley was enraptured, sitting up all night to watch the elephants go about their business: a sight more compelling than any other he had witnessed "on the material plane."[3]

Crowley didn't miss the shooting. He didn't really feel very involved in it. He would write how he felt in a curious state of mind all round, enjoying waking up daily to read Kant, Bishop Berkeley, and Persian poet Ferdowsi (935–1020 CE). He had hired a munshi in Calcutta to teach him rudimentary Persian and had it in mind to return to England with his wife via Persia, there to absorb knowledge on Sufism, a subject he wished to master, despite time spent considering it in Cairo the previous year in the company of Indian army general Dickson, who had converted to Islam.* Crowley says Persian fascinated him more than any other language, and he felt drawn powerfully to Sufism's ideas, imagery, and esoteric symbolism. He had begun trying to invent another poet in the manner of Sir Richard Burton's *Kasidah*, and had come up with "Abdullah al Haji (that is—with soft *h*—a satirist) of Shiraz." Crowley wrote a series of ghazals (amatory odes) in this name, purportedly

---

*See *Aleister Crowley: The Biography*.

composed around 1600 CE, entitled the *Bagh-i-Muattar* ("The Scented Garden"). Around this he invented an Anglo-Indian Major Lutiy who translated them, an editor to complete the poor deceased major's work (killed—alas—in South Africa), and high Anglican priest ("Rev. Carey") to provide "moral" comment on the poem. Crowley used the annotations to convey esoteric information he'd acquired in the East, or so he says; in fact, he uses excessive annotations to toy with every sodomitical-sexual implication he can wrench out of his very naughty (schoolboy-sophisticated), and often overaccomplished text: a vast paean to podex-oriented joys: an escape valve for Crowley's gay steam. It is also, he claims, a complete treatise on mysticism, and I daresay such can be wrung from it too, for symbols are often polyvalent and universal in utility. One may consider how the *Song of Solomon* has been taken as metaphor for Christ's love for his Church!

Crowley was making fun of everything he was really serious about at the time, and thus maintained sanity in the face of an overwhelming desire to commune with the "immanent soul of the universe," that is, to experience samādhi. Furthermore, Crowley regarded what he had written as a "symptom" of supreme significance.[4] By this he meant that the combination of the desire for samādhi with sexual symbolism was at the essence of his developing grasp of a new system of spiritual attainment.

Sex, on one level, was a satire on human folly, in the extreme; but it was also, potentially, the royal road par excellence. Turn the whole issue of sex around, he believed, and the human universe would change fundamentally. In the Persian satire, the "fundament" is certainly reached, but there is a hint of more. The first step was to undo inherited inhibition. He was going through a period of radical self-criticism, or so he later concluded. He would interpret strange things in the light of one being prepared for a great work, indeed, *the* Great Work: the uniting of the above and the below, as he saw it.

He had been arranging regular "astral" meetings with Elaine Witkowski, living (materially speaking) in Shanghai at the time. In these "meetings," their astral bodies were, according to Crowley, larger than their material ones. He says Elaine's was about six feet. It could be perceived in a kind of conscious lucid dream state, as though made of muslin, but clear enough to sense real intimacy. In a conference of Sunday, October 22, Soror Fidelis appeared accompanied by a golden hawk, which he took to be the presence of one of the "Secret Chiefs" of an order he was yet to establish on the material plane, the Astrum Argenteum, or "Silver Star," which name would appear in an astral vision entered into at Kobe dock, Japan, on April 24, 1906, after parting from Mrs. Witkowski.

The hawk in mysticism may be taken as a vision of an impending leadership role requiring thought and preparation. That is certainly what Crowley felt he was now approaching, though how much was retrospective analysis or contemporary awareness is difficult to say. His memory of the time was that he was basically ignoring *The Book of the Law* and heading back toward Buddhism. In the astral interview with Soror Fidelis, the "Great Work" was defined as the creation of a new universe, a thought that he wrote later left him spiritually prostrate. He had not settled his relations with the existing universe, never mind being ready for a new one, still less to promulgate such a thing. But he knew, by his own account, he could not delay in settling himself. And that meant understanding himself more fully, and it meant attaining samādhi, without which he was in no position to establish anything like a new order, being himself disordered.

He returned to Calcutta, not surprisingly perhaps, with Kali, the devourer, on his mind.

SIXTEEN

Get Out of Calcutta Quick!

Crowley returned to Calcutta in late October 1905. One of the first things he did was to go to Kalighat, close to the Tolly Canal, running south off the Hooghly River. There, Crowley sacrificed a goat at the ghat's temple to Kali, an animal sacred to the goddess. Reading that evening, the goddess appeared, inspiring his extensive poem "Kali," of which this is a short extract:

> There is an idol in my house
> By whom the sandal always steams.
> Alone, I make a black carouse
> With her to dominate my dreams.
> With skulls and knives she keeps control
> (O Mother Kali!) of my soul.

He felt insight into Kali's attributes aided his eventual perception of the place of evil and sorrow in the world; which, though ubiquitous, are never permanent, while perception of them may, Crowley came to believe, be transcended through initiation into the paradoxes of relativity. Crowley's sudden enthusiasm for Kali was perhaps inspired by Moharbhanj Palace's once having housed a temple to Kali, the *kuladeva* (or clan deity) of the Bhanj dynasty, also known as Chamunda. She was also the state deity. The idol for the palace's temple had been brought some ninety-three miles east from the family's old palace at Khiching, where there still stands the striking seventh- or eighth-century Kishakeshwari Temple to goddess Chamunda, with many remarkable life-size statues, including one of the Buddha.

Crowley's sudden devotion to Kali, goddess of time, is appropriate for his mental condition. Time controls us; we cannot control it. We are, effectively, devoured by time. Crowley's relations with time, process, and causality were in a gathering state of flux. This became evident one morning when riding with Thornton in the tum-tum by the Maidan, the largest park in Calcutta. Crowley blurted out to his friend: "I cannot formulate a plan of action of any kind because there is no true continuity in phenomena." Thornton turned on him, and said: "Quite so, but there is equally no continuity in yourself."[1]

This little exchange shows the impression Bishop Berkeley (1685– 1753) was having on Crowley in his blistering state. Berkeley refuted philosopher John Locke by emphasizing that we can never know any "thing in itself" or object external to our idea of it. We are aware of ideas, and to be aware of ideas indicates only a perceiving mind. Thus all our perception is of the mind—"Esse est percipi": to be is to be perceived.

So why can't we control the universe by thought?

Berkeley's reason is that ideas are not self-generated, to be willed into existence or out of it. There must be another mind that controls ideas, independent and greater than ours: God, or universal Mind (a Hermetic notion incidentally). Thus, ideas of mind do not disappear just because we do not perceive them. The idea of a tree exists when we have left it. Thus, God's existence, maintaining Mind, permits sense of *continuity.* We are not just a succession of ideas perceived. Crowley's problem here was that Berkeley's theist solution to discontinuity had been undermined by the Buddhist idea that there was no eternal essence, only process of change, involving sorrowful loss. Crowley did not know what the "right thing" was to do. He had lost both philosophical and moral compass.

Crowley noted in his *Confessions* that Thornton's answer mirrored philosopher David Hume's answer to Berkeley. Hume denied that ideas depend on God's existence. For Hume, it is not rational to insist God's existence cannot depend on our minds; for Hume, ideas derive from perceptions, which derive from sense-data alone. Hume even questioned causality, or what Theravadists called *kamma.* To Hume, we simply perceive successions of phenomena and choose to believe there is a causal connection. Necessity is not in things, but exists only in the human mind. Hume's challenge leaves the perceiver at the "mercy," so to speak of discontinuous perceptions, and Thornton was implying that Crowley's sense of disorientation was due to lack of continuity in his own sense of who he was. Had something in his mind gone under the pressure of the Kangchenjunga disaster, combined with a commitment to Buddhist detachment? For Crowley, reflecting on these events many years later, he interpreted it as having been all arranged by the gods to bring him to such a condition where a "new heaven and a new earth" could be taken into his being, as his old universe was devoured by circumstance.

Interestingly, Hume found the only thing that stopped him going mad from the force of his own skepticism about a rational basis for believing either in God or a material world external to impressions was the distraction provided by nature for taking the mind off such things in other sensual enjoyments. While such might have eased Crowley's mind in the past, he was fast approaching a time when his thoughts just might send him mad.

> The Secret Chiefs arranged for me to be in a situation where I was
> at their mercy. They meant to initiate me whether I liked it or not.
> And this is how they went to work.[2]

Perhaps mindful of Hume's madness preventative, Crowley recalled a "red light" area called "Culinga Bazar" he had been driven to, in the dark, from a distant part of Calcutta, back in 1901. The area concerned was Kalinga-Fenwick Bazar; the old Fenwick Bazar (off Chowringhee Street) having been demolished to make way for the New Market in 1874. The area of narrow streets is about three-tenths of a mile west of Janbazar, central Calcutta.

On a black night (October 27), only occasionally illuminated by flares and fireworks from the Durga Puja—then in full swing—he tried to find the infamous street from a corner of the Maidan, itself facing Chowringhee Street. Perhaps responding to the strangely abandoned atmosphere, Crowley tuned in to his "savage instincts" and smelt the path to his destination. However, his instincts also picked up a sense of danger, not merely fear, but real sense of peril; he was being followed. Crowley always admitted to being a complete coward, but one who nonetheless forced himself to confront his fears. This, of course, may be attributed to masochism rather than courageousness, but he was frank about his masochism too.

He became agitated, sure that human beings were on his trail. To pull himself together, he turned off a dim street into a darker alley, over which was a black archway. Lit by gloomy blue-gray sky, the alley, he realized, was a dead end. A group of white robes marching in single file approached. Dark of face and clothes, he held himself against the wall. Three passed him, then turned. Surrounded, his arms gripped, hands entered his pockets. Then he saw a knife. "Perhaps the long strain and horror of the Kangchenjunga tragedy had prepared me for this sudden outcropping of atavism."[3] Something told him he had lured the men; he was a "Q-ship," a merchant vessel with concealed armaments to fox hostile warships. Their ignoring his orders to cease, his life endangered, Crowley felt justified in pressing the trigger of his Webley, held since he had first glimpsed the men. He heard a click; the hammer seemed to have hit an empty chamber. With arms forced to his sides, he managed to lift the concealed pistol to the edge of his pocket, and fired. The figures backed off immediately in the explosion. Once darkness resumed, Crowley was blind. Did he step over bodies? He headed back to the archway, his finger still on the trigger. He walked back up the street quickly and quietly to the Dharamtolla Road (meaning "Holy Street" but now renamed "Lenin Sarani" by local communist government), took a gharry (horse-drawn taxi) for Edward Thornton's, and lit his pipe, enjoying the tobacco as one who feared he might never taste it again.

Crowley was proud of himself. Some dozen or so outrages had been committed against Europeans in the previous month, some ending in murder, but Crowley was the only Englishman to come out on top, albeit with the loss of four rupees and eight annas.

Waking Thornton up, he told his story, and found the first cartridge had failed to go off; there was a dent in its cap. Crowley asked Thornton whether he should report the incident to the police. Thornton gave a wizened look, recommending Crowley go to bed and return after *chota hazri* (a meal served at dawn in north India), when he'd take his friend to "the right man."

🏵

Next day, Crowley, again suggesting he go to the police, was taken to a Scottish solicitor he called "MacNair," who favored caution.* McNair recommended leading Calcutta barrister, William Garth (born 1848), eldest son of Sir Richard Garth (1820–1903), former chief justice of Bengal.† Crowley's recollection of their interview is amusing, reflecting important contemporary political facts.

> "Well," said Garth, "Curzon and Fraser are busy with the partition of Bengal, for reasons of purely administrative convenience; and it is singularly unfortunate that the measure will break the political power of the Bengali into a lot of dirty little bits. Their hearts bleed for Bengal. So, if you should have happened to hit somebody last night, they will be very indignant and bring you to trial. You will be instantly acquitted, but they will invent some scheme for having you tried again, and acquitted again, to show the sincerity of their love for the Bengali, whom they are out to smash."
>
> "Then you advise me," I said innocently, "to say nothing?" "Indeed no," he said tempestuously, "as a sworn barrister, it is my duty to advise you to report the whole affair immediately to the police." I became more innocent than ever. "Well, I don't see how I can throw any light on the matter." (I was still ignorant of the effect, if any, of the shot.)
>
> He bellowed with laughter. "You can throw a whole flood of light on it," he shouted. My Quaker ancestors knocked at the door of my dull mind, I suppose.
>
> "Would you do it yourself?" I asked meekly. "Well," he said more soberly, "you'd be acquitted of course. A man doesn't stroll out after dinner to murder strangers. But you'd be kept hanging about Calcutta indefinitely; and an unscrupulous man, I'm afraid, might be tempted to hold his tongue and clear out of British India p.d.q. [pretty damn quick.]"

---

*George Burgh McNair, solicitor of the High Court, Calcutta. His son George Douglas McNair became a Calcutta High Court judge. Crowley misspelt his name. (Thanks to William Breeze for this information.)

†Educated at Eton and Merton College, Oxford, William Garth was Calcutta High Court advocate 1880–1913, was knighted in 1914, became K.C. (King's Council) in 1919.

My Quaker ancestors told me what to do. I said sternly, but sadly, "then I suppose it is my duty to go to the police at once. Where is my gharry?" The great barrister wrung my hand in silent sympathy.[4]

Crowley had chosen a poor time to find himself a suspect in a possible interracial murder case. Curzon was still viceroy of India, and the "Fraser" Garth referred to was Sir Andrew Henderson Lieth Fraser, lieutenant general of Bengal (1848–1919), whom Crowley had met at the Masonic Lodge in Darjeeling, who, at the time, was preoccupied with the partition of Bengal. While partitioning the province gave more representative power to Muslims, it made Hindus a minority in East Bengal and Assam. Announced in July, partition had only been implemented on October 16, and was dangerously controversial. The administration was accused of exercising a divide-and-rule policy; Curzon retorted the measure would improve governance. Attempts were made to placate the feelings of angry Bengalis (the partition would be rescinded in 1911). While Crowley could claim he'd been set upon by *dacoits* (or ruffians), there was political capital to be obtained by nationalists and other Bengali political interests for challenging the claim. Three years earlier, Lord Curzon had condemned brutality exhibited by members of the Ninth Lancers when two Indians died after an assault. Curzon determined to punish the regiment. At the time it transpired that in the previous twenty years, there had been eighty-four recorded cases where Indians were killed clashing with Europeans, while only two Europeans had been hanged for murder of Indians since the Mutiny of 1857. Curzon wrote a minute, giving his views of the issue:

I know that as long as Europeans, and particularly a haughty race like the English, rule Asiatic people like the Indians, incidents of hubris and violence will occur, and that the white man will tend to side with the white skin against the dark. But I also know, and have acted throughout on the belief, that it is the duty of statesmanship to arrest these dangerous symptoms and to prevent them from attaining dimensions that might even threaten the existence of our rule in the future.

I have observed the growing temper of the native. The new wine is beginning to ferment within him, and he is attaining to a consciousness of equality and freedom.[5]

Curzon felt it necessary to check the tendency by controlling the temper of the European, lest the situation boil over in mutiny and rebellion. He was himself already embroiled in a crucial administrative crisis that would see him resign from his position in India and return to England in November 1905.

General Lord Kitchener had been made commander in chief of the Indian Army in 1902, and as such demanded sole military representative status on Curzon's governing council, rather than sharing the position with the military member of the government. Relenting to Kitchener's demand would have given Kitchener the largest part of India's budget. In 1904, convinced Russian railways were being constructed for offensive military purposes on Afghanistan's border, he said he'd resign if his demands were not met. Curzon assured the concerned prime minister Arthur Balfour that he'd look into the matter. Kitchener used the alleged Russian threat as leverage. In the spring and summer of 1905 he ensured the British press saw supposedly secret papers. The issue came to a head on Curzon's council on March 10, when Kitchener found himself in a minority of one. Curzon could not accept Kitchener's claim that India could not withstand Russian invasion under the existing system. The British Cabinet became convinced it was Curzon who leaked secret telegrams to the press. Under pressure, a poor compromise favoring Kitchener was reached, but in August 1905 Curzon realized he no longer had guarantee of Cabinet support and felt resignation inevitable, feeling bitter toward Kitchener who, he believed, lacked honor and truthfulness. Kitchener asserted he'd been misrepresented.

Meanwhile, the Bengal partition issue had enflamed nationalists and others. Young men, believing the Motherland was at stake, joined secret political societies. There was also, of course, the issue of threats to economic privileges enjoyed by dominant Hindus of West Bengal in an undivided province. Curzon stood fast against ensuing economic boycotts and terrorist bombs. In March 1905 he dismissed antipartition agitators as "petty volcanoes," throwing their "torrents of mud into the air," but by October recognized the agitators' methods as "open transgression and violence."[6]

Other than his immediate personal predicament, Crowley probably found the situation of some personal interest, but even if he did so at the time (he may have fancied being a rebel), he did not refer to it to any significant extent in his *Confessions.* Given his prophecies of 1900 (*Carmen Saeculare*), which foresaw the downfall of Britain in India in the wake of the great Indian famine of that period, when alleged inadequacies of conduct over government response had brought criticism on Curzon, one might think he felt some excitement at the prospect of revolt in India, as, perhaps, a sign of "Force and Fire," and the Aeon of Horus, the fiery youth avenger! If so, his attitude may still have been a mixed one, judging by his attitude to a Bengali doctor encountered at Tengueh (now Tengchong), some thirty-seven miles over the Burma-China border.

Crowley and family would be guests at Consul General George Litton's residence at Tengueh in January 1906. During their stay, Litton died mysteriously. Crowley suspected the consul general's Bengali doctor, Dr. Ram Lal Sircar, and personally whipped the doctor for refusing to examine Litton's corpse and give a proper account of cause of death. Crowley was convinced the Bengali doctor wrote anti-British articles for native Bengali newspapers. The doctor complained to William Henry Wilkinson (1858–1930), consul general at Yunnan-Fu (now Kunming), about the beating. When Crowley arrived there on February 19, 1906, Wilkinson was unable to offer hospitality until Sircar's complaints were investigated. Crowley settled the affair to his satisfaction before departure, leading intelligence writer Richard B. Spence to consider whether Crowley had not been rewarded for intelligence concerning the doctor's allegedly seditious propaganda. Given the paucity of evidence, however, other than another witness's recollection (botanist Dr. George Forrest) that the doctor had indeed refused or been unable to identify cause of death, it is impossible to say whether the doctor's seditious writing *in itself* annoyed Crowley. According to Brenda McLean,* the deceased George John L'Etablere Litton's good friend Scottish botanist George Forrest (1873–1932), whom Crowley met and admired (and with whom he buried Litton's body), recorded how "The Doctor, a Bengali and most incompetent could give the disease no name" (McLean, 80). Forrest also recorded being invited by Crowley to be botanist on Crowley's vaunted second Kangchenjunga attempt. Brenda McLean inspected

---

George Forrest: Plant Hunter (Edinburgh: Antique Collector's Club, 2004), 79.

Forrest's records held at Edinburgh's Royal Botanic Garden.* Kevin Mount, a researcher into George Forrest, emailed me January 11, 2013, after contacting "brilliantly helpful archivist" at the RBGE, Leonie Paterson. Mount's research revealed a letter Forrest wrote home on January 13, 1906, that confirmed Crowley's account of Litton's death. Mount kindly sent me a copy of a letter Forrest wrote to I. B. Balfour, his mentor at at the Royal Botanic Garden Edinburgh, that refers to Crowley's stay at the consulate in Teng Yueh, before Litton's death:

THE CONSULATE
TENG YUEH
YUNNAN
S.W. CHINA

30-12-1905

Dear Sir

Again I will have to ask you to excuse me writing a long letter to you. I have been so busy since I came back from the north. Mr Litton was called away suddenly to the frontier on business connected with the proposed railway extension from Bhamo to Teng Yueh and left me practically in charge here, to entertain any people who might be traveling through on their way east or west etc.

Unfortunately for me and my work there happens to be quite a number on the road this year. At present there are four Europeans in the Consulate. Mr Crowley, who is a member of the Alpine Club, his wife and child, and a Frenchman who is on his way north to buy musk and furs for some firm in Paris. His name is Peronne (?). I am the only person of the lot who understands a little Chinese, so you can quite easily understand that I have rather a busy time attending to their various needs. Later on I shall give you a full, or as full as possible account of our journey north and probably a number of photographs which may interest you. We reached lat. 27 15 1 ¼ degrees covering new ground. No roads, frightful

---

*I am grateful to "belmurru" a participant in the "LAShTAL" Aleister Crowley Society website, August 23, 2014, for this information.

travelling, people complete savages and the most barren country I have yet passed through. For days through grass 6–10 feet high. I have about 300 specimens for you, some of them new species I think, but as yet I cannot give you the correct number, as I have not had time to go over them and some are not yet dry. Of seeds I have only about 100 species I think and not by any measure those I wished most to secure. Therefore I shall have to go back on my tracks to Tsekou this next season as I cannot bear the thought of anyone else, especially a Frenchman, securing specimens and seeds of the plants I saw.

. . . I leave here about the middle of January. About that time I shall be sending off my plants but shall communicate with you regarding this later.

According to William Breeze,* the name of Ram Lal Sircar, medical officer to His Britannic Majesty's Consul in T'eng Yueh and the Chinese Maritime Customs, sometimes appears as Ramlal Sircar or R. L. Sircar. He was perhaps adopted son of notable Indian doctor Mohendra Lal Sircar C.I.E., editor of the *Calcutta Journal of Medicine.*†

In the event, Crowley hesitated going to the police, giving his reasons years later as it having been a guiding principle of his life never to enter a game without a sporting chance, on which basis it made no sense to stand trial without possibility of conviction! What he did was to wait and see if news arose of a serious wounding or death had resulted from his firing the revolver. After two days waiting he went to meet his wife and daughter off the ship. Rose asked how he was, to which he replied: "You've got here just in time to see me hanged!"

That night, Thornton hosted a dinner party for the couple, with Rose sitting at his right hand. While Crowley's wife seemed upset about something, Thornton kept making a curious gesture, raising two fingers.

---

*Endnotes to unexpurgated *Confessions.*
†See Sarat Chandra Ghose, *Life of Dr Mahendra Lal Sircar M.D., D.L., C.M.D.* (Calcutta, 1909). Ram Lal Sircar published "Secret Societies in China," *The Modern Review* 7, no. 2 (Feb. 1910): 182, Allahabad; "My Little Experiences in China," *The Modern Review,* probably vol. 7, nos. 1–6 (1910). On the insurrection in Yunnan, he contributed (as "Dr Ram Lal Sarkar, an Eye-Witness") to "The Revolution in China," *The Modern Review* 12 (July–Dec. 1912): 155, 349, 485, 612.

His intention was revealed after dinner when the host took the couple aside to inform them Crowley had in fact shot *two* dacoits. One bullet had gone clean through the abdomen of the first to lodge in the spine of the rogue behind him. Taken to hospital, they had confessed, which confession appeared as a story of attempted robbery in column three of next morning's *Standard* newspaper. The police were offering a reward for the apprehension of the shooter, believed to be a sailor from the harbor. Column five of the paper contained an interview with Crowley about Kangchenjunga!

"They will go round the ships," said Thornton, "and then they'll have a shot at the hotels. Get out and get out quick!"

"Darling sweetheart lovey-dovey silly great big she-ass!" I whispered to my wife, "would you rather walk across Persia or across China?" "My ownest own," she purred, "let's go through China!"[7*]

---

*In a typescript for a magazine article "A Brush with Dacoits" (1914), Crowley gives a slightly different exchange: "Wife of my bosom," said I, "suppose we walk across China?" "Darling," she cooed, "The exercise will do us good."

SEVENTEEN

Return to Burma

Such was the haste in which the Crowleys left Calcutta they felt compelled to take the first *ayah* (a servant nurse or nanny) they could find. As so often, haste made for ill luck, and they soon realized they'd engaged a hideous, ill-mannered, and untrustworthy person. Crowley said she claimed to be a Roman Catholic, which he took as concealing the likelihood that her own caste wanted nothing to do with her. Still, he had managed to secure the services of honest shikari, Salama Tantra, for whom no praise was too high: "The loyal staunch old hound! He never flinched, he never failed; he had all the innocence of a child and all the wisdom of Pythagoras; the courage to face the unknown—which Indians almost always fear to the limit—and the gentleness which goes with great strength of body and soul. Peace be to thee, old friend, where'er thou be."[1] As for the ayah, she would take a fancy to a muleteer encountered outside Tengueh in Yunnan province, China, and scarper overnight, leaving Rose holding the baby.

Crowley's comments about Allan Bennett and officialdom in Rangoon are interesting. While emphasizing that he experienced nothing but kind consideration from British authorities in Burma, he was aware that the social situation not being so well settled in Burma as it was in India, there was a feeling of superiority to indigenous peoples that generated a fear of "going native." Therefore, anyone saying a good word for the people was regarded poorly. Even officials who took a sympathetic interest in native beliefs and customs were regarded as "letting the side down"—so, for an Englishman to dress as a Buddhist monk (other than as a joke in a fancy-dress party), as Allan did, and to assert the superiority of that religion over that of his birth, and of his country-men to boot, and, furthermore, to concern himself with organizing a Buddhist *mission* to Blighty herself, *well*, that was not simply grounds for dislike, but for official suspicion on political grounds. Bennett's *Buddhism* journal would have been regarded as veering toward some-thing anti-British, a hostile and unwelcome development. The view was that such a person could be used to make British rule appear unneces-sary, a hindrance, even, God forbid, a deficit! Crowley considered the rationality of this view somewhat flawed, but then, neither the world, nor its average inhabitant, Crowley believed, was rational anyway. And Britain ruled well enough, convinced of what to reason might appear absurd or questionable. What worked without question in India was where British rule rested on superiority of courage, truthfulness, jus-tice, and self-control, it proved successful, thereby justifying itself. In Crowley's view, it needed no more reason. Excessive reasoning leads to doubt: poison to the ruler. Crowley was impressed by a letter signed "Duxmia" that appeared in *Vanity Fair* on October 13, 1907:*

> The British Empire was not built up by public school boys, for the excellent and all sufficient reason that while it was really being built up the public schools did not exist. The men who defeated Napoleon and crushed the Indian Mutiny were sons of country squires, edu-cated in private seminaries, or by tutors on their fathers' own estates, often left to run wild among grooms and stableboys, and obtaining their military or colonial posts through purchase or influence, cer-tainly not through examinations. And never let it be forgotten that the Navy, the one efficient service we possess, is officered by men who have not been to public schools.

It was, in Crowley's view, no good appealing to reason: sheer con-viction, sincerely held with a will was sufficient to impress. One argu-ment simply invites another. Politicians never cease arguing, and all

---

*Duxmia was probably Captain George Evelyn Cowley (1888–1918), who fought at Gallipoli (1915) and wrote short stories before World War One. He died of wounds after being captured by the Germans in 1918. Otherwise I might have thought that since the letter's date marked the 400th anniversary of the arrest of the Knights Templar, its author was Aleister Crowley. Crowley calls its author a "very wise bird" (*Confessions* 462).

assume themselves to be paragons of reason, philosophers likewise. And besides, Crowley's sense of reason was itself beginning to evaporate in the humid conditions that made any minor problem feel considerably more irritating.

Crowley hastened to meet up with Bennett, who had graduated, so to speak, from bhikkhu to sayadaw (a senior monk or abbot) at a monastery two miles from Rangoon. Crowley was troubled by Thornton's comment about there being no continuity in his ego. Bennett insisted samādhi could not be obtained unless one's "kamma" was ready for it, and if that was true of samādhi, even more so of arahatship: Buddhist enlightenment. To even have a chance, one would have to comply with the dhamma assiduously. Crowley countered that Allan's argument was basically on the same level of partisan dogmatism as Sri Parānanda's saying samādhi was impossible without Lord Shiva's grace. Bennett's reply was regrettable, from Crowley's perspective. The sayadaw could only say that Sri Parānanda's doctrine was not Buddhism! Crowley was unimpressed, convinced a man's progress depended on his prowess. So Crowley was, in the first instance, disappointed.

He moved the conversation on to what his kamma (or karma) might be. Bennett said he might best be able to trace his future by understanding his past and acquiring the "Magical Memory," which was taken to mean the same as Sammasati, or "Right Recollection," whose idea involves tracing back events one after another without thought for time. Now, as a Buddhist, it was not a question of looking into previous lives as being lives of oneself, for there is no perpetual essence or lasting ego, according to the doctrine. Even memories of "oneself" as a child boil down in Buddhist terms to saying, "I have a consciousness of a tendency to see a tendency for making some connection between what appears to be 'me' now and a figure in the past, who I have a consciousness of a tendency to see a connection with." As for previous lives, there may be causal links, but no continuity of essence or permanent identity. Nevertheless, if one can trace the past and see causal connections, one should gain knowledge of tendencies that may be repeated in the future.

The phenomenon of process of change gives the illusion of an ego as the subject of change, rather than a process subject to change. In science, as Crowley was quick to observe, it is possible to plot future coordinates from a limited set of indices, once one knows the rules of behavior and knowledge of their consistency over time. Crowley made an attempt at what he would call his "Kamma work," but it transpired to be an extremely tough, if ultimately illuminating exercise.

Crowley and his Buddhist friend also discussed poetry, and Crowley decided to try to make his poems more vivid, with a sense of immediacy of image, an example of which Bennett found in the line of Coleridge from the *Rime of the Ancient Mariner:* "And ice, mast high, went floating by," which put the reader in the position of the Mariner's companion. Crowley experimented with imagery and color in "The Eyes of Pharaoh" and in "Sir Palamedes the Saracen," about the mystic path. He also discussed with Allan ways of putting spiritual research on a scientific basis. A universal language was required. Bennett said all that was needed could be found in the *Abidhamma,* Buddhist doctrinal commentaries on the sutras. Crowley thought the terminology would strain the Western student, who would soon mistake wood for tree. Crowley reckoned the symbols of pure mathematics were most fit for purpose, Kabbalah being based on it.

Leaving Rangoon, the Crowleys availed themselves of the Irrawaddy Flotilla, taking freshly built paddle steamer *Java* on November 15, reaching Mandalay, far upriver six days later.* Crowley spent his time leaning over the rail, gazing at the wavelets and the flying fish, slowly drifting into insanity, which is to say, he could see one visual event after another, each having its own reason, and while all these reasons combined to make a phenomenon, there was no connection between one set of reasons and another. It all presented itself to his mind as unintelligible. As for himself, the perceiver, well, there was a kind of "I," but it was simply a machine recording phenomena. Reason had broken apart. This he took as proof of his criticisms of reason—a not untypical effect of genuine mystical experience—but the whole effect was profoundly miserable. It didn't help being aboard a paddle steamer going up a river surrounded by disordered jungle, desolation, pointlessly repeated dagobas, or as he put it: "stupid stalagmites of stagnant piety,"[2] while attached to the steamer were flat rafts of piles of putrefying fish that stank. It's

---

*Built by William Denny of Glasgow, the *Java* was shipped to Burma in May 1904. It was scuttled in 1942 to prevent its falling into Japanese hands.

surprising he didn't mention Conrad's *Heart of Darkness* (1899). One might have thought he was going the way of Kurtz.

Mandalay he found boring in its plethora of pagodas, bar one, the Arrakan, and a statue of a Buddharūpa said to be the sole one drawn from life. Crowley noted it did not have the oft-repeated smirk. Overall, he found Mandalay—practically under water for most of the summer—ghastly. Half the Europeans were, he wrote, on the sicklist; it was a white man's grave, and a half. Crowley was, however, encouraged by dark tales of the Salween valley, for he intended to cross it, and imagined its network of watersheds between the Salween, Yangtze Kiang, and Mekong Rivers would make for fascinating mountains.

Crowley soon found an immense array of bureaucratic restrictions imposed on anyone who wanted to explore the province beyond the China border. The party finally boarded the *Irrawaddy* for Bhamo, forty miles from the Chinese border, on November 23, but departure was delayed endlessly, or what seemed like it, until the twenty-ninth.

In a diary entry for November 19, Crowley had expressed great agony of mind: "I realise in myself the perfect impossibility of reason; suffering great misery." His exhausting meditation work had brought him to the realization that the god of Western philosophy, namely reason, held within itself the seed of its own absurdity. Every thought immediately evoked its opposite; where was reason without a conclusion? It was useless to understand by ordinary logic the structure of the higher planes of consciousness:

I am as one who should have plumed himself for years upon the speed and strength of a favourite horse, only to find not only that its speed and strength were illusory, but that it was not a real horse at all, but a clothes-horse. There being no way—no conceivable way—out of this awful trouble gives that hideous despair which is only tolerable because in the past it has ever been the Darkness of the Threshold. But this is far worse than ever before; I wish to go from A to B; and I am not only a cripple, but there is no such thing as space. I have to keep an appointment at midnight; and not only is my watch stopped, but there is no such thing as time. I wish to make a cannon [a billiards move]; and not only have I no cue, but there is no such thing as causality. This I explain to my wife, and she, apparently inspired, says "Shoot it!" (I suppose she means the reason, but, of course, she did not understand a word of what I had been saying. I only told her for the sake of formulating my thought clearly in words.) I reply, "If I only had a gun." This makes me think of Siegfried and the Forging of the Sword. Can I heat my broken Meditation-Sword in the furnace of this despair? Is Discipline the Hammer? At present I am more like a Mime than Siegfried; a gibbering ape-like creature, though without his cunning and his purpose. . . . But surely I am not a dead man at thirty.[3]

He was not. However, as the rock outcrops that bounded the river to Bhamo made for rapids that called on the captain's every skill, Crowley, felt acutely an interior dizziness from the slipping away like old mortar of accustomed mental coordinates. As far as the "outside world" was concerned, the family arrived at Bhamo on December 1. Crowley was not so "insane" as to be blind to the extraordinary trade in jade that flowed south down the Irrawaddy from mines at the river's head. Blocks of crude mineral were shipped down on rafts, being stopped for merchants on the way who had to gamble at auctions as to whether any particular block of ore would yield profit when split. The smallest blocks would eventually arrive in Rangoon, by which time fortunes had been made and lost. Crowley found the thought of the whole process exciting, which, when you think about it, should have helped him come to terms with processes of apparently disconnected events. One merchant did not know what was to happen to any given block at later stages, but one could trace the process back, at least, to the mine, and the process was intelligible: profit or bust.

Other incidents were less intelligible, though carried morbid meaning. An elderly official aboard the steamer was anxious because he'd been asked by Burma's lieutenant governor, Sir Herbert Thirkell White (1855–1931), to delay his return to retirement to help prepare arrangements for a visit from the Prince of Wales. The man succumbed to the country's abiding conversation on the immanence of death from cholera, dysentery, and typhoid, but attempted to conceal his fear by blurting that really, the three diseases were all forms of malaria. Crowley commented acerbically that the next time he got cholera, he trusted they'd administer quinine as a cure. Three days later, cholera carried the fellow to his ultimate retirement. It is unlikely quinine was dispensed.

Crowley was certainly not at a loss for mordant wit, even in psychological extremis where his sense of reality was concerned. While finding Bhamo a delightful outpost, being free of jungle squalor, his feelings turned on account of being detained seventeen days by the assistant commissioner, a Eurasian (like the bulk of middle officials in Burma), who, Crowley believed, was, in his master's absence, delighting in his power over "the white man." Having finally arranged things for a passport through contacting His Britannic Majesty's Consul at Tengyueh, with information about the assistant commissioner's conduct passed on to His Honour the Lieutenant Governor of Burma, Crowley wrote a politely formal but acerbic letter to the assistant commissioner, informing him he was likely to be contacted by the lieutenant governor whose observations would, he trusted, be greeted with the same "prompt courtesy" the official had extended to himself. He closed by asserting his confidence that the man had doubtless thoroughly enjoyed himself, and his bureaucratic victim could wish the assistant commissioner no more than the arrival of another "real white man" to treat the commissioner as *he* had been treated![4] Crowley did not think it inevitable on account of blood that the Eurasians he encountered exhibited what he considered low characteristics, but that the treatment they received as they grew up from their white and colored neighbors engendered resentments, in other words, persecution brought out the worst characteristics. Being outcast engendered shame, and shame breeds qualities their snobbish fellow men expected from those automatically regarded as inferiors.

Crowley tried to get to grips with his real state of mind. In this he was aided by the psychology of what he called the "Hebrews," in particular the distinction of *nephesch, ruach,* and *neschamah.* The first is that "animal soul" that animates the body. The ruach is the rational mind converging on a central consciousness, which appears to be the ego. "The true ego is, however, above Neschamah, whose occasional messages to the Ruach warn the human ego of the existence of his superior."[5] Communications from there may be resented, welcomed, repressed, or encouraged. Initiation consists, he found, in identifying the self with the divine, or receiving being from beyond ruach. Crowley's ruach or reason had simply become an obstruction, and the initial sense of that was to experience an "abyss" where it appeared the ego was lost, at sea, in a swirl of dispersed consciousness, with no root, or principle, or continuity, like sailing on an endless river, round and round, and going nowhere, and worse, assailed from all sides and no side, and a darkness of vision, with no center. The road to samādhi required breaking out of ruach and letting neschamah, or spiritual mind, flood the system, not to demolish, but to reconstruct according to higher order.

But for the time being, Crowley is on the road to China, where, crossing the border into a new world, he departed what was in those days a Crown Colony of Great Britain and province of India, and there we leave him leaving India for the last time.

Except that, from this point on, India will never leave *him*. The road to samādhi and beyond will keep him in spiritual union with the subcontinent to the end of his days.

PART TWO

INDIA IN CROWLEY

EIGHTEEN

Samādhi

Crowley's march to samādhi was certainly very different from established Hindu or Buddhist custom, and was certainly not reliant on any attempt at moral purification, or such doctrinal strictures as sayadaw Ananda Metteya had recommended. Crowley regarded moral dicta as accretions on what was originally a practical, scientific spiritual method, whose strictures concerned only matters that distracted practical progress.

Crowley saw attainment in terms of achieving what he believed was the essence of the knowledge and conversation of the Holy Guardian Angel (the Sacred Magic of Abramelin the Mage), combined with rāja yoga techniques related to the Kabbalah (assent up the Sephirotic Tree), and "Western" Hermetic-Egyptian and Neoplatonist conceptions permeating the Golden Dawn system. That is to say, Crowley was already synthesizing Western and Eastern techniques and conceptions of initiation. The basic ascent framework he worked from was that established in the Golden Dawn, derived from numerous esoteric antecedents. In this framework, he saw himself working toward the grade of Exempt Adept ($7° = 5°$), a grade requiring surrender of "everything" (the mind that converges on a false ego), or self-sacrifice, corresponding to what Bennett was suggesting with the destruction of karmic impedimenta, squaring and annihilating the karmic account. It would mean becoming receptive to the mind beyond the phenomenal material worlds, openness to noumenal worlds, or the intelligible world of spirit. In order to see from the point of view of the noumenal or spiritually intelligible state, the individual must "let go" of what has bound him to the lower world, and the "self" that has been made out of that knowledge. If he grabs too willfully at the higher knowledge, he shows himself unfit and will fall; he must be flung across in a climax of self-emptying, of letting go, that must involve in the process, a profound not-knowing, an agony. One may think of Christ's famous "agony" in the Garden of Gethsemane before surrendering to his destiny, involving his enemies serving, unbeknownst to themselves, as ignorant tools in the process of his rebirth. They knew not what they did.

The best method came to Crowley from indices in the "Sacred Magic of Abramelin." Having subdued the demonic world to his will (work undertaken at Boleskine 1899–1900), he was to enflame himself with prayer, and to "invoke often." Turning his head, as it were, into a temple, he would perform, while physically riding, walking, seated or standing, daily invocations of his "Higher Self" (a phrase Crowley disliked) by means of ritual repetition of what he called the ritual of the "Bornless One," adapted quite freely from a Graeco-Egyptian papyrus in the British Museum.* The first English translation from the Greek was given as "I call thee, the headless one [*akephalon*]," but Crowley regarded "headless" as a misunderstanding of the author's intention, a conception in Crowley's view that provides no straightforward English translation. The original appears to have been a ritual of exorcism, but its original purpose is debatable, though it bears all the characteristics of eclectic Graeco-Egyptian magic of the late antique period; it is a prayer for divine assistance, and as such lent itself to that traditional Rosicrucian method of communion with Adonai, "the Lord": *enflaming oneself* with prayer.

The actual wording taken by Crowley comes from Abramelin, book 2, chapter 13: "Humiliate yourself before God and His Celestial Court, and commence your Prayer with fervour, for then it is that you will begin to enflame yourself in praying, and you will see appear an extraordinary and supernatural Splendour which will fill the whole apartment, and will surround you with an inexpressible odour, and this alone will console you and comfort your heart so that you shall call for

---

*The ritual appears in Crowley's *Goetia,* vii (1904), and probably came to him through magical papers Allan Bennett left him when Bennett went to Ceylon in 1899. It derives from section four, beginning page 7 of a translation by Charles Wycliffe Goodwin, *Fragment of a Græco-Egyption Work upon Magic from a Papyrus in the British Museum* (Cambridge: Macmillan, 1852).

ever happy the Day of the Lord." "Invoke often" most probably came from Golden Dawn co-founder and S.R.I.A. member, William Wynn Westcott's 1895 introduction to the *Chaldaean Oracles of Zoroaster* (volume 6 of *Collectanea Hermetica,* 18): "Communion with the hierarchies of these constellations formed part of the Chaldaean theurgy, and in a curious fragment it is said: 'If thou often invokest it' (the celestial constellation called the Lion) "then when no longer is visible unto thee the Vault of the Heavens, when the Stars have lost their light the lamp of the Moon is veiled, the Earth abideth not, and around thee darts the lightning flame, then all things will appear to thee in the form of a Lion!" According to the theurgy of the oracles, beyond the constellations is the divine Light, their occulted power source, emanating from the paternal mind. In *Confessions* (516–17), Crowley says the idea "Invoke often" reached him in a flash, though the words derived from "Zoroaster" (the *Chaldaean Oracles*), which he had already paraphrased in his "song" of *Tannhaüser.*

The intuition to "invoke often" he associated with a dream he had of being visited by an angel holding an ankh, to comfort him: itself a response to a need he felt for a "G.R." (Great Retirement). He later realized that the Egyptian ankh symbol for "life" was a sandal strap, therefore the "Retirement" was to be the walk across Chinese territory, and so he imported into his mind the temple layout from Boleskine and performed his ritual movements by very great effort of interior will.

In order to enflame himself and identify his inmost being with the power invoked from above, Crowley now had additional skills of prāṇāyāma, which would assist in concentration and in vibrating god names, or "barbarous names of evocation," that is, taking the prāṇa of divine life energies through his being and into his heart, combined with dhāraṇā and dhyāna for single-pointed identification with the object. What the "object" was in this case we shall get to in a moment. Here are the words of Crowley's personally adapted, recomposed "Bornless Ritual":

> Thee I invoke, the Bornless one.
> Thee, that didst create the Earth and the Heavens:
> Thee, that didst create the Night and the Day.
> Thee, that didst create the Darkness and the Light.
> Thou art Osorronophris: Whom no man hath seen at any time.

Thou art Iabos:

Thou art Iapos:

Thou hast distinguished between the Just and the Unjust.

Thou didst make the Female and the Male.

Thou didst produce the Seed and the Fruit.

Thou didst form Men to love one another, and to hate one another.

I am Ankh f n Khonsu Thy Prophet, unto Whom Thou didst commit Thy Mysteries, the Ceremonies of Khem:

Thou didst produce the moist and the dry, and that which nourisheth all created Life.

Hear Thou Me, for I am the Angel of Apophrasz Osorronophris: this is Thy True Name, handed down to the Prophets of Khem.

Hear Me: Ar: Thiao: Reibet: Atheleberseth: A: Blatha: Abeu: Eben: Phi: Chitasoe: Ib: Thiao.

Hear Me, and make all Spirits subject unto Me: so that every Spirit of the Firmament and of the Ether: upon the Earth and under the Earth: on dry Land and in the Water: of Whirling Air, and of rushing Fire: and every Spell and Scourge of God may be obedient unto Me.

I invoke Thee, the Terrible and Invisible God: Who dwellest in the Void Place of the Spirit: Arogogorobrao: Sochou: Modorio: Phalarchao: Ooo: Ape, The Bornless One: Hear Me!

Hear Me: Roubriao: Mariodam: Balbnabaoth: Assalonai: Aphniao: I: Tholeth: Abrasax: Qeoou: Ischur, Mighty and Bornless One! Hear Me!

I invoke Thee: Ma: Barraio: Ioel: Kothà: Athorebalo: Abraoth: Hear Me!

Hear me! Aoth: Aboth: Basum: Isak: Sabaoth: Iao:

This is the Lord of the Gods:

This is the Lord of the Universe:

This is He Whom the Winds fear.

This is He, Who having made Voice by His Commandment, is Lord of All Things; King, Ruler, and Helper. Hear Me!

Hear Me: Ieou: Pur: Iou: Pur: Iaot: Iaeo: Ioou: Abrasax:

Sabriam: Oo: Uu: Ede: Edu: Angelos tou theou: Lai: Gaia:
Apa: Diachanna: Chorun.

I am He! the Bornless Spirit! having sight in the Feet: Strong,
and the Immortal Fire!

I am He! the Truth!

I am He! Who hate that evil should be wrought in the World!

I am He, that lightningeth and thundereth.

I am He, from whom is the Shower of the Life of Earth:

I am He, whose mouth flameth:

I am He, the Begetter and Manifester unto the Light:

I am He, the Grace of the World:

"The Heart Girt with a Serpent" is My Name!

Come Thou forth, and follow Me: and make all Spirits subject
unto Me so that every Spirit of the Firmament, and of the
Ether: upon the Earth and under the Earth: on dry land, or
in the Water: of whirling Air or of rushing Fire: and every
Spell and Scourge of God, may be obedient unto me! Iao:
Sabao: Such are the Words!

What was being invoked in these inner rituals Crowley chose to refer to
as the "Augoeides." Daily in his diaries for late 1905 and 1906, we see
A∴—his shorthand for that intriguing Greek word. The three dots are
a Masonic conceit indicating the presence of "higher activity" invoked
to be present; likewise the alchemical "Great Work" was also written
as "G∴W∴," and, as far as Crowley was concerned, the transformation
of base metal into gold was what Brahmins called "samādhi." This was
the Great Work of initiation, that is, identification with, or absorption
of the self in, the divine. Why *augoeides* was chosen as the literal symbol of that which was being invoked was, firstly, to lodge the process
in antique traditions of spiritual attainment (in this case, Neoplatonic
theurgy), and, secondly, because the word had real visual value. The
adjective *augoeides* derives from Greek noun *augē* (or dawn), and *eides*
referring to something seen: a form, image, sight, or appearance. So we
could translate it as "possessing the image of dawn," dawn light, or as
the dawn seen. The word *dawn* suggests radiance, glory, brightness,
shining, glittering, rebirth, and so on, even "the glittering one." We may
imagine the emergence of what has been concealed.

The symbolism here goes back to Neoplatonist assessments of the divine spirit's relation to the "vehicle," or person, on Earth. In Thomas Taylor's translation of the *Select Works of Porphyry* (1823) we learn about the "perception of intelligible natures," according to third-century CE philosopher Porphyry's interpretation of Plato. According to Porphyry, when the body, at death, releases the rational soul, or "sense of ether," it conjoins with the fire of pure ether, where a purgation occurs, rendering the purified vehicle *augoeides*, or luciform and divine, fit to dwell in the "intelligible world," or world of pure ideas. On Earth, however, the rational soul, being infused with matter and its desires, is in a falling state, which state is mortal, a desertion of the divine state. The body is not fit for the intelligible world and must be fled from: such is Neoplatonic wisdom.* Crowley was familiar with Blavatsky's reading of the status of the divine spirit in man. She distinguished between the Neoplatonist position—where a luciform augoeides is not entrapped but instead sheds its radiance on the aspiring inner man from outside the phenomenal universe, calling man forth to his intelligible source—and the belief of Christian Kabbalists, akin to radical gnosis, that the spirit was catastrophically detached from the pleroma, imprisoned in the "astral capsule" of earthly life, such being the meaning of the "fall of man." Crowley accepted the pagan Neoplatonist position, allowing access to the light of the higher being through invocation or mystical theurgy.

More light is thrown on Crowley's choice of "Augoeides" as the object of invocation by an unpublished diary entry from April 25, 1906, written at Kobe harbor, Japan:

> The word in my kamma-work was A∴ and the method "invoking often"! Therefore a Self-glittering One, whether my conscience approves or not, whether my desires fit or not, is to be my guide. I am to invoke often, not to criticise. Am I to lose my grade of $7° = 4^□$? I cannot go wrong, for I am the Chosen One; that is the very postulate of the whole Work. This boat carries Caesar and his fortunes.[1]

---

*In Platonist metaphysics, ether (Greek: *aithēr*) is the substance that fills the universe beyond the terrestrial sphere: translucent air, the purest, quintessential atmosphere, fit for gods.

This note followed the previous day's astral traveling encounter, also at Kobe, wherein Crowley's astral body reached a room where a cruciform table supported a man, nailed to it and being eaten by "venerable men"—"adepts, whom I might one day join."[2] He took this to mean that he would get the power of only taking spiritual nourishment, while suspecting there was more to it.

Next his astral form entered "an apparently empty hall" of Chinese ivory filigree decoration. An altar was there, and he felt himself asked what he would sacrifice upon it. "I offered all save my will to know A∴ which I would only exchange for its realization." Then Crowley saw vast Egyptian god forms, so huge he could only see their knees. He was then asked whether "knowledge of the Gods" would suffice. Crowley declined. He was accused of being rationalistic and told the A∴ was not necessarily made in his image. Crowley knelt at the altar, placing right hand over left.

> Then One human, white, self-shining (my idea after all!) came forth
> and put his hands over mine, saying "I receive thee into the Order
> of the Silver Star." Then with advice to return, I sank back to earth
> in a cradle of flame.[3]

In Israel Regardie's book *The Eye in the Triangle* (1970), dealing seriously with Crowley's immense spiritual achievement before World War One, Regardie heaps particular praise on Crowley's extraordinary efforts in undertaking this intense operation in the most trying conditions imaginable, walking and riding through rough, strange country, often among folk who regarded Crowley's group with suspicion. But as ever, he kept it up, good days and bad, and there was no Guillarmod to poor cold water on his excesses. Rose behaved like a "trooper," and really came into her own dealing with hardships without complaint. The effort extended beyond the "walk across China" to fill over nine extraordinary months.

He was also, it should be recognized, still involved in his "kamma work," assessing the tendencies of his developing mind and, through intense introspection, was coming to the conclusion that he had been saved from peril—involved on horseback in a forty-foot fall down a slope he emerged unhurt—for a purpose; his role was *to teach*. The next step for humankind was to make the "knowledge and conversation of the Holy Guardian Angel" open and accessible to all that aimed to find their higher genius.

February 9th. [1906] About this full moon Consciousness began to break through Ruach into Neschamah. Intend to stick to Augoeides.

. . .

9th March   A∴ [Augoeides Invocation] very poor (horseback, slippery wet road and cobbles)

10th March   A∴ good considering (horseback)

15th March   A∴ still poor (Rain, wind, loose, mud, cobbles)

. . .

17th March   A∴ slowly improving. (boat)[4][*]

From Hong Kong on March 28, 1906, Crowley wrote to Clifford Bax:[†]

Your letter reached me here on my arrival from Burma via Yunnan-Fan with the wife and child. We had a fine time—about four months on the road. . . .

I am myself just at the end of a little excursion of nearly seven years into Hell. The illusion of reason, which I thought I had stamped out in '98, was bossing me. It has now got the boot. But let this tell you that it is one thing to devote your life to magic at 20 years old and another to find at 30 that you are bound to stay a Magus. The first is the folly of a child; the second the Gate of the Sanctuary.[5]

---

[*]An argument with porters over payment had led to his having to brandish a rifle when casting off from the river bank. Crowley had hired a boat to negotiate the Hong Ha (Red) River from Mengtse southeast toward Hekou, on the French Indo-China (Tonkin) border, after journeying 650 miles through Chinese territory for some four months.
[†]They had met on January 23, 1905, when Bax, brother of composer Arnold Bax, was eighteen. For Crowley's activities in this period, please consult *Aleister Crowley: The Biography*.

Crowley never ceased drawing intimate comparisons of one mystical system to another. For example on May 1, aboard ship from Yokohama to Vancouver (Rose and Lilith, as far as he knew, were in transit from Hong Kong via Rangoon to England), he meditated on the seal of Solomon figure, that is, the two interlocking triangles ubiquitous to magical lore, and to alchemy: a figure of union (yoga!). He saw them as symbolic of the process of samādhi, where ▽ is "the divine force drawing nigh to man" and / "the human flame aspiring," expressed biblically as "Unto whosoever shall draw nigh unto Me will I draw nigh" (compare James 4:8). As symbols of the elements also, the analogy works, where ▽ is water (nourishment) and △ is fire (spiritual aspiration). This spiritual fire is, by the way, the "fire" of Horus's aeon of "force and fire."[6]

> It has struck me—in connection with reading [William] Blake, that Aiwass etc. = Force and Fire; the very thing I do lack and that my "conscience" is really an obstacle and a delusion, being a survival of heredity or education. Certainly to rely on it as on an abiding principle in oneself is wrong.[7]

He also speculated further on his ideas in *Berashith* (see page 233) of the universe being the product of the infinitely great and the infinitely small multiplied, that is: 0°. He now introduced conceptions from *The Book of the Law,* seeing the "two kinds of nothing" being symbolized respectively in the figures of Nuit and Hadit, with "Ra Hoor Khuit"—the god figure of *Liber AL's* chapter three—as consequent universe.

Further, on May 18, while in New York trying unsuccessfully to raise interest in the scientific possibilities of Kangchenjunga II, he again invoked A∴, and saw afterward that the Graeco-Egyptian compound name Osorronophris, called upon at the start of the Bornless Ritual, was simply *Asar-un-Nefer* transliterated: one of many epithets of Egyptian god Osiris, or Asar, father of Horus, where *un* means "to open, appear or make manifest," and *nefer* means "good, or beautiful." Crowley felt all this pointed to one who opened the gates, or paths (compare the nadī of yoga, and the paths of the sephiroth), so that the beautiful one might enter and the supplicant be visited: another way

Fig. 18.1. Aleister Crowley poses with meerschaum and climbing jacket to promote Kangchenjunga II, New York, May 1906. (The Spirit of Solitude)

of seeing augoeides that also, significantly, corresponds to the entering of the divine Paramātman through the brahmarandhra (aperture of Brahman) at the crown of the head in Sabhapaty's jñāna yoga system. Hence Crowley interpreted *Asar-un-Nefer* to mean "Myself made perfect," which attainment was samādhi. He had the bones for synthesizing initiation systems from India, Greece, Israel, and Egypt with Thelema, the basis of his "Magick." He would in due course add the Chinese wisdom of the philosophical Tao to the synthesis.

On May 31, on board ship in the Atlantic, returning to England, Crowley enjoyed his best invocation of A∴ to date:

> Vision quite perfect and I tasted the sweet kiss and gazed in the clear eyes of that radiant one. My own face (I am sure by the feel of the skin) became luminous.[8]

Arriving back in England on June 2, he was felled by news that his daughter Lilith had died of typhoid at Rangoon on May 1. Inconsolable, Crowley couldn't deal with the fact. Yet he maintained his invocations, meeting a badly nervous Rose off the SS *Himalaya* at Plymouth on June 7. Breaking down with grief at intervals, he was next beset with glandular problems of the throat, and a swollen gland in his groin that wanted an operation. He felt he was suffering a general nervous breakdown and in July moved into a nursing home. Around July 17, he began to experience superconsciousness, a clear distinction of his ordinary ego and a "real Crowley":

> This thinking seems little or no good: but the fault is that the real Crowley is actually not thinking of A∴.. When he is, the invocation was unnecessary; when he isn't, it's feeble. What *am* I to do? (Should suggest sticking to it).[9]

Still at the nursing home on the twenty-second, he experimented with five grains of hashish and a pipe of ganja and found it "remarkable." It opened whole trains of thought to analysis.

Leaving the nursing home four days later, he decamped to George Cecil Jones's house at Mistley, near Basingstoke, where on July 27, he had a vision of Christ as himself the aspiring adept, and "a certain vision of A∴. remembered only as a glory now attainable."[10] At the same time he caught a chill in his right eye, obstructing a nasal duct that required a number of painful operations, during which he suffered from neuralgia, which lasted months.

He also discovered Rose had become a serious alcoholic.

On August 3 Crowley went to Eastbourne, presumably to visit mother, Emily Bertha. His consciousness now started to move into a state of "realized eschatology" (from the Greek *eschaton* = the end). That is, he interpreted Christ's agony on the cross (surrender of the ego) as well as the essence of the Christian itinerary of the "second coming" as a personal, realized, and Self-realizing experience. The new heaven and the new earth becomes visible, he realized, when the blind can see, for "the kingdom of heaven is nigh and within you" (compare Luke 17:21). The coming of Christ was for Crowley, as for many Gnostics, reception into divine being. The divine responded to the flame of aspiration; if one draws near to the true Master and Will, "He" will draw near to thee. That is the formula.

On August 4 Crowley repeated the Aspiration of the Golden Dawn Adeptus Minor ceremony he had undertaken with Jones on July 26, for twenty-two minutes (in a crucifixion posture), along with the augoeides invocation: "It needed D.D.S. [Jones] but the Eli Eli feeling is perhaps induced and this is good."[11] The "Eli Eli" refers to Christ's quoting

Psalm 22 (v. 1) beginning, "My God, my God why hast thou forsaken me?" on the cross. The final leap must be made, unaided, in utter humility, purity, confidence, and aloneness. The vows attendant of Poverty, Obedience, and Chastity, meant to esteem nothing of value save the A∴; of Chastity to use the magical force only for the invocation; and of Obedience, to concentrate the will on the A∴ alone. The aspirant must "look expectantly always, as if He would instantly appear."

He repeated the oath: "I, Perdurabo, a member of the Body of Christ ('C[orpus] ∴ C[hristi]') . ∴., do hereby solemnly obligate myself, &c. to lead a pure and unselfish life; and will entirely devote myself to raise &c. myself to the K[nowledge] of my higher and d[ivine] G[enius] that I shall be Him. In witness of which I Invoke the great Angel הוא [HUA] to give me proof of his existence."

On August 10 he felt himself on the Threshold of the Augoeides:

Got the Threshold—the awful doubt whether one shouldn't walk away and throw up the whole thing—presented first as a temptation, then as a doubt. Wherefore the cry "Eli Eli [lama sabachthani]." But no further save for the sense as of dew distilling from the Eye in the Triangle by the Ray.[12]

On September 17, Mr. and Mrs. Crowley moved into a suite at the Ashdown Park Hotel in Coulsdon, Surrey,* and Crowley's health problems dried up suddenly and completely. September 21 marked the end of a thirty-two-week period of preparation for the Abra-Melin Operation. He decided to forego rituals and stick to the old order: invoke "OFTEN." Was he embarrassed at the Christian emphasis of the Adeptus Minor material?

Jones showed up at Coulsdon on September 22, and the tack changed again. They reduced the G∴D∴ Neophyte ritual to a quintessence and celebrated the autumnal equinox.† Nine days later, a hashish experiment combined with invocation and performance of the new

---

*The old Ashdown Park Hotel, between the Brighton Road and Farthing Downs, was demolished in 1971.

†This ritual would later be rewritten as *Liber 671*. It concerns the ascent of the Mountain of Initiation.

ritual coincided with the unexpected culmination of the Operation of the Sacred Magick of Abra-Melin the Mage.

On October 9, Crowley remarked in a diary full of cryptic references: "Tested new ritual and behold it was very good! Thanked gods and sacrificed for—[Crowley subsequently added the word 'Lola.']"[13]

LOLA DAYDREAM

"Lola" would play a fascinating part in the climax to Crowley's march to samādhi. We know he met her at the Ashdown Park Hotel, Coulsdon, but whether that was their first meeting, remains unclear. He may have met her at Eastbourne in August, for a diary entry for August 18 records: "Came back to Eastbourne. Reobligated ♀ [Venus symbol] though ill." The *V* of Venus (goddess of love, of course) could well stand for Vera Blanche Neville Snepp (1888–1953), an extremely beautiful, young Virgoan (possibly Leo) who would come to the stage as Vera Neville, but called herself Lola.*

---

*The 1901 UK Census shows Vera living in Mayfair (her birth was registered in the borough of Marylebone, in which district Mayfair was included for census purposes), London, aged twelve, with her parents, Alfred Neville Snepp (apprentice electrician) and Laura Kate Snepp, at 23a Old Bond Street, where currently (2018), Stella McCartney has her flagship shop. Vera was baptized at Lyneham, Wiltshire, on September 5, 1888, and registered in the July–August–September 1888 period. The baptismal record shows the family abode as London, Vera's father's occupation as "gentleman," while the vicar officiating was "Mr. Snepp." This was the Rev. Edward Maitland Snepp, Vera's paternal grandfather, Associate of King's College London, who became incumbent at Lyneham in 1888.

In 1909, twenty-year-old Vera Neville married Henry Algernon Claude Graves (1877–1963), who became 7th Baron Graves of Gravesend upon the death of his cousin in 1937. Their son Peter Graves (1911–1994) was an actor who married actress and singer, Vanessa Lee (1920–1992). Vera divorced Graves in 1922 and married property developer and financier, Philip Ernest Hill (1873–1944); they divorced in 1933.

One of Miss Neville's earliest engagements was as understudy to Gabrielle Ray. More substantially, she played Perlie in Grossmith and Laurillard's production of Victor Herbert's musical play *The Only Girl*, which opened at the Apollo Theatre, London, September 25, 1915. She appeared in *Mr Manhattan,* a musical play at the Prince of Wales's Theatre, London, March 30, 1916; and in the musical comedy *Houp La!* (St. Martin's Theatre, London, November 23, 1916), with Nat. D. Ayer and Gertie Millar. She appeared in the *War Economy Revue* (Ambassadors' Theatre, London, April 1917); and finally in *A Certain Liveliness* by Basil Macdonald Hastings (St. Martin's, February 1919).

Fig. 18.2. "Lola"—stage name Miss Vera Neville (1888–1953).

Crowley's account in his *Confessions* is that he met Vera at Coulsdon:

At Coulsdon, at the very moment when my conjugal cloudburst was impending, I had met one of the most exquisitely beautiful young girls, by English standards, that ever breathed and blushed. She did not appeal to me only as a man; she was the very incarnation of my dreams as a poet. Her name was Vera; but she called herself "Lola." To her I dedicated *Gargoyles* with a little prose poem, and the quatrain (in the spirit of Catullus) "Kneel down, dear maiden o'mine." It was after her that my wife called the new baby![14]

The new baby was Lola Zaza (born December 3, 1906). Crowley's quatrain for his 1905 accomplished poetry collection *Gargoyles* does indeed reflect the sexual candor of Catullus:

> Kneel down, dear maiden o'mine, and let your eyes,
> Get knowledge with a soft and glad surprise!
> Who would have thought you would have had it in you?
> Say nothing: on the contrary, continue!

Crowley not only dedicated *Gargoyles* to young Lola, but she also served as inspiration for maiden "Lola Daydream" in "The Wake World," an allegory on the path to initiation with the Holy Guardian Angel, published in Crowley's profound, inspired collection *Konx Om Pax: Essays in Light,* 1907. Her presence also informs, directly and indirectly, aspects of the antinomian sexual satire of the poem *Clouds without Water* (1909), five of whose sections begin with "LOLA" as an acrostic, with Lola the name of the ecstatic poet's repeatedly declared "maiden o' mine." Perhaps something of the real Lola breathes in the opening lines of the exquisite "Wake World":

My name is Lola, because I am the Key of Delights, and the other children in my dream call me Lola Daydream. When I am awake, you see, I know that I am dreaming, so that they must be very silly children, don't you think? There are people in the dream, too, who are quite grown up and horrid; but the really important thing is the wake-up person. There is only one, for there could never be any one like him. I call him my Fairy Prince. He rides a horse with beautiful wings like a swan, or sometimes a strange creature like a lion or a bull, with a woman's face and breasts, and she has unfathomable eyes.

On October 9, 1906—the day of the breakthrough—one has the strong impression that Lola was in the vicinity, though he seems, from his diary entry to have been suffering acutely the short-term memory loss familiar to devotees of the "herb dangerous."

Hashish 10 p.m. acting—taken at 8. Many very strange illusions of sight, sense of proportion, locality, illusions of muscular distortion, the pen actually writing good legible English, but appearing to do so only as a vector of two enormous counterpoises. (Hours to write that sentence—and this.) None of the illusions seriously interfere with small fine coordinated movements. I think of a word and forget it before I can write it down. This happens by lapses: a question of attention held and released.

10th. [October] I am still drunk with samādhi all day. Curious observation S.D. looks like a symbol. Curious feeling that one has a foreign body in one's mouth. Enough, these are all dog-faced demons. I will see Adonai. [the Lord, the inmost fire, the Holy Guardian Angel][15]

The anagram "S.D." is intriguing. Given the context, it could refer to hashish, or to a person. The anagram might be "Sweet Dream," which could work either for hashish or a girl. It could be "Servus Dei" (Servant of God), which, again in the context of samādhi, could equally be either of those, or indeed both. Given Crowley's story where the path to the Holy Guardian Angel is taken with Lola Daydream, S.D. might be a sweet-dream anagram for Vera Snepp, lest Rose be alerted to the love affair.

Crowley's diary for October 10 remarks of the "thanksgiving and sacrifice": "I did get rid of everything but the Holy Exalted One, and must have held Him for a minute or two. I did. I am sure I did. I expected Rose to see a Halo round my head."

> But the hashish enthusiasm surged up against the ritual-enthusiasm; so I hardly know which phenomena to attribute to which. Noticed at the time that S.D. made A∴ enthusiasm possible; was therefore good. Yet I would not pray for one more Kiss having already had my deserts. The more I think of it the more I am sure that I got into samādhi. (somehow) not like a human at all.[16]*

Relating aspects of the story in his *Confessions* years later, he recorded how people everywhere seemed to be drawn to him as if he were aglow. On October 20 he visited industrial chemist Jones's home at Mistley in Essex to discuss samādhi. It irked somewhat that it may have been influenced by hashish. Jones, however, was deeply impressed, and thought hashish had "nothing to do with the samādhi, though possibly useful as a starter."[17]

> 21st. A somewhat disappointing day, nearly all the talk being talked. Also I am still "polarized" a good deal; my indifference "titiksha" is pronounced. I am truly indifferent even to L.[18]

"L" is of course Lola, and his indifference would not last long. *Titiksha* is Sanskrit, literally speaking, for a desire to leave. Its usual

---

*Worth noting that this entry uses *hashish* without an anagram, the which appears in relation to "one more Kiss," though the "Kiss" could refer to the presence of "the Holy Exalted One."

application is showing forbearance to someone that one could punish, while in Vedanta it denotes bearing with indifference opposite conditions, such as pleasure and pain—the latter seems the strongest idea here.

Two days later, his diary confesses being lovesick "with lack of Lola—a still pool of clear water in which L.V.X. is reflected."[19] After L.V.X., Crowley inserted a drawing of a dharmachakra, symbolic wheel of Buddhists and Jains, whose eight spokes reflect the Eightfold Path to Nibbana. "L.V.X." refers to the divine "Light" force as expressed in the Golden Dawn Neophyte and Adeptus Minor rituals, emphasizing a threefold death and rebirth cycle (Isis mourning; Typhon-Apophis—death triumphant; Osiris risen). High praise for Lola!

Despite disturbing rushes of imagery at bedtime, Crowley was getting insight into the point of view of the divine, that is, when his ordinary self, or his thoughts, were not in the way:

31st. . . . There is nothing but d[og] f[aced] d[emon]s after I get to bed; but there is always the consciousness behind thoughts. Thus when the consc[iousness] realizes that "I am apart from my thoughts" that thought itself is pictorially shown as a thought. Thus the Bhagavad Gita, "I am all and in all, yet apart from all—I who am all, and made it all, abide its separate Lord."* This consciousness is the real Self in all probability; it would never trouble to command its thoughts, for all are alike to it. The spine should be vertical as the Hindus justly say.[20]

During November 1906, the sense of divine glory about him began to fade and reaction set in, and with it, doubt. When the experience was not being experienced it could not be recalled in any of its fullness, leaving a feeling of empty achievement, vain effort.

It happened that a book had recently appeared: *A Real Mahatma: A Personal Study* (London: Luzac & Co, 1906) by T. C. Crawford. The subject of study was Agamya Guru Paramahamsa. It seems likely this publication may have had something to do with the fact that on November 13 Crowley wrote to the guru, who was in London:

---

*A translation of the last line of chapter 10 of the Bhagavad Gita.

13th. [Nov.]

Wrote to Sri Agamya Guru Paramahamsa "If you are the one I seek, this will suffice—name and address."

He replies: "Ask your own intelligence."

Crowley made a tarot divination to assess whether zodiacal intelligences favored the meeting.

I reply "My question concerned myself. Your answer emboldens me to ask for an interview. I need hardly add that in such matter all days and hours are alike to me."

He answers "Come ☽ [Monday] noon."[21]

Mr. Crawford's book might have been made for Crowley's doubting. On page 4, Crawford wrote: "Those who do not know this higher self are called ignorant. Those who do, are wise. So when, in the Vedanta philosophy, you read of the wise man, you read of him who knows all things through the All Knowledge of his Higher Self." Crawford goes on to say that Agamya Guru Paramahamsa is one of India's most conspicuous gurus: "He is called the Tiger Mahatma, on account of his energy and force of character"—and his rudeness, according to the late Karl Kellner, who had walked out on the guru, disgusted by his ill temper. Crawford's interview with the guru would have commended itself to Crowley, for Crawford insisted the guru did not want proselytes, while his attitude to the world was one of cheerful indifference, favoring jewels of wisdom to the world's illusory gold. Why illusory? Because to the spirit, the world is a projection of mind, and to mind, matter is illusory.

Crowley duly turned up to meet the guru at midday Monday, November 19, 1906, a day after the eighth anniversary of what he called his "birth," that is initiation into the Golden Dawn. Crowley felt a good impression of the guru after leaving, stronger than when in the man's presence. He saw him again on the twenty-first. The guru prescribed three things: Devotion, Mystery, and "Omnibenevolence." Crowley assessed him coolly: "He has attained a high grade, but has no Viveka [discrimination] concerning men. He thinks of all the world as either inside or outside his little fold, and sheep or goat according. Which is unusual folly for such an illuminated bugger.

Another lesson not to attribute objective value to one's *samādhi* results."[22]

On the twenty-third Crowley began work on the three "gunas." In Hindu Sānkhya philosophy, the gunas are qualities that serve as tendencies, and are tamas (darkness); sattva (beingness); rajas (activity). Sattva is a positive quality of balance, purity, and creativity. Rajas suggests passion, movement, dynamic activity, egocentric but neither good nor bad. Tamas is the quality of imbalance, disharmony, dullness, lethargy, even to violence, viciousness, and ignorance. Human nature represents a combination of these qualities and tendencies. In order to change, there must be a higher force, as to change only one quality produces inertia in the other two gunas.

On December 2, he attended what either he or the guru called a "business meeting" of the latter's disciples at 60 South Audley Street, Mayfair. Crowley was underwhelmed: "His whole plan perfectly ridiculous; a fine object lesson in what to avoid."[23]

Taking a break from the guru, Crowley entertained a spiritually inspired George Cecil Jones on the tenth who reckoned Crowley an $8° = 3^□$ (Magister Templi grade). Jones's recognition of his advancement made Crowley genuinely a "master" of himself, "without scruple or diffidence. No personality."[24] He experienced samādhi again; this time, he *knew*.

On the eleventh "no personality" Crowley returned to Bournemouth, for his health, where he received a letter from Jones that made him think Jones was also a truly advanced adept, able to hail another, and see through the cloud of the superficial self. Jones reckoned he'd attained to the grade of Master of the Temple, but Crowley would wait until he had well and truly traversed the Abyss, which he believed accomplished in Algeria in 1910.

Crowley spent most of the rest of the month working on tables of correspondences. These would eventually comprise his concordance of comparative symbolism, *777* (1909), intended as a work-in-progress. Jones contributed to the effort until he "broke down" from the labor on December 26 (British Boxing Day). On that day Crowley noted it was now 320 days since he had written in his diary in the Far

East: "Ruach breaking through into Neschamah."* The figure was deemed significant because 320 was 32 × 10, that is, the thirty-two paths of wisdom adumbrated in the *Sefer Yetzirah* (Kabbalist *Book of Formation*), multiplied by the ten sephiroth, which made a nice personal message that he was well on the Path. He called the process a "Truth game."[25]

Returning to town (St. Mary's Mansions, Paddington, London) on the twenty-seventh he "broke down" himself. Rose asked him: "Who is Lola?" Crowley answered: "The Flapper": a kind of put-down of indifference. He confided to his diary: "really very difficult to do without using tone of voice of a lying nature."[26]†

Crowley experienced a vision of what he called the Gate of $10° = 1^\square$, that is, the highest grade of the Golden Dawn system, "His own Very Self," or identification with God. The vision consisted of himself as a mage in his magic circle, breaking it down, and the universe rushing in as lions and dragons and all manner of symbols that vanished as they entered. The next day he began to see the possibilities of what he now called the "Truth Scheme." He had attained to a remarkable objectivity, and who knows what else.

Confessions dates this realization to February 8, 1906, but Crowley's transcript 1906 diary dates it as February 9, with different language: "About this full moon Consciousness began to break through Ruach into Neschamah." The 1906 typescript omits the sentence following: "Intend to stick to Augoeides." William Breeze (endnotes, unexpurgated *Confessions*) suggests the anomaly may be because there was a now lost, original diary used when writing *Confessions,* and that therefore the February 8 date may be correct.

†The term *flapper* in 1906 did not have all the overtones of meaning it came to enjoy in the Roaring Twenties. In the 1900s, it could mean a vivacious girl in her mid-teens; theatrical slang for an acrobatic young female actress; a dancer who flapped her arms; a young girl not ready to wear her hair up or wear long dresses; a maiden of about sixteen, perhaps wearing a plain long dress with a sash carelessly knotted. A flapper could also be a stage-type of girl, flirtatious and mischievous. It could also mean a young prostitute. In context, Crowley seems to have been saying that Lola was not someone to be taken seriously, at least by Rose.

NINETEEN

I Came from God the World to Save: 1907

> BURY me in a nameless grave!
> I came from God the world to save,
> I brought them wisdom from above:
> Worship, and liberty, and love.
> They slew me for I did disparage
> Therefore Religion, Law, and Marriage.
> So be my grave without a name
> That earth may swallow up my shame.
>
> "THE POET," FROM *KONX OM PAX:*
> *ESSAYS ON LIGHT,* 1907 E.V.

The poet would come to see 1907 as a year of fulfillment. As his married life fragmented, his mystic quest attained the heights. Rose's alcoholism strained everything, and the year began with pain. On New Year's Day Crowley returned to bourgeois Bournemouth on England's south coast for amelioration of throat trouble. He concentrated on his book of correspondences of religious, mythological, and occult symbolism, while making further experiments with hashish.

Appear to have got into the Fruit of which Jones' "Hail! All Hail!" was the Blossom. In short, recognizing that *I am He* in the same way that I recognize "Snow is white"—not arguing it, nor announcing it triumphantly. I acted on that basis without self-consciousness, and wrote various letters.[1]*

That was January 6. Lying in bed that night. Crowley experienced *ātmadasharna:* a vision of divine Ātman as a "Universal Peacock," that "is One."

> The "millions of worlds" game—the peacock multiform with each "eye" of its fan a mirror of glory wherein also another peacock—everything thus.
>   1.20.A.M. Head still buzzing; wrote above. *Samādhi is* Hashish, an ye will; but Hashish is not *samādhi.* (It's a low form this *atmadarshana.*)[2]

The implication is that only an adept can use hashish to excite samādhi, while, in itself, hashish has no necessarily divine constituent. That is, hashish of itself won't make a spiritually blind person into a spiritually perceiving person—it cannot "pass on" of itself any attainment; hashish is not the answer: *samādhi* is—so long as one can recall the question! Crowley systematically explored—often to his bafflement—the value of introspective analysis gained from taking measured quantities of hashish, a substance held sacred to Shiva by devotees. If there was a mystical and magical benefit, Crowley wanted to discover precisely what it was. His pioneering analysis resulted in a detailed study, "The Psychology of Hashish" the following year.

The problem, as he soon discovered, was that memory cannot cope with communicating the depth and wonder of what becomes an interior reality to the enlightened user, because words are, as it were, exterior to the complexity of the experience of what thoughts may actually consist of. Clearly under the influence, Crowley tried to express this problem in writing: "Oh for a memory—in flesh to tell people about this; in spirit to bind together and organize the analyzed thoughts, so that one's consciousness should normally observe the second rank crowd [of thoughts]. This is (*would be*) constant ecstasy, but the actions

---

*Note the pun on Theosophist Mabel Collins's novel, *The Blossom and the Fruit: A True Story of a Black Magician* (1887).

of the man (*would*) go on as usual, and it is only a certain instinct in one's hearer if they perceive that one is not oneself."[3] From references to the formation of words from pictures, and to *saññna* (that is, *perception*, formed from aggregation of personal identities—Crowley refers to "the Hierarchies of me") and from sense experience in the body, or "picture ideas," he had been thinking on the Buddhist doctrine of five aggregates that compose perception. Perhaps he was trying to overcome his illness by withdrawing or distancing himself from his perception, the latter being formed of materiality and sensation, which perception becomes an experience, passing into memory, which then repeats, unless stopped.

A reference in Crowley's diary from March 11 suggests that he was indeed combining yoga with hashish as a means of withdrawing the five senses from objects, to be replaced by divine vision: "I think the hashish has had little or no effect—perhaps just less than the desired waking of *pratyahara*. But no hallucinations; no loss of time-sense. Possibly slight self-consciousness; but one wouldn't like to assert it."[4]

Pratyāhāra constitutes the fifth element of the eight stages of Patañjali's ashtāṅga yoga, which for Patañjali bridges the external yoga of yama, niyama, āsana, prāṇāyāma, and the internal yoga: dhāraṇā, dhyāna, and samādhi. Sufficient mastery of pratyāhāra should enable practitioners to "turn off," as it were, particular senses. Where nose and throat were concerned, Crowley had every motive for doing so.

Quitting Bournemouth on January 29 ("hopefully for ever"), he returned home to Paddington to find Rose dangerously neglecting the baby on account of drink addiction. Crowley claimed he only just saved the baby's life by timely provision of oxygen, and subsequently by forcibly ejecting from the apartment Rose's mother Blanche—on the end of his boot, Blanche Kelly having ignored doctor's strict instructions to keep out the child's room. Suffering from operations on his nasal ducts* performed by celebrated ear, nose, and throat specialist Dr. Herbert Tilley (1866–1941) at 72 Harley Street, Crowley became passionately involved with twenty-eight-year-old sculptress Kathleen Bruce who sculpted her pained lover as an "Enchanted Prince," which sculpture

---

*Crowley refers to his nostrils in terms of the nadīs: "iḍā" for the left channel, "piṅgāla" for the right. According to yogic theory, the operations would have affected his currents of prāṇa.

appears lost—while continuing to enjoy assignations with Vera Snepp (Lola), sincerely believing these experiences helped to bring him close to God—especially when punctuating Patañjali's disciplines of mind.

On Sunday, March 17, Crowley received from himself as seer, or "Master of the Temple,"* by some divinatory method or other, the "word" of the spring equinox, which word *catena* (Italian for "chain") he took to indicate a chain of penance and a chain of power. He should then, he concluded, form a "chain of brethren by tapas."[5] *Tapas* is Patañjali's third niyama and means something that "burns" away impurities, a discipline or austerity passionately pursued. Niyama is the second of Patañjali's eight limbs of yoga, and is a recommended practice to ensure wholeness of life.

> To this end will I subdue this my body by fasts and by scourging, by vigils and meditations, by yama and niyama, āsana and prāṇāyāma. In short, I will confirm unto myself the true grade of 6° = 5□ [Adeptus Major] (which before I held but nominally) and thus fit myself wholly for the sorrow of Binah,† the drinking of the Cup of Tribulations, which is the Cup of Iacchus.
>
> He should sleep upon a plank bed wrapt in his ranch poncho. His weight should be one hundred and forty-four pounds. He shall urgently acquire money.
>
> It shall no longer be lawful to will Initiation, but only to do the appointed Work. He should not buy things.[6]

On Thursday March 21, the sun entered Aries, and Crowley arranged an apartment for himself at 60 Jermyn Street, Piccadilly. The apartment is still there, on the top floor at the north side of the street. He forbade himself thick soups, eel, mackerel, salmon, herrings, sardines, pork, duck, goose, macaroni, potatoes, peas, beans; pastry and sweets; sugar, cocoa, milk, butter, save in small quantity.

---

*The 8° = 3° grade had two mottos: *Vi Veri Vniversum Vivus Vici,* "By the power of truth, I, while living, have conquered the universe," or "V.V.V.V.V.," and the Greek double negative ὀυ μη: *ou mē,* meaning "certainly not."

†The "sorrow of Binah" (Understanding) refers to the sephira corresponding to the grade of Magister Templi 8° = 3°, complete attainment of which was Crowley's next magical aim.

He was to have more exercise, less sleep, and aim to free his bowels and skin. He would also take regular Turkish baths and limit liquid intake to forty ounces a day. He would permit himself "Fish, lean meats, eggs, fruit, green vegetables and heroin." One may presume the heroin was a prescription to ease the pain in his tubes.

In order perhaps to pick up some initiated tips on hatha yoga, Crowley again visited Punjabi Yogi Mahatma Sri Agamya Paramahamsa Guru Swamiji, author of *Sri Brahma Dhara,* whom he had first met at 70 Margaret Street in November 1906 on the guru's second English visit. The guru had been in America and, returning in 1907, sent Crowley a card inviting him to a general meeting.* In Crowley's later account of their latest encounter (see footnote below), Crowley described the guru's book as containing:

> some of the most astonishing balderdash ever put in print . . . a stewed-up hash of Yoga, Vedanta, and outrageous verbosity. "Love," he writes, "is the force of the magician Maya, and is the cause of all disorder" (it seems to be so even in his exalted position). "This force of love—in the state of circumgyration in the extended world—is the cause of all mental movements towards the feeling of easiness or uneasiness: but the mind enjoys eternal beatitude with perfect calmness, when the force of love is concentrated over the unlimited extension of silence" ("silence" is really choice!).[7]

Subsequent encounters offered little more enlightenment. However, Crowley's diary reveals that before they came (nearly) to blows, as recounted in the *Equinox* account, there was something to be gained from meeting, though Crowley's basic intention seems to have been to take some of the guru's "tiger-cubs"—as the swami called his better disciples or "chelas"—and train them himself in his vaunted "chain of brethren." On Tuesday, April 2, Crowley had an interview with "guru S.A.P. etc." without his "dog-faced *chelas.* He is good to talk to and has a very fine aura. One departs stronger in every way." Crowley

---

*See Crowley's humorous account of their meetings in the *Equinox* 1, no. 4 (1910): 284–90: "Half-Hours with Famous Mahatmas" by "Sam Hardy" (= samādhi!), a skit on the popular book *Half-Hours with the Best Authors.*

noted the guru was off again on the twentieth, and that during the self-styled tiger-mahatma's absence Crowley might "select any comparatively human *chelas,* if to be found, and teach them." He then recorded he was to see the guru again to demonstrate his "meditation act," and wondered if it would be a good idea to take him a gift of snuff, since the guru was always reaching for his snuffbox. "And he must give me *hathayoga. Aum!*"[8]

The next day, Crowley describes himself as "messing about with chemicals all day." He took a very small dose of hashish at 9:10 p.m. When nothing happened he took more than he'd done in Bournemouth. Ten minutes later he found expectation with some apprehension disturbed his thoughts. At 9:46 he undertook twenty minutes of prāṇāyāma in his hood, invoking Adonai, but nearly dropped off to sleep twenty-four minutes later, and "abandoned the unequal contest" at 10:35 p.m.

On April 20, Crowley amused himself with a visit to the New Gallery at 121 Regent Street, round the corner from his apartment. Built where a fruit market used to stand, to a design by Edward Robert Robson F.S.A. and opened in 1888, the gallery had encased cast-iron columns in marble, with gilded Greek capitals, with architraves, friezes, and cornices above the columns decorated in platinum leaf. Oil paintings occupied the west and north galleries on the ground floor, while smaller works in oil were displayed around a first-floor balcony. It had been particularly friendly to Pre-Raphaelite and Aesthetic movement art, having exhibited works by Burne-Jones, Lawrence Alma-Tadema, William Holman Hunt, G. F. Watts, and Lord Leighton. The *Spectator* magazine reviewed the new show on April 27, 1907, to which Crowley a week earlier had gained ingress at a private view. He bemoaned the general lack of quality of the Burne-Jones type, but was nonetheless full of praise for portraits by American painter John Singer Sargent (portraits of Mrs. Harold Harmsworth and Rev. E. Wane, for example), and one of a "Monsieur Simon" by Jacques Emile Blanche.

E. R. Frampton's *The Passage of the Holy Grail* was compared to Burne-Jones to Frampton's disadvantage, though one feels Crowley might have liked its medieval perspective and curious atmosphere, while probably disliking its Englishness and absence of Parisian verve. One wonders if Crowley was accompanied by sculptress Kathleen Bruce to

Fig. 19.1. John Singer Sargent's portrait of Mrs. Harold Harmsworth (née Mary Lilian Share, d. 1937). Newspaper proprietor Harold Harmsworth (1868–1940) cofounded the Daily Mail *with brother Alfred in 1896 and the* Daily Mirror *in 1903.*

Fig. 19.2. The New Gallery, 121 Regent Street, London.

*Fig. 19.3. Kathleen Scott (1878–1947),
née Edith Agnes Kathleen Bruce, sculptor and sometime
lover of Crowley, with husband, Antarctic explorer,
Robert Falcon Scott, whom she married in September 1908.*

an event that exhibited sculpture by the now-uncelebrated Joubert, such as the Earl of Warwick (the "Kingmaker"), a historic subject possibly to the Scottish artist's taste.

The next day (a Sunday) found Crowley reading works by Spanish "Quietist" mystic, Miguel de Molinos (1628–1696) whose *Guide* (1678) Crowley held in some regard, and for whose daring Molinos himself suffered greatly at the Inquisition's hands, dying in prison. Molinos believed the most profound contemplation came from an abandonment of meditative practices, practices associated particularly with the Jesuits' founder, Saint Ignatius of Loyola. Molinos seems to have inspired a sense of a need in Crowley the modern mystic for meditation on "How to spike the Dvaitist guns." Molinos could be seen as being close to the (opposing) Advaitist position, that there is, at a certain level of self-negation, an identity of essence in the divine spirit available to the advanced contemplative.

On Tuesday May 21, he recorded "a *dhyāna* today," a remarkably light reference to what on October 1, 1901, had been a life changer! He took to disciplined practice of prāṇāyāma again, gaining advancing results. On June 19, he found he could forget everything, and nearly himself altogether. At one point his arms began to levitate involuntarily. When he finished, the year 1907 did not seem a clear reality; it seemed "a very long way back."[9]

> Saturday 13 [July]
> ... The curious sense that I have the Power of samādhi is again with me. No doubt I have attained; only a question of waiting without attachment for the reward.

On the diary's opposite page, he wrote:

> I think this stamps me clearly as an $8° = 3^\square$ elect."[10]

Six days later he received more intimations that he was progressing to complete experience of the Master of the Temple grade, which entailed experiencing the negative side of intimacy with Binah (Understanding): "In my Irrawaddy ordeal, the mortar of the Universe gave way. Today the stones themselves crumble and dissolve. There is no meaning in any idea; all statements are not only false and true, but unintelligible. (This is the hell of Binah.)"[11]

On Monday September 30 he noted that at 5:30 p.m. he'd settled down to working "on Agamya's lines." His more mortal part, however, was concerned with the nonarrival of a person whose identity he concealed with the Enochian letter *Ur*. *Ur* corresponds to the English letter *L*, so we may suppose that Lola had failed to show up as expected, and Crowley would have to give more time to his formal, as opposed to informal yoga. He was finding the discipline tough going, and at the start of October composed some questions to put to the guru:

> Is it better to go on until one gets so sick of it one has a bust, or to avoid impulse by anticipation?
> What is it when one forgets everything, who one is, what one is doing, etc.

What are signs of good progress?

Give me a hathayoga practice to make body strong

What is the cause of that extreme distaste for meditation which catches one and is almost insuperable?[12]

Crowley noted that if in ordinary life one's thought wandered as much as it does when meditating, one would be considered an idiot! The mahatma's answers were that one shouldn't be alarmed that problems would defeat one; one just had to get up and fight again. When it came to forgetting who one is, or what one was doing and the like, well, this was a good sign! The sign of progress was interest in the work itself. Just persisting with hatha yoga would help make the body strong. The cause for the distaste for meditation was the thought-wandering's reflection in the will.

On October 3, things got worse: a day of utter, abject misery. He couldn't settle for any mortal things, never mind yoga. A symbol for Venus in the diary at 12:50 a.m. would seem to indicate the late arrival of Lola. But the following comments seem to relate to the ongoing yoga work rather than his perception of the beautiful flapper: "One gets vague feelings of calm, indifference, detachment, solitude, non-existence of everything etc. Quite as [*sic:* an?] experience, yet not fulminating and of catastrophic vividness. Just before going to sleep, a sharp single clear bell."[13] The next day he meditated "off and on—mostly off." On Monday the seventh he saw "L" by chance in Ludgate Hill and waved wildly. Then he met Mrs. "J.R." and discussed the "hathayoga scheme." He seemed, he wrote in his diary, to be full of prāṇa, so that he attracted folks. "Perhaps from Yoga, perhaps from Chastity."[14] Chastity might mean he was abstaining from sexual activity or more probably that he was following the discipline required and keeping clean of distractions from his purpose. He read the mahatma's book and made notes of its errors.

Tuesday 8 [October]

. . . (Good *hathayoga* practice: Hold one leg in opposite hand. Repeat <u>mantra</u>. When practised, revolve body on hips, rhythmically. Simple balance for 5 minutes can be done right off.)

About 9.35. Light-blaze on head—very brilliant. Later head

swelled and became like the bright night-sky filled with fleecy clouds.

9.48–10.3. *Pranayama* 10.20.30 [breathing cycle in seconds].

The Goddess Kali appeared very black but strangely beautiful. Also tried to reach her glory, and I was too fearful or dull—I know not which.

10.20. Very sleepy. Heard astral bell again—the r-r-r-r-r-r-r one.[15]

On Friday October 11, he had what he called a "long silent interview with Mahatma" and had more of the same next day.[16] Crowley intoned the Gāyatrī mantra from the *Rig Veda* when he saw the new moon. The name refers to the meter in which the mantra, dedicated to sun deity Savitṛ, is written. It is recited by "second born" (*dvija*), or spiritually reborn, men in their daily rituals. Preceded by "Aum," the "great utterance" goes "*bhūr bhuvah svah.*"

On Sunday October 13—the 400th anniversary of King Philippe IV's attack on the Knights Templar, incidentally—far from a silent conversation, Crowley had a blazing altercation with the guru, recounted as follows in "Half-Hours with Famous Mahatmas No. 1" by "Sam Hardy" (Crowley):

It was towards the close of last October, when I received from a friend of mine—also a so-called disciple—a letter in which he wrote: "There was a devil of a row at 60 [South Audley Street] last night. M[ahatma]: pressed me to come to his weekly entertainments; so I came. He urged me to speak; so I spoke. He then revealed his divine self in an exceptionally able manner; I refrained from revealing mine. His divine self reminded one rather of a 'Navvy's Saturday Night, by Battersea Burns.'"* He further urged me to go and see the Mahatma himself on the following Sunday; and this I did.

I arrived at 60 South Audley Street at seven o'clock. There were already about twenty sheepish-looking tigers present, and when the Mahatma entered the room, I sat down next to him; for, knowing,

---

*John Burns 1858–1943, a trades unionist and socialist party founder, born of a Scottish father in Battersea, London. 60 South Audley Street, Mayfair, is currently occupied by Sinai and Sons, antique dealers.

in case a scrimmage should occur, that a Hindoo cannot stomach a blow in the spleen, I thought it wisest to be within striking distance of him. The Mahatma opened the evening's discussion by saying: "Humph . . . I am Agnostic, you are believers. I say 'I don't know,' you contradict me." And during the next hour and a half more Bunkum was talked in that room than I should say in Exeter Hall* during the whole course of the last century. At last it ended, and though I had made various attempts to draw His Holiness into argument, I had as yet failed to unveil his divinity. He now started dictating his precious philosophy, and in such execrable English, that it was quite impossible to follow him, and I once or twice asked him to repeat what he had said, and as I did so I noticed that several of the faithful shivered and turned pale. At length came the word "expectation" or "separation," and as I could not catch which, I exclaimed "what?" "You pig-faced man!" shouted His Holiness, "you dirty fellow, you come here to take away my disciples . . . vat you vant vith this: vat! vat! vat! vat! . . . You do no exercise, else you understand vat I say, dirty man!" And then turning to his three head bell-wethers who were sitting at a separate table he sneered: "X——" (my friend present at the previous revelation of his divinity) "send this pig-one . . . eh?" "I don't know why . . ." I began. "Grutch, butch!" he roared, "you speak to me, you coeater! . . . get intellect," he yelled, "get English," he bellowed, and up he sprang from the table.

As I did not wish to be murdered, for he had now become a dangerous maniac, I rose, keeping my eyes on him, and taking up my hat and stick, which I had purposely placed just behind me, I quietly passed round the large table at which his terror-stricken fold sat gaping, and moved towards the door. The whole assembly seemed petrified with fear. At first the Blessèd One appeared not to realize what had happened, so taken aback was he by any one having the audacity to leave the room without his permission: then he recovered himself,

---

*Exeter Hall on the Strand's north side, London, opened in 1831, could seat 4,000 people and was used by the antislavery lobby, and a large number of Protestant religious, activist, and philanthropic organizations, protest meetings of many kinds, including an Australian independence movement. In July 1907 it was acquired by J. Lyons and Co. for a restaurant (Lyons was a famous chain restaurant company, specializing in tea), and demolished in 1909.

and at the top of his tiger-roar poured out his curses in choicest Hindustani.

On reaching the door I opened it, and then facing him I exclaimed in a loud voice in his native tongue: "Chup raho! tum suar ke bach-cha ho!" ["Shut up! You are the child of a pig."] With gleaming eyes, and foaming lips, and arms flung wildly into the air,—there stood the Indian God, the 666th incarnation of Haram Zada, stung to the very marrow of his bones by this bitterest insult. Beside himself with fury he sprang up, murder written on every line of his face; tried to leap across the table—and fell in an epileptic fit. As he did so, I shut the door in his face.

Aum.[17]

As Crowley mentions in his diary that day that he had lunch with "Tweed," one might guess that Tweed* was the fellow referred to as "X" in the humorous account of an evening that ended Crowley's association with the "Tiger Mahatma." It was inevitable. Crowley was his own guru now, knew the ropes, and was willing to show them to enquirers. On Sunday, November 17, he heard that his new friend Captain J. F. C. Fuller had been to 60 Great Audley Street where the mahatma threatened to murder him and fell paralyzed as if dead!

On October 22, Crowley's attention turned again to Buddhism when he received a letter from Lt. Col. Dr. Ernest R. Rost of the Indian Medical Service, then on home leave from Rangoon, requesting six copies of each of Crowley's books for the Buddhist Society of England, 14 Bury Street, near the British Museum. Honorary secretary of Ananda Metteya's international Buddhasasana Samagama—whose first meeting took place on March 15, 1903—Rost had been introduced to R. J. Jackson through Jackson's new acquaintance Col. J. R. Pain (sometimes "Payne"), an ex-soldier from Burma who had committed to Buddhism. Rost, Jackson, and Pain founded the Bury Street Buddhist bookshop. Lectures were given in a little room at the back of the shop as well as at events in parks

---

*"The British Rodin," John Tweed (1869–1933), a Glaswegian sculptor, referred to in *The Equinox*, vol. I, no. 1 (March 1909), "Special Supplement: John St. John," 127, line 11, in the context of a letter of Swami Vivekenanda, who, according to Tweed, wrote that his "sanctity" prevented him from enjoying a drinking bout.

with a portable platform painted bright orange bearing the device, "The Word of the Glorious Buddha is sure and everlasting," which attracted much attention. The shop purveyed the six issues of Secretary General Ananda Metteya's *Buddhism* that ran from 1903 until he brought the first Buddhist sangha to Britain in 1908.[18]

Crowley's relations with the Bury Street bookshop were strained. He called there on Monday, November 18, and would appear to have had some disagreement with whoever was running the shop at the time, for on November 22 he wrote to Rost about "the extraordinary conduct of his man."[19] Rost replied on December 2, saying he'd enquire as to what was wrong. On December 30 Crowley sent a demand to the Buddhist Society. Its Honorable Secretary Rost, came round the next day and refused to pay, presumably, for books Crowley had provided them with. Further evidence for poor relations between Crowley and at least one member of the Buddhist Society emerges after Ananda Metteya had left London in the fall of 1908, following his pioneering missionary journey of that year. The new *Buddhist Review's* third issue (July 1909, pp. 221–20) contained the following supercilious notice of *777*, Crowley's book of correspondences:*

> This work comes to us from a member of the masonic fraternity, to whom it is dedicated, and professes to be "an attempt to systematize the date of mysticism and the results of comparative religion." To this end, a number of tables have been drawn up, in which the "correspondences" of certain subjects are supposed to be indicated. Thus the Ten Fetters of Buddhism "correspond" with The Chakras or Centres of Prana (Hinduism), The Soul (Hindu), and Egyptian Attribution of Parts of the Soul. No Buddhist would admit such correspondence, or consider it worth while to pass from the crystalline clearness of his own religion to this involved obscurity. Some of the language is extremely undignified.

Unsigned, the review may have been the work of the journal's editor, Captain J. E. Ellam, general secretary of the Buddhist Society of

---

*I am grateful to William Breeze for drawing this issue of the *Buddhist Review* to my attention.

Great Britain and Ireland. He was perhaps Rost's "man" referred to above by Crowley. We do not know what Bennett thought about this dismissal of a work built upon his own original notes, compiled when he was in the Golden Dawn, but one might suppose it might have vexed his sensitivities. While there may be a case that the reviewer was concerned with the poor reputation of Buddhism in the general public's domain, being anxious to remove it from hints of doctrinal perversity, there is no reason to suppose the review reflected Allan Bennett's attitude either to his old friend, or to Thelema, as some authors have stated.* Well, Crowley's personal resonance with Buddhism was fading anyway, though he would be happy to include Ananda Metteya's essay "The Training of the Mind" in his own journal the *Equinox* (vol. 1, no. 5, March 1911). Besides, something else was happening to Crowley that was putting him in something of a religious class of his own, and it was happening fast.

On Tuesday October 29, around lunchtime, he was reading a brand-new science book, *Two New Worlds* by Edmund Edward Fournier d'Albe (Longmans, 1907). Intended to penetrate the mystery of space and time with the most modern scientific research, the "two worlds" consisted of the "infra-world" and the "supra-world," and the book was divided in two, likewise—as Crowley was himself about to be, after lighting a pipe of kif, a kind of cannabis smoked in Morocco and elsewhere. At ten to seven he turned to meditation and prayer. At 7:40 he recorded: "Nuffin' came of anyfink. (This sample of Hashish was quite inert through age.)"[20]

However, about eleven o'clock he began writing what became the first of what he would call the "Holy Books," because the manner of their reception was so extraordinary: *Liber Liberi Vel Lapidis Lazuli, Adumbratio Kabbalae Aegyptiorium Sub Figura VII.* This "7-fold Word" consisted of 5,700 words, written in two and a half hours.[21] One can imagine the horse-drawn taxis clip-clopping outside in busy Piccadilly in the cold and dark . . .

---

*For example, *Aleister Crowley: Magick, Rock and Roll and the Wickedest Man in the World* by Gary Lachman (2014) apparently repeats Lawrence Sutin's error in *Do What Thou Wilt: A Life of Aleister Crowley* (2002) where Sutin erroneously describes the *Buddhist Review* as "Bennett's journal," confusing it with its predecessor, *Buddhism*.

My God, how I love Thee!

With the vehement appetite of a beast I hunt Thee
    through the Universe.

Thou art standing as it were upon a pinnacle at the edge
    of some fortified city. I am a white bird, and perch
    upon Thee.

Thou art My Lover: I see Thee as a nymph with her
    white limbs stretched by the spring.

She lies upon the moss; there is none other but she:
    Art Thou not Pan?

I am He. Speak not, O my God! Let the work be
    accomplished in silence.

Let my cry of pain be crystallized into a little white fawn
    to run away into the forest!*

A note for 1:30 a.m. for Wednesday, October 30 informs us
"a.c." (the ordinary Crowley) had been meditating a book on *bhakti,*
or devotional yoga, for some time. (The "Holy Books" are highly devotional.) A note for 1:00 p.m., twelve hours later tells us: "Now there
wasn't a shadow of any Samādhi [crossed out], yet this morning I feel
just as if there had been." In the evening, he noted he could now actually see a reason for having a temple again, with an exclamation mark.
"Expecting an august visitor, one gets everything ready."

> Wrote I & II Liber Cordis Cincti Serpente ["The Book of the Heart
> Girt with the Serpent"]. Again, no shadow of *samādhi;* only a feeling
> that V.V.V.V.V. was in His *samādhi,* and writing by my pen, i.e., the
> pen of the scribe, and that scribe not *ou mē,* who reasons, etc., nor
> a.c., who is a poet & selects, but of some perfectly passive person.[22†]

Liber Liberi Vel Lapidis Lazuli, Adumbratio Kabbalae Aegyptiorium Sub Figura VII,
chap. 1, lines 1–9.

†V.V.V.V.V. (*Vi Veri Universum Vivus Vici*): Crowley's motto as 8° = 3° A.·.A.·., Magister
Templi (October 1906–December 1909); "ou mē" (Greek: ου μη)—"Not Not" (the
Greek is an emphatic double negative: "absolutely not")—was Crowley's motto as 7° = 4°
A.·.A.·., Adeptus Exemptus, attained October 1905, his official grade in the order at the
time, denoting a fully realized state of consciousness, on the path to Magister Templi,
"Master of the Temple"; "a.c." is Aleister Crowley.

On Friday November 1, at 11:30 p.m., "he" wrote section III *of Liber Cordis Cincti Serpente* and half of section IV, not stopping until 3:00 a.m. on the Saturday when he slept a few hours. At midday he completed section IV. *Liber Cordis Cincti Serpente Sub Figura LXV* was completed on Sunday, November 3.

> No doubt I am in Binah; "absence of definite *samādhi* only meant 'no *ananda*.'" [*ananda* = bliss] Now this absence of all the phenomena is just what constitutes 8° = 3□. I can, I know, get into touch with Adonai at will, and I have not gone back for a single moment since. . . . E.g. the old dreary purposeless misery of vacillation in the streets continues at times, but is enjoyed. I want nothing; but to do my work with confidence and no hope or fear. ([P.S.] True. Nov. 29.)[23]

And so, for the rest of the year "Holy Books" kept coming from his pen: *Liber XLVI* on November 25; *Liber CCXXI* (minus the verses) on December 5–6, and December 14; *Liber X* on December 12; *Liber CD* on December 13; *Liber XXVII* on December 14; and *Liber DCCCXIII* during the winter of 1907–08. The remaining "Holy Books" were not received until 1911.

It is interesting how the real human being Aleister Crowley enters the "Holy Books." A peculiarly sacred conception of sex was of course supremely important to him and the many affairs that illuminated his life were not infrequently woven into his spiritual writings. Thus, for example, in Holy Book *Liber LXV*, the invocation, "*A*donai, *d*ivine *A*donai . . . !" (v. 43; my emphasis) simultaneously spells out the name of his lover, Ada Leverson. Ada had helped him perceive his Adonai, his Holy Guardian Angel, or Higher Genius. "Thus I concealed the name of Her name that inspireth my rapture, the scent of whose body bewildereth the soul, the light of whose soul abaseth this body unto the beasts" (v. 43). On Saturday, November 23, his diary records "A.L." was in town: "A.L." being Ada Leverson (1862–1933), writer, novelist, and wit known for her friendship with Oscar Wilde (maintained after Wilde's imprisonment and social rejection). He called her "Sphinx." She wrote for *Punch*, the *Yellow Book*, the *Saturday Review,* and the *Referee,* often anonymously. Crowley refers to Ada as "Sphinx" in his diary

Fig. 19.4. Ada Esther Leverson
(1862–1933).

of Monday, December 2, when he notes of her visit, semicryptically: "Sphinx all A.M. [morning] One long continuous etc."[24]

What "long continuous etc." might have involved may be found in Crowley's poem "The Sphinx," published in his fascinating collection, *The Winged Beetle* (1910):

> Beneath the cruel splendid Sphinx
> My soul lies supine still, and drinks
> Damnation from the emerald eyes,
> Death from the painted mouth that dies
> As, drunk on life, she sucks it in!
> O crimson masterpiece of sin,

The mouth that maddens me and slays
My youth in many molten ways!
All her adulterous ardours wake
The god, the tiger, and the snake.
I yield; her soft, her strenuous breath
Fills me and feeds my soul on death.
O Sphinx, more sacred than the stars!
O beast! O God! thy passion chars
This life. Beneath thy claws I writhe.
For like a lion thou art lithe
And like a bull exceeding strong.
Thine eagle's scream beats down my song.
Ah slay me, slay me now! Have done! . . .
The torture is but half begun.

After having written *Liber X Porta Lucis. Viarum Viae* over Wednesday, December 11, and Thursday, December 12, Crowley had to take Rose to Leicester on the Friday to an establishment there specializing in treating alcoholics.*

Fig. 19.5. Advertisement in journal the Hospital *for treatment of "inebriety" at Melbourne House, Leicester: almost certainly the establishment that treated Rose Crowley for chronic alcoholism.*

---

*I found an advertisement for "INEBRIETY" (polite and professional term for alcoholism) in specialist medical journal the *Hospital* (June 9, 1906): "Melbourne House, Leicester, Private Home for Ladies; Medical Attendant: Robert Sevestre M.A. M.D. (Cantab.); Principal: H. M. Riley; Assoc. Soc. Study of Inebriety. *Thirty Years Experience*. Telegraphic Address: MEDICAL, LEICESTER." Melbourne House is still standing at 263 London Rd., Leicester, run as a care home for the elderly. It is doubtful another specialist home in Leicester for alcoholics in this period, or indeed perhaps elsewhere existed in England, especially one dedicated to women. Robert Sevestre, M.D. (1868–1949) was admitted to Trinity College, Cambridge—Crowley's alma mater—in 1886.

On Sunday, December 15, he looked back on the year:

☉ [Sunday] Looking back on the year, it seems one continuous ecstasy, save for the Rose trouble and the Tankerville nagging.*

The Morocco poems seem about the best I have ever done.

Not since my Attainment in October has there been any falling away whatever.

I am able to do automatic writing at will and the absence of great *ananda*-full [blissful] *samādhi* is rather a sign of my Attainment than its reverse. I cannot doubt that I am an 8° = 3□; i.e. a 1° = 10□ of the Supernal Order. My work as a scribe seems the 3° = 8□ [*Practicus*] exam as Founder of new Order, the 2° = 9□ [*Theoricus*] and as ? the 4° = 7□ [Philosophus] . . . and yet all this Supernal Order seems vague and unreal. At last I've got to a stage where desire has utterly failed: I want nothing.[25]

A guru should want nothing. Crowley had learned many lessons, and, like his friend Allan Bennett, he was ready and willing to bring the fruits of India to the waiting West—or as "a.c." put it in his diary on Christmas Day 1907:

God helping me, I will this next year perform the irrational abominable things that I should ere this have done. That I may Yield.[26]

---

*In July 1907, Crowley took on the case of George Bennet, 7th Earl of Tankerville. Tankerville attributed his suffering vexatious derangements to occult hostility in his family. Perceiving a "persecution complex," Crowley assumed the role of alienist and took "Tanky" to unwind in Spain and North Africa. The case proved impossible. See *Aleister Crowley: The Biography* for details of a journey that also produced some of Crowley's best poetry.

TWENTY

777 and *Book 4*

Crowley was becoming a teacher, a guru. A teacher needs pupils, indeed, a school. In 1908 Crowley and George Cecil Jones followed what they regarded as the will of the "Secret Chiefs" to melt down the G∴D∴ structure, rituals, and teaching, to forge a new sword of initiation. Its name had come to Crowley via astral vision at Kobe, Japan, in 1906: the Order of the Silver Star, or *Astrum Argenteum*. The A∴A∴ was a reorganized, trimmed, and augmented Golden Dawn–inspired system in tune with Crowley's gathered experience and enlightenment. A key innovation of the new Order, sanctioned, Crowley believed, by the Secret Chiefs from whom Mathers (Crowley believed) had deviated, was that the A∴A∴ would not be a social body. Student contact was intended to be restricted to a member from a higher grade deputed to guide from knowledge and experience. The kind of interpersonal strife endemic to Mathers's now-fragmented body would be eliminated. As a result of this discipline, the issue of publications naturally arose, since members could not, as in Masonic bodies, learn the ropes from imitative group activity and conversation. Study of texts was paramount. What became very clear to persons interested in the A∴A∴ was that the required texts involved many strange words and ideas absorbed by Crowley, chiefly from India, and that traversing these new landscapes would require ability to negotiate elements from a number of different and hitherto independent systems.

What was common to all the elements comprising the new system was a single aim: what Crowley called "the Knowledge and Conversation of the Holy Guardian Angel," expressed poetically as "One Star in

Sight." Crowley had found his understanding of this idea to be the key aspect of all systems of magical and mystical initiation proven by time. The idea was to strip the process down to scientific essentials. This aim was embodied in the Order's magazine, the *Equinox,* launched in March 1909 under the rubric: "The Method of Science. The Aim of Religion." The perception was that religion and science had come apart, to the detriment of both, and that a new temporal dispensation promised reunion.

It had been a belief of more enlightened Freemasons since at least the seventeenth century that the original science and the original religion of humanity were one, but over time, truth had too often been sacrificed to convenience, even as the source of truth was thrust out of practical touch into realms of superstitious mystery. Crowley's name for the ancient knowledge base was "Magick," indicating the knowledge of the first Magi: men who knew, and could do. He shared an assumption absorbed by Theosophy that a once noble civilization had enjoyed dominance through mastering the keys to this knowledge. Its remains were universally diffused, particularly in India, where yoga and Buddhism had, amid much moralism, maintained certain more or less scientific attitudes to spiritual knowledge, with Buddhism a kind of protest at accretions and unscientific conclusions advanced in Vedanta, while Crowley himself believed Buddhism had itself absorbed a freight of misplaced strictures, burdensome mythology, and common custom. It was time for the birds to come home to roost.

Now we can see why Crowley devoted so much time in 1907 to augmenting his "tables of correspondence." They were to demonstrate, in practical terms, how conceptions of spiritual being and their natural analogues related to one another, or found equivalence, expressing identical energies. Near Rangoon in 1905, Crowley had discussed with Bennett establishing a simplified, unified, comprehensible system of relation between phenomena, disagreeing with Bennett's view that Buddhist terminology sufficed. Westerners simply could not, Crowley believed, be expected to grasp the Pāli and Sanskrit terminology, which required specialized scholarship. Crowley decided that *number* furnished the cleanest approach. Therefore, since Hebrew gematria related numbers mathematically to letters, words, and essences, Kabbalah or

"Qabalah" (Crowley preferred the Arabic spelling) seemed to Crowley best suited to relate corresponding principles required to ascend the "Tree of Life," that is, to ascend from a material level to a realm, or consciousness, of the "Holy Guardian Angel."

THE TREE OF LIFE

We have already seen in our account of Sabhapaty Swami's system its analogy and correspondence to the sephiroth of the Tree of Life: a crucial realization for Crowley in synthesizing Indian and so-called Western systems.

Most likely drawing on Gnostic antecedents, the Tree of Life first appeared as "the tree of emanation" in the "Book of Illumination" (*Sefer Bahir*), composed by Isaac the Blind (fl. 1190–1210). Based on "received" tradition that God emanates (and is known by) ten balanced attributes called sephiroth, each divine aspect is called a sephira (sephiroth is the plural). *Sephira* means "number." Each number was given a name. Beyond these attributes God is unknowable to man's rational faculties. Mystical and magical progress requires a conscious return up the inner tree.

First appearing in print in Joseph Gikatilla's *Portae Lucis,* (Augsburg: Johann Miller, 1513), the tree constitutes a model of the microcosm or "mirror of the universe." It may be regarded as Man's invisible structure, for Man is made in the "image of God." As man mystically rises, he encounters the downward flow of the divine emanations—hence the numerical inversions in the Golden Dawn system: steps upward correspond to the Light's descent. Human consciousness encounters principles involved in man's supposed primal "fall" from union with God. To reach the heights of the angels and archangels—the hidden structures of being—man must retrace the steps of the "Fall" from knowledge. Through progressive purifications he may in theory return himself to highest, hidden divinity.*

---

*The numerical Golden Dawn grade system works in this wise: the sephiroth are numbered from one to ten, with one being the highest sephira (Kether, Hebrew for "crown") and ten the lowest (Malkuth, Hebrew for "kingdom"). Thus, the Zelator grade or first degree (1°) begins at the lowest sephira, Malkuth (the tenth sephira), so the Zelator grade

The Golden Dawn system had joined the Tree of Life to the tarot card system (understood as a compendium of initiation secreted in a "game") because the twenty-two trumps were taken to correspond both to the twenty-two paths or lines joining the sephiroth and the twenty-two letters of the Hebrew alphabet (all of which had a numerical equivalent). Crowley's correspondences draw on his interpretation of the Golden Dawn tarot system, as well as other magical and religious lore. The Golden Dawn system had integrated astrological and alchemical symbolism. Crowley's correspondences were intended to assist in relating the systems to each other.

From the very first issue of the *Equinox* (March 1909), methods Crowley had acquired in India played paramount roles in the A∴A∴ teaching regimen. Already by page 27 readers were confronted with a section on āsana, with photographs of recommended postures. Chapters on dhāraṇā and prāṇāyāma followed. The "Course of Reading" included eight Indian texts out of a total of twenty-four, the Indian texts being the Upanishads; the Bhagavad Gita; *Raja Yoga* by Swami Vivekānanda; the *Shiva Sanhita; The Aphorisms of Patanjali;* the *Hatha Yoga Pradipika; The Dhammapada* [S.B.E. Series, Oxford University Press]; and *The Questions of King Milinda* [S.B.E. Series].

(*cont.*) was written as $1° = 10°$. The use of the little square was to represent formative emanations. Each degree represents harmonization of forces, symbolized by the circle and square in balance. The second degree, Theoricus, was thus written as $2° = 9°$ (where 9 is the ninth sephira called Yesod, or Foundation); Practicus $3° = 8°$ (where 8 is the sephira Hod, or Splendor); Philosophus $4° = 7°$ (seventh sephira is Netzach, or Victory); Adeptus Minor $5° = 6°$ (sixth sephira is Tiphareth, or Beauty); Adeptus Major $6° = 5°$ (fifth sephira is Geburah, or Strength); Adeptus Exemptus $7° = 4°$ (fourth sephira is Chesed, or Mercy); Magister Templi $8° = 3°$ (third sephira is Binah, or Understanding); Magus $9° = 2°$ (second sephira Hokmah, or Wisdom); Ipsissimus $10° = 1°$ (first sephira is Kether, or the Crown).

Most members of the order worked with the lower degrees. The highest grade, called *Ipsissimus* ("his own very self," the divine, of which personality and mind are expressions) was practically speaking, an ideal, really only suitable for a Secret Chief. Invariably, the Secret Chief had a message for human beings since, by definition, a Secret Chief or Ipsissimus enjoyed overview of the human situation, being above and beyond limitations of the rational mind. Our word *angel* comes from the Greek for "messenger," so the Secret Chief might be described as an angel.

The reading list also included the freshly published *777,* limited to 500 copies, at ten shillings for its 64 pages bound in scarlet buckram.*

Crowley's *777*'s table of correspondences (Columns XXII–XXXIV) show correspondences between a "small selection of Hindu deities," the "Forty Buddhist Meditations," "Certain of the Hindu and Buddhist Results" (or trances), "Some Scandinavian Gods," and "Some Greek Gods." Thus, we find a correspondence between the Hindu creative word *Aum* with Buddhist meditation on Nothing, Space, and Consciousness, related to the trances of Nerodha-samāpatti, Nirvikalpa-samādhi, and Shiva darshana, and on to the Greek *Pan* (All). Likewise a correspondence is shown between "Parabrahm," Buddhist meditation on Indifference, trances of Unity with Brahma, and Atmadarshāna, related in turn to the Scandinavian Wotan, and the Greek Zeus and Iacchus (a name given to Dionysos in the Eleusinian Mysteries, as son of Zeus and Demeter). Bhavani and all forms of sákti, prāna (as Force), and yoni, correspond to Buddhist meditation on "Compassion," and to Frigga in Scandinavian lore, and Cybele, Demeter, Rhea, and Heré among Greek deities.

Tables LXXX to LXXXIII relate Olympic Planetary Spirits of magical lore to metals, the Noble Eightfold Path, and the "Attribution of the Hexagram." Not surprisingly, Buddhist "Samma Samādhi" corresponds to gold, planetary spirit Och, and to the center point of the hexagram. Tables CXVI to CXIX make correspondence between Egyptian Attributions of the Parts of the Soul to the Hindu Soul, to the chakras or Centers of Prāna in Hinduism, and the Ten Fetters of Buddhism. Thus, the Egyptian *Kha* or *yekh* corresponds to the Ātma, the Sahasrara chakra, and the Buddhist fetter of Arūparāga (craving for immaterial existence).

BOOK 4

Crowley's desire to wed magick with meditation lies at the core of *Book 4,* whose genesis has been related adequately in several biographies,

---

*The book was called "777" because that is the sum of the supposed eight paths taken by the "lightning flash of creation" down the Tree from Kether to Malkuth (four diagonals, three horizontals, one vertical), where Aleph is 1; Daleth 4; Gimel 3; Teth 9; Lamed 30; Nun 50; Pé 80; Resh 200; Tav 400. Total: 777. Incidentally the tarot trump numbers corresponding to those paths add to 93, the Greek gematria of "Thelema."

Fig. 20.1. Crowley with Rose and daughter Lola Zaza on the day divorce was granted, January 10, 1910. (Courtesy of Ordo Templi Orientis)

most fulsomely in Crowley's *Confessions,* and of course in the actual record of the "Abuldiz Working" from which the instruction from the Secret Chiefs allegedly initiating the idea of a new magical "primer." Several key events preceded the instruction. By December 1909, Crowley was satisfied he'd completed the ordeals admitting him to the grade of Magister Templi: he'd sacrificed his ego, and crossed the "Abyss" to Binah (Understanding). Crowley's divorce from Rose followed in January 1910, though they spent time together occasionally until a crisis of dementia in September 1911 precipitated permanent separation.

On October 11, 1911, Mary d'Este Sturges was at the Savoy Hotel, London, celebrating her birthday. Crowley arrived in search of Mary's close friend, famous dancer Isadora Duncan. Setting eyes upon the woman born Mary Dempsey in Quebec forty years earlier, Crowley tuned directly into her vibes, and the two entered a passion. Crowley followed Mary to Europe. At Zurich, at midnight on November 21, she became hysterical. This state led to a profound calm in which she revealed the "head of the Five White Brothers" was communicating with her. He told her that there was a book to be given to Perdurabo called "Aba," its number 4 (the gematria of Aba is four).

To cut a long story short, parts 1 and 2 of *Book 4* were composed in late December 1911 and early January 1912 at the Villa Caldarazzo, Posilippo, near Naples, following indices from "Abuldiz" (or Ab-ul-Diz), encountered in astral conference by seer Mary. Part 3 (a treatise on theory and practice of Magick) was dictated to Crowley's assistant and lover Leila Waddell at Fontainebleau in spring 1912; it included material originally intended for part 2, with which Crowley was dissatisfied. In September 1912's edition of the *Equinox* (vol. 1, no. 8), part 1 of *Book 4* was announced as "NOW READY" at the back of the issue in a strikingly modern advertisement on a yellow background, the book attributed to Frater Perdurabo and Soror Virakam (Mary d'Este Sturges) as "A Treatise on Magic and Mysticism for Beginners," available from "all Booksellers," price one shilling, and published by Wieland & Co., 33 Avenue Studios, South Kensington, London WC (Telephone 8987 City). Part 2 was announced as "READY SHORTLY" in the March 1913 *Equinox*. Crowley had not the means to publish parts 3 and 4. He'd hoped to complete the galleys when World War One broke out. Composition and rewriting continued in Sicily after the war, based on comments and queries from students, but it would not be until 1929 that the still-unfinished work appeared in Paris as *Magic in Theory & Practice,* published by Lecram Press. It should be stressed that the original *Book 4,* part 1, of ninety-four short pages that appeared in 1912 was devoted to "Meditation or The Way of Attainment of Genius or Godhead Considered as a Development of the Human Brain," consisting of seven chapters on Āsana; Prāṇāyāma, and its Parallel in Speech, Mantrayoga; Yama and Niyama; Pratyāhāra; dhāraṇā; Dhyāna; Samādhi; followed by a summary. In the latest, comprehensive edition of *Liber Aba,* edited by Hymenaeus Beta (Weiser, 1994) in 884 pages, the original part 1 material is presented, revised and edited, in part 1 under the overall title of "Mysticism," subtitled "Meditation."

As editor Hymenaeus Beta emphasizes in his introduction to the completed text, Crowley saw the confluence of Magick and yoga in the principle that both yoga and Ceremonial Magic are arts for uniting the mind to a single idea. Where yoga has four methods of jñāna yoga, rāja yoga, bhakti yoga, hatha yoga (to which may be added mantra yoga and karma yoga), Ceremonial Magic has four methods: Holy Qabalah, Sacred Magic, Acts of Worship, and the Ordeals (to which may be added

Invocations and Acts of Service). And these four principal methods and subsidiaries correspond respectively as Union by Knowledge (jñāna yoga and Qabalah); Union by Will (rāja yoga and Sacred Magic); Union by Love (bhakti yoga and Acts of Worship); and Union by Courage (hatha yoga and the Ordeals), to which may be added Union through Speech (mantra yoga and the Invocations), and Union through Work (karma yoga and Acts of Service).[1]

In Crowley's "Preliminary Remarks" to *Book 4,* part 1, he makes a powerful, trenchantly expressed case that the experience of samādhi at some level is precisely what made otherwise ordinary men become prophets of religions. They were in contact with their genius, while the existing attainment of of their minds necessarily shaped interpretation of the experience, perhaps uncritically or indiscriminately. The purer the mind, the purer and more spiritual the experience. The experience being self-transcending, even self-annihilating, remembered content will be registered as owning absolute divine sanction. Crowley makes the case that such attainments ought to be repeatable and useable once one has located the method and subjected the mind to discipline. For Crowley, Magick is above all the method for communicating with discarnate intelligence. As he says of Buddha: "Buddha goes into details too elaborate to enter upon in this place; but the gist of it is that in one way or another he got hold of the secret force of the World and mastered it."[2] Buddha had found relief from a given of human existence (sorrow) by transcending that which bound him formerly to it. Enlightenment was synonymous with liberation.

Crowley found the Buddha's testimony the most compelling since he explained his system thoroughly, and showed his ability to recognize mental limitations by resisting dogmatism. Crowley therefore recommends studying his testimony.

Crowley then observes that methods associated with Buddha, Jesus, Muhammad, Moses, and Saint Paul have common features. First they go into a deserted place to be alone; then they come back with a transformative message that compels interest. "They recommend 'virtue' (of various kinds), solitude, absence of excitement, moderation in diet, and finally a practice which some call prayer and some call meditation. (The former four may transpire on examination to be merely conditions favorable to the last.)"[3] Prayer and meditation have this in common: the restraining of the mind to a single act, state, or thought. This is quite distinct from normal human experience, with its wandering and distraction without fixity of attention. Here of course is the essential case for yoga, to unite unalloyed, subject and object. Crowley observes that in general, the larger, stronger, more highly developed animal moves about least, and when it it does, movement is slow and purposeful. Solitary habits characterize the more intelligent animals.

In order to see something of the truth of things, it is necessary to free the mind from external influences. This means mastering the mind, and that is yoga's purpose, and a prerequisite of Magick. Quieting the mind is objective number one, and nothing must prevent the will to so concentrate. One thinks of Izaak Walton's motto: "Study to be Quiet," as Crowley was thinking both of yoga and of "Quietist," Miguel de Molinos.

This necessity explains the usual rules over monks, taken as virtues, in Crowley's view, for the wrong reasons. It should be seen simply that if you have no property, you have nothing to be anxious about. Chastity saves you from being anxious for another, who, anyway, may distract you. As to a vow of obedience, you are relieved of having to worry about what to do; you simply obey: a weight off the spirit. Many men have felt freer in uniform.

Pursuing the goal produces a result. Something happens that can be expressed as the blotting out of consciousness of ego and non-ego, seer and thing seen, knower and thing known. One becomes "One."

Crowley sums up his preliminary remarks thus: "we assert a secret source of energy which explains the phenomenon of Genius. We do not believe in any supernatural explanations, but insist that this source may be reached by the following out of definite rules, the degree of success depending on the capacity of the seeker, and not upon the favor of any Divine Being. We assert that the critical phenomenon which determines success is an occurrence in the brain characterized essentially by the uniting of subject and object. We propose to discuss this phenomenon, analyze its nature, determine accurately the physical, mental and moral conditions which are favorable to it, to ascertain its cause, and thus to produce it in ourselves, so that we may adequately study its effects."[4]

Āsana

Chapter one opens with a treatment of posture. A person desires to control their mind? Think one thought as long as desired without interruption. First problem: the body. It does not want to sit still, so āsana is first port of call. Still that body! According to Vivekānanda, *Rāja-Yoga* (sutra 46, 184), "Posture is that which is firm and pleasant." Vivekānanda quotes Sānkhya (one of the six principal philosophical systems derived from the Upanishads): "posture is that which is steady and easy."[5] Of course, initial discomfort will have to be overcome, and that is hard.

Prāṇāyāma and Its Parallel in Speech, Mantrayoga

Crowley recommends breathing is best timed by use of a mantra, with a stopwatch. The mantra acts upon thoughts as prāṇāyāma does on breath. Thought is bound to a recurring cycle. The mantra casts off intruding thoughts; the swifter the wheel, so to speak, the less sticks. One recommended mantra is "Aum sivaya vasi," and one may note that *si* means "rest"—the absolute or male aspect of the Deity, while *va* is "energy," the manifested or female side of the Deity. The mantra therefore expresses the course of the Universe, from Zero through the finite back to zero. Crowley observes that Sri Sabhapaty Swami gives a particular mantra for each chakra, but recommends students select a single mantra and master it thoroughly. Crowley owed his *Liber HHH*, to Sabhapaty.

Yama and Niyama

As we have observed, Crowley has little time for yama and niyama as he believed the principles had been misapplied over centuries of priestcraft. Moral qualities and good works were supposed to promote mental calm. The point, again, was mental calm. Yama involves non-killing, truthfulness, avoiding theft, continence, self-denial in the matter of gifts. Crowley's view of yama is that breaking its injunctions would excite the mind. The codes of behavior were intended as purely practical, of no value in themselves. That is to say, "the cleanliness which assists the surgeon in his work would prevent the engineer from doing his at all."[6]

Pratyāhāra

Crowley notes that pratyāhāra is purely to do with the mind, whereas the previous sections relate to body and speech. Now is recommended a practice of introspection, a kind of general examination of one's mind to assess power of thought.

Dhāraṇā

Having learned to observe the mind, gaining some knowledge of its workings, while developing the idea and practice of control, it is recommended to embark on assembling the powers of mind so as to focus on a single point. Crowley notes that if students found acquiring ease of āsana was tough, nothing compares to the aridity of dhāraṇā! He goes on to explain the whole matter of breaks, and the use of a stopwatch.

Dhyāna

Crowley informs us that *dhyāna* is the same word as the Pāli *jhāna*. The Buddha counted eight jhānas, or different degrees and kinds of trance. While some Hindu yogis regard dhyāna as a lesser form of samādhi, others treat it as no more than dhāraṇā intensified. According to Patañjali, dhāraṇā means holding the mind onto some particular object. When knowledge in that object flows unbroken, that is dhyāna. When that, giving up all forms, reflects only the meaning, it is samādhi. Patañjali combines the three into *saṃyama.*

Crowley warns of exaggerations that abound in Indian lore regarding the benefits of trance. *Śiva Samhitā,* for example, insists that the one who daily contemplates on this lotus of the heart is eagerly desired by the daughters of gods, and enjoys clairaudience, clairvoyance, and can walk in the air. Other wonders have included the ability to make gold, discover medicine for a disease, and to see hidden treasures. Crowley's conclusion: "All this is filth."[7] Crowley sticks to science: "One extra fact may destroy some existing theory; that is common enough. But no single fact is sufficient to construct one."[8] He makes a fine job of trying to describe what others have found indescribable:

> In the course of our concentration we noticed that the contents of the mind at any moment consisted of two things, and no more: the Object, variable, and the Subject, invariable, or apparently so. By success in dharana the object has been made as invariable as the subject.
>
> Now the result of this is that the two become one. This phenom-

enon usually comes as a tremendous shock. It is indescribable even by the masters of language; and it is therefore not surprising that semi-educated stutterers wallow in oceans of gush.

All the poetic faculties and all the emotional faculties are thrown into a sort of ecstasy by an occurrence which overthrows the mind, and makes the rest of life seem absolutely worthless in comparison.[9]

Crowley notes how conditions of thought, time, and space are abolished. Now this, he admits, is impossible to explain; experience only furnishes apprehension. He then draws attention to the appearance of the Form universally described as human, though many details are not infrequently added that are not human at all. The appearance is assumed to be "God." A person with such experience is likely to reenter the world, so to speak, armed with intense conviction and authority. Crowley notes that the value of the experience can be lost should the seer forget a signal component of dhyāna, that is, within the trance, the ego is annihilated. To put the experience back, as it were, into the hands of the ego risks hideous inflation. While the one who has experienced the more intense forms of dhyāna is liberated, that may not necessarily guarantee all will be well. The experience may have liberated a lunatic from all but his lunacy! The Universe having been destroyed for the seer, it is well that his ego is also; then the Will can go on its way unhampered.

Crowley makes many important points and caveats about this catastrophic experience, for example, that what the mind brings back from the experience may not be the dhyāna itself, but only his image or impression of it. However, he concludes that a Hindu metaphor expresses the matter simply, and well, so long as we interpret the last lines regarding the "Sun" as "some unknown thing whose presence has been masked by all things known, and by the knower":

That image is that of a lake into which five glaciers move. These glaciers are the senses. While ice (the impressions) is breaking off constantly into the lake, the waters are troubled. If the glaciers are stopped the surface becomes calm; and then, and only then, can it reflect unbroken the disc of the Sun. This Sun is the "soul" or "God."[10]

Samādhi

Crowley begins succinctly: "More rubbish has been written about Samādhi than enough; we must endeavor to avoid adding to the heap."[11] Crowley finds the most reasonable statement in the words of Yājñavalkya: "By prāṇāyāma impurities of the body are thrown out, by dharana the impurities of the mind; by pratyahara impurities of attachment, and by Samādhi is taken off everything that hides the lordship of the Soul."[12] Crowley takes a lot of his expressions from Vivekānanda's book on *Rāja Yoga* in whose book this quotation appears.

Etymology is a good way to start: *sam* in Sanskrit is the Greek *syn,* meaning "together with"; *ādhi* means "Lord." A reasonable translation then is union with God. Crowley notes that Buddhists use *samādhi* to express attention: to think of a cat is "to make samādhi" on that cat. "This is excessively misleading, for as we saw in the last section, dhyana is a preliminary of Samādhi, and of course jhāna is merely the wretched plebeian Pāli corruption of it."[13]

There are many kinds of samādhi. Some authors, says Crowley, consider *ātmadarshana,* the Universe as a single phenomenon without conditions, to be the first real samādhi. If this is accepted, many less exalted states need to be relegated to the class of dhyāna. In samādhi, Death has lost all meaning, for the idea of death depends on the ideas of the ego, and of time, which in samādhi have been destroyed. He quotes Saint Paul: "Death is swallowed up in victory" (1 Cor. 15:54). As in dhyāna, Duality in any form is abolished. Since our idea of time involves two consecutive things, and space involves two coincident things, and causality two connected things, normal thought conditions are contradicted, and this phenomenon is even more marked in samādhi. Crowley talks from experience: "He [AC] can produce dhyana at will in the course of a few minutes' work, and it often happens with apparent spontaneity; with Samādhi this is unfortunately not the case. He probably can get it at will, but could not say exactly how, or tell how long it might take him; and he could not be *sure* of getting it at all."[14] Crowley writes that he'd rather not say with certitude if he got dhyāna from common objects, because he desisted trying after a few months and concentrated instead on the chakras. In fact, you can meditate on anything especially appealing, but beware: one does not want the mind getting excited.

He notes how some Hindus regard lower samādhis as able to confer "magic powers," or *yogapravritti*. He suggests meditating on the tip of the nose, and one may indeed find a wonder: the idea of a smell that is not a smell. Crowley remarks that the experience being contrary to reason, it is only reasonable the words describing it should be contrary to reason too. In a footnote he cheekily compares the perception to the Athanasian Creed!

The samādhi par excellence is, we are confidently informed, *ātmadarshana*. While it is normal for ideas of God and Self to be tainted by form, in ātmadarshana the All is manifested as the One: the Universe freed from its conditions. Not only are all forms and ideas destroyed, but also those conceptions implicit in our ideas of those ideas. Each part of the universe has become the whole, and phenomena and noumena are no longer opposed. This happened, so to speak, to Crowley in Bournemouth in January 1907, as we may recall.

"But it is quite impossible to describe this state of mind. It is impossible for anyone who experiences it to bring back any adequate memory, nor can we conceive a state transcending this."[15]

However, there is said to be an even higher state: *śivadarshana*. What can one say of it? It is a destruction of the previous state, its annihilation; and yet the ensuing Nothingness is paradoxically not negative, but positive.

One can find a simile for dhyāna, such as the normal mind is a candle in a darkened room. When the shutters are thrown open, sunlight makes the flame invisible. But there is no such simile for ātmadarshana. One might say it is the recognition that the positive is merely the negative. The ultimate truth is perceived not only as false, but truth's logical contradiction. How, Crowley asks, can one elaborate on this theme? It has baffled all minds hitherto. "It is enough if we say that even the first and most transitory dhyana repays a thousandfold the pains we may have taken to attain it.

"And there is the anchor for the beginner, that his work is cumulative; every act directed towards attainment builds up a destiny which must someday come to fruition. May all attain!"[16]

SUMMARY

Crowley concludes by asserting it his life's work to prove, from studying each religious practice of each great religion on the spot, that there is

Identity-in-diversity of all, and that it is therefore possible to formulate a method free from all dogmatic bias, based only on ascertained facts of anatomy, physiology, and psychology.

"The main idea is that the Infinite, the Absolute, God, the Oversoul, or whatever you may prefer to call it, is always present, but veiled or masked by the thoughts of the mind, just as one cannot hear a heartbeat in a noisy city."[17] I paraphrase Crowley's summary of method: To obtain knowledge of That, it is necessary only to still all thoughts. First the body is stilled by āsana, its ease is secured and the regularity of its functions by prāṇāyāma. No messages from the body disturb the mind. Second, by yama and niyama, we still emotions and passions and prevent their arising to disturb the mind. Third, by pratyāhāra we analyze mind more deeply, and begin to control and suppress thought in general. Fourth, we suppress thoughts by direct concentration on one thought. This process has three parts: dhāraṇā, dhyāna, and samādhi, grouped as saṃyama.

"For further knowledge consult the A∴A∴."

Students were advised to read: *777; Konx Om Pax;* Crowley's essays "Time" and "Eleusis"; *Rāja Yoga* by Vivekānanda; *Śiva Saṃhitā* or *Hatha Yoga Pradipika;* the *Tao te Ching* (Chuang-Tzu); the *Guide* by Miguel de Molinos; *Dogme et ritual de la Haute Magie* by Éliphas Lévi; the *Goetia of Lemegeton of Solomon the King,* and Crowley's *Magick: Elementary Theory.*

TWENTY-ONE

Sit Down, Shut Up, Get Out!

The A∴A∴ system's indebtedness to its creator's Indian experience is evident from Crowley's "glimpse" of the grade system and those grades' basic requirements, adumbrated in his *One Star in Sight*.*

The first stage before taking the Probationer's Oath was that of "Student," requiring a "general intellectual knowledge of all systems of attainment," for which Crowley established a reading list, a portion of which we have seen already, containing Hindu and Buddhist classics, amongst a wide trawl of global wisdom. The stage ends formally with a written examination and a small ritual involving the Order's History Lection (Liber LXI), before passing to the grade of Probationer, first step in the Order of the G∴D∴ (Golden Dawn), the first Order of three constituting the A∴A∴.

Kenneth Grant (1924–2011) published the contents of *his* Student examination,[1] set by Crowley in April 1945, when Grant was twenty.

---

*One Star in Sight: A Glimpse of the Structure and System of the Great White Brotherhood A∴A∴ (in *Magick*, ed. H.B. [2004] appendix II, 488–98). In *Magick* Crowley maintained the true name of the A∴A∴ was secret. James Eshelman[2] has taken two occurrences in Crowley's handwriting to indicate the secret name was not the Latin, but the Greek form of "Silver Star": *Astron Arguron*, whose gematria—451—is that of *Konx Om Pax*. According to Blavatsky's *Theosophical Glossary* (1892, 179), "Konx-Om-Pax" are Greek, mystic words "used in the Eleusinian mysteries. It is believed that these words are the Greek imitation of ancient Egyptian words once used in the secret ceremonies of the Isiac cult. Several modern authors give fanciful translations, but they are all only guesses at the truth."

1. Buddhism may be divided into these classes:
   1. Hinayana (Burma, Siam, Ceylon)
   2. Mahayana (Tibet)
   3. Twelve sects in Japan
   4. Chinese Buddhism

What divisions of Christianity correspond to each, and why?

2. What is the meaning, and why, of the following numbers:
   148.
   210.
   831.

Reconcile the two apparently conflicting series of meanings of the number 65.

Work out the equation 3 = 4 especially in relation to the Sephiroth and the Planets.

3. State the difference between Vedantism, Sufism, & Molinism. Can you trace any historical sequence in these branches of Mysticism?

4. A friend's cows suffer from some epidemic disease. How would you set to work to discover the cause; if due to bewitchment, how to detect the agent; and how would you proceed to avert the evil?

5. Describe a woman with ♅ ☌ ⛢ △ ♀ rising in 8° {?} ♑

The answers to these questions are to be submitted on An Ixix ☉ ☍ ☾ in ♊ 6°

666

I wonder how many readers would feel confident to fulfill this basic task today!

According to *One Star in Sight*, the first grade of the A∴A∴'s Order of the Golden Dawn was Probationer (0° = 0□). The Probationer may begin with preferred practices, keeping a record for a year. The Neophyte (1° = 10□) was expected to "perfect control of the astral plane."

Dedicated to mastery of āsana and prāṇāyāma, the Zelator ($2° = 9°$) was also required to study the "formula of the Rosy Cross." The Practicus ($3° = 8°$) had to complete intellectual training with particular attention to Qabalah. The Philosophus ($4° = 7°$), having completed moral training, would be tested in "Devotion to the Order."

The link to the second Order was called *Dominus Liminis* (Master of the Threshold), requiring demonstration of "mastery in *pratyāhāra* and *dhāraṇā*."

Entry into the Order of the R.∴C.∴ (Rosy Cross) began with the grade of Adeptus Minor (Without) ($5° = 6°$). The Lesser Adept (Without) had to "perform the Great Work and attain the Knowledge and Conversation of the Holy Guardian Angel," following which the Adeptus Minor (Within) ($5° = 6°$) was "admitted to the practice of the formula of the Rosy Cross on entering the College of the Holy Ghost."

The Greater Adept or Adeptus Major ($6° = 5°$) had to attain "general mastery of practical Magick, without comprehension." The Adeptus Exemptus ($7° = 4°$) or Exempt Adept had to perfect all these matters, after which the Adept could become (a) a "Brother of the Left-Hand Path" or, (b) be "stripped of all attainments and of himself as well, even of his Holy Guardian Angel," to become a "Babe of the Abyss, who, having transcended the Reason, would do nothing but grow in the womb of its Mother," before finding itself a Master of the Temple.

The Magister Templi ($8° = 3°$) has entered the Order of the S.∴S.∴ (Silver Star), and the Master of the Temple's principal business is "to obtain perfect understanding of the Universe," involving annihilation of the personality that limits and oppresses the true self. A Master of Mysticism, the Magister Templi's Understanding (corresponding to Binah) is entirely free from internal contradiction or external obscurity; his Word is to comprehend the existing Universe in accordance with his own Mind. Crowley associated the grade with Śivadarśana and with four Formless States of Buddhism, whilst cautioning against treating these criteria as sufficient for the grade.

The Magus ($9° = 2°$) "attains to Wisdom, declares His Law, and is a Master of all Magick in its greatest and highest sense." His will is entirely free from internal diversion or external opposition;

his work is to create a new Universe in accordance with his Will. The grade corresponds to Hokmah (Wisdom) on the Tree of Life.*

The ultimate degree, Ipsissimus (10° = 1°) is "beyond all comprehension of those of lower degrees." Being free from limitations and necessity, the Ipsissimus lives in perfect balance with the manifest universe, corresponding to Kether on the Tree of Life. A condition of the grade was named by Crowley as the trance *nirodha-samāpatti,* meaning absorption in nibbana itself, the achievement of the *arhat* (Sanskrit) or *arahat* (Pāli), meaning "one who is worthy." It is attainment of extinction, also called *saññā-vedayita-nirodha,* extinction of feeling and perception, the temporary suspension of all consciousness and mental activity, following immediately upon the semiconscious state called "sphere of neither-perception-nor-non-perception" (the eighth jhāna). The absolutely necessary preconditions to its attainment are said to be perfect mastery of all eight absorptions (jhāna), as well as the previous attainment of *anāgāmī or arahatship.* While Buddhist monks traditionally attain nirodha-samāpatti by producing the Formless States one after the other, perceiving in each the Three Characteristics: sorrow or tendency toward sorrow, change or unreliability, and insubstantiality or lack of self. Crowley's A∴A∴ sought to replace this threefold view with the quest for balance as both a motive for discipline and the means of achieving their end goal. In *Liber B vel Magi* the Magus who seeks to progress is urged to identify the Buddhist Three Characteristics with the opposite states. "Wherein Sorrow is Joy, and Change is Stability, and Selflessness is Self." Crowley's version of nirodha includes seeing first the truth and then the falsity of the Three Characteristics. This well reflects his Indian experience as adumbrated in *The Sword of Song* (1904). The Ipsissimus should keep the achievement of this final grade secret, even from the rest of the Order, and continue with the work of the Magus while expressing the nature of an Ipsissimus in word and deed: a proscription on announcement analogous to the bodhisattva who returns to earth, or incarnation, out of compassion for those who may follow.

---

*For Crowley's complex passage to this grade, please consult the author's *Aleister Crowley in America,* which offers a comprehensive account.

THE GURU IN ACTION

Numerous accounts have survived of some of Crowley's pupils' progress (or otherwise) on the Path of the Wise. All testify to the emphasis Crowley laid on yoga, Buddhism, and Vedanta, and they all demonstrate how this knowledge was integrated into Crowley's unique synthesis in practice. Anyone looking at the ideal itinerary of the A∴A∴ student outlined above will recognize the enormous difficulty that most students of Magick would experience on the path, and may sympathize with the fact that few got beyond the first Order. Had Crowley's system received serious financial backing, and acquired status in his lifetime, one may suspect the number of outstanding students would have increased. Crowley's personal presence seems to have been a key factor in students gaining understanding, for, as Gerald Yorke maintained, Crowley was, among so many things, a *jīvanmukta*, a liberated soul whose presence could open the "eternal worlds" to the conscious eye of the seeker of pure heart. When people saw things through Crowley's eyes, what had appeared obscure could suddenly make sense. We see this potential very clearly in the case of Crowley's Lancashire-born pupil, Frank Bennett (1868–1930) who attempted, largely without success, to promote Crowley and his system in Australia in the second and third decades of the twentieth century.

Frank Bennett—*Frater Progradior*—arrived at Crowley's Abbey of Thelema on a hillside overlooking the sea at Cefalù, Sicily, on July 18, 1921. The Villa Santa Barbara was already crowded, with the Beast's assistants Leah Hirsig and Ninette Shumway, and their children Hansi and Howard, and Crowley's daughter with Ninette, Lulu Astarte (1920–2014) in residence. Also present were writer Mary Butts, her partner Cecil Maitland, former U.S. sailor Cecil Frederick Russell, and American movie actress Jane Wolfe—and, of course, the Beast himself.

Jane Wolfe had just returned from a long "magical retirement," alone in a leaky tent by the seaside, in solitude and contemplation, meditating, and practicing her āsana and prāṇāyāma and dhāraṇā, and finding a peace of mind she could never find in Hollywood. She had maintained concentration despite aggressive taunts from local children, and even when mildly concussed by a stone hurled at her by a xenophobic local peasant. She had earned her place back under the abbey roof, but *someone* was going to have to move to make way for Bennett, who was entitled, as was the rule, to a week's hospitality. Frater Genesthai (C. F. Russell) had been there seven months, and Crowley suggested the young man quit his room for yoga and meditation. Refusing, Crowley had to threaten Russell with expulsion, whereupon, Genesthai stormed off in high dudgeon to a ruined shepherd's hut on a high crag, without food or drink. Bennett arrived at the abbey soon after, while a sympathetic Ninette climbed up to the American's hut with provisions.

Bennett was introduced to the community schedule, including a four-times-a-day ritual to the sun, to Ra at dawn, to Hathor at midday, to Tum at sunset, and Khephra at midnight. In morning and evening a ritual of "Pentagram" was performed, based on the Lesser (Banishing) Ritual of the Pentagram familiar to the Golden Dawn.

While at the abbey, Bennett received a letter from Crowley's American representative, Charles Stansfeld Jones, one of whose tasks in the A∴A∴ was to instruct Bennett, then approaching the degree of Zelator (2° = 9□). Jones commented on Bennett's Magical Record, sent to Jones for monitoring. Jones's own instructor in the A∴A∴ during the wartime period had been Crowley himself, who had even written a (then-unpublished) book especially for Jones's encouragement and instruction, *Liber Aleph, the Book of Wisdom or Folly.* Addressing Jones lovingly as his "magical son," *Liber Aleph*'s concise chapter "De Gautama" maintained Gautama's essential doctrine was "no Soul," meaning a substance incapable of change. "Then He, like Lao-tze, based all upon a Movement, instead of a fixed Point."[3] Crowley's Thelemic view was that the "core of the Star" could be seen as *both* process *and* as irreducible essence, analogous perhaps to the quantum notion of light quanta being both waves and particles, depending on conditions of observation.

On July 22, Crowley heard Bennett's oath of the Zelator, and Bennett commenced grade work, concentrating on āsana and prāṇāyāma. O.T.O. member Bennett was finding the idea of the IX° troubling. As Keith Richmond observed in his compelling account of Bennett and Crowley,* the O.T.O.'s sex magic was intended as yoga for the mind and body, like the tantrics' secret assemblies of which Crowley had gained

---

*Keith Richmond, *Progradior and the Beast, Frank Bennett and Aleister Crowley,* 167.

some knowledge in India, and perhaps from works such as Sir John Woodroffe (Arthur Avalon's) *The Serpent Power: The Secrets of Tantric and Shaktic Yoga* (1919), though he nowhere mentions Woodroffe. Crowley hoped Bennett's problem might come to the surface with a magical retirement. This was consistent with the ideal program for visitors to the abbey, which required, after the first week, four weeks of silence and work, three weeks likewise in weeks seven to nine, and more silence and work in weeks eleven to thirteen, the remaining weeks reserved for instruction.

Before the retirement was due to commence on September 1, 1921, Bennett descended to the Bay of Caldara on a glorious morning (Friday, August 19), and listened to Crowley expatiate on the role of sexuality and of the subconscious in initiation. In simple language, 666 explained what initiation meant, and what the Real Self was. Initiation could be seen as bringing the subconscious to the fore, so that one could say truly "I AM what I'm doing." Crowley's identification of the Holy Guardian Angel with the subconscious came to Bennett as a staggering personal revelation. As night wore on, it grew in his mind until he felt like his head would split.

While Crowley had made the connection with Carl Jung's *Psychology of the Unconscious* the year Jung's book appeared in New York (1915) while on a magical retirement near Bristol, New Hampshire,* the idea came to Bennett as a bolt from the purest blue. He felt he had been getting his whole life wrong, fundamentally. He had thought of the H.G.A. as an exalted being far above the earth, with earth as the setting of the sexual instinct that needed to be repressed as impure, inappropriate for spiritual regions, in which ether the Holy Guardian Angel breathed, free of lusts. Crowley explained to him that the sexual organs corresponded to God's creative power and were therefore closest to the Holy Guardian Angel, so long as that is how the experience was understood: a glory of God, not something to be ashamed of. The shame lay in *not seeing that,* or understanding it, or celebrating it, and instead treating sex as something base and shameful, furtive and disgusting. This was what Crowley could not forgive Christian tradition for, for denigrating what he took to be God. Purity, or chastity,

---

*See *Aleister Crowley in America* (Inner Traditions, 2018).

to Crowley did not mean anything more than being "true to God," and sex was an aspect, perhaps most central aspect of the divine sun in humankind. It was for him critical in Magick, for to suppress it meant distortion of mind and body, and therefore bad magic: obsession and uncleanness. Those who actively suppressed sexual knowledge were the most unclean, and could never be trusted; they blackened love and the sacrament of love. When love was raised, love could raise.

While Bennett felt bitterness at what he suddenly saw as his wasted years, we may ask ourselves what the implications of Crowley's idea of the unconscious as agent of the soul's salvation (what Jung called the "self-regulating psyche") would be for Indian thought; for by extension, samādhi becomes communing with the Unconscious, or subconscious; so of what *is* man unconscious in his normal state?—Why, his essential divinity, to be sure, and in this sense, Crowley concurs with the Advaitist school, and with Sabhapaty: cleanse the chakras, and Parabrahm appears. The "subconscious" of Crowley then is not buried facts, but gnosis of God. The task of the modern Magus, Crowley believed, was to dissolve "complexes" obstructing access to that truth. And here, in the case of Frank Bennett of Worsley, Lancashire, he had complete vindication of his theory. The Beast, it transpired, was a golden Lion, and had turned lead into gold!

Crowley finished composing *Liber Samekh,* his recomposing of the "Bornless" ritual, for Bennett's retirement, to bring Bennett and his Holy Guardian Angel into closer relations. Crowley did an I Ching divination on Bennett's retirement, obtaining hexagram Ku, interpreted by Crowley as a binding of mind and body: *hatha yoga.* He instructed Bennett to take the contents of the Chinese hexagram apart, and in doing so, to "explore the tangle of being a separate being."[4] This would hopefully involve a meditation of the sammasati or "right recollection" type, to establish the history of Bennett's relations with the Universe, his tendencies, and possible future. Crowley was doubtless reflecting on his own mental struggle in Burma in late 1905.

Bennett began his retirement in a tent close to the abbey, returning for meals. Otherwise he was engaged in prāṇāyāma to balance his energies and command his body, so as to make him more attentive to the internal mind. On September 5, he did prāṇāyāma for fifteen minutes.[5]

On the twelfth he did "a little Cabbala and Prāṇāyāma. Very sick and weary towards night."[6] On September 24, similarly to other days, he'd go for dinner, then back to the tent. He'd go through *Liber Samekh,* then do an hour's exercise and prāṇāyāma; then an hour's study of *The Book of the Law,* with tea at 5:30 p.m., and "Pentagram" at 6:30, "and it rained like hell."[7]

The next day: some exercise and prāṇāyāma until twelve. On October 8, from ten to eleven, Bennett sat in meditation, "inflaming himself with invocations to get the full consciousness of the Absolute Self."[8] He then read some Nietzsche before returning to his invocations.

Another pupil of Crowley's who left an idea of what his training under the Beast involved was Gerald Yorke (1901–1983), who joined the A∴A∴ on December 9, 1928, quitting after a legal dispute with Crowley in 1932 to embrace Buddhism, while preserving his friendship and interest in 666 and his work to the end of his days, despite aversion to much of *The Book of the Law.* When Coptologist and musician David Tibet interviewed Yorke shortly before Yorke's death in 1983, Yorke informed him: "Crowley taught me the initial stages of yoga— breathing exercises—which he had learned under the Solicitor General of Ceylon, Sri Ramanathan, who had an English wife."[9] For Yorke, the magical retirement or retreat was also deemed essential practice, as such breaks from ordinary life had proved to be for the Beast.

Yorke's second significant magical retirement was made in July– August 1931 in a Welsh cave—Bishop Asser's Cave—on the cliffs of Strumble Head, Pembrokeshire. Apart from scanty Western clothing, Yorke had a camel-hair burnoose from North Africa, to shield him from the elements. It proved to be a struggle to concentrate on either the tip of his nose or on a mantra 250 feet above the roaring sea. It was not only the draught and the noise, but he was plagued by thoughts.

Ānāpānasati was Yorke's main practice, a Pāli word for mindfulness of breathing, as taught by Gautama in the *Ānāpānasati Sutta.* The practice of concentration on inhalation and exhalation, when worked and refined in approach through the Seven Factors of Enlightenment— mindfulness, analysis, persistence, rapture, serenity, concentration (Buddhist samādhi), then to equanimity—should conclude in release from suffering in realizing nibbana. Combined with prāṇāyāma and the

Bornless Ritual, Yorke did not approach nibbana. Crowley, however, was impressed by the pointedness of Yorke's Magical Record, regarding it as packed with promise of achievement to come. Yorke himself was irritated by problems encountered in the chosen set and setting, and his own busy and frustrated thoughts—his father Vincent had set himself against the connection with Crowley, and threatened his son's income. Yorke undertook a more successful retirement at the Franciscan Monastery of St. Mary at the Cross, Glasshampton, Worcester. There, conditions were truly made for practices of reading, meditation, and yoga, and Gerald Yorke felt the benefit in clarity of direction, though not one Crowley approved of: leaving Europe for China as a Reuters correspondent.[10]

We get a glimpse of Crowley taking the odd pupil on for personal tuition in the 1930s from notes in his diaries. He rarely took money directly for magical instruction; it depended on what was required in expenses, providing books and so on, and the nature of the case. On Tuesday March 31, 1936, Crowley drew up an account for Frenchman André Pigné's training in London. This is what Crowley offered at least one pupil and at what price:

> Masonry. Qabalah. Astrology. Geomancy. Mantra-Yoga. Sammasati.
> Dharana. AP [André Pigné] 14 lessons £14.14.0
> Paid £6.17.0
> Due £7.17.0
> Pd. Apr.1 £1.10.0
> £6.7.0. P[ai]d on April 6[11]

We obtain another glimpse into the facets of Crowley's approach, influenced and guided by his experience of India when we look at his record of his first sexual encounter with twenty-one-year-old Deirdre Patricia Maureen Doherty (1915–1992). Known to Crowley's friends as "the Girl Pat," she declared her intention to Crowley that she would bear his child. The necessary precursor to that event took place on Friday July 31, 1936:

> Linga-yoni mudra with G[irl] P[at]. 93 AL Mrs Turner Coles
> began an unprovoked and furious attack on Miss Doherty, calling

her trollop, harlot, whore, and slut in the course of a spate of venomous abuse.[12]

Crowley and Pat's spiritual union was special for Crowley since he describes the rite purely, and uniquely, in terms of a "mudra" or mystical gesture of mutual tantric-style divine worship. She duly bore him a son, Randall Ghair, whose upbringing was assisted by the O.T.O; he died in 2002.

We cannot speak of "India in Crowley" without referring to that portion of India he offered to put inside all his dinner guests in the mid- to late-1930s, namely: very hot curries! Crowley was a British curry-loving pioneer, stimulating early biographer Charles Cammell to refer to Crowley's "ordeal by curry." The Beast's diary informs us that on Thursday, August 6, 1936, spiritualist medium Vyvyan Deacon was treated to one of his mouth-igniting recipes: "Real Vindalu of Bhindi—lowest layer. Madras Chutney. Lamb with red and green Chillis. Usual rice—top layer," Crowley vainly sought support for a London curry house, trading humorously on his reputation—the "Black Magic Restaurant" or "Bar 666." Had he succeeded in 1936, the 666 would have been one of only two curry houses for Europeans in London— Edward Palmer's "Veeraswamy" having graced Piccadilly since 1926. The first Indian to run a London curry establishment was former surgeon in the East India Company's army, the Bengali, Sake Dean Mahomed (1759–1851), whose "Hindoostane Coffee House," opened in 1810: a true pioneer. Crowley may not have been first, but Crowley's dishes would have been the hottest in Britain, for sure. Where Crowley led, you might say, millions now follow, though they do not see the footsteps trod before them.

YOGA FOR YAHOOS AND YELLOWBELLIES

Crowley would have liked the whole world to know what was involved in yoga, and what was the best way to approach the subject. It wasn't just something for initiates of his Orders. To this end, on February 17, 1937, he left his Richmond lodgings to give the first lecture in a series divided into two sets of four lectures: "Yoga for Yahoos," and "Yoga for Yellowbellies." The lectures were open to the public, and held in sympathetic circumstances at the Eiffel Tower restaurant at 1 Percy Street, London Borough of Camden, between Tottenham Court Road, Charlotte Street, and Rathbone Place. It was a favorite place of meeting for Crowley's friend Nancy Cunard and her many associates and friends. Patronized by George Bernard Shaw, and by Crowley's friend, artist Augustus John, the "Eiffel Tower" had been a haunt of the Prince of Wales, before becoming king, and subsequently abdicating for love in 1936. Crowley gave the second lecture on yoga on Wednesday, February 24, 1937, while Republicans fought Nationalists at the Battle of Jarama, southeast of Madrid during the Spanish Civil War.

The lectures were extremely funny, terse and erudite where appropriate. No pomposity, however, remains unpricked, as the guru lays waste the myths of centuries, and delivers what is arguably the clearest exposition of the eight limbs of yoga ever: the work of a master of his subject, displaying real willingness to communicate, as well as entertain.

> There is more nonsense talked and written about Yoga than about anything else in the world. Most of this nonsense, which is fostered by charlatans, is based upon the idea that there is something mysterious and Oriental about it. There isn't. Do not look to me for obelisks and odalisques, Rahat Loucoum, bul-buls, or any other tinsel imagery of the Yoga-mongers. I am neat but not gaudy. There is nothing mysterious or Oriental about anything, as everybody knows who has spent a little time intelligently in the continents of Asia and Africa. I propose to invoke the most remote and elusive of all Gods to throw clear light upon the subject—the light of common sense.[13]

"Yoga means Union." The statement was deliberately repeated, mantra-like. Nobody hearing the lecture could be in any doubt as to what yoga meant!

The initial seven lectures deal with the preparation for trance, the trances themselves, and what the trances mean: called trances, he says, because they transcend the conditions of normal thought. It all leads powerfully to a consideration of yoga and Magick in the eighth and final lecture, with Crowley boldly declaring: "Yoga training was an admirable aid to that final concentration of the Will which operates the magical ecstasy."[14] He wants it understood what he means by "Magick," and why he thinks it a way of life valuable to all. "Magick is the science and art of causing change to occur in conformity with the Will. How do we achieve this? By so ordering every thought, word and act, in such a way that the attention is constantly recalled to the chosen object." [15] To Crowley's brain, profundities seem commonplace:

> At this point we begin to see an almost insensible drawing together of the path of Yoga which is straight (and in a sense arid) with that of Magick, which may be compared with the Bacchic dance or the orgies of Pan. It suggests that Yoga is ultimately a sublimation of philosophy, even as Magick is a sublimation of science. The way is open for a reconciliation between these lower elements of thought by virtue of their tendency to flower into these higher states beyond thought, in which the two have become one. And that, of course, is Magick; and that, of course, is Yoga.[16]*

In the fifth lecture the guru explores the analogy between yoga and the sexual process, with, as usual, penetrating and interesting asides, or relevant digressions:

> It would be easy to develop this thesis by analogies drawn from ordinary human experiences of the growth of passion, the hunger accompanying it, the intense relief and joy afforded by satisfaction. I like rather to think of the fact that all true religion has been the artistic, the dramatic, representation of the sexual process, not merely because of the usefulness of this cult in tribal life, but as the veil of this truer meaning which I am explaining to you tonight. I

---

*It is also useful to see how, in a sense, the yogic process—especially in Sabhapaty's scheme—mirrors the classic Gnostic creation myth, but in reverse, so to speak. In the Valentinian creation scheme, for example, the universe and its false god stems from a disturbance in Mind that leads to an emanatory fall into time and space, with attendant sorrow and yearning. The yoga process entails beginning with realizing the fallen state of disturbed mind, and through rising back to the source of mind, aims through union, to heal the breach and overcome spiritual distress, replacing the false self with the True Self, or ego with divinity and so on.

think that every experience of life should be regarded as a symbol of the truer experience of the deeper life. In the Oath of a Master of the Temple occurs the clause: "I will interpret every phenomenon as a particular dealing of God with my soul."[17]

He makes a particular case for the relevance of yoga to art; he had chosen the right venue for such a point. The consciousness and practice of what he calls the "true artist" constitutes the aim of the yogi or the magician, but artists who embark on yoga will, nevertheless, especially benefit from the disciplines. Artists were not the only intended beneficiaries, for sure, as we shall see. But who could not be moved by Crowley's "Concise Compendium of Initiated Instruction"? I refer to something elicited from Crowley on the *terrasse* of the Café des Deux Magots where he was asked to proclaim the entire doctrine of yoga in as few words as possible. He did so:

Sit still. Stop thinking. Shut Up. Get Out![18]

On March 9, 1939, with the Second World War just seven months away, Crowley designed the dustcover for a new book: *Eight Lectures on Yoga*. That same day the first proofs arrived, much to his joy and relief. He celebrated with a walk, feeling free. The next day V. D. Freedland photographed him extensively for the dustjacket and frontispiece. There he appears as "Mahatma Guru Sri Paramahamsa Shivaji," author of the

Fig. 21.1. Mahatma Guru Sri Paramahamsa Shivaji (Aleister Crowley), Eight Lectures on Yoga. *(Portrait by V. D. Freedland, 1939; courtesy of Ordo Templi Orientis)*

work. One wonders if Crowley would have enjoyed more success in his life if he had impersonated this creation of his from the beginning of his teaching career, for experience has shown that people will believe practically anything if it emerges from someone who to Western eyes looks a bit exotic and mysterious; Typically, Crowley toyed with the image, but when it came to choosing the best image for the book, Crowley, interestingly, rejected the warmer image of himself (fig. 21.2).

Fig. 21.2. Aleister Crowley as guru. (Portrait by V. D. Freedland, 1939; courtesy of Ordo Templi Orientis)

Fig. 21.3. "Aleister Crowley as a yogi in an Indian village"; caption incorrectly given to this studio portrait used in the prospectus for The Spirit of Solitude—*Crowley's "Autohagiography" (Mandrake Press, 1929).*

YOGA AND THE WAR

Crowley's diaries are nearly always interesting, but sometimes one is teased by information, and left wondering how much more of a story lies behind brief references to many people largely or completely forgotten. For example, on Monday, February 24, 1941, with the war entering its most painful phase for Great Britain, he wondered if one "Major Penny" might "help in Magical Symbol scheme." The scheme referred to here was Crowley's plan for the famous "V for Victory sign," whose creation by Crowley is detailed in my *Aleister Crowley: The Biography*.

But who was Major Penny?

The *Aircraft Engineer & Airships* magazine of June 9, 1927, records, in its Birthday Honors section, the award of an O.B.E. (Order of the British Empire medal) to Major Rupert Ernest Penny, Principal Technical Officer, Air Ministry (late of the R.A.F.). Major Penny also appears in that capacity in the *Edinburgh Gazette* of June 7, 1927.

Rupert Ernest Penny was born in Nagpur and baptized in Kamptee, Bengal, in 1884. A flight lieutenant in the Royal Navy Air Service during World War One, he subsequently joined the R.A.F. where he distinguished himself as an engineer in the design of seaplanes.

In February 1941, Major Penny was on sick leave in Torquay, on the Devon coast, where Crowley was also living at this time. The Palace Hotel, Torquay, was the R.A.F.'s officers' convalescent establishment. On February 25, Crowley recorded how his doctor, Dr. Lodge, "sent his Xmas 'Yoga' [Crowley's *Eight Lectures on Yoga*] to Major Penny who is here [Torquay] on sick leave." Having been born in India, perhaps Major Penny had personal or sentimental reasons for wanting to read a (relatively) new book on yoga by Aleister Crowley. Crowley's diary records he sold him his "last available *Yoga*," adding that Major Penny wanted a course of training, if only Crowley had been in London. "I will suggest a correspondence," noted Crowley.[19] Was Crowley teaching yoga to other military officers? Rāja (royal) yoga would have been excellent training for officers under stress of interrogation as well as other stresses connected with covert operations. Crowley was an acknowledged authority on a subject that was still new and mysterious to most people. At this time, Torquay hosted an important R.A.F. Aircrew Reception Centre (A.C.R.C.) with extensive training facilities. The

Torquay area would also become an important area for drafting suitable volunteers for S.O.E. (Special Operations Executive), engaged in undercover operations on the German-occupied continent. It may also be worth observing that Crowley attributed his arrival at Torquay to preternatural forces, that is to say, the will of his Holy Guardian Angel, as he related in his diary of March 23: "These works from Feb. 19 are most interesting, I was entirely controlled by my H.G.A. [Holy Guardian Angel] acting swiftly, secretly, and 'irrationally': i.e. according to a plan based on facts of which A.C. [Aleister Crowley, himself, the man or instrument of the H.G.A] had no knowledge whatever." He described his journey to Torquay as "automatic."[20]

In March 1943, in the midst of war, Crowley met Mrs. Anne Macky,* whom he would affiliate to the O.T.O. as *Soror Fiat Yod,* even though she was already a Co-Mason. In August 1943 they agreed to a contract whereby she would write him some fifty letters enquiring about any subject relating to Magick that she felt wanted a plain answer, or an answer at any rate. It began as "Aleister Explains Everything" and was intended to fill a gap *Magick,* the magnum opus, had failed to fill, that is, a perceived need for an easily accessible, even colloquial manual that, as it were, got onto the level of the ordinary intelligent enquirer in a practical manner with no fuss. After his effort, and reasonable success, in *Eight Lectures on Yoga,* Crowley felt up to the challenge, and the correspondence began. Sadly, Crowley did not live to see the finished work in print, and while his successor in the O.T.O. Karl Germer in the 1950s made a very limited rough typescript edition of what Crowley

---

*Anne Macky (b. Fitzroy, Australia, February 8, 1887, d. Melbourne, Australia, 1964.) Born Anne Maria Hawkins, Macky received the Senior Certificate of the Royal Academy of Music, London, and taught music at Williamstown, Ballarat, and Brighton in Victoria, Australia. She married her second husband, New Zealander Dr. Stewart Macky, in 1916, sharing with him a belief in the soul-elevating power of music as well as enthusiasm for Rudolf Steiner's anthroposophy. After establishing a "People's Conservatorium" in Victoria, the couple immigrated to England in 1932 where they joined spiritually minded artistic and musical circles. Mrs. Macky met Crowley on March 12, 1943. A mostly friendly relationship, it, being creative, had its ups and downs. This information comes thanks to recent research by Heather Schubert. Her essay about Anne Macky, "The Unknown Soror," appears in the anthology *Daughters of Babalon,* vol. II, and includes confirmatory research by Barbara Chapman.

had cheekily retitled *Magick without Tears,* Israel Regardie's basic edited version did not appear until 1983. We must await Stephen King's new, properly prepared edition with keen anticipation; it is a thrillingly entertaining and highly communicative work.

Magick without Tears gives us a new slant on the place of Buddhism in what Crowley calls "The Three Schools of Magick." It is included in what he calls the "Black School," with no inference relating to black magic, but rather on account of its negative assessment of life in this world. The "White School," however, is wholly in the active, and therefore optimistic realm; it is worth doing things; will has purpose other than its own annihilation. The "Yellow School" is reserved for an indifferentism, something like Taoism, for example, content to observe, and accept that "going with the flow," passionless, may constitute wisdom, and that only the slightest adjustments need be made to accord life its harmony with the eternal Tao of the universe. All in all, it is a thought-provoking, eminently useful series of letters.

Crowley also relates certain Buddhist practices to the vital maintenance by students of the Magical Diary: "The construction of this Record is, incidentally, the first step in the practice called Sammasati, and leads to the acquisition of the Magical Memory—the memory of your previous incarnations."[21]

Having said what he willed about the Magical Record, he declares "the way is now clear to set forth our Method. This is twofold. (1) Yoga, introversion. (2) Magick, extroversion. (These are rough but useful connotations.)[22] As in *Eight Lectures,* Crowley is keen to assert the unity of the yogic and the Magical methods.

> To study Yoga, you have my *Book 4, Part One,* and my *Eight Lectures on Yoga.* Then there is Vivekānanda's *Rāja Yoga* and several little known Hindu writers [like Sabhapaty]; these latter are very practical and technical, but one really needs to be a Hindu to make much sense of them. The former is very good indeed if you remember to switch off when he slides into slipperiness, which luckily is not often.[23]

Again Crowley emphasizes the practical point that the various practices are intended to prevent the body from interrupting the mental process:

"The process of analyzing, developing, and controlling the mind is the essence of all Yoga practices."[24]

In the light of what we shall discuss in the next chapter, Crowley had interesting things to say in *Magick without Tears* regarding Indian tantriks, seeing them as an early stage of his "White School of Magick."

> Paradoxical as it may sound the Tantrics are in reality the most advanced of the Hindus. Their theory is, in its philosophical ultimatum, a primitive stage of the White tradition, for the essence of the Tantric cults is that by performance of certain rites of Magick, one does not only escape disaster, but obtains positive benediction. The Tantric is not obsessed by the will-to-die. It is a difficult business, no doubt, to get any fun out of existence; but at least it is not impossible. In other words, he implicitly denies the fundamental proposition that existence is sorrow, and he formulates the essential postulate of the White School of Magick, that means exist by which the universal sorrow (apparent indeed to all ordinary observation) may be unmasked, even as at the initiatory rite of Isis in the ancient days of Khem.[25]

Perhaps Aleister doesn't explain *everything,* but he certainly gives the impression that everything *has* an explanation, but you may have to rise very high indeed to find it. It has been said that experience is a fine teacher, but her fees are very high. Aleister Crowley paid the fees, and gave to us the benefit, for which gift he has been accorded the customary gratitude of this world.

TWENTY-TWO

The Coiled Splendor

It has been widely stated, and inferred, that Crowley's knowledge of "sexual magic" derived from India, and in particular, from varied traditions known to the West collectively as "tantra." "Tantriks" use sex as part of devotional, meditative, and magical rites. There is, however, much confusion on the issue. For example, yoga focusing on the *kuṇḍalinī* or coiled energy in the mūlādhāra chakra has sometimes been considered a privilege of tantric, that is, spiritual-sexual knowledge. This is not so, as we have seen in Sabhapaty Swami's treatment of Vedantic rāja gnosis where the ecstasy of samādhi is the reward of the able, sole practitioner.

The Book of the Law seems to exhibit specific knowledge of kuṇḍalinī yoga, or something akin, in several passages, to be directed toward Nuit, goddess of infinite space.

> But to love me is better than all things: if under the night stars in the desert thou presently burnest mine incense before me, invoking me with a pure heart, and the Serpent flame therein, thou shalt come a little to lie in my bosom. For one kiss wilt thou then be willing to give all; but whoso gives one particle of dust shall lose all in that hour. . . . Put on the wings, and arouse the coiled splendour within you: come unto me! (*AL* I:61)

Again, it should be emphasized that the English translation *kuṇḍalinī* derives from a Sanskrit word referring to a "coil." The English *splendour* may allude to the sephira "splendor" (Hod; also "glory") on the

Tree of Life, while "splendour and pride" occur earlier in this passage in the context of triumph, and there may be an allusion to Hod's complementary sephira Netzach, understood as "victory," "eternity," and "awe," with further allusion to the "power and the glory for ever and ever" of the Paternoster. Already in summer 1904, Aleister Crowley outlined a ritual involving himself and his wife Rose, with an obvious erotic component, as each performed the office of divine powers Nuit and Hadit.

> I am the secret Serpent coiled about to spring: in my coiling there is joy. If I lift up my head, I and my Nuit are one. If I droop down mine head, and shoot forth venom, then is rapture of the earth, and I and the earth are one. (*AL* II:26)

The idea of tantra as a, or even *the* source for sexual magic has been attributed to O.T.O. founder Carl Kellner's yoga research and, more pointedly, from Kellner's colleague in matters masonic, Theodor Reuss. Once Reuss realized Crowley had already grasped the essential nettle concerning the "mystic rose" and the "mystic rood," (in Crowley's *Book of Lies*) he decided to entrust the O.T.O.'s secret of the IX° to Crowley in 1912, making the Englishman head of a British branch of the Order (Mysteria Mystica Maxima). Scholar of Western esotericism Henrik Bogdan, while emphasizing Reuss and Kellner's overwhelming debt regarding sex magic to the neo-Rosicrucian Hermetic Brotherhood of Light, and to its offshoot, Max Theon's Hermetic Brotherhood of Luxor (embodying Paschal Beverley Randolph's sex magic), nonetheless located an element of Reuss's interest in Indian theories and practices.

In September 1912, O.T.O. journal *Oriflamme* contained Reuss's thoughts on the nadīs (described as "nerve centers") and the *vāyus,* or five "winds" of prāṇa associated with head, throat, navel, heart and lungs, and lower abdomen, which Reuss seems to confuse with the chakras: "Now, sexual magic deals with the Vayus Napa (in the reproductive organ), specified in the sixth place."[1] Reuss referred specifically to tantric tradition in his short article on "Mystic Anatomy," in July 1913's issue of the *Oriflamme:* "The Sympathicus is played on by the Tantrikas, the writings of Sakti, or worship of female energy."[2]

Crowley himself, in Part XVI of his restricted treatise *De Arte Magica* (1914), paid attention to prāṇa residing in *bindu* (semen), and its mystical and magical use, distinguishing between semen obtained in mystical rites, requiring reabsorption into the body; and magical rites where semen constituted an elixir for consumption or talismanic smearing on significant objects. Gerald Yorke's copy of Kenneth Grant's *Aleister Crowley and the Hidden God* in the Warburg Institute contains Yorke's marginal note that Crowley "did get Tantrik knowledge from Subhapati-Swami [*sic*] in Madras, or so he told me." Yorke may have misremembered, as Crowley made no written reference ever to meeting the swami in person, which he would surely have done had they met. Indeed, on several occasions Crowley made it plain his encounters with Indians in south India in 1901 were brief and modest. He did recall obtaining information about Sabhapaty Swami's work while in Madura, however, though Sabhapaty Swami was not, as far as we know, a tantrik practitioner, and it should be emphasized that in India, *tantras* can be used as a general term for spiritual writings. It is possible Crowley obtained his actual copy of Sabhapaty's work on rāja yoga in Madras, where the Theosophical Society was based. Col. Olcott possessed his own copy in south India (see page 88). Crowley makes no reference to Sir John Woodroffe's translations of tantric sexual works, though it seems unlikely he was unaware of them.

The fact is that Crowley's conception of sexual magic had been formed predominantly from Persian sources (such as Hafiz) accessed by his hero Sir Richard Burton, enriched by neo-Rosicrucian writings and imagery, which included alchemical imagery (sun and moon combined in *mysterium coniunctionis*), further adumbrated by the P. B. Randolph–influenced sex magic of the Hermetic Brotherhood of Luxor through Reuss, and by Hargrave Jennings's phallicist *The Rosicrucians, Their Rites and Mysteries* (1879). Crowley did practically nothing in the way of systematic experiment until charged with the secret's rudiments by Theodor Reuss in 1912.

Sex, for Crowley, was essentially magical anyhow. After intense experimentation in using sex specifically for willed ends in the United States 1914–1919, he would come to refer to IX° sex magic in his diaries with a symbol of a cross superimposed over a smaller circle ⊕. This figure represented a combined rose and cross and denoted a fecund rite of "sacrifice," that being Crowley's interpretation of the chief symbol of Rosicrucianism. What he obtained from yoga in the matter was not so much the theory, as the training of the will to one-pointedness, to concenter, or concentrate energy.

In point of fact, we owe the idea that O.T.O sex magic should be seen as predominantly tantric chiefly to enthusiasms engendered within a young Kenneth Grant, who had first written to Crowley for magical guidance in November 1944 when the mage was living at the Bell Inn, Aston Clinton, Buckinghamshire. By the end of December, Grant had become a student in the A∴A∴, assisting Crowley with chores connected with his move to Hastings, Sussex, in early 1945. Until July 1945, Crowley attempted to train Grant as his secretary, but eventually Grant's father persuaded young Kenneth to find a "proper job." Despite Crowley's protests to Mr. Grant senior that working for an international Order could bring great experiential benefits, Grant, as Crowley put it, needed his "greens," being in Crowley's disappointed view what was in those days called a "rabbit," someone who needed to be kept at home.

Grant developed a sometimes intense, lifelong curiosity for a man who first wrote to Crowley on September 1, 1944, desperate, after years of largely fruitless study, to see for himself some real magic! This was David Curwen (1893–1984), practicing alchemist, professional furrier, and member of the second grade of the "Order of Krishna," apparently based in India. Crowley would observe Grant's growing interest in Curwen in 1945 and 1946, and, while willing to concede Curwen knew "a hundred times" more about tantra than he (Crowley) did, he "would not advise it" (letter to Grant, spring equinox, 1946).[3] Crowley had his reasons, as we shall see, but Grant's respect for Curwen grew nonetheless.*

Thanks to Tony Matthews—David Curwen's grandson—and Henrik Bogdan, editor of Crowley and Curwen's correspondence (*Brother Curwen, Brother Crowley,* Teitan Press, 2010), we know a lot more about what passed between Crowley and Curwen on the subject of tantric secrets. In the course of a frequently unpleasant, irritable

---

*Henrik Bogdan in *Brother Curwen, Brother Crowley,* draws attention to Grant's acknowledgements in his *The Magical Revival* (1972), where Grant states he was initiated into the *vama marg,* or left-hand path, by a tantric adept. The "adept" was most likely Curwen, with knowledge from an unpublished typescript Curwen received from a supposed Indian guru in the 1930s of "an initiated Tantric work on the worship of the Supreme Goddess, by an Adept of the Left hand Path,"[4] the which, adapted by Grant, would constitute the sexual magic of his "Typhonian trilogy."[5]

correspondence of protest and counterprotest, humilities and forgiveness, exhortation and exasperation, Curwen not only badgered Crowley with impatiently expressed—if understandable—questions and demands for "signs," but felt forced to conclude that Crowley's knowledge of sex magic—the secret for which Curwen would needs pay a substantial sum should he, as he eventually did, enter the IX°—was inferior to, being already encompassed by, that vouchsafed to himself by an Indian swami Curwen had studied under for six years in the 1930s. Confronted by documentation, Crowley took Curwen's charge of inadequacy seriously and investigated, an investigation that led to puzzlement, the essential reason for which we can now discover.

THE SECRET TYPESCRIPT

In 1945, Curwen sent Crowley a typescript of what he had received from his guru. It was a commentary by one "Swami Pareswara Bikshu"* (Curwen treasured a photograph, allegedly of this otherwise untraced swami) on the *Ananda Lahari* ("Wave of Joy"), first part of tantric text *Soundarya Lahari,* attributed to eighth-century advaitist, Shankara: a hymn in praise of Shiva's consort, Parvati. Curwen had hoped to impress Crowley in his first letter (September 1, 1944) with the news that *his* teacher not only imparted the "Bhairavī Dīkshā" but was actually a friend of Crowley's "teacher" at Madura, India: a claim Crowley denied in a letter to Curwen of September 11, 1945:

> I cannot understand why your teacher should be so careless of fact. His letter says: "He [Crowley] was the student for a time of a brother of mine staying at Madura." I was only at Madura for three days and was nobody's pupil. I had a casual conversation for a couple of hours one morning with a local Camille,† but there was no suggestion of any sort about tuition.[6]

---

*"Swami Pareswara Bikshu" is not really a name. It means "the teacher *belonging to* the supreme god (or simply, *The Supreme Lord*), with "Bikshu"meaning either a Buddhist monk or a Hindu renunciate, who has accepted Sannyasa, subsisting on alms.
†The word *camille* here can mean a perfect girl, kind in every way, a virgin, or a virgin acolyte at an altar, male or female.

However, as Crowley's letter to Curwen goes on to recount, there is the possibility that it wasn't Crowley's "teacher" (be it male or female) that Curwen's alleged guru knew, but simply someone who, *if* we choose to give the tale the benefit of the doubt, helped Crowley into exclusive temple precincts, and who might plausibly have exaggerated that role in conversation with another. It may seem more likely, however, as we delve more deeply into the matter, that the Madura story was simply lifted out of the second volume of Crowley's *Confessions* (published by Mandrake Press in December 1929), or from one of Crowley's magazine articles about India, in expectation that it would never be checked. Crowley tried to enlighten Curwen about his Madura experience:

> One incident at Madura is however very interesting, though it does not bear on the point at issue. I got on the right side of the local *mahant** and persuaded him to introduce me to a part of the temple where he said no European had previously been allowed, and there sacrificed a goat. At this time I was travelling entirely alone, except for a servant that I had brought from Ceylon. When I got to Madras I sent him back and awaited the boat to Calcutta. The weather being very stormy the steamer was not able to get into the harbor and I was shipped on to it in a wherry of sorts. In this way my connection with the past was completely broken.†
>
> I don't know why you think that I shall think more kindly of your teacher because he speaks so well of me. If he did, it would make no difference, but I cannot see that he gives me credit for anything except the value of my publications.[7]

---

*Priest in charge of temple or shrine.

†It remains a mystery as to why Crowley's "connection with the past was completely broken," by leaving Madras, or *who* it was he had ceased communicating with. Crowley then more or less repeated the story told in his *Confessions* of how servants at Lambe and Thornton's Calcutta lodging knew he had sacrificed a goat at Madura, and that he was a magician, even though Crowley was sure no one could have got this information to Calcutta before his arrival by natural means. See page 94. However, it is worth mentioning that in 1901 there *was* in fact a train from Madras to Calcutta, the line having been completed in 1900. It took thirty-six hours to cover the 1,032 miles in wooden coaches, and there were no services on the train of any kind. Crowley says his passage by sea took over three days, so in point of fact, somebody *could* just have got the story about him to Calcutta before he arrived.

Judging from Grant's comments on the typescript document that came from Curwen's Indian teacher, its unique contribution seems to have come from criticism made of Crowley's attempts to prepare the elixir of life, that is, for not having recognized the value of what Grant called the "kalas, or psycho-sexual emanations of the woman chosen for the magical rites."[8] Well, by Crowley's own account of his elixir of life experiment in New York and New Hampshire in 1916, his recipe had worked only too well! (see my *Aleister Crowley in America* for a full account.) However, Crowley had done no specific work on the "kalas," and if this constituted the special point of the typescript, then there *was* something new in it for Crowley.

The word *kala* is, note, a masculine noun for "time," and also "black" since that is what "light" came out of at the creation (the power of the creation is what is harnessed in sexual magic and in tantra). Kala is obviously related to goddess Kali, of whom Crowley had intimate poetic experience, as we have seen.

Kali is in fact kala deified. Thus we see why the tantrik has been called devotee of the left (lunar, feminine) path; it is worship of the goddess primarily, or rather, worship *through* the goddess, hence the need for a sympathetic *suvacini,* or female partner and co-worshipper. It is a Shaivite nostrum that Shiva *is* in one aspect kala, and *therefore* his consort is Kali.

Now, Grant clearly associates kalas with feminine sexual fluids and magical force (perhaps a conclusion from the lost typescript commentary). This interpretation may be derived from writings such as the *Mahānirvana Tantra* where, during the dissolution of the universe, Kala (time) devours the universe, and is himself engulfed by the supreme creative force that is his wife, the blackness beyond time. This becomes a type for the creative sexual act, the absorption of the male within the female, the divine consummation, mirrored on earth by absorption of male sexual fluids within the female.

Crowley knew of the "eagle of the gluten," or female sexual fluids, primarily as the "solvent" of the "lion" or bindu. In fact, discussion on this point led, according to Grant, to one of Crowley's practical jokes, in that he sent Curwen round to Gerald Yorke's London apartment at 5 Montagu Square in search of "suvacini juice," bottled! Yorke was most amused. Nevertheless, it must have made Crowley at least wonder whether the state of mind and body of the sexual partner was even *more* important than he had hitherto suspected, and that the woman had a considerably more magically and spiritually active part to play than he may have allowed. Even though Thelema in its revealed writings is full of feminine energy (Shakti, if you like) and absolutely insistent on female complementarity, Crowley labored with deeply embedded, negative personal attitudes toward women, and this subconscious prejudice may have influenced his view of feminine sexual energies as being practically passive and even destructive in the negative sense. He was afraid of being dominated, but fantasized about it too: his sadomasochistic streak, which psychology might seem as being bound up with his peculiar relationship with his repressed mother.

Having seen the criticism in Curwen's document, he may have asked himself: had he *really* got a *complete* spiritual, as opposed to intellectual grasp of the potential of the "Scarlet Woman" or indeed every partner in IX° rites? His religion was, as he adumbrated frequently, "solar-phallic," and it is surely significant that there is no obvious feminine equivalent to this phrase, such as lunar—? —i.e: Have we been missing something? Well, none of Curwen's extant correspondence with Crowley suggests that *he* had seen the full significance of the lacuna in Crowley's conception of sexual magic, perhaps because as far as we may know at the time, Curwen's knowledge of tantric sex was not practical, a point Crowley repeated in their correspondence.

Now, as for the "Bhairavi Diksha," this phrase, which has been copied and repeated so confusingly from work to work, boils down to a tantric approach to the worship through sexual communion of Mahāvidyā goddess Bhairavī, a consort, naturally we may say, of Shiva. The name *Bhairavī* also means "terror" and "awe-inspiring," and she seems a worthy sister-in-law to Kali. Overflowing with Shakti, Bhairavī is a path to Shiva consciousness, as an aspect of Brahman.

And the *Dīkshā?* The "dīkshā" is something given in preparation for an act of devotion, so it can be a mantra, or a rite of initiation, or method or teaching. In a tantric context, it means Curwen's swami gave him means to commune through the goddess to attain samādhi, a kind of divine intoxication with the god and goddess mutually annihilating one another in absolute bliss—or what Crowley implied by multiplication of the infinitely great with the infinitely small (in *Berashith*), or Nuit and Hadit (after 1904), that produces "the" alogical positive Nothing.

When Crowley wrote to Gerald Yorke for his views on Curwen's document, Yorke informed Crowley that the Bhairavī Dīkshā came from what he called the "Kaula Circle." Well, a *kaula* or *kula is* a "circle," or family or group, or band of mutually supportive devotees of tantra who have chosen to identify themselves with a god or goddess. A kula consists of yogis and yoginis, known for flouting convention (as Crowley did) with a deliberately antinomian spirit, outrageous in any but a spiritual context, that binds the group together. In fact, a kind of Thelemic "kula" is somewhat akin to what Crowley had hoped to establish through his base at Cefalù, but perhaps he had not quite grasped all that was necessary for success. On the other hand, one suspects if he had established his community in India, he might have attracted thousands! However, that said, the so-called Kaula Circle has a more involved, and not at all scholarly, origin.

Crowley's unpublished diary for Monday, November 12, 1945, reveals Curwen eventually sent a book, *The Secrets of the Kaula Circle* by Elizabeth Sharpe (born 1888), to Crowley: "Chit [note or letter] from D[avid] C[urwen] with book *The Secrets of the Kaula Circle* by that snotty mongrel weasel Elizabeth Sharpe. Q[uer]y. Criminal libel on pp. 48–49? Saved by title page?"

Crowley's latter point referred to what could be taken as a disclaimer on the book's title page: "A tale of fictitious people faithfully recounting strange rites still practiced by this cult." Crowley's concern with possible criminal libel on pages 48–49 is borne out by Elizabeth Sharpe's text:

> I met a European who was one of X.Y.Z.'s pupils. He called himself by a number. In the beginning he was extremely handsome, afterwards he grew gross. The man of God is beautiful. He had many women at his disposal: and he spoke of them quite calmly and openly. He said that he had several children born to him by them thro' magic. He learned many magical processes by which he drew into his circle great phantoms.
>
> I witnessed one of his evocations: he had, with him, a pupil, a thin, long-nosed boy for whom I conceived a great pity. He was so

eager, so thrilled at all and so sincere: he sat very still, his eyes on the tip of that long nose of his, his long thin hands resting on each other, his legs crossed in the lotus posture. I wondered why he had followed the man whose number was 666: for his soul's sake, for the acquisition of good, or, for the acquisition of power? I suspected, always, that the last was the greatest force of all—for the poison of desire is hidden so insidiously in the flower that calls itself goodness as to be unseen before it darts out too late to recognise, to kill.

666 wore a ceremonial robe, had a pentacle, a wand, a sword and a cup. I watched him from my corner solemnly cleansing the altar with water shaken in drops from a blade of grass: and heard him chant Sanscrit mantras; whilst Tibetan acolytes waved censors of incense.

To the beasts the consolation of laughter is denied. I wished that 666 and the thin boy could have laughed. I can still see 666: he was tall and handsome. He had a strong jaw on a massive neck and in strange contrast, he had small, womanly hands showing up in the dusk, clear white patches, against his black robe. I watched that day the spirits he evoked with the help of the Lamas. They came first in smoky vapor, emanation of the impurity that comes from desire, and surrounded him like a smoke cloud. I saw spots form in that cloud, and each spot dragged round itself a little mote, a little less of his vital force; then enlarge and fall into the shape of phantom-figures called from the forgotten sarcophagi of the world: one of whom crowned with a diadem and wearing an Egyptian headdress of sorts came forward threateningly.

All 666's own life-force—expended at will on concubines, or evocations, and—afterwards? Afterwards! These withered husks of rash men and women declaim against God, and man; and vainly cry out for the happiness that life, no longer, holds for them. Have they who cried out ever added an iota to the happiness of the world? They, who expect gods, men and beasts unceasingly to contribute to their needs?

I saw 666 fall to the ground frothing at the mouth; yet he was training his pupil for the same ordeal. 666 wanted his pupil to strengthen his willpower and alertness. He told him not to use the word "the" or "no" in any conversation: and should he unwittingly transgress this injunction, he must gash himself on the arm with a knife to make the boy remember his mind's desire. This method, he thought, made the brain watchful. The poor boy was covered with gashes.

I am saddened for these wasted lives; and I hope the reading of this slender treatise will prevent the misguided enthusiasts of the world spilling the enthusiasm of youth before strange altars to unknown gods.

It is plain in Elizabeth Sharpe's book of "fictitious" characters that "666" is obviously Crowley, allegedly operating a so-called Kaula Circle, dominated by an evil character that Sharpe's story calls "X.Y.Z." who, according to Sharpe, was 666's teacher! This is likely the source of Curwen's alleged teacher's claim that he taught Crowley at Madura. According to Sharpe's story: "The cult of the Circle is already in vogue in Europe in secret places; and I must tell the world of it all."* Curwen is obviously very confused—not surprisingly, though we shall get to the root of that confusion in due course.

A month before receiving Sharpe's book, Crowley had sent Curwen's typescript commentary on the "Wave of Bliss" to Yorke. Having read Yorke's assessment, Crowley replied:

Thanks for yours. I do not know who wrote the typescript but the style of typing is very familiar to me, and I think it is a Babu [hired clerk] of some sort, as you yourself apparently do.

I could give you a whole lot of information, but not by writing, the subjects which these MSS. treat being unsuitable for that medium. The MS. was lent to me by Mr. David Curwen, 7a Melcombe Street, N.W.1, but I am not at all sure whether he will be pleased at me having disclosed his name. He is a very curious person.

I quite agree with you about the inherent difficulties in the Manuscript. One of the troubles is that, as you know, the Hindus have got an Anatomy of their own. That too, you seem to have noticed.

It is true that from what he writes it would appear that he is making everything depend almost exclusively upon the physical or physiological basis; but when you go into that with him you find there is

---

*The Secrets of the Kaula Circle (London: Luzac & Co., 1936), 44.

a whole lot of additional stuff about mantras and various magical methods, including secret medicines and the like. In a letter I got from him a day or two ago Curwen talks about their sending him certain Salts from India and speaks of a great deal of magical work having been done in India.*

It is all very puzzling. Naturally I got into contact with this subject quite a lot while I was in India, and on the whole I was repelled, though I had no moral scruples on the subject. I came to the conclusion that the whole thing was not worthwhile. They do a sort of Cat and Mouse game with you; they give you the great secret, and then you find there is something left out, and you dig up this and go for a long while in a rather annoyed condition, and then you find there is yet another snag. And so on, apparently for ever.

In any case it did not square with my ideas of initiation. I never wanted to do Hatha Yoga, "seek ye first the kingdom of God" etc.

I am interested and a little surprised at the extent of your knowledge of all these subjects. You must have put in a great deal of hard work."[9]†

A further letter, of November 7, 1945, from Crowley to Yorke, emphasizes that even his road to samādhi did not come through ordinary yogic channels:

I cannot agree that Asana and Pranayama are exclusively Hatha Yoga studies. The point surely lies in the motive. I have never wanted anything but spiritual enlightenment; and, if power, then only the power to confer a similar enlightenment on mankind at large.

I think you are wrong about my history. I did practically no Yoga of any kind after my return from my first journey to India. I attempted to resume practices at Boleskine and elsewhere, and could not force myself to do them. The Samādhi is a sort of by-product of the operation of Abramelin.[10]

---

*Note also the following advertisement on the title page of Sharpe's book on the "Kaula Circle": "*An Eight Hundred Year Old Book of Secret Indian Formulas and Medicine* (in the press). (Luzac & Co., London)." One might presume Curwen possessed the book.
†It is likely Yorke got his idea of the Kaula Circle from Sharpe's book.

Crowley had expressed a similar attitude to the Bhairavī Dīkshā when replying to Curwen's letter on the subject on August 21, 1945, where he attempted to get Curwen to see that had Curwen been familiar with the real India, then he would have known that he could find there umpteen recipes promising the sun and the moon, and any number of groups practicing accordingly. He insisted the O.T.O. provided disciplined teaching regarding otherwise dangerous "Ophidian Vibrations" (that is, "serpent" energy, or kuṇḍalinī).

> I have never come across what you call the Bhairavi Diksha, but in my wanderings through India I came across, I suppose, something like fifty different systems which made similar claims, and the training for which was equally eccentric.[11]

Crowley's frustration with an equally frustrated David Curwen is again evident in a letter of October 23, 1945:

> Dear Brother Curwen
> [. . .]
> I wish you would not jump to conclusions about other people's knowledge. If you had ever been to India you would know very differently. I was simply overwhelmed with all kinds of teachers and systems and books and mantras, and *shastras,* etc. most of it utterly worthless superstition, and I cannot help adding in many cases peculiarly disgusting, at least to me, and I feel quite sure to the average civilized human being. After a time one learned to recognize this sort of stuff at a glance and reject it, perhaps with undue haste without further consideration.[12]

Crowley was trying to impress upon Curwen that the O.T.O. IX° had its own doctrine and structure, and knowledge base, independently arrived at through years of experimentation. Curwen, a wary man fearful of being fleeced for knowledge of something he may already have known, was trying to come to a rational basis for paying considerable admission fees for the IX° degree. Crowley was not prepared to haggle over specific knowledge, only repeating that the value of the knowledge could only be arrived at by regular, attentive practice in a disciplined setting. He spoke also of other social benefits of the Order. In a letter of November 7, 1945, Crowley attempted to offer a taste of some practical knowledge from the Order's approach to sex magic, accepting that he was addressing an intelligently informed brother.

As you know certain schools teach that the amrita flows naturally and normally from the brahmarandra-Cakra [or "Sahasrara" chakra above the head crown]. This however caught by the fires of Agni in the stomach and its virtue destroyed. . . . You must not swallow the Elixir; it must be allowed to soak into the system through the mucus membrane.

The Elixir has of course to be treated as a talisman; that is to say, it has to be properly charged with magical energy so that it will perform the particular task for which you have created it. Nature can never be bought; when *Yod* impregnates *He, Vau* and *He* must finally be produced. Therefore if this *Vau* is inert and caused to waste, it may become the vehicle for one of the wandering Qliphoth.

. . . I have been assuming by the way that the use of mantras is the Indian equivalent of our methods of invocation and the like, by which we charge the Talisman.

. . . I have worked upon this crude secret as it was given to me for many years, and made literally thousands of experiments, but there are still many conditions of success which elude me. I consider myself doing very well if I am successful twice in three times. Much research still remains to be done.[13]

Curwen began to warm to the idea of investing in the IX°, perhaps encouraged by Crowley's words of December 5, 1945: "Another reason perhaps is that all along I have taken pains with you such as I have hardly ever taken with anyone else. I should have got rid of you long ago if I had not been certain—I cannot tell you why—that you were destined to play some very important role in this extraordinary drama."[14]

Curwen was initiated into the IX° on December 10, 1945, with Crowley's old friend, author Louis Wilkinson (Louis Marlow)—out of his depth—serving as witness as a favor to Crowley. Two days later, Curwen informed Crowley his motto would be Hebrew for "I trust in God," (*Ani Abthilal*) providing a careful kabbalistic account of its significant gematria. He became *Frater A.A.L.*, but was soon bitterly disappointed by the almost total lack of O.T.O. activity (in Great Britain, that is), finding Wilkinson vague and useless in giving him answers about the degree or the Order itself. In order to convince Curwen, there *was* life—and young life at that—in the O.T.O., he suggested Curwen contact Kenneth Grant; and much would come of that!

So, now we must attempt to address the question of who wrote the controversial commentary on *Ananda Lahari* and whence came Curwen's prior initiation?

THE LATENT LIGHT CULTURE

Kenneth Grant held the view that Swami Pareswara Bikshu was high priest of a Shakta temple in Travancore, a now-vanished kingdom of southwestern India, having been absorbed into Kerala state in 1949. Grant offers no information as to what temple this swami was "high priest" of.

However, what we do know is that Curwen's contact with the alleged swami came as part of a correspondence course run by the "Latent Light Culture," a still-extant organization aimed at revealing to members divine light within them, as part of which effort the Latent Light Culture offered members graded access to an inner "Order of Krishna."

Founded by a Dr. T. R. Sanjivi in Tinnevelli (now Tirunelveli in south Indian state Tamil Nadu, some eighty-seven miles south of Madurai), we may observe its inspirational antecedents were in fact Western, Theosophical-type organizations, given a Hindu face, esoteric doctrine, and coloring. Interestingly, Tinnevelli was only twenty-eight miles west of the port known to Crowley as Tuticorin (now Thoothukudi), where he read Robert Browning during his 1901 sojourn in south India, contemporary with his encountering Theosophical leader, Col. Henry Steel Olcott, possessor and promoter of the work of Sabhapaty Swami.

A first look at material about the Latent Light Culture available today on the Net offers a striking apology from 1931. Blogger Phil Hine found the following announcement in two issues (vol. 26, issues 3–4) of the *Kalpaka,* the Latent Light Culture's magazine—itself closely modeled on Papus's Martinist-led organ of French occultism in the late nineteenth and early twentieth centuries, *L'Initiation.* The apology was current around the time Curwen became interested in Latent Light Culture.

> We are once again being taken to task for some of our writers quoting often the slogan of verse 18.63 of the Bhagavad Gita "Yatha ischasi tathha kuru"—of which we accepted Crowley's "Do what thou wilt shall be the whole of the law" as the best English paraphrase; and if there is so much public opposition to the very mention of Crowley's name we have to bow thereto, and do so. But that is not to deny that Crowley had been trained in India of men who were great Yogis such as Karunananda [the name means "bliss of compassion"], Sabapati Svami's disciple. In deference to occidental opinion we shall paraphrase the Gita dictum by the English in "Fulfill thy Will."[15]

Now here is something! It appears that we have Indian esotericists finding essential spiritual guidance from a Western occultist—not at all the way round we've come to expect.

In fact, scholar Henrik Bogdan had already noticed Crowley's presence in documents sent to Curwen by the Order of Krishna. On applying for the Order's third grade, the member had to state that "he (a) has accepted the First and greatest of all the Privileges of the Order, namely the Law of the Gita: *Yatha Ischasi Tatha Kuru—Do thy Will and Rejoice.*"[16] We now know why it did not state "Do what thou wilt." Indeed, one of those who complained to the Order about Crowley's doctrinal presence in the Order of Krishna was Dion Fortune (Violet Firth), founder of the Order of the Inner Light, and later herself a Crowley admirer, though wary of admitting it publicly!

Not all references to Thelemic doctrine were expunged. Curwen's Order of Krishna papers indicating he'd made the second grade were headed: "Do what thou wilt shall be the whole of the Law."[17] On page 17 of "Bhikshu's" *A Series of Eleven Lessons in Karma Yoga (The Yogi Philosophy of Thought-Use) and the Yogin Doctrine of Work,* published in 1928 by the Yogi Publication Society, Chicago—whose Indian agents were none other than Latent Light Culture, public manifestation of The Holy Order of Krishna—we find the following:

> Act Thou, therefore, when opportunity confronts you; responding to it, meeting it bravely, utilizing it, actively. "*Do* what thou wilt," say the Masters, "Shalt be the whole of the Law," of Dharma of Karma—only he who doeth is the Karmi; he who wills to do and doeth is the Karmi Yogi; the *Deed* is the *Karma,* his future, his destiny the harvest of his Thoughts and Acts. Your Deed is the expression of your will, the will in you; say then to yourself "I will" and the Act. So acting shalt thou not sin, says the Lord Krishna. . . . In this shall be the Ordinance (*Sastra*) for you Karmi Yogi, in the dictum of "Do what thou wilt" which shall be for thee the whole of the law, teaching you comprehensively what to do, what to avoid, this is only ordinance; "do what thou wilt, then do nothing else"; we shall repeat it constantly, without end, that you may be unified of will, that in all your act you may bring all the universe that is of you, that in your act the whole of you and not the puny portion of you miscalled the "I" at the threshold, at the outer gate of consciousness may act, and impress itself on the event that anyhow must be.[18]

Crowley would have been most interested, to say the least, to see how his work was being used, or manipulated, without his knowledge, and, further, that this was precisely where Curwen's superior-toned challenges to Crowley were coming from!

The Order of Krishna structure is, on analysis, close to Theosophical and fringe-Masonic organizations like Reuss's O.T.O., Co-Masonry, or others advertised in *L'Initiation* in Paris before World War One. It is no surprise in Krishna Order literature to find directions to becoming "Entered Apprentice" or to find the Third Grade "Prince" (*Rajanah*), nodding in the direction of such Masonic additional degrees as "Prince of the Royal Secret," and the like in the Ancient & Accepted and Ancient & Primitive Rites. No wonder Curwen's teacher claimed sympathy with Crowley! Crowley's work was being effectively plagiarized by what was effectively a New Thought–style self-help organization, with an implication that Crowley got his teaching from enlightened friends of the Latent Light Culture!

More information on the *Kalpaka** comes from Pat Deveney, writing for the *International Association for the Preservation of Spiritualist and Occult Publications* (IAPSOP) website.[19] Founded as a monthly in 1908 by the Latent Light Culture, *Kalpaka*'s masthead was very similar to that of its contemporary *L'Initiation* in Paris: "A Magazine of Knowledge / The Psychic Review of the East (India's Only Psychic and Spiritual Review) / The Quarterly Journal of Psychic, Occult, Spiritual Sciences, Joga and Tantra Shastra." Editors were R. T. Sanjivi, K. T. Ramasami, S. V. Rengasami; with Swami A. P. Mukerji, associate editor.

Theosophical-type journal the *Swastika* in June 1907 announced the *Kalpaka*'s aim as "the discussion of occultism in all its branches." It attempted to combine Indian wisdom with Western occultism. It promoted in India what Deveney calls "American-style magical New Thought," with interests in publishing (and plagiarizing) American New Thought authors like William Walker Atkinson (1862–1932)— claimed by one scholar as likely the real "Bikshu," though Atkinson himself died before Curwen's supposed correspondence with the swami ended. It is also interesting that the Yogi Publication Society, Chicago, published two books by Crowley's representative (at the time) C. S. Jones, in 1923. The *Kalpaka*'s principals' works were printed in America by Sydney A. Flower's Psychic Research Company and the Yogi Publishing Society, Chicago. Associate Editor Swami A. P. Mukerji's works received U.S. publication by the Yogi Publication Society (copyrighted there by the Latent Light Culture). As Deveney puts it, the Yogi Publication Society "returned the favor by plagiarizing Ramacharaka's (i.e., Atkinson's) lessons on drawing up, transmuting and storing the reproductive energy—the same lessons that Theodor Reuss had 'paraphrased' in the Jubilee Edition of the *Oriflamme*—publishing them in the United States in the 1920s as authentic Oriental Wisdom."

The journal's most successful correspondence course "in Occult Sciences" was "India's Hood Unveiled! Occult Mysteries Revealed!!" Purchasers could acquire "practical and simple ancient Hindoo methods for Clairvoyance, Vayusthambam (Levitation) and Samādhi (Burial Alive) and Spirit Sight at Will." Price: $3.00. Plagiarized by L. W. de Laurence of Chicago, the latter offered the same goods for

---

*The kalpaka tree was a tree that was said to give people whatever they wanted.

$2.00. *Kalpaka* came back with an advert in the *Swastika* in 1909 for lessons "in the development of the inner or occult powers. . . . The instruction includes development in such subconscious powers as: Personal Magnetism, Hypnotism, Mesmerism, Suggestive Therapeutics, Psycho-Therapeutics, Mind-Reading, Telepathy, Magnetic Healing, Development of the Will, Clairvoyance, etc., and their practical application to specific cases." There was plentiful interchange of articles with a great many U.S. periodicals. *Kalpaka* editors soon obtained university degrees when the magazine advertised in the Oriental University Register, the school catalogue of Helmuth P. Holler's degree mill in Washington, D.C. Favor for favor, the Latent Light Culture functioned as a "branch" of Oriental University, conferring its degrees widely (for a suitable fee) in its south India franchise area.

An advertisement in the *Occult Digest* of January 1939 informs us that the Latent Light Culture's Order of Krishna was "more ancient than the Masonic, Rosicrucian and other Mystic Orders." Aleister Crowley's work was picked up in 1931 when the journal accepted Crowley's "Do what thou wilt shall be the whole of the law" as best translation of a New Thought–style injunction found in the Bhagavad Gita—at least until it became a source of embarrassment after the Holy Order of Krishna's "Practical Instruction in Occultism (Yoga)" was reviewed in the December 1929 edition of the *Occult Review* by Dion Fortune.

> There is one point that may be raised, however. The Order appears to have for its slogan the words "Do what thou wilt shall be the whole of the law." This phrase has somewhat sinister associations in English ears and the organizers of the Holy Order would be wise not to employ it in literature intended for European circulation.[20]

The magazine changed its wording accordingly, as we saw above. Nearly a decade later, a letter from the institute's founder, T. R. Sanjivi, dated May 4, 1937, was reproduced in Elizabeth Sharpe's book *Indian Tales* (1939): "I find the translation of the MSS, on the 'Science of Breath' appended to your work 'The Secrets of the Kaula Circle' contains some useful notes to practitioners of prāṇāyāma, especially for those who seek material advantages. Have I your permission to reprint it and circulate same among the members of the 'Order of Krishna?'"

And that's where Yorke's and Curwen's—and Grant's—"Kaula Circle" came from. And we owe it to Phil Hine for finding this following little endorsement for the *Kalpaka*'s latest tantra wares in its July–September quarterly issue of 1950 (note: the "endorsement" could have been sent years earlier):

> Regarding the TANTRA LESSONS which you have sent, I have and have been reading them with considerable interest. . . . I am rather fascinated by it. I feel that with all my study that here indeed is one of the missing pages turning up at last. DAVID CURWEN. (London-England)

So much, I suspect, for Kenneth Grant's high priest from a Shakta temple in a lost kingdom! Crowley needn't have worried. It seems the only reason Curwen knew a "hundred times" more about tantra than Crowley did was because Crowley was not a paid-up subscriber to the *Kalpaka*!

> "Do what thou wilt shall be the whole of the Law" is the mantra of this lesson of Karma Yoga. There is no law beyond "Do what thou wilt"—Ishta Poorti—the ordinance is called in the Vedas.*

So what have we found? Only this, that unbeknownst to himself, Crowley's teachings had now, for some Indians anxious to construct an East–West spiritual ideas link through, and for, profitable business, become inseparable from those of the Indian masters! India was not only *in* Crowley, but now, Aleister Crowley was secreted in India's spiritual culture—imported for export, so to speak—as component of an allegedly authentic Indian yogic spiritual culture! Crowley would surely have seen the hilariously ironic aspect of this development, and would certainly have recognized, had he been made fully party to the information, that had he died in India, rather than in Hastings, in Sussex, he would very likely have been venerated with a shrine, as a saint.

---

*Bhikshu, *A Series of Eleven Lessons in Karma Yoga* (*The Yogi Philosophy of Thought-Use*) *and the Yogin Doctrine of Work* (Chicago: Yogi Publication Society, 1928), 33.

INDEPENDENCE

Only I see the century as a child
   Call Truth and Justice, Light and Peace,
    To guide;
Wisdom and Joy, and Love the undefiled,
   Lead up true worship, its eternal bride.
Stormy its birth; its youth, how fierce and wild!
   Its end, how glorified!

Crowley's prophecy of the oncoming century made in *Carmen Saeculare*—a prophetic poem written while sailing to the United States in July 1900—of a world unbound, tearing away from its chains toward a new freedom, would come true, in India's case, only a few months before the Beast himself departed the bounds of this world in December 1947. As Crowley slowly slipped away, India was reborn.

Addressing "the American people on the anniversary of their independence" from the decks of the SS *Pennsylvania* on July 4, 1900, Crowley had asked whether the United States would properly heed a global cry of the spirit for true freedom—and that cry, made, as he put it, in the "Hour before Revolt" was coming from India, racked with famine and disease:

From Ind—shall her summons awaken?
   Her voices are those of the dead!
By famine and cholera shaken,
   By taxes and usury bled,
In the hour of her torture forsaken,
   Stones given for bread!

Sadly, we do not have a record of Crowley's thoughts when, on August 14, 1947, India became independent of the British Empire. He was very ill that summer, and fading from this life, and made no diary entries at the time the British finally quit the jewel in the imperial crown. However, I think it fair to say that he would not have regarded the final settlement of India's independence as an unalloyed good in the direction of spiritual freedom. The move to Indian nationalist control was accomplished in great haste under the direction of Britain's Labor Party prime minister, Clement Attlee. Crowley's view of Attlee comes out in this diary snippet from the moment Attlee suddenly awarded the United Kingdom two days' holiday following the capitulation of Japan to the Allies in August 1945:

> Imbecile "nobody with a grocer's moustache" sprang two days "holidays" V.J. ["Victory in Japan"] on us at Midnight, breaking up everybody's plans and giving them no time to make new ones! Inconceivable asininity.[21]

The cause of the V.J. day came as a result of the United States dropping nuclear explosives on Hiroshima and Nagasaki on August 6 and 9, respectively, causing Japanese surrender. Crowley was much attuned to prophecies coming true in these times. Thus, he wrote to Louis Umfraville Wilkinson, suggesting the atom bombs were fulfillment of a prophecy in *The Book of the Law* whereby the god Ra Hoor Khuit promises "I will give you a war engine" whereby "ye shall smite the peoples; and none shall stand before you" (*AL* III:7–8). In Crowley's diary for August 23, he noted: "Wrote L.U.W. [Wilkinson] suggesting to panic the world with *AL*. III." That is, he could show them that current events were in tune with the establishment of the Law of Thelema!

"Nobody with a grocer's moustache" was Clement Attlee, who, by some horror of national stupidity (in Crowley's—and many others'—view), had wrested Britain's premiership from Winston Churchill in the country's democratic general election of July 1945, promising a socialist paradise. *Asinine* means extremely stupid, foolish, ridiculous, doltish, and other words of that type.

It was under Attlee's "watch" that Lord Louis Mountbatten, last viceroy of India, had been empowered to agree to a settlement for India's independence from the British Empire with nationalist leader Jawaharlal Nehru and Muslim representative Muhammad Ali Jinnah, that involved partition of the country into sovereign territories for the Hindu majority (India) and the Muslim minority (Pakistan), with Pakistan itself divided between east and west (East Pakistan is now Bangladesh). Partition would lead to unimaginable numbers of deaths, mass displacement, riots, arson, terrorism, murders, disease, starvation, and war, and many of the issues stemming from the original settlement; subsequent adjustments and conflicts continue to bring misery to the subcontinent. Crowley would have remembered the partition of Bengal in 1905, and the destabilization that that had caused, and would doubtless have preferred transition to have been a responsibility for deposed prime minister Churchill, whom Crowley greatly admired (they had much in common), who understood the profound character of the "darkest hour."

While fully recognizing the vast achievements of post-partition India, as we must, Crowley would certainly not have found it a boon to the future of the planet that a territorial settlement of such profound magnitude was based on a principle of religious incompatibility, for in the end, Crowley was of the conviction that the leaders of thought and action in the world should acknowledge the best of all inherited spiritual systems and work for the practice of a dynamic synthesis. Crowley's work in integrating many of the spiritual traditions of East and West gives us a legacy toward such a perhaps eventual accommodation, which Crowley saw as evolutionary, even though it would likely encounter the bitterest resistance from vested interests of the "Old Guard" of domineering and repressive religions, and novel enthusiasms.

In 1937, aware that another great war was coming, Crowley reissued *The Book of the Law,* given symbolically to representatives of all races, containing as an addendum his assessment of "The Next Step" for humanity:

Democracy dodders.

Ferocious Fascism, cackling Communism, equally frauds, cavort crazily all over the globe.

They are hemming us in.

They are abortive births of the Child, the New Aeon of Horus.

Liberty stirs once more in the womb of Time.

Evolution makes its changes by anti-Socialistic ways. The "abnormal" man who foresees the trend of the times and adapts circumstance intelligently, is laughed at, persecuted, often destroyed by the herd; but he and his heirs, when the crisis comes, are survivors.

Above us today hangs a danger never yet paralleled in history. We suppress the individual in more and more ways. We think in terms of the herd. War no longer kills soldiers; it kills all indiscriminately. Every new measure of the most democratic and autocratic governments is Communistic in essence. It is always restriction. We are all treated as imbecile children. Dora, the Shops Act, the Motoring Laws, Sunday suffocation, the Censorship—they won't trust us to cross the roads at will.

Fascism is like Communism, and dishonest into the bargain. The dictators suppress all art, literature, theatre, music, news, that does not meet their requirements; yet the world only moves by the light of genius. The herd will be destroyed in mass.

The establishment of the Law of Thelema is the only way to preserve individual liberty and to assure the future of the race.

In the words of the famous paradox of the Comte de Fénix—The absolute rule of the state shall be a function of the absolute liberty of each individual will.

All men and women are invited to cooperate with the Master Therion in this, the Great Work.

Aleister Crowley's epic engagement with the land and thought of India had made such insight possible. Whether that engagement will render his vision any more likely as a reality is a question we may leave to you the reader, and to posterity, into whose hands this account is given.

Notes

INTRODUCTION. TIPPING POINT FOR INDIA: CATALYST FOR CROWLEY

1. Edwardes, "The Coming of the Raj," 336.
2. Crowley, *Confessions*, 282–85.
3. Edwardes, "The Remote Elite," 869.
4. Edwardes, "Revolt against the Raj," 1905.
5. Dilks, "A Most Superior Person," 1632.

CHAPTER ONE. GO EAST, YOUNG MAN!

1. Wachtmeister, *Reminiscience of H. P. Blavatsky and the Secret Doctrine*, 56–57.
2. Cranston and Williams, *The Extraordinary Life and Influence of Helena Blavatsky*, 50–51.
3. Johnson, *The Masters Revealed*, 19.
4. Johnson, *The Masters Revealed*, 23.
5. "H. P. Blavatsky's Adieux," *Daily Graphic* (New York), Dec. 10, 1878, 266. In Caldwell, *The Esoteric World of Madam Blavatsky* (selection 7g).
6. Sinnett, *The Occult World*, cited in Caldwell, *The Esoteric World of Madam Blavatsky*, 127.
7. Caldwell, *The Esoteric World of Madam Blavatsky*, 129.
8. Olcott, *Old Diary Leaves*, in Caldwell, *The Esoteric World of Madam Blavatsky*, 130–31; also in "Voyage with Madame Blavatsky: The

Summary Manner in Which She Silenced a Sceptical First Officer," *Philadelphia Enquirer,* May 11, 1891, 5; reprint in *Canadian Theosophist* 70 (Jan.–Feb. 1990): 121–23.

9. Dharmapala, "On the Eightfold Path," 720–27, 769–70.

10. Caldwell, *The Esoteric World of Madam Blavatsky,* 134.

11. Caldwell, *The Esoteric World of Madam Blavatsky,* 134.

12. Caldwell, *The Esoteric World of Madam Blavatsky,* 135.

13. Caldwell, *The Esoteric World of Madam Blavatsky,* 135.

14. Caldwell, *The Esoteric World of Madam Blavatsky,* 137.

15. Caldwell, *The Esoteric World of Madam Blavatsky,* ch. 10, para. 3.

16. Roy, *From Hinduism to Hinduism,* ch. 8, para. 1–2.

17. Roy, *From Hinduism to Hinduism,* in Caldwell, *The Esoteric World of Madam Blavatsky,* 192.

18. Arvidsson, *Aryan Idols,* 21.

19. Arvidsson, *Aryan Idols,* 24.

20. Arvidsson, *Aryan Idols,* 25.

21. Conway, "The Theosophists."

22. Conway, *My Pilgrimage to the Wise Men of the East,* chapter 10, 195–214.

23. Conway, *My Pilgrimage to the Wise Men of the East,* chapter 10, 195–214.

24. Hodgson, "Account of Personal Investigations in India, and Discussion of the Authorship of the 'Koot Hoomi' Letters," 207–380.

CHAPTER TWO.
FALL-OUT AND FALL-IN

1. Bell, "Being Creative with Tradition," 4–9.

2. See Gombrich, *How Buddhism Began,* 17–18, 60, 97, 142.

3. Bell, "Being Creative with Tradition," 6.

4. Reproduced in Holroyd, *Magic, Words and Numbers,* 120. The handwritten heading reads: "The Adeptus I.A. CHAB.A.Mac.G." (Bennett called himself "Allan MacGregor," in line with Mathers's assumptions of Jacobite MacGregor lineage; Crowley would also take the name on occasion) above a composite photo of Bennett, under which is handwritten: "Al Ayn ben Ayt [Allan Bennett]—Ananda Metteya."

5. See Harris, "Ananda Metteyya," 172.

6. Gombrich, *How Buddhism Began,* 28.

7. Gombrich, *How Buddhism Began,* 31.

8. Gombrich, *How Buddhism Began,* 33.

9. Obituary in *The Buddhist,* April 28, 1923, 6. Cited by Harris, "Ananda Metteyya," 172.

10. Pereira, "Why Do I Renounce the World?" *Ceylon Daily News,* No. 2491 (Colombo, Sri Lanka), dated "Vesak," that is, Sri Lanka's "Buddha Day" (first full moon in May), 1947, 67. Cited in Harris, "Ananda Metteyya,"172–73.

11. Crowley, *Confessions,* 249.

12. Pereira, "Why Do I Renounce the World?" 67.

CHAPTER THREE.
THE BEAST IN COLOMBO

1. "The Writings of Truth," Yorke Collection (Y.C. N20); Japanese vellum diary; August–October 1901, Ceylon. The version of the diary used by William Breeze in his unpublished AC Diaries is from Gerald Yorke's typed transcript of contemporary "written-up" versions of the 1901 diary, copied in 1954 from a holograph notebook of Dr. Jan P. Kowal (present whereabouts unknown). The typescript used by Breeze is a carbon copy by Yorke sent to Kowal, which passed to successors in the Universal Brotherhood, acquired by O.T.O. Archives from The Book Baron in Anaheim, California, 1995. The notebook with the original working diary is in the Y.C. (consulted by the author). Both sources were used in "The Temple of Solomon the King" in the *Equinox* 1, no. 4 (1910).

2. Crowley, "The Writings of Truth."

3. Crowley, *Confessions,* 232.

4. Crowley, *Confessions,* 233.

5. Crowley, *Confessions,* 233–34.

6. Crowley, *Confessions,* 236.

7. Crowley, *Confessions,* 235.

CHAPTER FOUR. TO KANDY

1. Y.C. D6.

2. Crowley, *Confessions,* 236.

3. Crowley, *Confessions,* 246–47.

4. Crowley, *Confessions,* 236.

5. Crowley, *Confessions,* 246.

6. Y.C. D6. A.1a, Crowley to Gerald Kelley from "Marlborough," Kandy.

7. Crowley, *The Sword of Song.*

8. Crowley, *The Sword of Song.*

9. Crowley, *Magick, Liber Aba,* 199.

10. Crowley, *Confessions,* 240.

11. Crowley, *Confessions,* 240.

12. Crowley, *Confessions,* 241.

13. Crowley, *Confessions,* 242.

14. Crowley, *Confessions,* 243.

CHAPTER FIVE.
BIG GAME, SMALL GAMES

1. Crowley, "On A Burmese River," part four, February 24, 1909: 232.

2. Crowley, *Confessions,* 255.

3. Crowley, *Confessions,* 225.

4. Crowley, *Confessions,* 255.

CHAPTER SIX.
THE AIM IS BEING: CALCUTTA

1. Crowley, *Confessions,* 256.

2. Crowley, *Confessions,* 256.

3. Crowley, *Confessions,* 257.

4. Crowley, "On A Burmese River."

5. Crowley, "On A Burmese River."

6. Crowley, *Confessions,* 259.

7. The 1902 Indian diary, currently being edited by William Breeze, was formerly in Major General J. F. C. Fuller's collection, his having used Crowley's typescript for compiling "The Temple of Solomon the King" for the *Equinox.*

8. Crowley, *Confessions,* 260.

9. Crowley, *Confessions,* 261.

10. Unpublished 1902 diaries, edited by William Breeze. These two extracts cited by Crowley in *Confessions,* 262.

11. Crowley, *Confessions,* 262.

12. See Martin, *Under the Absolute Amir.*

CHAPTER SEVEN.
BURMA—BY TRAIN, BOAT,
AND PADDLE STEAMER

1. Crowley, *Confessions*, 262.
2. Crowley, *Confessions*, 264.
3. Crowley, "On A Burmese River."
4. Photographs exist of the Dalla Dockyard, as well as the *Amherst* and *Pulu* at the Royal Museums Greenwich, UK.
5. Crowley, *Unpublished Diaries*, January 30, 1902.
6. Crowley, *Unpublished Diaries*, February 4, 1902.
7. Crowley, *Confessions*, 268–69.
8. Crowley, "On a Burmese River."
9. Crowley, *Unpublished Diaries*, February 8, 1902.
10. Crowley, *Unpublished Diaries*, February 12, 1902.
11. Smart, *Burma Gazetteer, Akyab District*, vol. B, 17.
12. See Gombrich, *How Buddhism Began*, 143.
13. Harris, "Ananda Metteyya," 174n30. Citing *Buddhism* 1, no. 1 (1903): 27.
14. Harris, "Ananda Metteyya," 174n30. Citing *Buddhism* 1, no. 4, 677–78.
15. Crowley, *Unpublished Diaries*, February 15, 1902.
16. Crowley, *Unpublished Diaries*, February 16, 1902.
17. Crowley, "On a Burmese River": "We were able, however, to talk of Buddhism, and our plans for extending it to Europe, most of the day. The next four days were occupied in the same way."
18. Crowley, *Unpublished Diaries*, February 16, 1902.
19. Crowley, *Confessions*, 273.

CHAPTER EIGHT. ACROSS INDIA

1. Crowley, *Unpublished Diaries*, February 23, 1902.
2. Crowley, *Unpublished Diaries*, March 2, 1902.
3. Crowley, *Unpublished Diaries*, March 8, 1902.
4. Crowley, "On a Burmese River."
5. Crowley, "On a Burmese River," part four, February 24, 1909.
6. Crowley, "Warning," preface to *Orpheus: A Lyrical Legend*.
7. Crowley, "On a Burmese River."
8. Crowley, *Unpublished Diaries*, March 14, 1902.

9. Crowley, *Unpublished Diaries,* March 15, 1902.
10. Crowley, "On a Burmese River."
11. Crowley, *Unpublished Diaries,* March 18, 1902.
12. Crowley, *Unpublished Diaries,* March 22, 1902.

CHAPTER NINE. K2

1. Crowley, *Unpublished Diaries,* March 24, 1902.
2. Crowley, *Confessions,* 279.
3. Crowley, *Confessions,* 283.
4. Guillarmod, *Six Mois dans l'Himalaya,* 151.
5. Guillarmod, *Six Mois dans l'Himalaya,* 161–62.
6. "The Expedition to Chogo Ri," part 4; originally published as an eight-part series in *Vanity Fair,* July 8, 1908: 51–52; July 15, 1908: 71–72; July 22, 1908: 106–7; August 5, 1908: 179–80; August 19, 1908: 246–47; September 2, 1908: 310–11; September 9, 1908; and September 16, 1908: 372–73.
7. Crowley, *Confessions,* 310.
8. Crowley, *Confessions,* 311.
9. Crowley, *Confessions,* 314.
10. Crowley, *Confessions,* 322.
11. Crowley, *Confessions,* 328.

CHAPTER TEN.
RETURN TO CEYLON, VIA BOLESKINE

1. Crowley, *Confessions,* 460.
2. Crowley, *Unpublished Typescripts,* June 9, 1903. In possession of O.T.O. made by G. J. Yorke from original notebooks—one is apparently a worked-up version of the other—in possession of Dr. J. P. Kowal; ed. William Breeze. Note by William Breeze: "From June 22 to July 6 there are two diaries, a pencil notebook that was probably the original record, given at left, and a 'written up' version, on right. Added only in brackets if extra information to right version. Or on right if completely additional."
3. Crowley, *Unpublished Typescripts,* June 11, 1903.
4. Crowley, *Unpublished Typescripts,* June 12, 1903.
5. Crowley, *Unpublished Typescripts,* June 16, 1903.

6. Crowley, *Unpublished Typescripts,* June 17, 1903.

7. Crowley, *Unpublished Typescripts,* June 23, 1903.

8. Crowley, *Unpublished Typescripts,* June 30, 1903.

9. Crowley, *Unpublished Typescripts,* June 30, 1903.

10. Crowley, *Unpublished Typescripts,* July 2–July 13, 1903.

11. Y.C. D6, Aleister Crowley to Gerald Kelly, 1903 undated.

12. Crowley, *Confessions,* 384; see also 276.

13. Crowley, *Confessions,* 374.

14. Crowley, *Unpublished Diaries,* February 1924.

15. Crowley, *Confessions,* 384.

16. Crowley, *Confessions,* 384.

17. Crowley, *Why Jesus Wept.*

18. Crowley, *Why Jesus Wept.*

19. "I MASQUERADE AS A PERSIAN PRINCE," Y.C. NS18: undated typescript, series of articles, 1930s.

20. Crowley, *Unpublished Diaries,* February 1924.

21. Crowley, *Unpublished Diaries,* February 22, 1904.

22. Crowley, *Unpublished Diaries,* February 22, 1904.

CHAPTER ELEVEN. THE WORKS 1901–1904

1. Crowley, *The Works of Aleister Crowley, with Portraits,* 261.

2. Crowley, *The Works of Aleister Crowley, with Portraits,* vol. 2, 36.

3. Crowley, *The Works of Aleister Crowley, with Portraits,* 36.

4. Crowley, *The Works of Aleister Crowley, with Portraits,* 38.

5. Crowley, *The Works of Aleister Crowley, with Portraits,* 44.

6. Crowley, *The Works of Aleister Crowley, with Portraits,* 44.

7. Crowley, *The Works of Aleister Crowley, with Portraits,* 45.

8. Crowley, "Time—A Dialogue between a British Sceptic and an Indian Mystic" in Crowley, *The Works of Aleister Crowley, with Portraits,* vol. 2, 276.

9. Crowley, *The Works of Aleister Crowley, with Portraits,* 49–51.

10. Crowley, *The Works of Aleister Crowley, with Portraits,* 51.

11. Crowley, *The Works of Aleister Crowley, with Portraits,* 201 (Notes to *The Sword of Song*).

12. Crowley, *Confessions.*

13. Crowley, *Confessions.*

14. Crowley, *The Works of Aleister Crowley, with Portraits,* 234.

15. Crowley, *The Works of Aleister Crowley, with Portraits*, 235.
16. Crowley, *The Works of Aleister Crowley, with Portraits*, 235.
17. Crowley, *The Works of Aleister Crowley, with Portraits*, 236.
18. Crowley, *The Works of Aleister Crowley, with Portraits*, 237.
19. Crowley, *The Works of Aleister Crowley, with Portraits*, 238.
20. Crowley, *The Works of Aleister Crowley, with Portraits*, 238.
21. Crowley, *The Works of Aleister Crowley, with Portraits*, 239.
22. Crowley, *Confessions*.
23. Crowley, *The Works of Aleister Crowley, with Portraits*, 244.
24. Crowley, *The Works of Aleister Crowley, with Portraits*, 249.
25. Crowley, *The Works of Aleister Crowley, with Portraits*, 249.
26. Crowley, *The Works of Aleister Crowley, with Portraits*, 250.
27. Crowley, *The Works of Aleister Crowley, with Portraits*, 252.
28. Crowley, *The Works of Aleister Crowley, with Portraits*, 253.
29. Crowley, *The Works of Aleister Crowley, with Portraits*, 254.
30. Crowley, *The Works of Aleister Crowley, with Portraits*, 255.
31. Crowley, *The Works of Aleister Crowley, with Portraits*, 257.
32. Crowley, *The Works of Aleister Crowley, with Portraits*, 258.
33. Crowley, *The Works of Aleister Crowley, with Portraits*, 258.
34. Crowley, *The Works of Aleister Crowley, with Portraits*, 260.
35. Crowley, *The Works of Aleister Crowley, with Portraits*, 260.
36. Crowley, *The Works of Aleister Crowley, with Portraits*, 261.

CHAPTER TWELVE.
THE WORKS II: "ASCENSION DAY" AND "PENTECOST"

1. Crowley, *The Works of Aleister Crowley, with Portraits*, vol. 2, 201.
2. Crowley, *Confessions*, 257.
3. Crowley, *The Works of Aleister Crowley, with Portraits*, 192–95.

CHAPTER THIRTEEN. 1905: JÑĀNA YOGA

1. A.C. to Gerald Kelly, October 12, 1904, Y.C. D6.
2. Crowley, *Unpublished Diaries*, O.T.O. typescript, 1905 diary, transcribed by G. J. Yorke circa 1954 from pencil notebook of Dr. Kowal; present whereabouts of original unknown, ed. William Breeze. Wednesday March 29, 1905.

3. Crowley, *Unpublished Diaries.*

4. Crowley, *Unpublished Diaries.* Gerald Yorke, transcribing Crowley's diary entries, copied his paraphrased summary of the method, which appears in a later section of the notebook.

5. Crowley, *Unpublished Diaries,* Friday, March 31, 1905.

6. For analysis of the biography, and an account of Sabhapaty's place in "Western Esotericism" and Indology, see Keith E. Cantú, "Śrí Sabhāpaty Swami: The Forgotten Yogi of Western Esotericism"; paper delivered at the American Academy of Religion annual meeting, San Antonio, Texas, November 2016.

7. Sabhāpati, *Om: The Philosophy & Science of Vedanta and Raja Yoga.*

8. Cantú, "Śrí Sabhāpaty Swami: The Forgotten Yogi of Western Esotericism," 6.

9. Sabhāpati, *Om,* 2–3.

10. Sabhāpati, *Om,* 6–7.

11. Sabhāpati, *Om,* 10.

12. Sabhāpati, *Om,* 12.

13. Sabhāpati, *Om,* 19.

14. Sabhāpati, *Om,* 24.

15. Sabhāpati, *Om,* 25.

16. Sabhāpati, *Om,* 26.

17. Sabhāpati, *Om,* 26–28.

18. Diary editor's note (William Breeze): "The Character of Breaks" appears in the typed transcript of the 1903 pencil diary, but dates after August 1905, as the last paragraph refers to two years of marriage. It appears in "The Temple of Solomon the King" by J. F. C. Fuller in the *Equinox.*

19. Crowley, *Unpublished Diaries,* Saturday, April 1, 1905.

20. Crowley, *Unpublished Diaries,* Sunday, April 2, 1905.

21. Crowley, *Unpublished Diaries,* Monday, April 3, 1905.

22. Crowley, *Unpublished Diaries,* Monday, April 3, 1905.

23. Crowley, *Unpublished Diaries,* Wednesday, April 5, 1905.

24. Crowley, *Unpublished Diaries,* Saturday April 8, 1905.

CHAPTER FOURTEEN.
KANGCHENJUNGA

1. Crowley, *Confessions,* 419.

2. Crowley, *Confessions,* 420.

3. Guillarmod, notebook entries for April–May 1905, my translation. Transcript is available in French from the website of the Fondation .lignieres.org.

4. Guillarmod, Notebook XIII, 11.

5. Crowley, *Confessions,* 422.

6. Guillarmod, Notebook XXIV, 11. July 31, 1905.

7. Guillarmod, Notebook XXIV, 11. August 17, 1905.

8. Crowley, *Confessions,* 429–30.

9. Crowley, *Confessions,* 430.

10. Guillarmod, Notebook XXIV, 12. August 22, 1905.

11. Crowley, *Confessions,* 431.

12. Crowley, *Confessions,* 432.

13. Crowley, *Confessions,* 434.

14. Guillarmod, Notebook XXIV, 12. August 28, 1905.

15. Crowley, *Confessions,* 438.

16. Crowley, *Confessions,* 439.

17. Guillarmod, Notebook XXIV, 12.

18. Crowley, *Confessions,* 439.

19. Crowley, *Confessions,* 440.

20. Guillarmod, Notebook XXIV, 13.

21. Guillarmod, Notebook XXIV, 14.

CHAPTER FIFTEEN. MOHARBHANJ

1. Crowley, *Confessions,* 447.

2. Crowley, *Confessions,* 448.

3. Crowley, *Confessions,* 451.

4. Crowley, *Confessions,* 452.

CHAPTER SIXTEEN.
GET OUT OF CALCUTTA QUICK!

1. Crowley, *Confessions,* 453.

2. Crowley, *Confessions,* 453.

3. Crowley, *Confessions,* 454.

4. Crowley, *Confessions,* 457–58.

5. Dilks, "A Most Superior Person," 1639.

6. Edwardes, "Revolt against the Raj," 1905.

7. Crowley, *Confessions,* 458.

CHAPTER SEVENTEEN.
RETURN TO BURMA

1. Crowley, *Confessions,* 458.

2. Crowley, *Confessions,* 465.

3. Crowley, *Confessions,* vol. 4, unabridged, ed. Hymenaeus Beta (William Breeze).

4. Crowley, reproduced in full in *Confessions,* 468.

5. Crowley, *Confessions,* 469.

CHAPTER EIGHTEEN. SAMĀDHI

1. Crowley, *Unpublished Diaries,* O.T.O. typescript by G. J. Yorke from pencil notebook original, ed. Hymenaeus Beta.

2. Crowley, *Unpublished Diaries.*

3. Crowley, *Unpublished Diaries.*

4. Crowley, *Unpublished Diaries.*

5. Y.C. D6. A.C. to Clifford Bax, March 28, 1906.

6. Crowley, *Unpublished Diaries,* May 1, 1906.

7. Crowley, *Unpublished Diaries,* April 30, 1906.

8. Crowley, *Unpublished Diaries,* May 31, 1906.

9. Crowley, *Unpublished Diaries,* July 17, 1906.

10. Crowley, *Unpublished Diaries,* July 27, 1906.

11. Crowley, *Unpublished Diaries,* August 4, 1906.

12. Crowley, *Unpublished Diaries,* August 10, 1906.

13. Crowley, *Unpublished Diaries,* October 9, 1906.

14. Crowley, *Confessions,* 556.

15. Crowley, *Unpublished Diaries,* ed. William Breeze, October 9–10, 1906.

16. Crowley, *Unpublished Diaries,* October 10, 1906.

17. Crowley, *Unpublished Diaries,* October 20, 1906.

18. Crowley, *Unpublished Diaries,* October 21, 1906.

19. Crowley, *Unpublished Diaries,* October 23, 1906.

20. Crowley, *Unpublished Diaries,* October 31, 1906.

21. Crowley, *Unpublished Diaries,* November 13, 1906.

22. Crowley, *Unpublished Diaries*, November 21, 1906.

23. Crowley, *Unpublished Diaries*, December 2, 1906.

24. Crowley, *Unpublished Diaries*, December 10, 1906.

25. Crowley, *Unpublished Diaries*, December 26. 1906.

26. Crowley, *Unpublished Diaries*, December 27, 1906.

CHAPTER NINETEEN.
I CAME FROM GOD THE WORLD TO SAVE: 1907

1. Crowley, *Unpublished Diaries*, January 6, 1907.

2. Crowley, *Unpublished Diaries*, January 6, 1907.

3. Crowley, *Unpublished Diaries*, January 6, 1907.

4. Crowley, *Unpublished Diaries*, March 11, 1907.

5. Crowley, *Unpublished Diaries*, March 17, 1907.

6. Crowley, *Unpublished Diaries*, March 17, 1907.

7. Hardy, "Half-Hours with Famous Mahatmas," 287.

8. Crowley, *Unpublished Diaries*, April 2, 1907.

9. Crowley, *Unpublished Diaries*, June 19, 1907.

10. Crowley, *Unpublished Diaries*, July 13, 1907.

11. Crowley, *Unpublished Diaries*, July 19, 1907.

12. Crowley, *Unpublished Diaries*, entry facing entries for Monday September 30, and Tuesday October 1, 1907.

13. Crowley, *Unpublished Diaries*, October 3, 1907.

14. Crowley, *Unpublished Diaries*, October 7, 1907.

15. Crowley, *Unpublished Diaries*, October 8, 1907.

16. Crowley, *Unpublished Diaries*, October 11–12, 1907.

17. Hardy, "Half-Hours with Famous Mahatmas," 290.

18. Shine, *Honour Thy Fathers*, 20. This book is a tribute to the late Venerable Kapilavaḍḍho Bhikkhu (William August Purfurst, known later as Richard Randall) for whom the English Sangha Trust was formed. He started and developed the founding of the first English Theravāda Sangha in the Western world.

19. Crowley, *Unpublished Diaries*, November 22, 1907.

20. Crowley, *Unpublished Diaries*, October 29, 1907.

21. Crowley, *The Holy Books*, xix.

22. Crowley, *Unpublished Diaries*, October 30, 1907.

23. Crowley, *Unpublished Diaries*, November 1907.

24. Crowley, *Unpublished Diaries*, December 2, 1907.
25. Crowley, *Unpublished Diaries*, December 15, 1907.
26. Crowley, *Unpublished Diaries*, December 25, 1907.

CHAPTER TWENTY. 777 AND BOOK 4

1. Crowley, *Magick, Liber Aba, Book Four*, lviii–ilx.
2. Crowley, *Magick, Liber Aba, Book Four*, 9.
3. Crowley, *Magick, Liber Aba, Book Four*, 10.
4. Crowley, *Magick, Liber Aba, Book Four*, 14.
5. Vivekānanda, *Rāja Yoga*, 227, quoting Sānkhya, book III, v. 30.
6. Crowley, *Magick, Liber Aba, Book Four*, 23.
7. Crowley, *Magick, Liber Aba, Book Four*, 31.
8. Crowley, *Magick, Liber Aba, Book Four*, 31.
9. Crowley, *Magick, Liber Aba, Book Four*, 31–32.
10. Crowley, *Magick, Liber Aba, Book Four*, 34.
11. Crowley, *Magick, Liber Aba, Book Four*, 37.
12. Crowley, *Magick, Liber Aba, Book Four*, 37.
13. Crowley, *Magick, Liber Aba, Book Four*, 37.
14. Crowley, *Magick, Liber Aba, Book Four*, 39.
15. Crowley, *Magick, Liber Aba, Book Four*, 39.
16. Crowley, *Magick, Liber Aba, Book Four*, 41.
17. Crowley, *Magick, Liber Aba, Book Four*, 42.

CHAPTER TWENTY-ONE.
SIT DOWN, SHUT UP, GET OUT!

1. Grant, *Remembering Aleister Crowley*, 52.
2. Eshelman, *The Mystical and Magical System of the A∴A∴*, 23.
3. Crowley, *Liber Aleph vel CXI, The Book of Wisdom or Folly*, 70.
4. Richmond, *Progradior and the Beast*, 178.
5. Richmond, ed., *The Magical Record of Frater Progradior*, 51.
6. Richmond, ed., *The Magical Record of Frater Progradior*, 72.
7. Richmond, ed., *The Magical Record of Frater Progradior*, 72.
8. Richmond, ed., *The Magical Record of Frater Progradior*, 80.
9. Yorke, *Aleister Crowley*, 210.
10. Yorke, *Aleister Crowley*, xxxi–xxxiii.

11. Crowley, *Unpublished Diaries,* March 31, 1936.

12. Crowley, *Unpublished Diaries,* July 31, 1936.

13. Crowley, *Eight Lectures on Yoga,* 7.

14. Crowley, *Eight Lectures on Yoga,* 74.

15. Crowley, *Eight Lectures on Yoga,* 72.

16. Crowley, *Eight Lectures on Yoga,* 71.

17. Crowley, *Eight Lectures on Yoga,* 44.

18. Crowley, *Eight Lectures on Yoga,* 32 (fourth lecture, "Yoga for Yahoos").

19. Crowley, *Unpublished Diaries,* February 25, 1941.

20. Crowley, *Unpublished Diaries,* March 23, 1941.

21. Crowley, *Magick without Tears,* 492. Unless otherwise noted references are to the 1983 Regardie edition.

22. Crowley, *Magick without Tears,* 492.

23. Crowley, *Magick without Tears,* 493.

24. Crowley, *Magick without Tears,* 493–94.

25. Crowley, *Magick without Tears* (Germer edition), 34–35.

CHAPTER TWENTY-TWO.
THE COILED SPLENDOR

1. Theodor Reuss, "Mysteria Mystica Maxima," *Oriflamme* 7 (Sept. 1912): 21–22. Cited in Crowley and Curwen, *Brother Curwen, Brother Crowley,* xxxii.

2. Theodor Reuss, "Mystic Anatomy," *Oriflamme,* July 1913, 4–7. Cited in Crowley and Curwen, *Brother Curwen, Brother Crowley,* xxxiii.

3. Grant, *Remembering Aleister Crowley,* 47.

4. Bogdan, introduction to *Brother Curwen, Brother Crowley,* xxviii.

5. Grant, *Remembering Aleister Crowley,* 49.

6. A.C. to David Curwen, September 11, 1945, in Bogdan, *Brother Curwen, Brother Crowley,* xxviii, 49.

7. A.C. to Curwen, Sept. 11, 1945, in Bogdan, *Brother Curwen, Brother Crowley,* 49–50.

8. Grant, *Remembering Aleister Crowley,* 49.

9. Y.C. A.C. to G. J. Yorke, October 20, 1945, cited by Bogdan in *Brother Curwen, Brother Crowley,* xxx.

10. Y.C. A.C. to G. J. Yorke, November 7, 1945, cited by Bogdan in *Brother Curwen, Brother Crowley,* xxxv.

11. A.C. to Curwen, August 21, 1945, cited by Bogdan in *Brother Curwen, Brother Crowley,* 45.

12. A.C. to Curwen, October 23, 1945, cited by Bogdan in *Brother Curwen, Brother Crowley,* 63.

13. A.C. to Curwen, November 7, 1945, cited by Bogdan in *Brother Curwen, Brother Crowley,* 65–66.

14. A.C. to Curwen, December 5, 1945, cited by Bogdan in *Brother Curwen, Brother Crowley,* 90.

15 Phil Hine, "East meets West: New Thought, Thelema, and The Holy Order of Krishna." Posted in "History, Occult, Tantra," July 1, 2013. Quoting from *The Kalpaka* 26, nos. 4–5 (1931). Article is available on the Enfolding.org website.

16. Cited in Crowley, Curwen, Bogdan (ed.), *Brother Curwen, Brother Crowley,* xliv.

17. Bogdan, introduction to *Brother Curwen, Brother Crowley,* xliii.

18. Bogdan, introduction to *Brother Curwen, Brother Crowley,* xliv–xlv.

19. Pat Deveney, database on "The Kalpaka." Available on the IAPSOP.com website.

20. Phil Hine received this information from Clive Harper for the blog (see n. 14).

21. Crowley, *Unpublished Diaries,* August 15, 1945.

Bibliography

Arvidsson, Stefan. *Aryan Idols: Indo-European Mythology as Ideology and Science*. Chicago: University of Chicago Press, 2006.

Bell, Sandra. "Being Creative with Tradition: Rooting Theravāda Buddhism in England." *Journal of Global Buddhism* 1 (2000): 4–9.

Bogdan, Henrik, ed. *Brother Curwen, Brother Crowley*. Introduction by Henrik Bogdan and foreword by Tony Matthews. York Beach, Maine: Tietan Press, 2010.

The British Empire. 7 vols. London: Time-Life Books, 1971–73.

Caldwell, Daniel, comp. *The Esoteric World of Madame Blavatsky*. Wheaton, Ill.: Quest Books, 2000.

Cantú, Keith E. "Śrī Sabhāpati Svāmī: The Forgotten Yogi of Western Esotericism." Paper presented at the Annual Meeting of the American Academy of Religion, San Antonio, Tex., 2016. (A revised version of this paper will appear in the forthcoming *The Occult Nineteenth Century: Roots, Developments, and Impact on the Modern World*. Edited by Lukas Pokokny and Franz Winter.)

Churton, Tobias. *Aleister Crowley: The Biography*. London: Watkins Publishing, 2012.

———. *Aleister Crowley in America: Art, Espionage, and Sex Magick in the New World*. Rochester, Vt.: Inner Traditions, 2017.

Conway, Moncure Daniel. *My Pilgrimage to the Wise Men of the East*. New York: Houghton, Mifflin and Company, 1906.

———. "The Theosophists." *Religio-Philosophical Journal* (Chicago) 10 (May 10, 1884): 1. First published in the *Glasgow Herald,* April 11, 1884; see BlavatskyArchives.Net.

Cranston, Sylvia, and Carey Williams. *The Extraordinary Life and Influence of Helena Blavatsky, Founder of the Modern Theosophical Movement.* Santa Barbara, Calif.: Path Publishing House, 1993.

Crowley, Aleister. *The Confessions of Aleister Crowley* [Abridged]. Edited by John Symonds and Kenneth Grant. London: Routledge and Kegan Paul, 1978.

———. *Eight Lectures on Yoga.* Introduction by Israel Regardie. Phoenix, Ariz.: Falcon Press, 1987.

———. *The Holy Books.* Edited by Hymenaeus Beta [William Breeze]. York Beach, Maine: O.T.O./Weiser, 1988.

———. *Liber Aleph vel CXI, The Book of Wisdom or Folly.* York Beach, Maine: Weiser, 1991.

———. *Magick, Liber Aba, Book Four, Parts I–IV.* 2nd rev. ed. Edited by Hymenaeus Beta [William Breeze]. York Beach, Maine: Weiser, 2004.

———. *Magick without Tears.* Edited by Israel Regardie. Phoenix, Ariz.: Falcon Press, 1983. First published in 1954 as edited by Karl Germer. Hampton, N.J.: Thelema Publishing Co.

———. "On A Burmese River: Part Four." From the Note Book of Aleister Crowley." Originally published in *Vanity Fair.* Editions of February 3, 1909: 135; February 10, 1909: 169; February 17, 1909: 201; February 24, 1909: 232; March 3, 1909: 269; and March 31, 1909: 393.

———. *Orpheus: A Lyrical Legend.* Inverness: Society for the Propagation of Religious Truth, 1905.

———. *The Spirit of Solitude, Re-Antichristened The Confessions of Aleister Crowley.* Edited by John Symonds and Kenneth Grant. London: Routledge and Kegan Paul, 1979.

———. *The Sword of Song.* Paris: Philippe Renouard, 1904.

———. Unpublished Diaries. Edited by William Breeze. Private collection of William Breeze. Property of O.T.O., O.T.O. Archive.

———. *Why Jesus Wept.* New York: Hill and Wang, 1969.

———. *The Works of Aleister Crowley, with Portraits.* Vols. 2–3. London: Foyers, Society for the Propagation of Religious Truth, 1906.

———. "The Writings of Truth." Unpublished diary, August–October 1901. Yorke Collection N20.

Dharmapala, Anagarika. "On the Eightfold Path: Memories of an Interpreter of Buddhism to the Present-Day World." *Asia* (New York): September 1927.

Dilks, David. "A Most Superior Person." In *The British Empire.* Vol. 5. London: Time-Life Books, 1971–73.

Edwardes, Michael. "The Coming of the Raj." In *The British Empire*. Vol. 1. London: Time-Life Books, 1971–73.

———. "The Remote Elite." In *The British Empire*. Vol. 3. London: Time-Life Books, 1971–73.

———. "Revolt against the Raj." In *The British Empire*. Vol. 5. London: Time-Life Books, 1971–73.

Eshelman, James A. *The Mystical and Magical System of the A∴A∴: The Spiritual System of Aleister Crowley and George Cecil Jones Step-by-Step*. Los Angeles: College of Thelema, 1993. 1st hardcover edition issued 2000.

Gombrich, Richard F. *How Buddhism Began: The Conditioned Genesis of the Early Teachings*. New Delhi: Munshiram Manoharlal Publishers, 1997.

Grant, Kenneth. *Remembering Aleister Crowley*. London: Skoob Publishing, 1991.

Guillarmod, Jules. *Six Mois dans l'Himalaya*. Neuchâtel: Sandoz, 1904.

Hardy, Sam [Aleister Crowley]. "Half-Hours with Famous Mahatmas." *Equinox* 1, no. 4 (1910): 284–90.

Harris, Elizabeth J. "Ananda Metteyya: The First British Emissary of Buddhism." WH 420/22 in *Collected Wheel Publications*, vol. 27: nos. 412–30, 161–222. Kandy, Sri Lanka: Buddhist Publication Society, 2014.

Hodgson, Richard. "Account of Personal Investigations in India, and Discussion of the Authorship of the 'Koot Hoomi' Letters." *Proceedings of the Society for Psychical Research* 3 (1885): 207–380.

Holroyd, Stuart. *Magic, Words and Numbers*. London: Aldus, 1976.

"H. P. Blavatsky's Adieux." *Daily Graphic*. New York. In Caldwell, *The Esoteric World of Madame Blavatsky*, 266 (Selection 7g), Dec. 10, 1878.

Johnson, K. Paul. *The Masters Revealed: Madame Blavatsky and the Myth of the Great White Lodge*. Albany: SUNY Press, 1994.

Martin, Frank. *Under the Absolute Amir*. London: Harper and Bros., 1907.

Olcott, Henry Steel. *Old Diary Leaves: The Only Authentic History of the T.S.* Vol. 2. London: Theosophical Publishing Society, 1878–1883.

Pereira, Cassius A. "Why Do I Renounce the World?" *Ceylon Daily News*. No. 2491 (1947), Colombo, Sri Lanka, 67. Cited in Harris, "Ananda Metteyya," 172–73.

Richmond, Keith, ed. *The Magical Record of Frater Progradior*. Chicago: Neptune Press, 2004.

Richmond, Keith. *Progradior and the Beast, Frank Bennett and Aleister Crowley*. Chicago: Neptune Press, 2004.

Roy, Parbati Churn. *From Hinduism to Hinduism*. Calcutta: W. Newman Co., 1896.

Sabhāpati, Svāmi. *Om: The Philosophy & Science of Vedanta and Raja Yoga*. Edited by Srīṣa-Candra Vasu. Lahore: New Lyall Press, 1895.

Sharpe, Elizabeth, *The Secrets of the Kaula Circle: A Tale of Fictitious People Faithfully Recounting Strange Rites Still Practised by This Cult,* London: Luzac & Co., 1936.

Shine, Terry. *Honour Thy Fathers*. 2009. This ebook may be downloaded/printed from either www.aimwell.org or www.buddhanet.net eBooks.

Sinnett, Alfred Percy. *The Occult World*. London: Trubner, 1881.

Smart, R. B., comp. *Burma Gazetteer, Akyab District*. Volume B. Union of Burma, Rangoon: Settlement Office, Supdt., Government Printing and Stationery, 1917.

Spence, Richard B. *Secret Agent 666, Aleister Crowley, British Intelligence, and the Occult*. Seattle: Feral House, 2008.

Vivekānanda, Swami. *Rāja Yoga*. Revised Edition. New York: Ramakrishna-Vivekānanda Center, 1953, 1984.

Wachtmeister, Constance. *Reminiscence of H. P. Blavatsky and the Secret Doctrine*. London: Theosophical Publishing Society, 1893. 2nd ed. Wheaton, Ill.: Theosophical Publishing House, 1976. Page references are to the 1976 edition.

Yorke, Gerald. *Aleister Crowley, The Golden Dawn and Buddhism: Reminiscences and Writings of Gerald Yorke*. Contributions by Keith Richmond, David Tibet, Timothy d'Arch Smith, and Clive Harper. York Beach, Maine: Tetan Press, 2011.

Index

BOOKS OF RELATED INTEREST

Aleister Crowley in America
Art, Espionage, and Sex Magick in the New World
by Tobias Churton

Aleister Crowley: The Beast in Berlin
Art, Sex, and Magick in the Weimar Republic
by Tobias Churton

The Spiritual Meaning of the Sixties
The Magic, Myth, and Music of the Decade That Changed the World
by Tobias Churton

Occult Paris
The Lost Magic of the Belle Époque
by Tobias Churton

Deconstructing Gurdjieff
Biography of a Spiritual Magician
by Tobias Churton

Gnostic Philosophy
From Ancient Persia to Modern Times
by Tobias Churton

Gnostic Mysteries of Sex
Sophia the Wild One and Erotic Christianity
by Tobias Churton

The Mysteries of John the Baptist
His Legacy in Gnosticism, Paganism, and Freemasonry
by Tobias Churton

INNER TRADITIONS • BEAR & COMPANY
P.O. Box 388 • Rochester, VT 05767
1-800-246-8648
www.InnerTraditions.com

Or contact your local bookseller